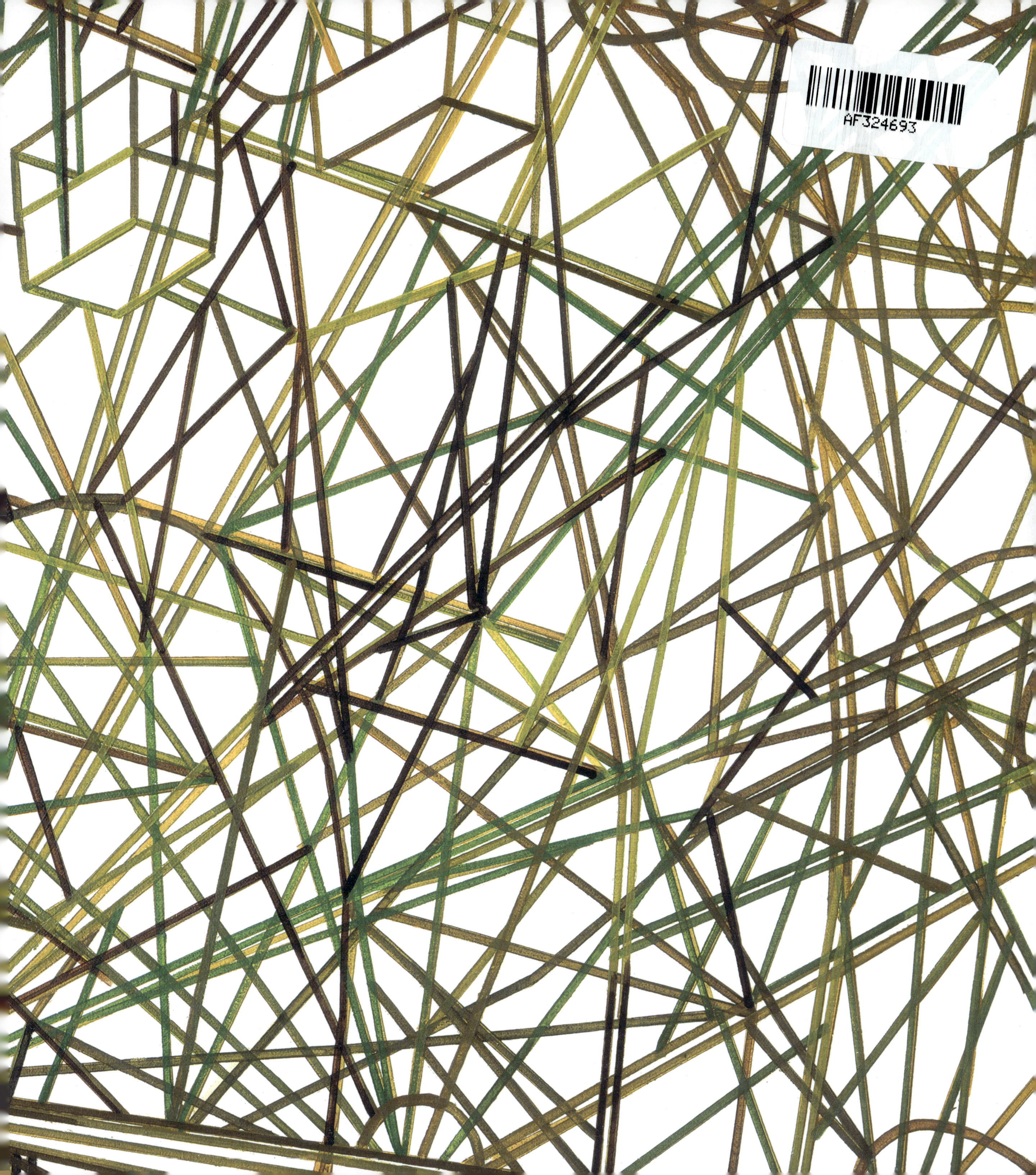
AF324693

WILLIAM STEIGER
TRANSPORT

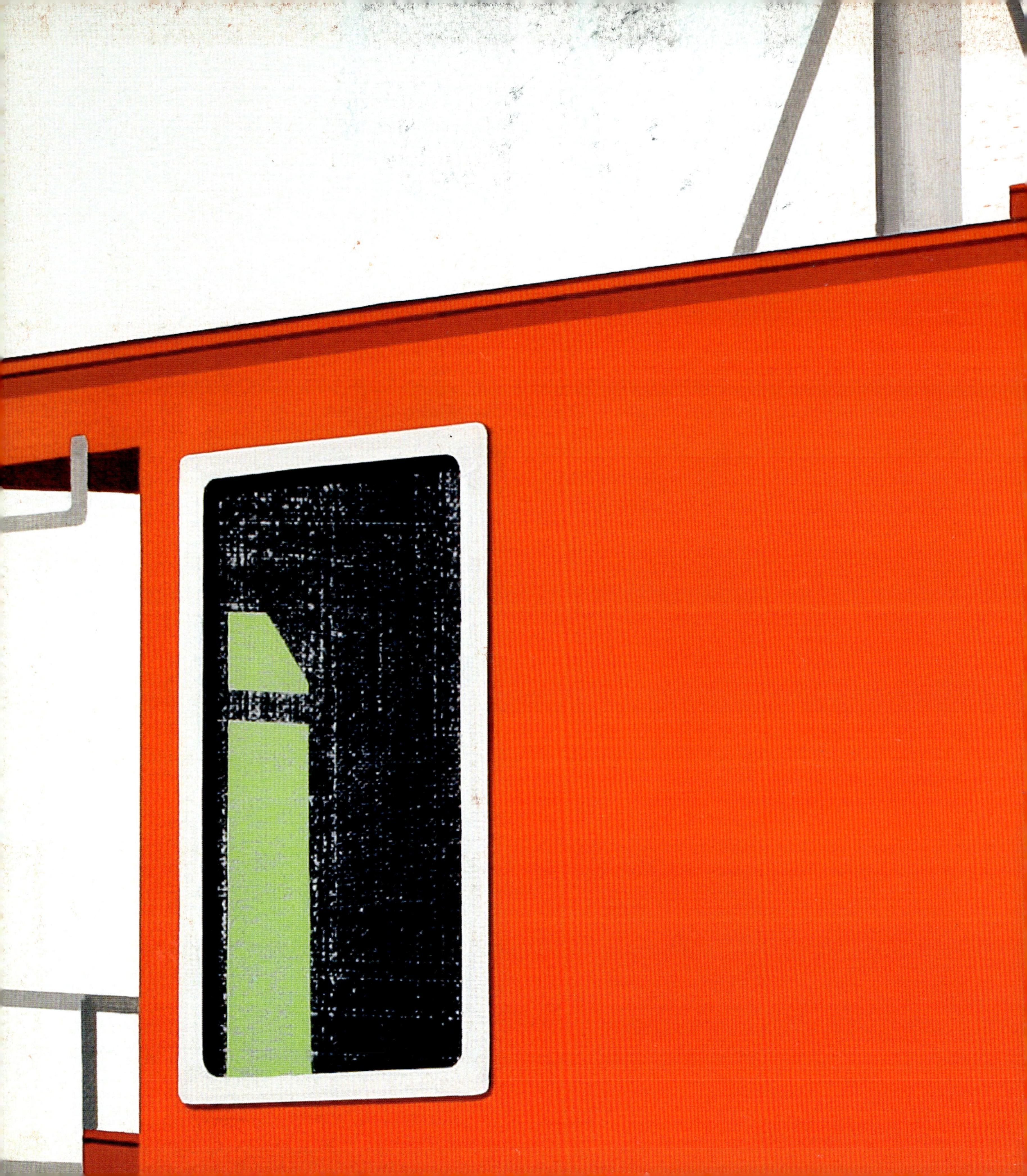

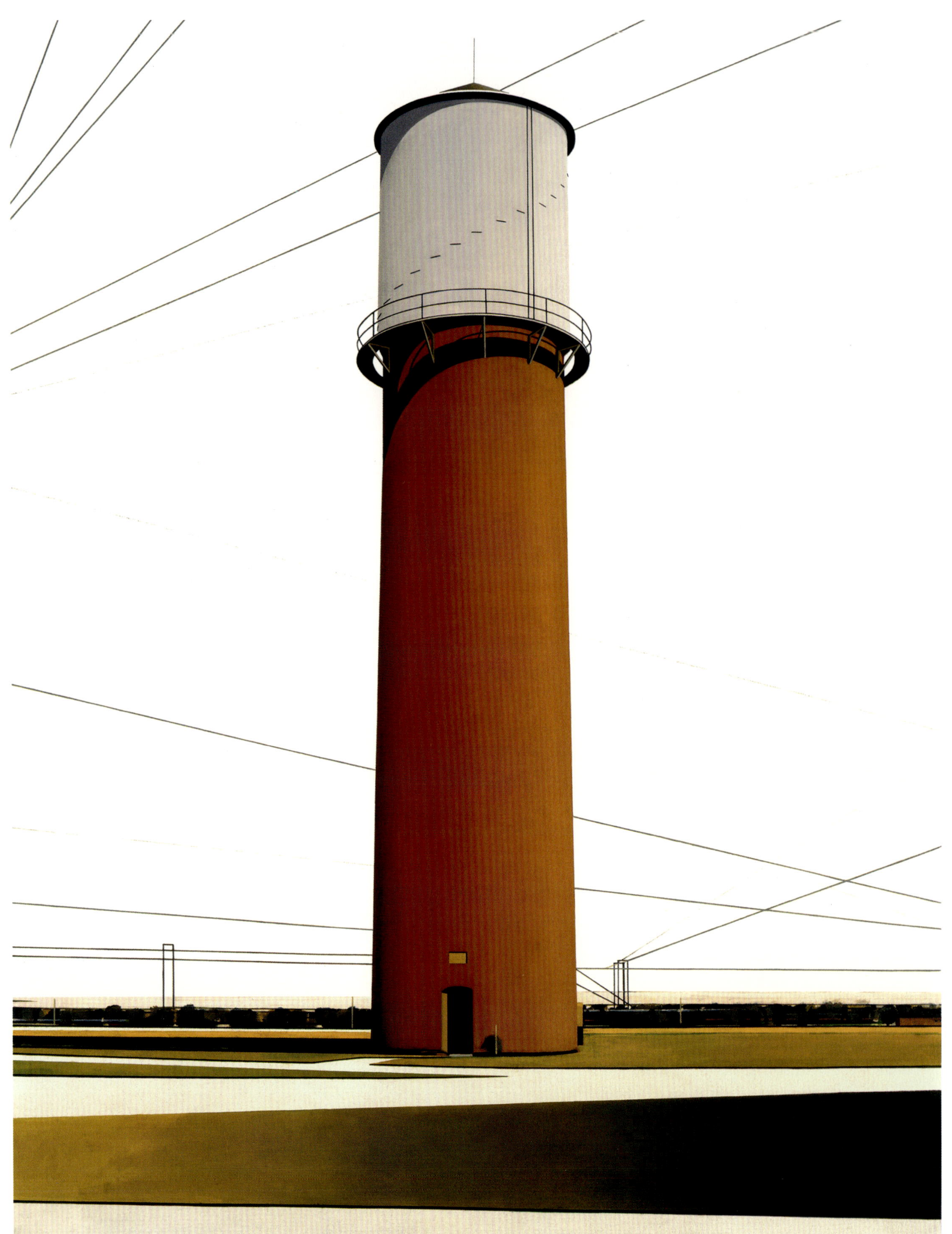

WILLIAM STEIGER
TRANSPORT

Richard Vine and Christopher Gaillard

WITH CONTRIBUTIONS BY

TURAN DUDA   BETTINA PRENTICE   ALLISON PETERS QUINN

MELISSA MILGROM   LISA HATCHADOORIAN   LOWELL PETTIT

MAURA ROBINSON   BRUCE W. FERGUSON   CESAR PELLI

FRED CLARKE   RICHARD SOLOMON

HUDSON HILLS PRESS
MANCHESTER AND NEW YORK

First Edition

Copyright © 2011 by William Steiger

All rights reserved under International and Pan-American Copyright Convention.

Published in the United States by Hudson Hills Press, LLC
P.O. Box 205, 3556 Main Street, Manchester, Vermont 05254

Distributed in the United States, its territories and possessions,
and Canada by National Book Network, Inc.
Distributed outside of North America by Antique Collectors' Club, Ltd.

Publisher and Executive Director: Leslie Pell van Breen
Production Manager: David Skolkin
Design: David Skolkin / Skolkin + Chickey
Editor: Ted Gilley
Proofreader: Deborah Thompson
Production Editor: Marisa Crumb
Printed and bound by The Imago Group
Founding Publisher: Paul Anbinder

Manufactured in China

Library of Congress Cataloging-in-Publication Data

Vine, Richard, 1948-
  William Steiger : Transport / Richard Vine and Christopher Gaillard ; With contributions by Turan
Duda [and ten others].
     pages cm
  Includes bibliographical references and index.
  ISBN 978-1-55595-358-4
  1. Steiger, William, 1962—-Themes, motives. I. Gaillard, Christopher. II. Duda, Turan. III. Title.
  ND237.S68275V56 2011
  759.13—dc22
                    2010054418

Cover: **Wonderwheel**, 2002, oil on canvas, 60 x 48 inches. Collection of Richard Lorenti and Andrew Flatt.
Frontispiece: **Watertank Somonauk**, 1999, oil on canvas, 60 x 48 inches. Collection of Tim Mott.

CONTENTS

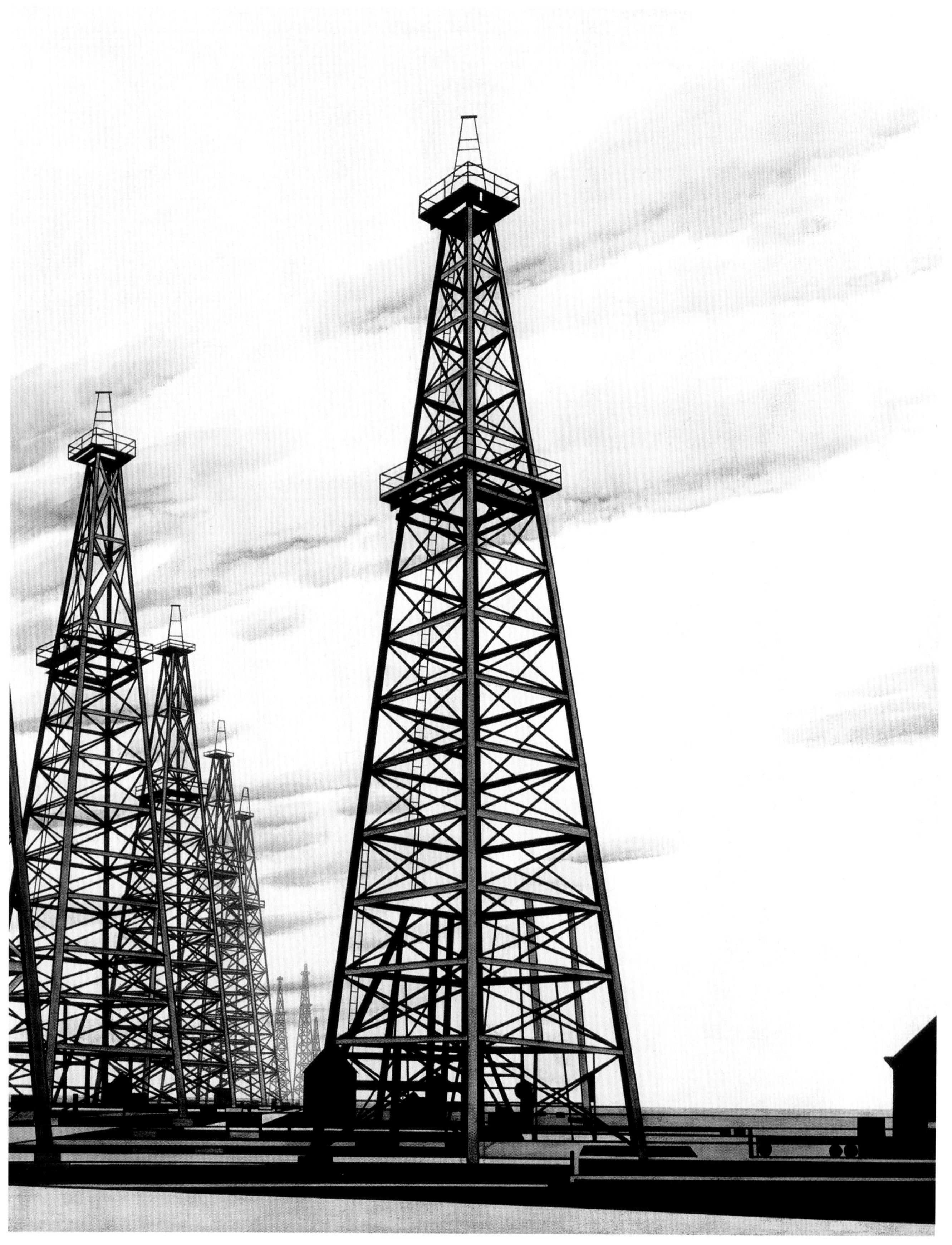

Figure 1. William Steiger, *Oil Derricks*, 2000, oil on canvas, 60 x 48 inches. Collection of Gerald and Dianna Peterson.

THE ARTIST OF ABSENCE
BY RICHARD VINE

The eternal silence of these infinite spaces frightens me.

— BLAISE PASCAL

SINCE THE BEGINNING OF WILLIAM STEIGER'S SOLO EXHIBITION career twenty years ago, critics have systematically—and repeatedly—identified the numerous influences, subjects, and formal characteristics found in his distinctly schematized work. Readers have been informed, very legitimately, that his canvases, drawings, and prints owe a debt to classic American landscape painting as well as to the machine-age Precisionism of Charles Sheeler (fig. 2) and Charles Demuth; that his bridges, train cars, dirigibles, railroad signals, and cable gondolas convey a nostalgia for a pre-electronic era (as imagined, if not as actually lived); and that his simplified forms and flat surfaces partake of the geometric reductivism that has been central to modern art from Cubism through Minimalism to neo-Geo and beyond. Some writers have noted a particularly strong affinity with the urban and industrial semi-abstractions of Ralston Crawford (fig. 3). Others have identified the exact airships and park rides that served as models for particular Steiger images. Several have dwelt on the consistent allover illumination that permeates his scenes, and the starkly graphic nature of his compositions.

Despite the accuracy and thoroughness of these identifications, there is something deceptively simplistic in this taxonomic approach. Looking at Steiger's art, reading about it, and looking again, one can almost come to believe that these trained observers have entered into a conspiracy of silence with the artist. Critics, curators, and art historians remark at length on what is so clearly there before us in Steiger's pictures but neglect, mysteriously, what is *not* there. This is no small omission. For, in an important sense, the most compelling aspect of a Steiger image is all that ought to be present—logically, structurally, and emotionally—is in fact consistently absent. What, one wants to ask, does this sum of omissions mean?

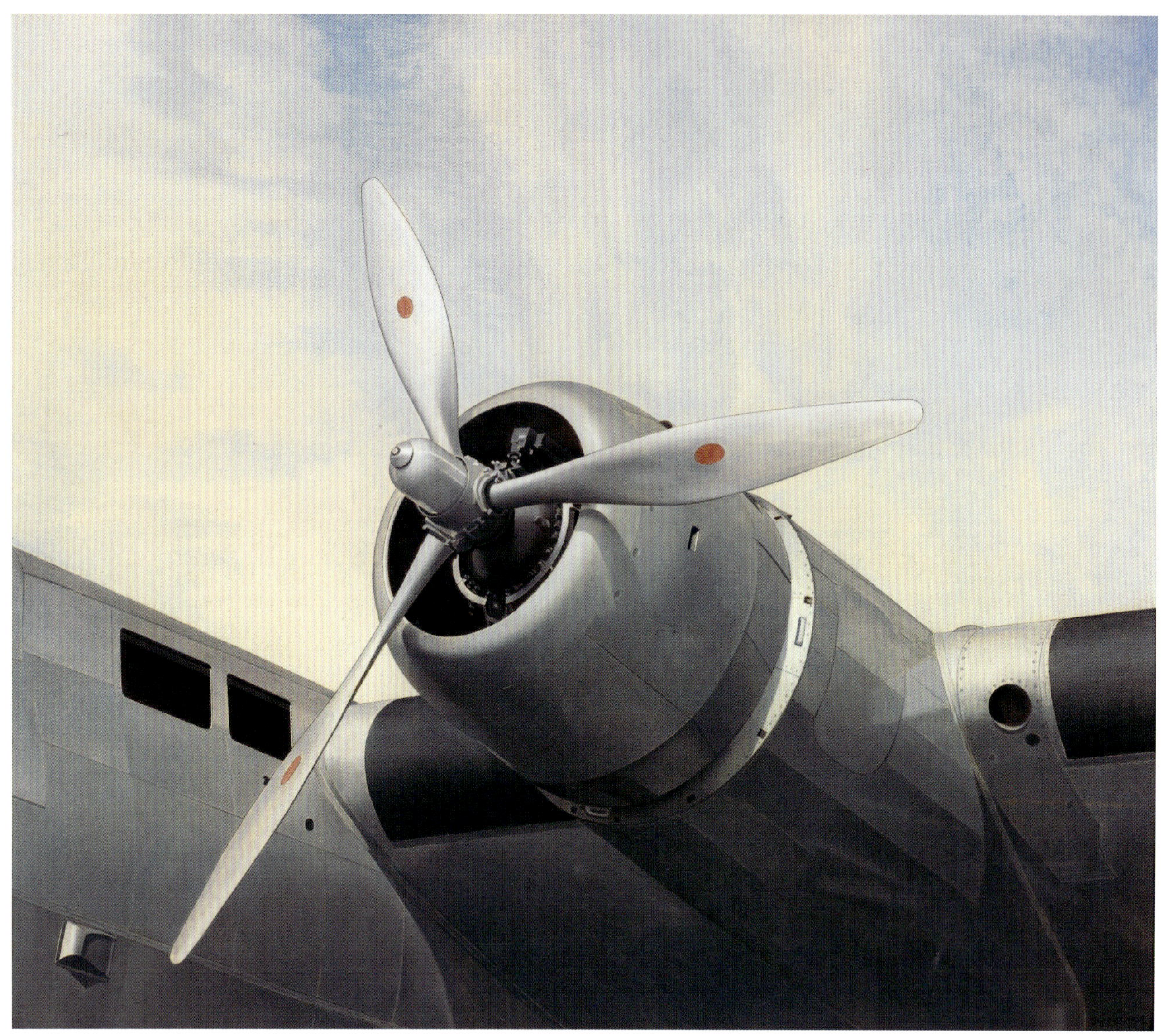

Figure 2. Charles Sheeler, *Yankee Clipper*, 1939, oil on canvas, 24 x inches. Museum of Art, Rhode Is School of Design, Providence. Jes Metcalf and Mary B. Jackson Fun Photograph: Erik Gould, Museum Art, Rhode Island School of Desi Providence.

To begin with the most salient example, these works are utterly devoid of people—a strange state of affairs for an artist who closely scrutinizes man-made objects and has more than once been termed a contemporary "realist." Think of all the places in the Steiger universe that human beings might—or even should—naturally appear but somehow never do; think of the cable cars, cabooses, train yards, carnival rides, gondolas, grain-elevator compounds, doorways, windows, factory floors, island shorelines, and quiltlike farm fields seen from above. Such a consistent exclusion can result only from willful, repeated acts of choice.

There could be many plausible reasons for this imaginative depopulation. In a Columbia University lecture, the experimental architect Zaha Hadid once complained that human figures inserted in a proposal drawing "spoil the geometry of the buildings." Likewise Steiger's elision of everyday details (no rust, no bent nails, no sun-faded boards) and living beings (no animals in his barnyards or fields) seems to aid the formulation of rationalized essences—the culmination, paradoxically, of a long process of cumulative viewings. The artist must have looked repeatedly at myriad places and objects (both in reality and in reproduction) to have arrived at this clean visual typification of each. Perhaps a thousand grain-processing facilities were seen and analyzed in order to yield, through composite memory, the single Platonic image that is *Blue Mill* (2004) (plate 102). "One should learn from nature," said the eighth-century Chinese painter Zhang Zao, "and paint the image in one's mind."

Why, then, are people not remembered and painted? It is not because Steiger, in architectural mandarin fashion, simply dismisses them. No, his rigorously attentive images are too rife with the products of human hands and minds—our many cultural fabrications

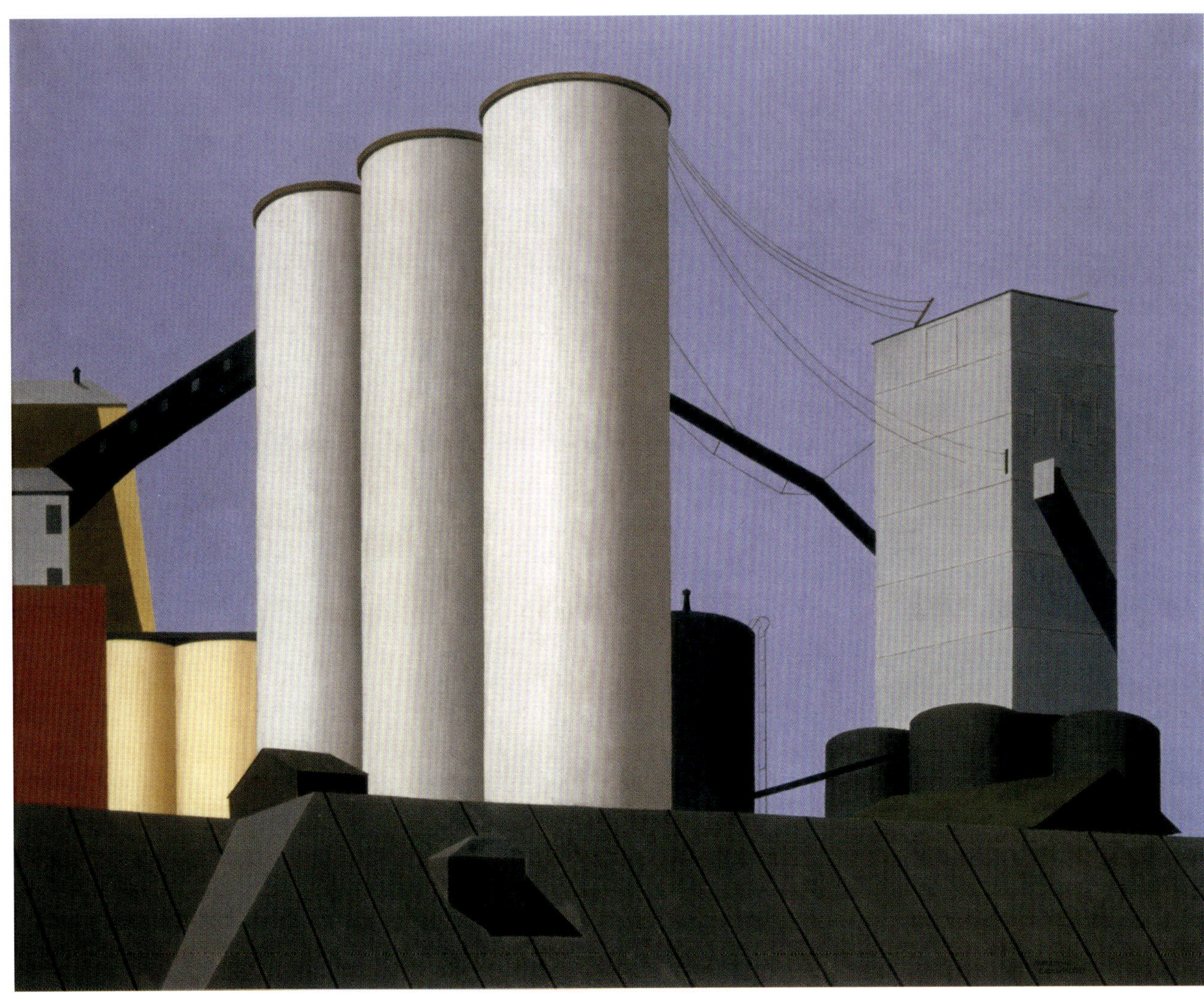

3. Ralston Crawford,
Grain Elevators, 1937,
canvas, 40¼ x 50¼ inches,
onian American Art Museum,
m purchase 1976.

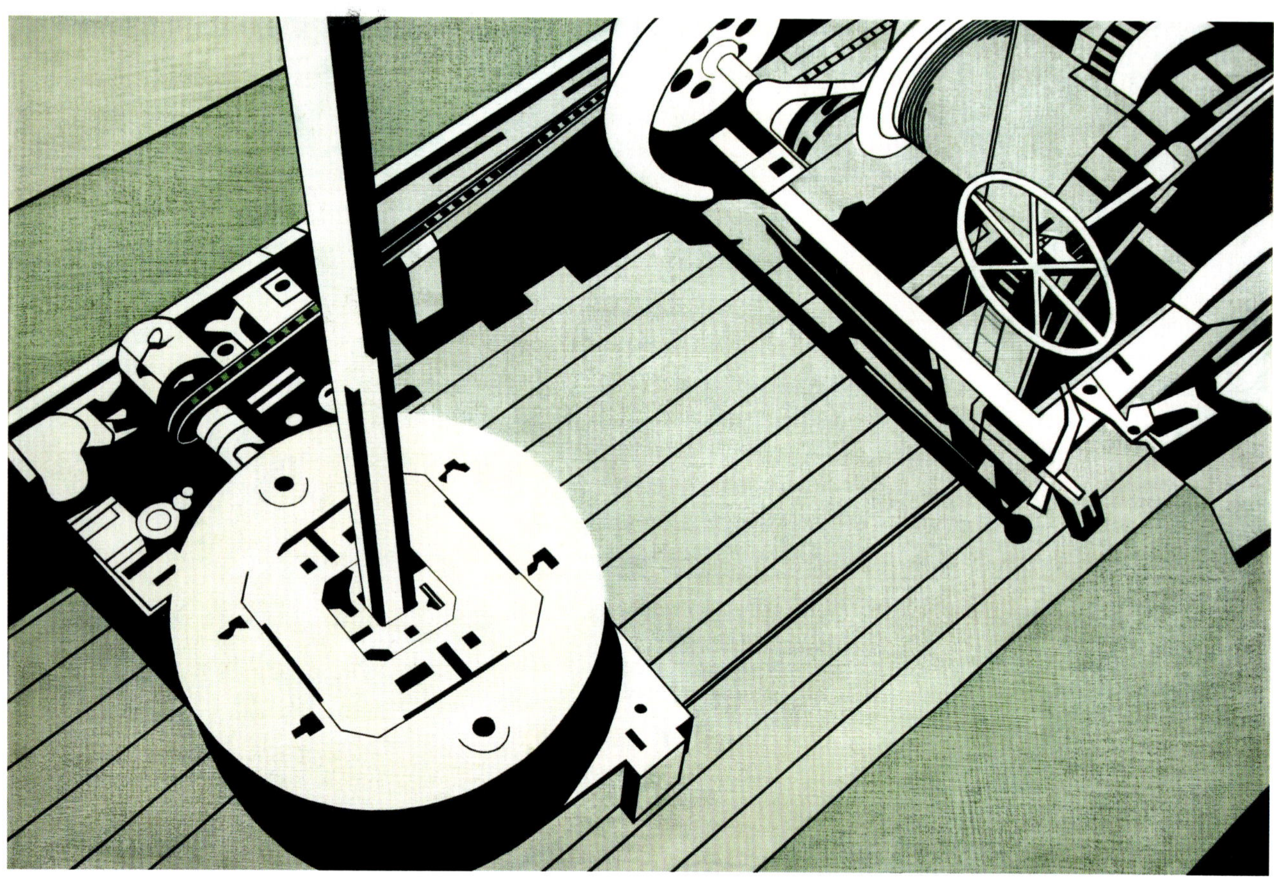

Figure 4. William Steiger,
Green Machine, 2007,
oil on linen, 20 x 30 inches.
Collection of John R. Eckel, Jr. Est

(homes, farms, rail systems, amusement parks)—for that to be the case. In instances like *Green Machine* (2007) (fig. 4), viewers are invited to contemplate the very belts, bolts, and gears that routinely serve our human needs. Indeed, having experimented with pure geometric abstraction in early works like *Formation I* (1990) (fig. 5), restricted to layered grids in black-on-white, Steiger has since moved inexorably toward an ever more elegiac representation. Pictures such as *Kinderhook* (1994) (fig. 6)—an outmoded water tower set against a blank sky and an extinct industrial building—seek to commemorate, obliquely and with stately restraint, the passing away not simply of a lifestyle or one individual consciousness but of all creatures. Subdued, decorous, yet unblinking, such works are visual odes on mortality.

What, we are left to ponder, could be more poignant than those implied Steigerian journeys; on Ferris wheels that pause on their eternal round and round; on train cars that go nowhere; on unseen boats that pass deserted shores; on cable trams suspended over the abyss; on phantom aircraft tilting over empty fields where a river winds sinuously through? This semiotic quality is reinforced by another great omission in the artist's mise-en-scène: volumetric space. Although depth is sometimes cannily suggested by hard, slant shadows

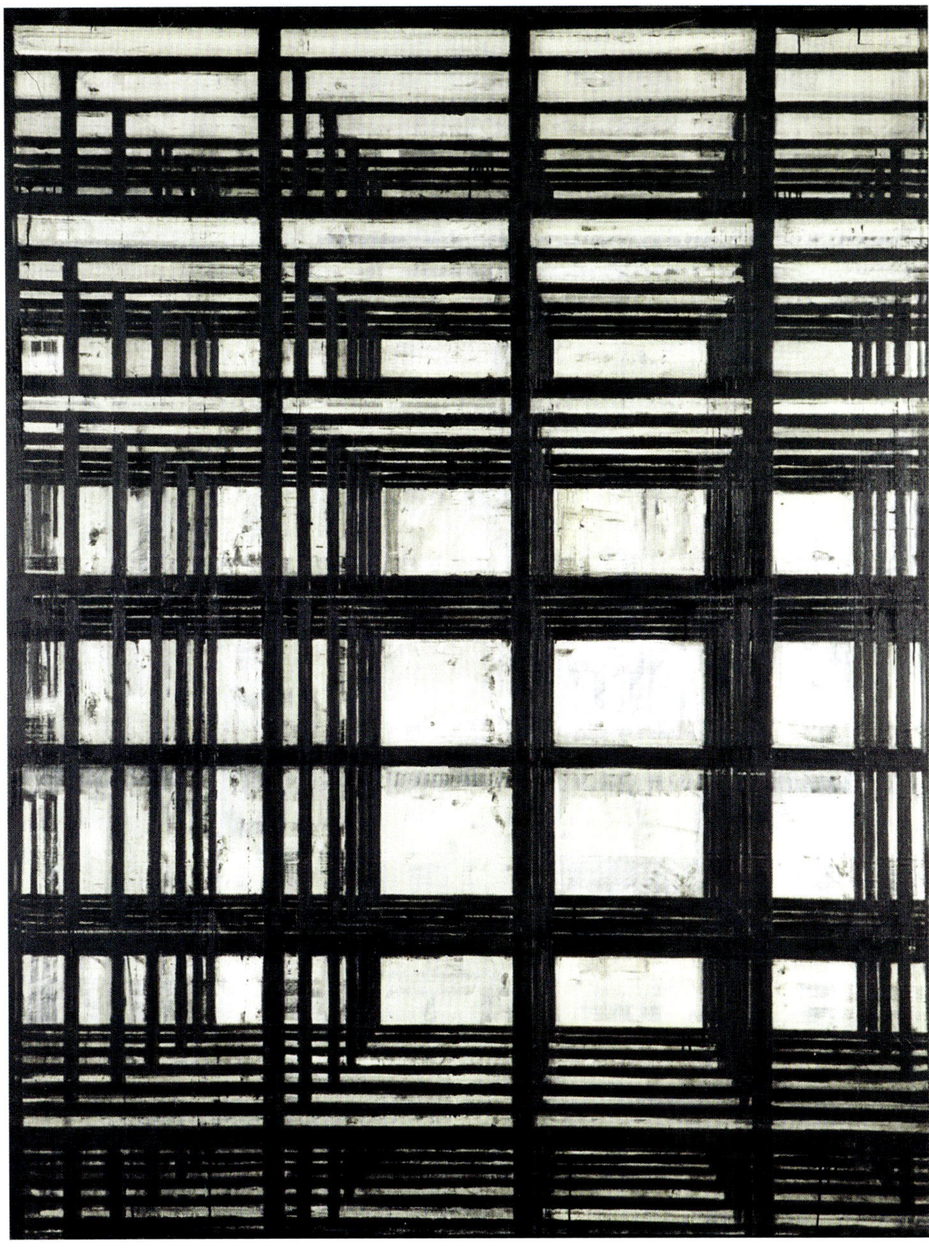

and a Hans Hofmannesque push–pull between figure and ground, the overriding attribute of a Steiger image is uniform flatness, fostering the all-at-once retinal imprint of graphic design. No complex of vanishing points, no modeling, no chiaroscuro, minimal varying of line thickness, limited overlaying of forms—one seemingly in front of the other—no distant hazing of color.

In part, this austere look is an outgrowth of the modernist revolt against naturalistic conventions, particularly as that impulse was channeled through the ad-influenced Pop art of 1960s America. But Steiger also melds this anti-illusionism with a contemporary emphasis on mediation—the insistence that the world we experience is a dynamic construct of signs (not of things in themselves), delivered to our minds through technological and cultural systems that imprint their own natures on the messages they transmit. His preoccupation, however, is not with the mass publications, films, TV programs, and new-media platforms that obsess his more au courant peers. In his research, Steiger goes back beyond the visual cataloguing of Bernd and Hilla Becher (fig. 7), behind the physical variations of

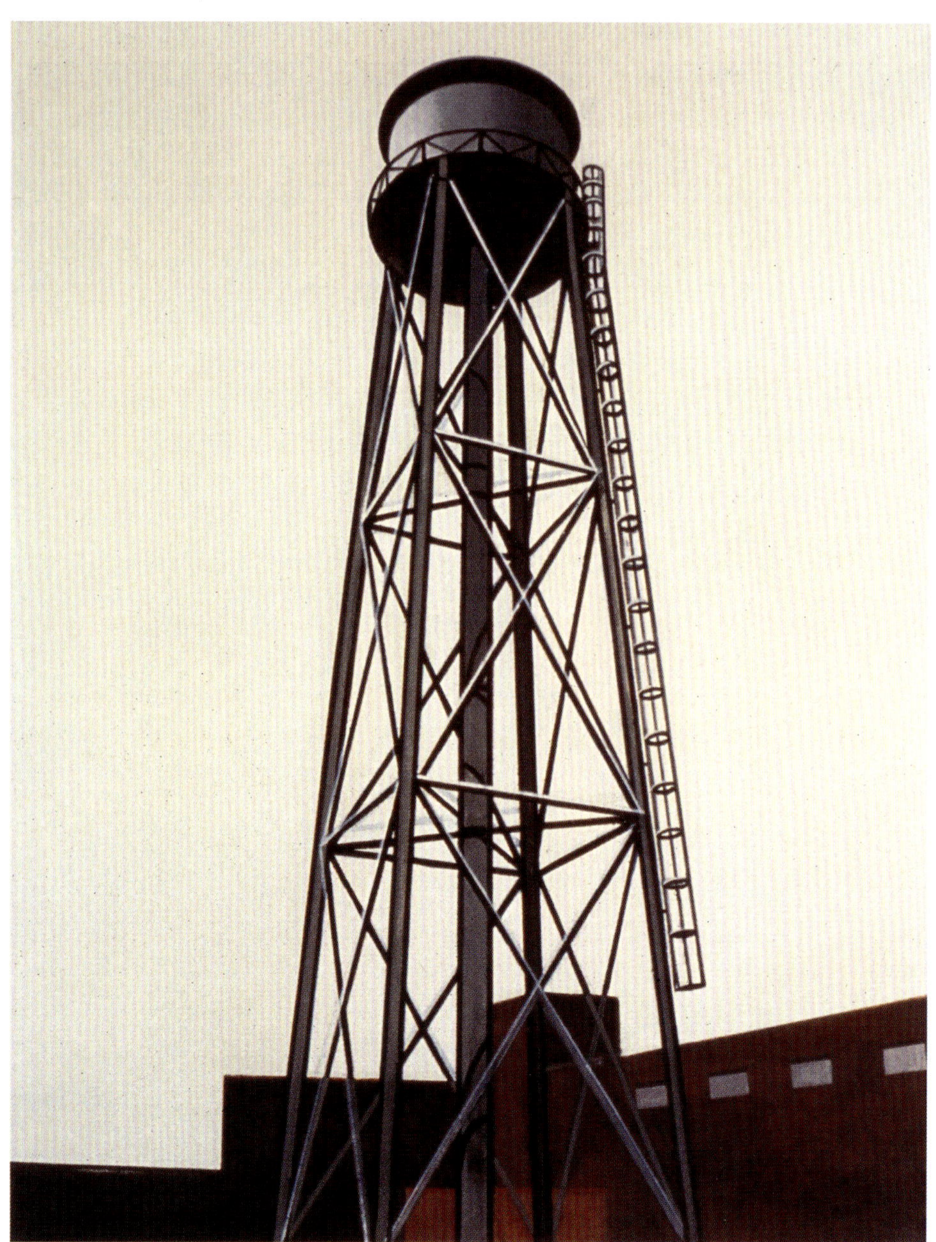

Figure 6. William Steiger, *Kinderhook*, 1994, oil on canvas, 38 x 30 inches. Collection of Jeffrey and Johanna Longnecker.

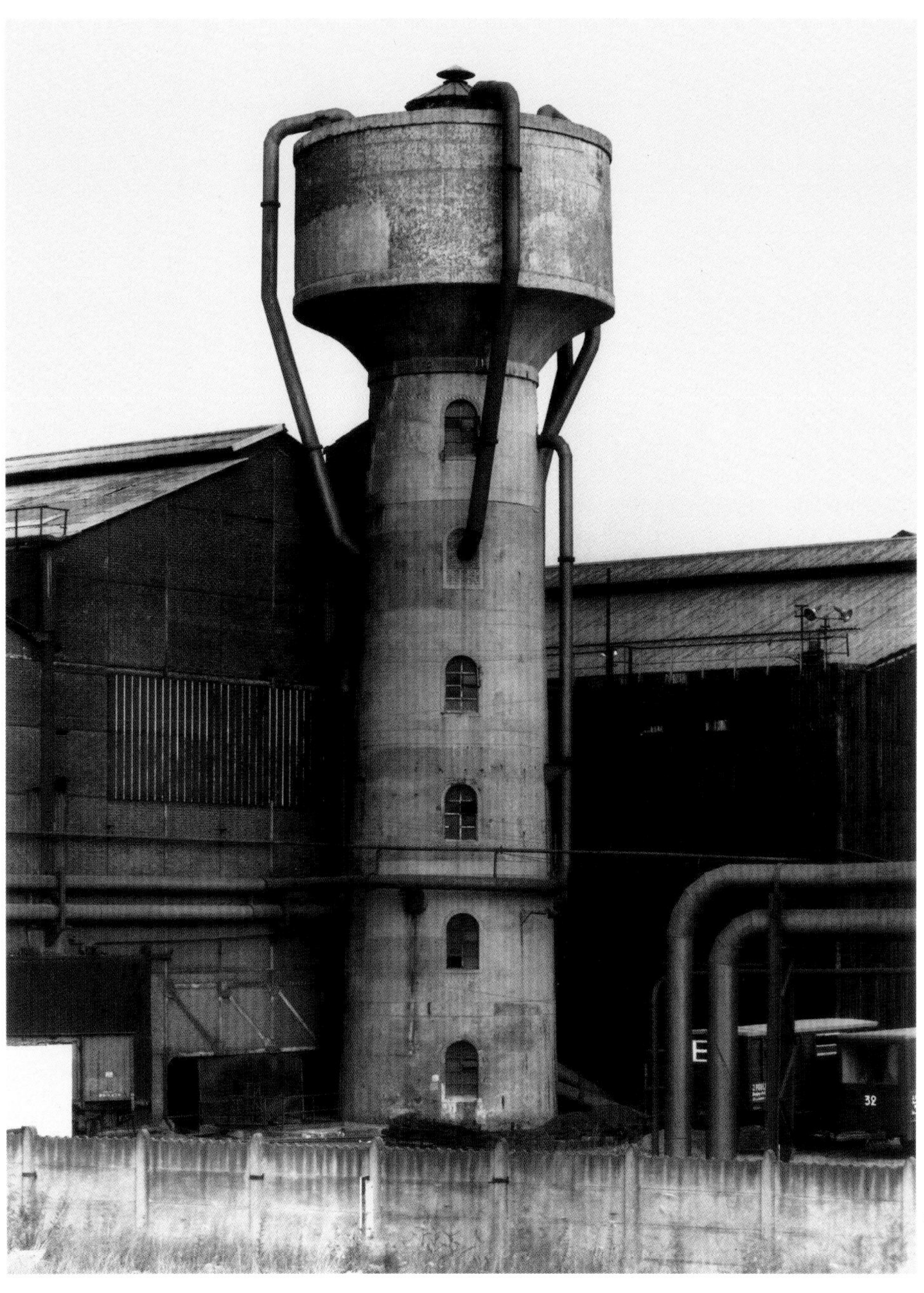

Figure 7. Bernd and Hilla Becher, *Charleroi-Marchienne, Belgium 1971*. Courtesy Sonnabend Gallery.

engineering in the built environment, to study the fundamentals of visual coding per se (*this* signifies barn, *that* water tower; *this* means tanker car, *that* caboose), like a linguist analyzing the rules of a vanishing dialect. His source material includes vintage railroad operating manuals (fig. 8a–b), "real photo" postcards and social-documentary photographs (fig. 9a–d) from the 1930s, and such esoteric trade publications as the Caldwell Tank & Towers catalogue of 1929 and the Des Moines Bridge and Iron Company catalogue from the 1930s

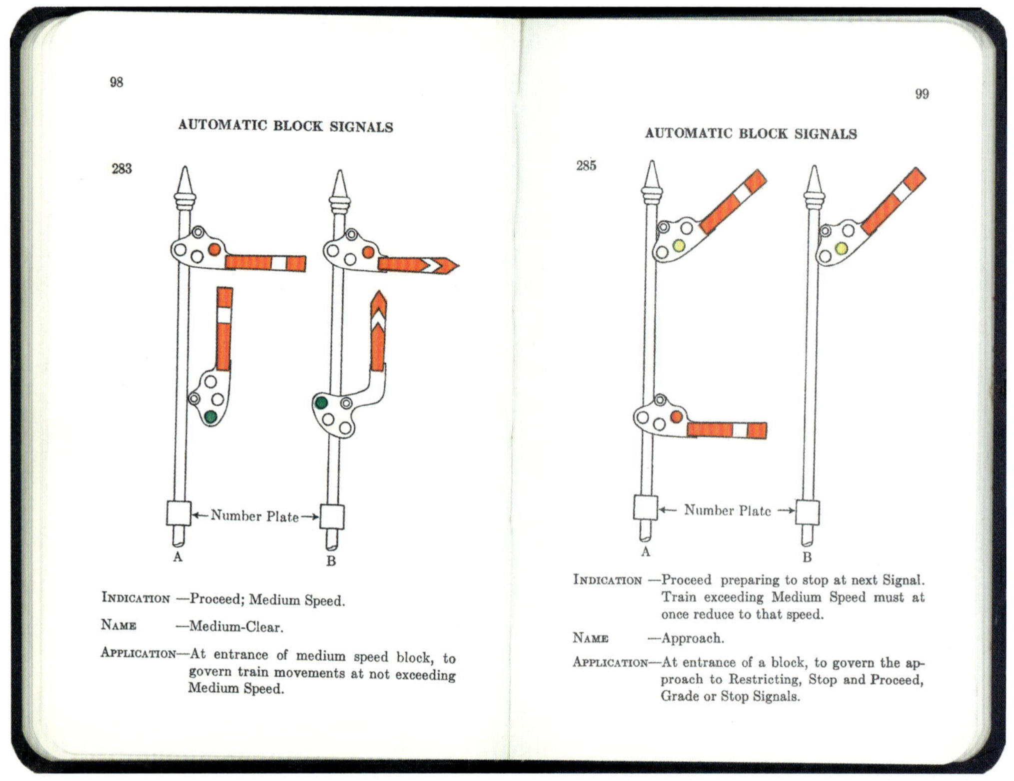

Figure 8a. *Western Maryland Railway Company*, operating manual (pages 98–99), 1939.

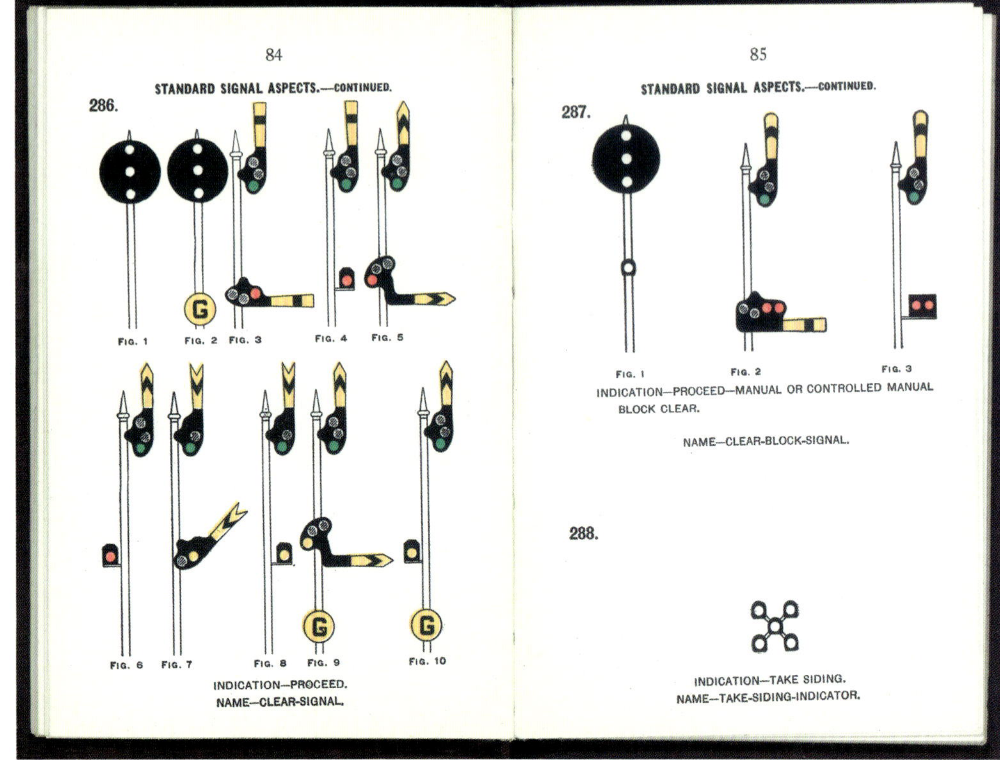

Figure 8b. *Pennsylvania Railroad System*, operating manual (pages 84–85), 1925.

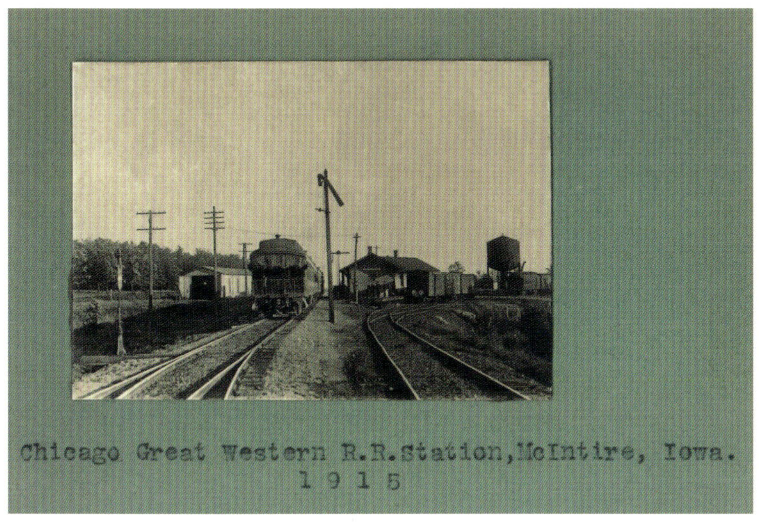

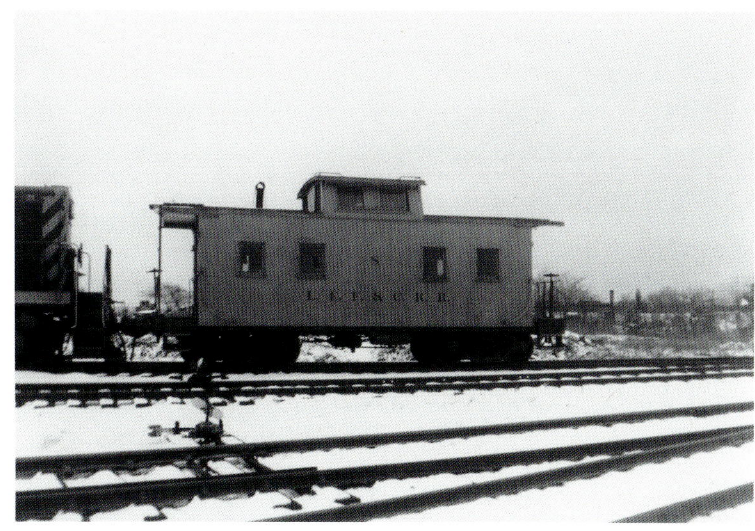

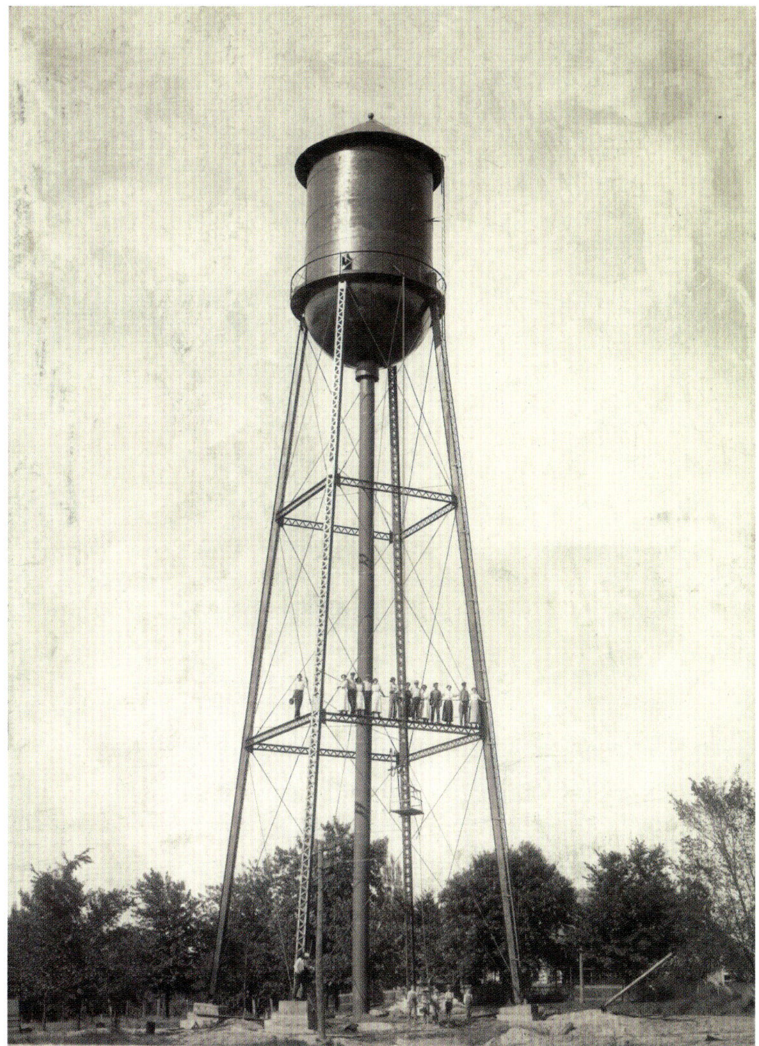

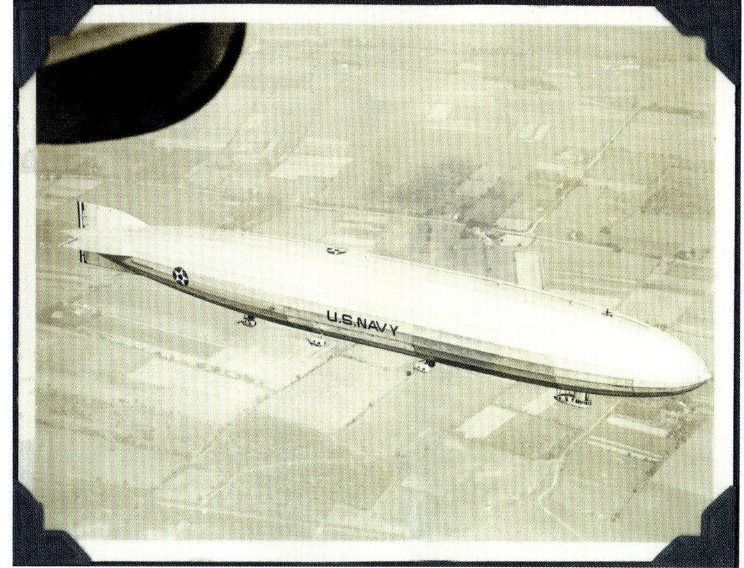

Figure 9a (top left). Anonymous photograph, Chicago Great Western Railroad Station, McIntire, Iowa, 1915.

Figure 9b (top right). Anonymous photograph, L.E.F. & C.R.R. Caboose, 1962.

Figure 9c (bottom left). Anonymous photograph, Water Tower, New Athens, Illinois, 1912.

Figure 9d (bottom right). Anonymous photograph, Dirigible, c. 1930s.

(fig. 10a–c). We are confronted, consequently, with imagery that comes close to the graphic legibility of signage, the consensual order of language.

For the Word, as Steiger's signs attest, exists in a mental space without depth. Fittingly, one is reminded, given the national character of these images, of the America of sweeping vistas and abundant land, whose seeming limitlessness can itself become a form of confinement—an emptiness, like that of Pascal's cosmos, which through its very vastness entraps us. In silence resides the possibility to say anything, as once in the great vacancy of America there existed the potential to build anything that the human mind could conceive. But as soon as one begins to speak (which for Steiger is to paint) or to build, choices are already made. As some opportunities are thereby opened up, many others are automatically closed. Sensing this, one is tempted, in desperation, to build, to say, to paint more furiously. Dwelling on that existential dilemma, that vacillation between structure and chaos, is, as Jackson Pollock discovered, an invitation to madness.

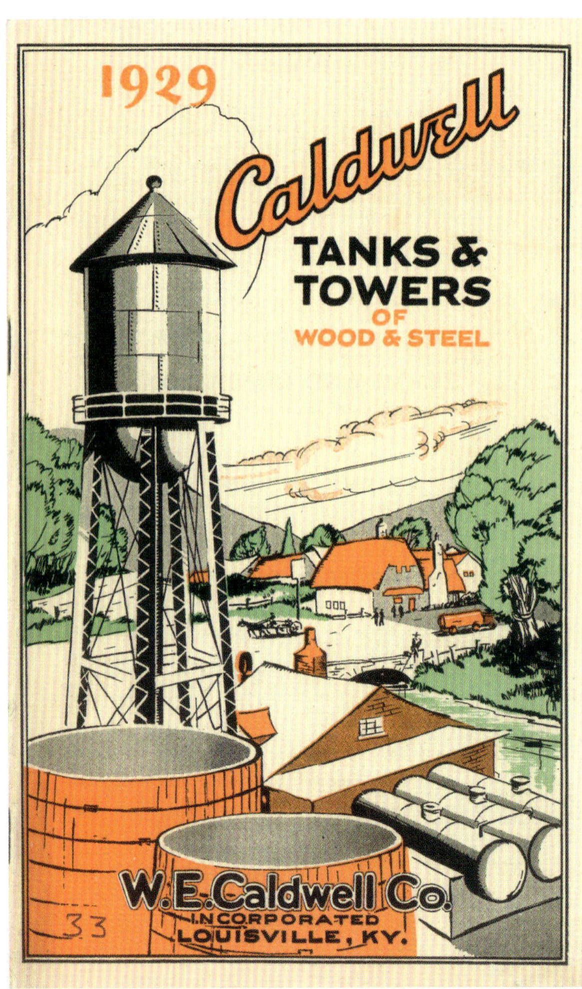

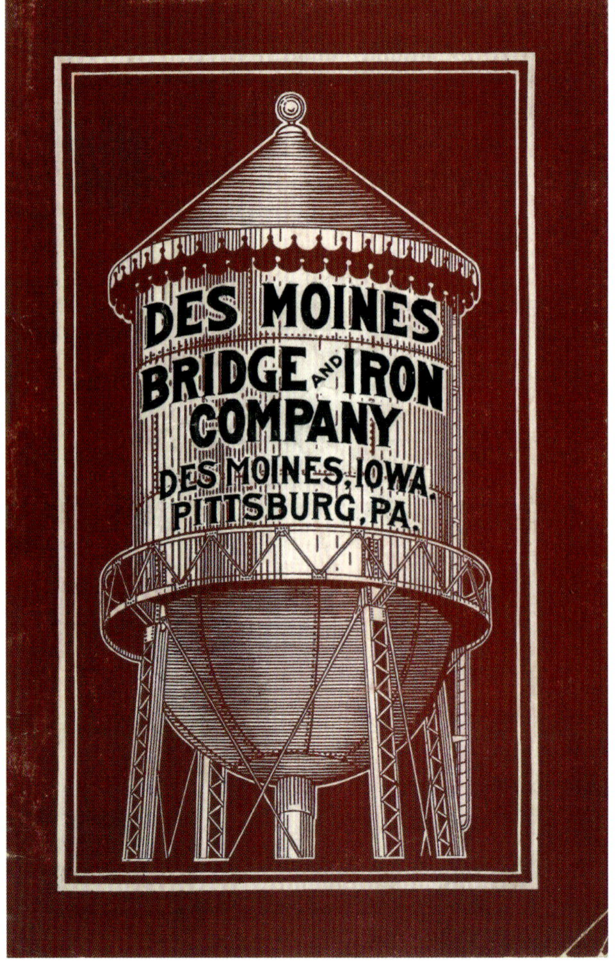

Figure 10a. *Caldwell Tanks & Tower* catalogue (cover), 1929.

Figure 10b. *Des Moines Bridge and Company*, catalogue (cover), c. 193

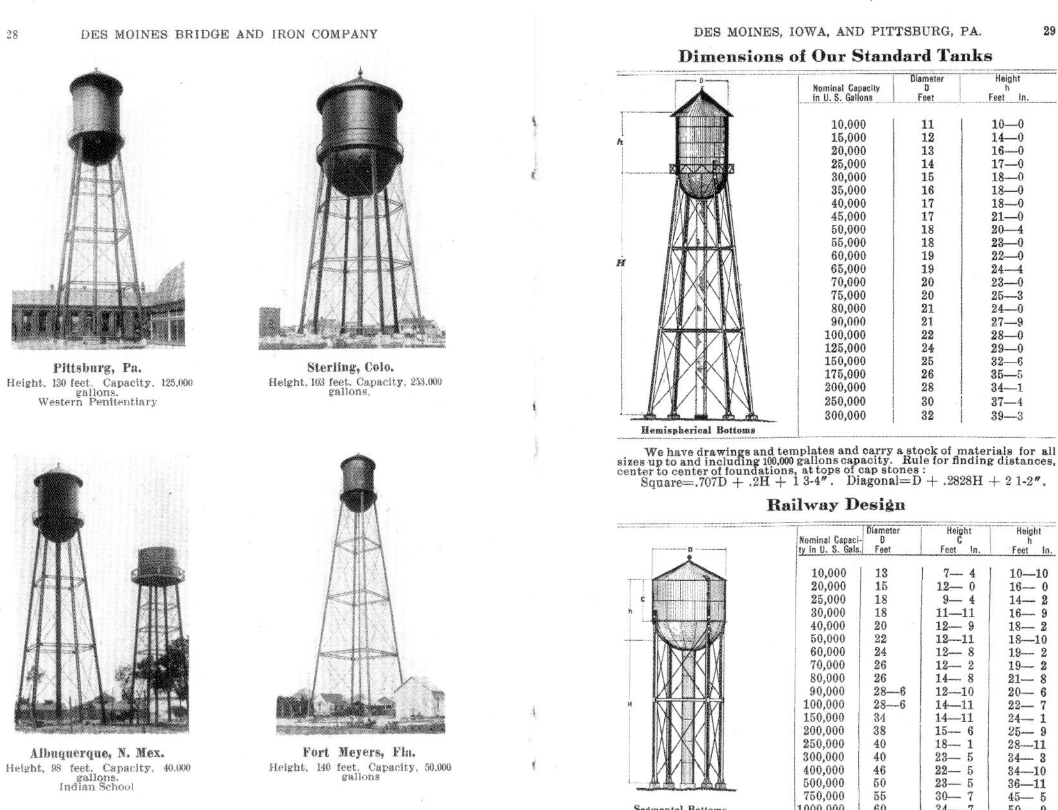

Pittsburg, Pa.
Height, 130 feet. Capacity, 125,000 gallons.
Western Penitentiary

Sterling, Colo.
Height, 103 feet. Capacity, 253,000 gallons.

Albuquerque, N. Mex.
Height, 98 feet. Capacity, 40,000 gallons.
Indian School

Fort Meyers, Fla.
Height, 140 feet. Capacity, 50,000 gallons.

Water Towers all Over the United States.

Dimensions of Our Standard Tanks

Nominal Capacity in U. S. Gallons	Diameter D Feet	Height h Feet—In.
10,000	11	10—0
15,000	12	14—0
20,000	13	16—0
25,000	14	17—0
30,000	15	18—0
35,000	16	18—0
40,000	17	18—0
45,000	17	21—0
50,000	18	20—4
55,000	18	23—0
60,000	19	22—0
65,000	19	24—4
70,000	20	23—0
75,000	20	25—3
80,000	21	24—0
90,000	21	27—9
100,000	22	28—0
125,000	24	29—0
150,000	25	32—6
175,000	26	35—5
200,000	28	34—1
250,000	30	37—4
300,000	32	39—3

Hemispherical Bottoms

We have drawings and templates and carry a stock of materials for all sizes up to and including 100,000 gallons capacity. Rule for finding distances, center to center of foundations, at tops of cap stones :
Square=.707D + .2H + 1 3-4″.   Diagonal=D + .2828H + 2 1-2″.

Railway Design

Nominal Capacity in U. S. Gals.	Diameter D Feet	Height C Feet—In.	Height h Feet—In.
10,000	13	7—4	10—10
20,000	15	12—0	16—0
25,000	18	9—4	14—2
30,000	18	11—11	16—9
40,000	20	12—9	18—2
50,000	22	12—11	18—10
60,000	24	12—8	19—2
70,000	26	12—2	19—2
80,000	26	14—8	21—8
90,000	28—6	12—10	20—6
100,000	28—6	14—11	22—7
150,000	34	14—11	24—1
200,000	38	15—6	25—9
250,000	40	18—1	28—11
300,000	40	23—5	34—3
400,000	46	22—5	34—10
500,000	50	23—5	36—11
750,000	55	30—7	45—5
1,000,000	60	34—7	50—9

Segmental Bottoms

Figure 10c. *Des Moines Bridge and Iron Company*, catalogue (pages 28–29), c. 1930s.

One can see the dichotomy—and feel the tension it elicits—by comparing two modes of Steiger's production. The degree-zero economy of, say, *Green Elevator* (2006) (plate 103)—a study of architectural forms that are almost not there at all—contrasts markedly with the manic elaboration of *Wonderwheel* (2002) (plate 141) and other amusement park pictures. In the latter, we discover Steiger's addition of trusses and spaghetti-like swirls of armature that bespeak an apparent compulsiveness, pushing at the very boundary of reason.

Another remarkable absence here is the lack of darkness, either natural or expressionistic. This is a bold disavowal, since the interplay between light and dark is a standard device, in Western art, for suggesting depth—not only for situating objects in perceived space but for endowing them with a sense of psychic profundity. Rembrandt is not possible in a sun-flooded room. For an artist to deliberately eschew the potential of shading and sudden contrasts in chromatic value (the drama of forms and luminosity epitomized in Caravaggio) is to forgo—and perhaps to guard against—the darker aspects of existence and the

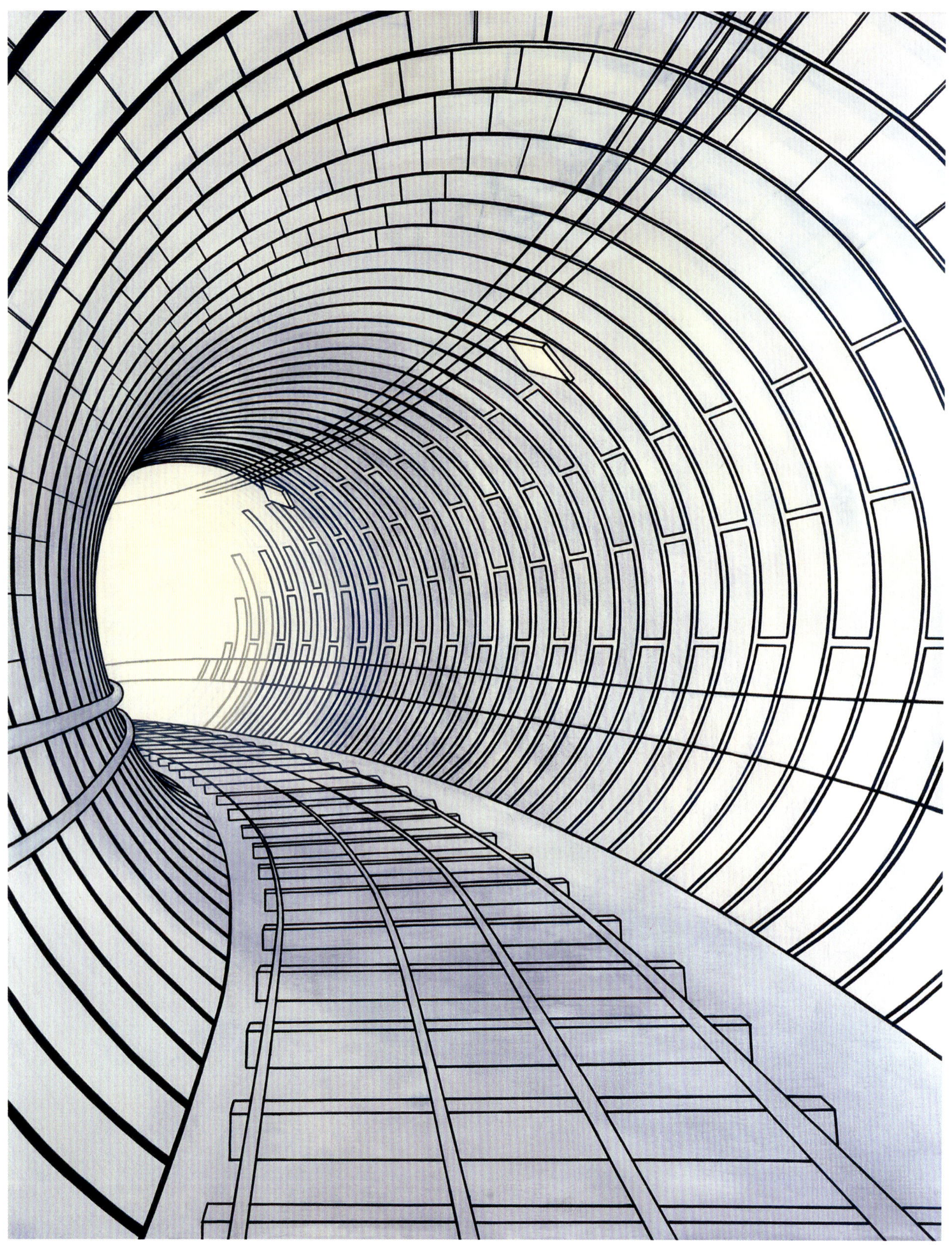

Figure 11. William Steiger, *Tunnel*, 2000, oil on canvas, 60 x 48 inches. Courtesy Roy Boyd Gallery.

human mind. Not for Steiger an investigation of the dark satanic mills; his workplaces are sites of pure functionality.

Such consistent denial suggests a vivid awareness—however sublimated, however transformed into its daylight contrary—of all that is suppressed. Let us look at the things we have fashioned, Steiger's pictures seem to implore: the buildings for shelter and industriousness, the odd contraptions for amusement, the continually outdated vehicles for transport. Leave aside, if we can, the inner contradictions and ultimate end of man the builder, immersed in the void. Let us endorse the systematic defiance of nothingness that is human endeavor. Let us look at our creations in the calm, even light of reason. For perhaps, as America's deistic forefathers would have it, the Divine is expressed in a rational, clockwork order that is susceptible to understanding of its mechanics, if not of its transcendent purpose.

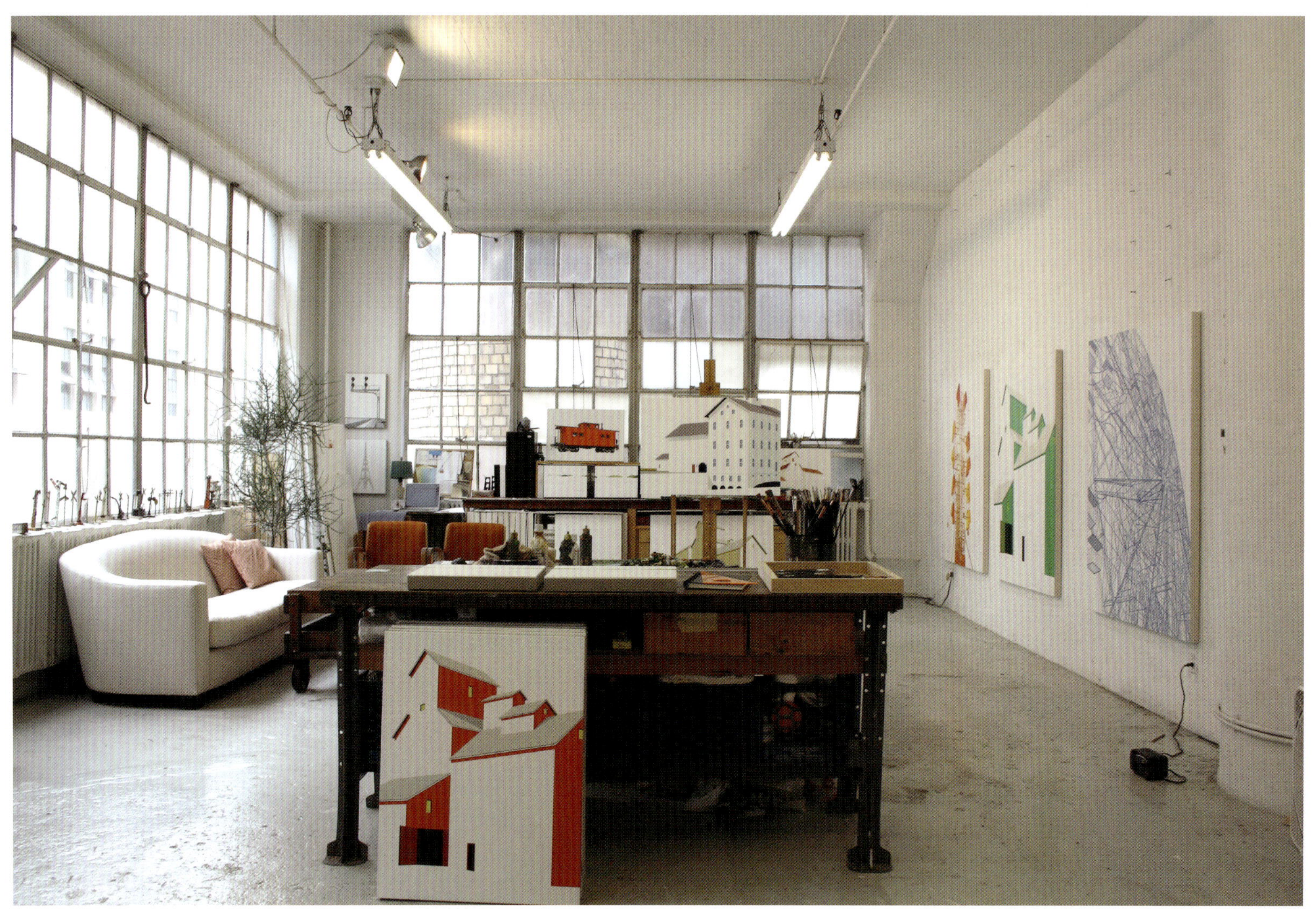

Figure 12. **Studio**, 508 West 26th Street, New York City, 2006.

TRANSPORT

BY CHRISTOPHER GAILLARD

UPON ENTERING WILLIAM STEIGER'S WORKSPACE you will immediately see materials that are essential to any artist's studio: primed canvases, wet paint, brushes of every size. But after spending time there, as I have over the course of several years, one notices other elements of the works in progress. Source material is present in various forms: parts of old train sets, printed ephemera of the early twentieth century, or other relevant objects he has found at a recent postcard fair or flea market. Beneath a windowsill, covered by antique toy train signals, sit binders filled with old photographs of structures now deemed obsolete. Steiger can readily produce a 75-year-old magazine to show you an intriguing image, or a catalogue from which you might once have ordered your own water tower. He will have you read a passenger's description of flying on an early zeppelin, or let you peruse a manual on early railroad rules. Your mind will be quickly transported to another time and place and you will easily appreciate what fascinates this artist.

The studio, located in the Chelsea gallery district of New York City, is housed in a vast 100-year-old factory with windows overlooking the High Line, a defunct elevated train track that is in the process of being transformed into a park. The ceilings are high and the room is flooded with natural light. The industrial space feels like one that would be difficult to find in this neighborhood of glossy, new construction—like something from the past existing in the present day, and not unlike the subjects in a Steiger painting.

Born in New Jersey and raised in Chicago and San Francisco, William Steiger grew up in a family in which his father and grandfather were guiding forces. Both men possessed great curiosity and an encyclopedic knowledge on a wide variety of subjects, and each practiced photography as a hobby. Neither had formal art-related backgrounds; their livelihoods came from business and science. As such, artistic pursuits seemed secondary to Steiger and upon enrolling at the University of California, Santa Cruz, in 1980, geology appeared to him to be a logical course of study. That focus, however, was promptly eclipsed by the allure of art classes, which offered a greater scope of challenges, particularly in learning to draw from life.

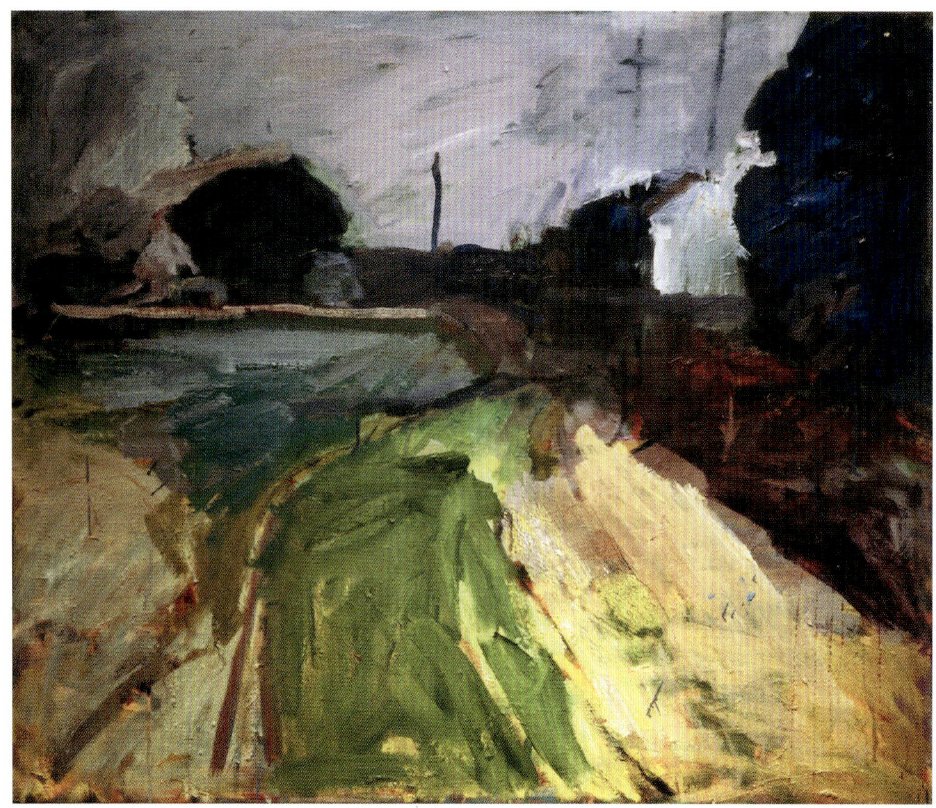

Figure 13. Terry St. John, *Old Benicia Road*, 1981, oil on canvas, 30 x 36 inches.

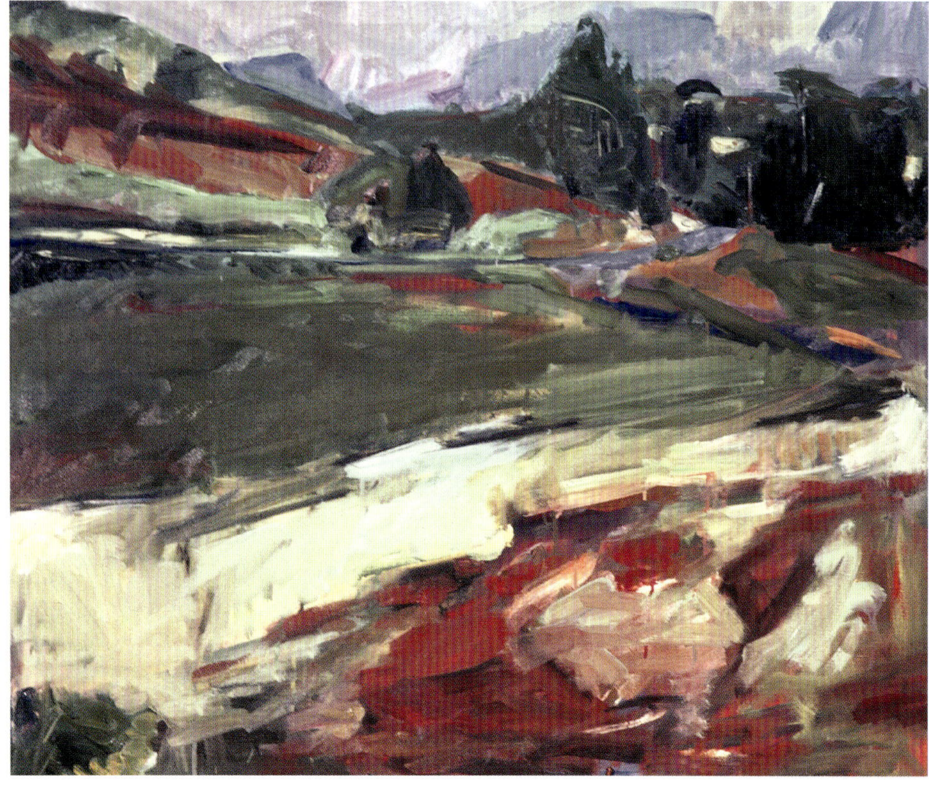

Figure 14. William Steiger, *Watsonville*, 1984, oil on canvas, 30 x 36 inches. Collection of artist.

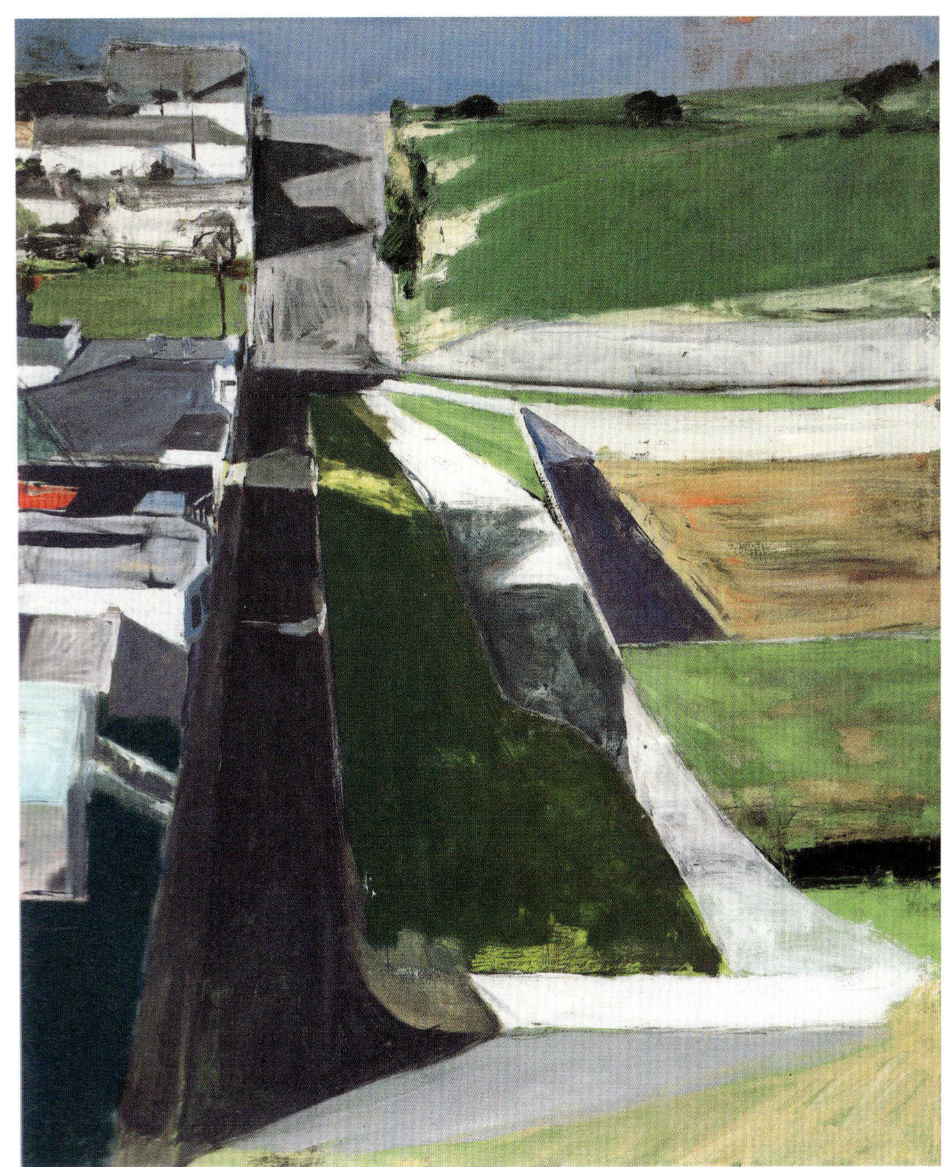

Figure 15. Richard Diebenkorn, *Cityscape I* (formerly *Landscape I*), 1963, oil on canvas, 60¼ x 50½ inches. San Francisco Museum of Modern Art. © Estate of Richard Diebenkorn. Purchase with the funds from trustees and friends in memory of Hector Escobosa, Brayton Wilbur, and J.D. Zellerbach.

It was at UCSC that Steiger met artist Terry St. John (fig. 13), who taught the seminal Outdoor Painter's Project class. St. John's own work was heavily influenced by the San Francisco Bay Area painters, including Richard Diebenkorn (fig. 15) and David Park, whose painting styles engaged California's landscape and light. The impact of Diebenkorn's lush colors, heavy impasto, and lovingly crafted canvases, exemplified by *Cityscape I* in the collection of the San Francisco Museum of Modern Art, is evident in many of Steiger's paintings of this period (fig. 14). Subsequently, an Edward Hopper retrospective at SF MoMA sparked a fascination in him with an even earlier era. Hopper's paintings (fig. 16), revered

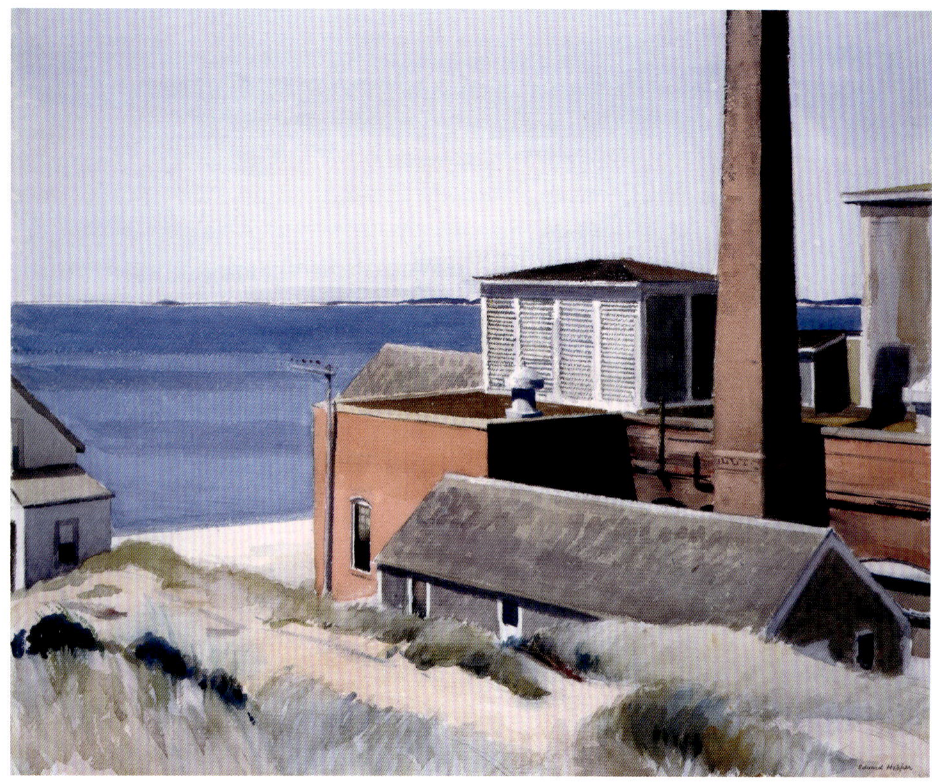

Figure 16. Edward Hopper, *Cold Storage Plant*, 1933, watercolor, 20 x 25 inches. Harvard Art Museum, Fogg Art Museum, Louise E. Bettens Fund, 1934.62. Photograph: David Matthews. © President and Fellows of Harvard College.

for their forlorn, haunting presence and their sensuous brushwork, gradually led Steiger away from nature as a primary subject and toward more defined architectural elements and more controlled brushwork (fig. 17).

In 1987, Steiger enrolled in the Master of Fine Arts program at Yale University and became immediately intrigued both by the linear and spatial concerns of the Minimalist movement, and how these could be employed in landscape painting. The demands and constraints of the aesthetic, along with its cool detachment, affected the stylistic course of the artist's work; his paintings evolved to absorb Minimalism's formal qualities and strict ideology. At this time, one can begin to see the influence of Donald Judd's radical manipulation (or absence) of color, as well as Sol Lewitt's conceptual methodology and meticulous execution. While aesthetically very different from Minimalism, early Pop art shared a similar aloofness, precision of execution, and intentional flattening of the picture plane. In particular, Roy Lichtenstein's (fig. 18) almost stencil-like brushwork and bold use (or dismissal) of color proved influential, as did the mundane or commercial objects depicted in his works. Jasper Johns boiled down the significance of Pop's easily recognizable images to its essence when he famously defined them as "things the mind already knows."

Sources of inspiration available at Yale were also found beyond the painting studio. Steiger enrolled in film courses taught by Michael Roemer, a screenwriter and docu-

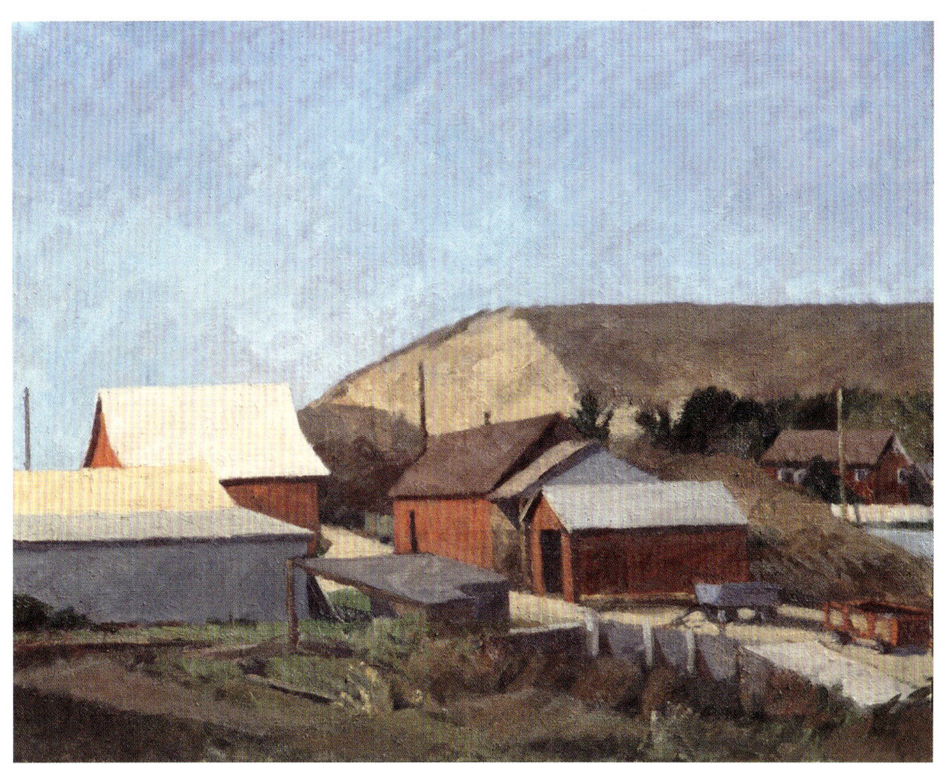
Figure 17. William Steiger, *Coast Road Farm*, 1984, oil on canvas, 18 x 24 inches. Private collection.

mentary filmmaker, and became captivated by what he saw. Roemer's unfettered, head-on style of filming allows the viewer to see the subjects of his work without the use of cinematic or theatrical devices to aggrandize or dramatize them; what comes through are scenes as they are—straightforward and frank—a concept Steiger believed could translate well into painting. A small class taught by Frank Gehry paired students of the painting and architecture schools, forcing each team to understand the influences of one discipline upon the other. This opportunity to study structure and design, combined with his part-time job reproducing architectural drawings, would have a clear impact on Steiger, both generating his interest in buildings and underscoring the importance of including or eliminating particular details.

During his time in New Haven, Steiger read and was deeply intrigued by Robert Smithson's essay in *Artforum*, "A Tour of the Monuments of Passaic, New Jersey." Smithson writes not of the pollution and steely ugliness of the place, but of its power and magnificence. Overlooking the sheer mess and decay of the city, he describes "failed immortality and oppressive grandeur," a deeply emotional response to what the casual viewer may see only as a blighted landscape. Steiger has said that in his work he hopes to create "new places that contain or embody specific emotions," a statement that mirrors the haunting majesty that Smithson found in New Jersey.

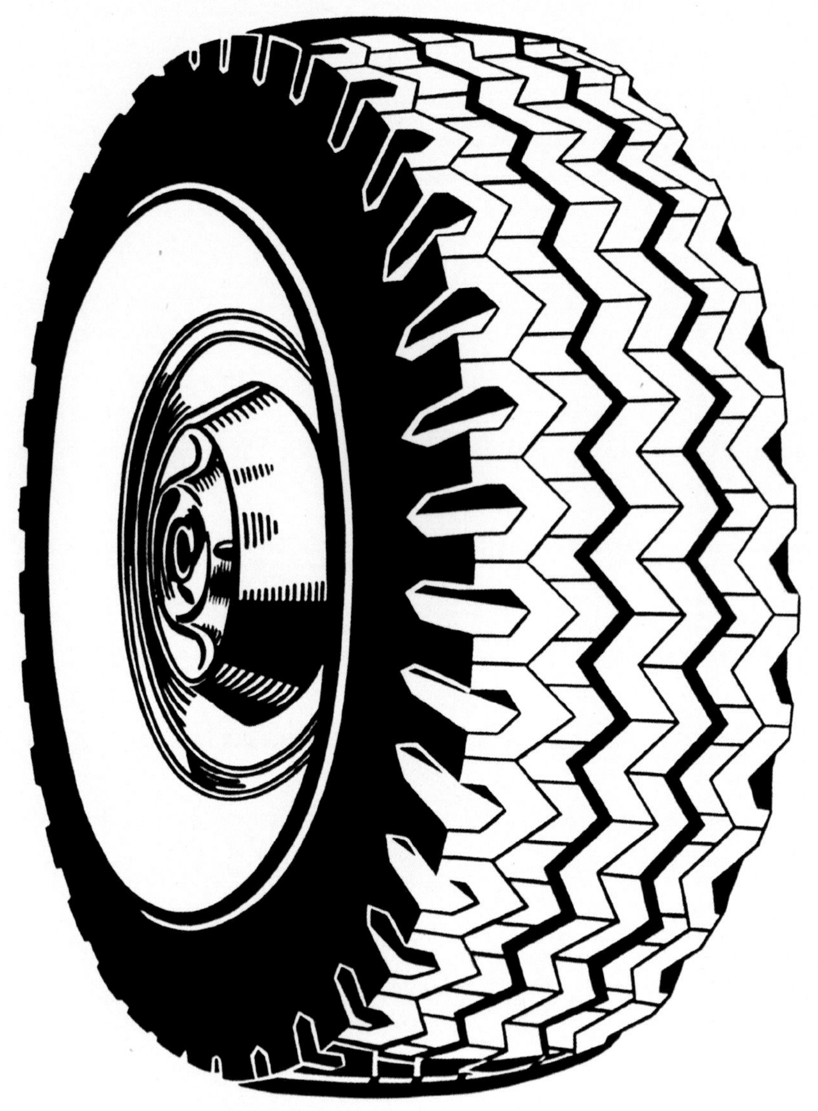

Figure 18. Roy Lichtenstein, *Tire*, 1962, oil on canvas, 68 x 56 inches. © Estate of Roy Lichtenstein.

The photographs taken during Smithson's visit to Passaic (fig. 19) reflect his words in their colorlessness and cinematic aura. He writes of how the "noon-day sunshine cinema-ized the site, turning the river into an over-exposed picture," declaring this to be a place imbued with a kind of aesthetic holiness. Smithson captures Passaic in photographs but also abstracts and elevates it to high art; one clockwise turn and pipes spewing sewage become smokestacks belching purposefully; a particular view of a sandbox is called a "monument." Similarly intriguing to Steiger was the work of the German photographers Bernd and Hilla Becher (fig. 7). Their portraits of industrial facades, tanks, and towers capture site- and time-specific panoramas in stark architectural photographs juxtaposing form and function. The Bechers document things built with little or no aesthetic merit but which in their hands—or in Robert Smithson's or William Steiger's—become significant, memorable, and elegiac.

Following graduate school, Steiger's first show, *New Work*, at the John Slade Ely House in New Haven, Connecticut, included paintings from the Formation series (fig. 5). Executed with a limited palette of gray, black, and white, and only scant traces of other color, the works depict imaginary structures rooted in the rigors of Minimalism. The quasi-painterly style of the surfaces belies Steiger's earlier Bay Area influence, but with added restraint. What is most apparent is the structures' psychic edge; the rigid geometry and repetition also evoke a nervous uncertainty, as we cannot know if they are in the midst of being built or dismantled. The artist has said of his work, "The images . . . all suggest the beginning *or* end of industrial progress." Paintings from this series also appeared in 1990 at his first New York City exhibition at the Condeso/Lawler Gallery.

Condeso/Lawler in New York and Hackett-Freedman Gallery in San Francisco continued to represent Steiger for the next six years. During this period, the paintings evolved

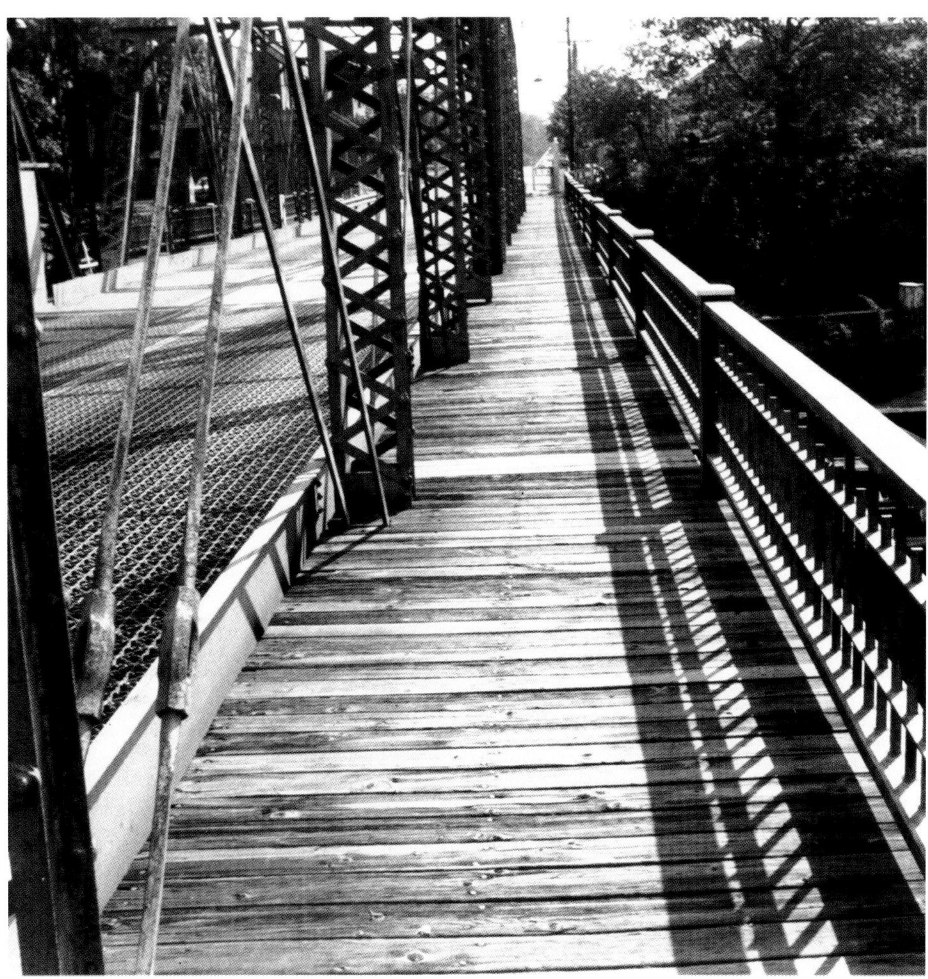

Figure 19. Robert Smithson, *Monuments of Passaic (The Bridge Monument)*, 1967, Instamatic snapshot. Collection of National Museum of Art Oslo, Oslo, Norway. © Estate of Robert Smithson/Licensed by VAGA, New York. Photograph courtesy of James Cohan Gallery.

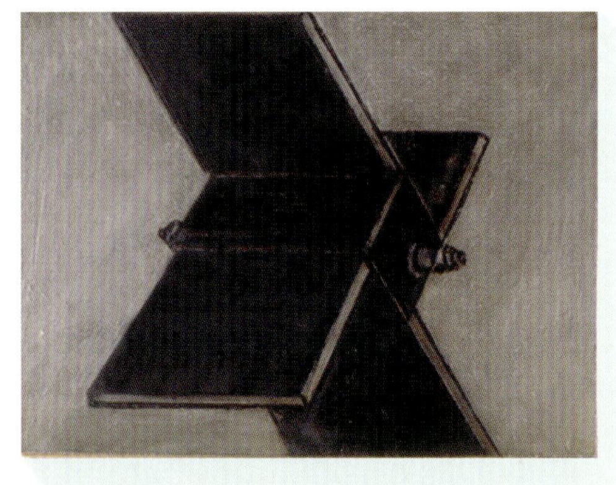 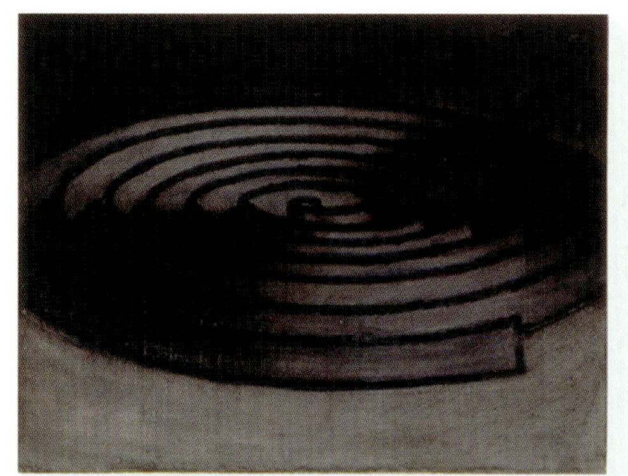 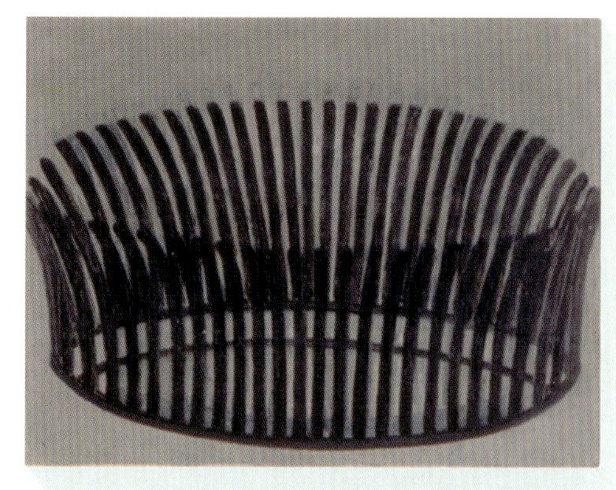

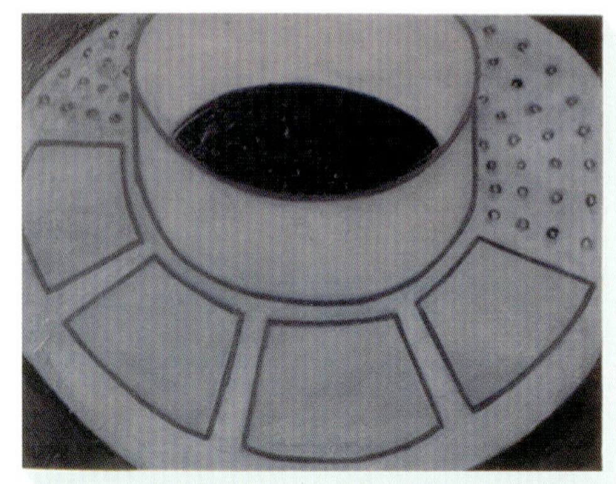 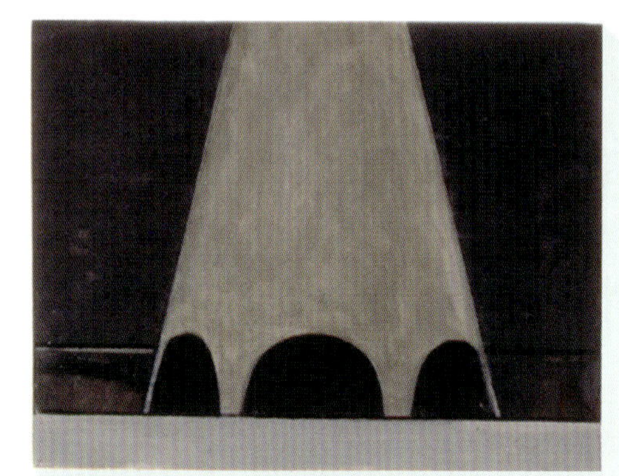 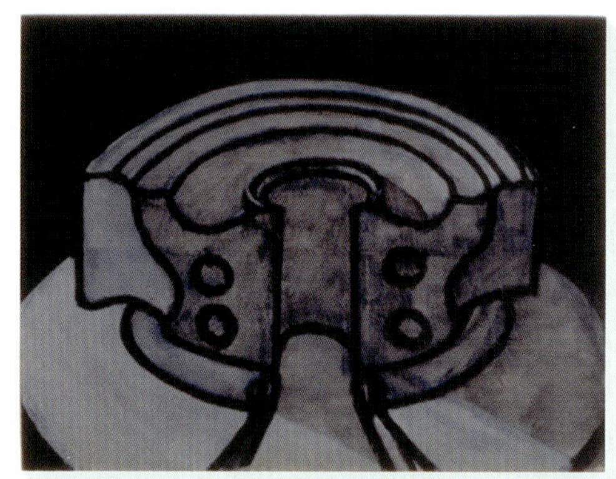

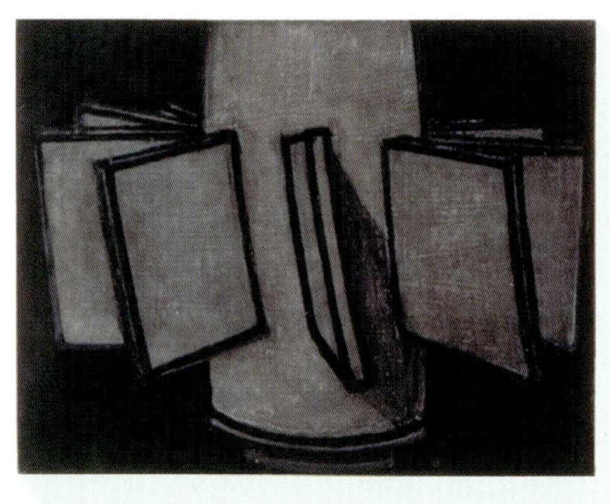 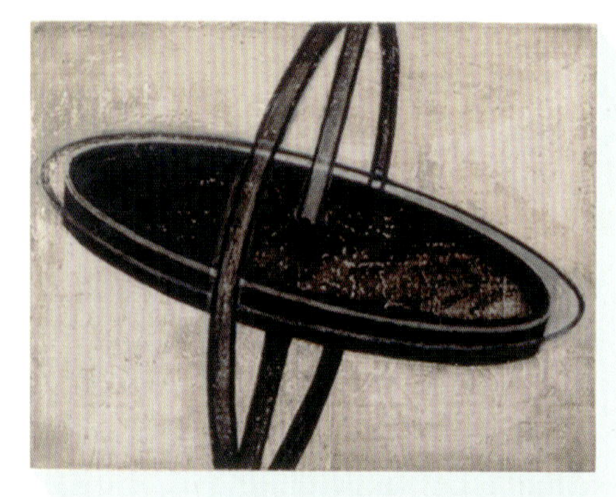 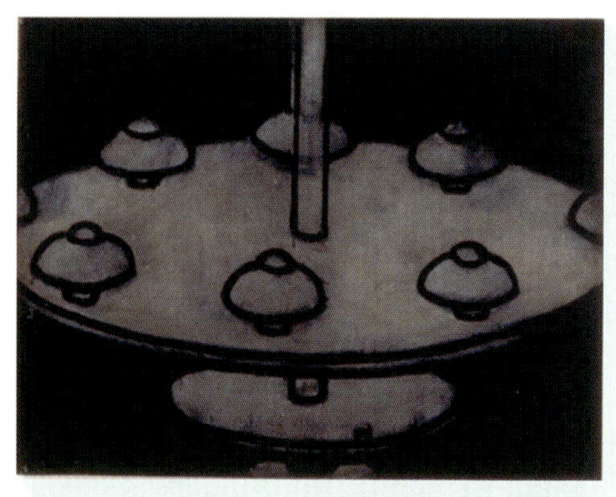

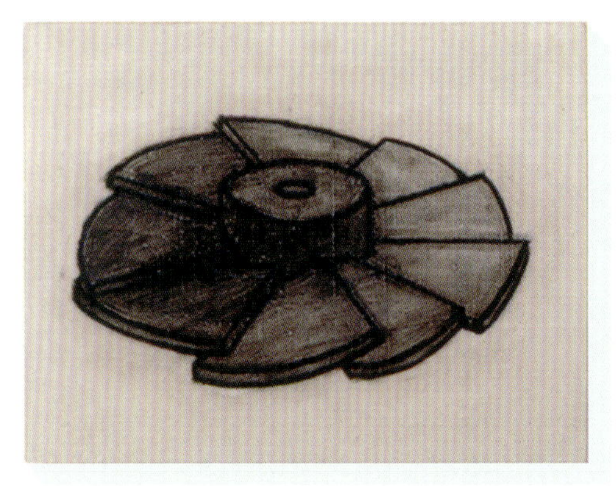 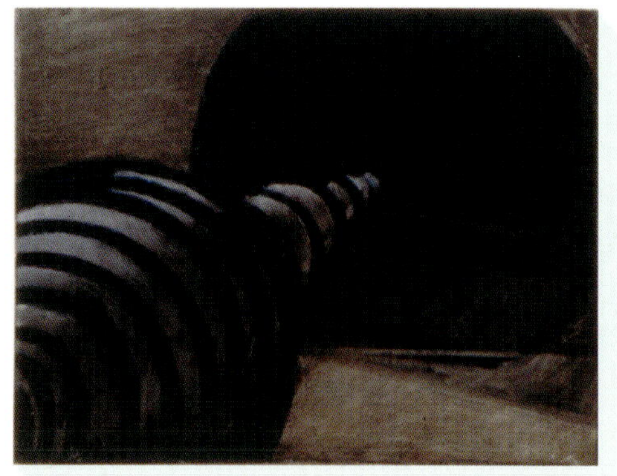 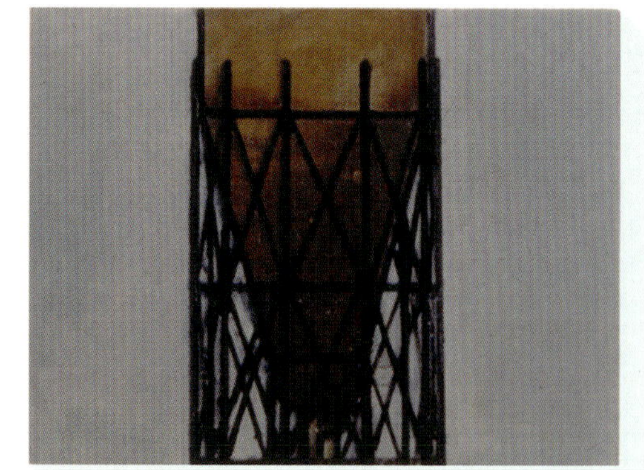

from geometrical constructions toward a focus on machine parts, dirigibles, and water towers. These subjects and a gradual introduction of color first appeared in a series entitled *Rotations and Limited Movements* (fig. 20). Here the central elements of the structure were, isolated on the canvases, with bold outlines of the forms tinted in pale color. The aesthetic continued to rely on mathematical proportion and symmetry, but the examination of archaic machinery would be a precursor to Steiger's depiction of decaying or obsolete Americana.

As he began to revisit outmoded America, in the form of machines, biplanes, and amusement park rides, Steiger was drawn to vintage *Fortune* magazine covers (fig. 21) from the 1930s to 1950s that produced some of the most memorable commercial images from the mid-twentieth century. The most esteemed graphic designer on staff was Thomas Maitland Cleland, renowned for his designs rooted in Art Deco stylization and graphic punch. Of equal importance to the publication was its art director, Eleanor Treacy, whose eye for discovering new talent and encouraging established artists and designers helped create some of the most memorable magazine covers of the time. Launched just after the 1929 crash on Wall Street, it was this sleek manner of depicting the great industries of America that aided in *Fortune*'s decades of success—a surprise, considering the economic climate during which the magazine was established. In the words of its founder, Henry Luce, "American business has importance—even majesty—so the magazine in which we are able to interpret it will look and feel important—even majestic." There was indeed both visual heft and cultural relevance to images depicting the machine age as portrayed by contributors and contemporary painters of the period such as Charles Sheeler and Ralston Crawford (figs. 2 and 3).

As a painter, Sheeler, in particular, holds sway with Steiger's themes and technique. His glorification of the American machine and factory are full of optimism and pride, mirroring the successes of the 1920s, and lending hope during the painful Depression. Sheeler was a witness to developing technology and was in awe of the burgeoning mechanized world. Steiger examines these same machines at the end of their life cycle, still beautiful objects but ones whose promise and power have now dwindled.

It is a well-known fact that Sheeler's eye as a photographer greatly influenced his own painting style and construction. His work for *Fortune* was directly sourced from photographs of the steam engines and other machines depicted, and generally edited out the human form and landscape in favor of man-made objects. The steady, methodical application of paint and near-invisible brushwork also gives the illusion that they are part photographic in nature. Similarly, both the elimination of the human figure from the composition and a precise aesthetic are adopted by Steiger and gradually become hallmarks of his work.

When Steiger moved to New York, the once lively and now all-but-forsaken Coney Island Amusement Park became an obvious source of inspiration. Steiger read extensively on the history of the area and wandered through the park taking photographs and trying the rides. The mechanics of the Wonder Wheel and the Cyclone roller coaster incorporated the intricacies of his own earlier mechanical or structural images. The-now defunct Parachute

Figure 20. William Steiger, *Rotations and Limited Movements*, 1992, oil on wood, 12 x 16 inches (each panel), 54 x 52 inches overall. Collection of Patricia Brett and Thomas Butcher.

Drop and the atmosphere of the run-down boardwalks evoked the minutiae of Sheeler's engines and the melancholia of Hopper's lonely streets.

Critical to his examination of America's urban and rural past is Steiger's fascination with vintage postcards (fig. 22 a–g) and photographic ephemera, the latter executed mostly by anonymous commercial artists. These documents, while avidly pursued by passionate collectors, offer information that, for the most part, no longer exists; they are often the only record of that place at a particular time, recorded for a mundane reason, but now possessing true historic meaning. The railway bridges, water towers, gritty industrial scenes, inert factories, or amusement parks are of particular interest to Steiger, as they, like the

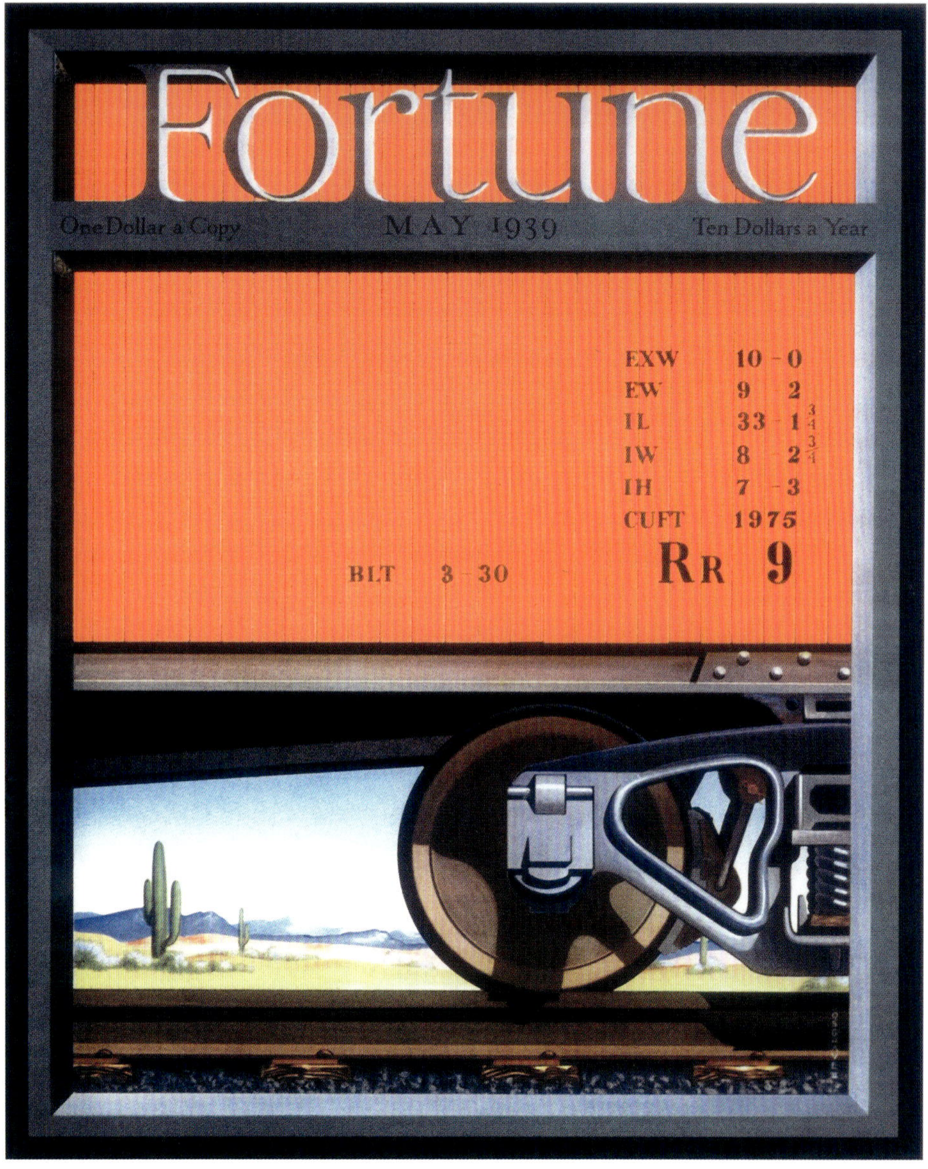

Figure 21. *Fortune* magazine cover, May 1939. © Time, Inc. All rights reserved. Used by permission and protected by the Copyright Laws of the United States. The printing, copying, redistribution, or retransmission of the material without written permission is prohibited.

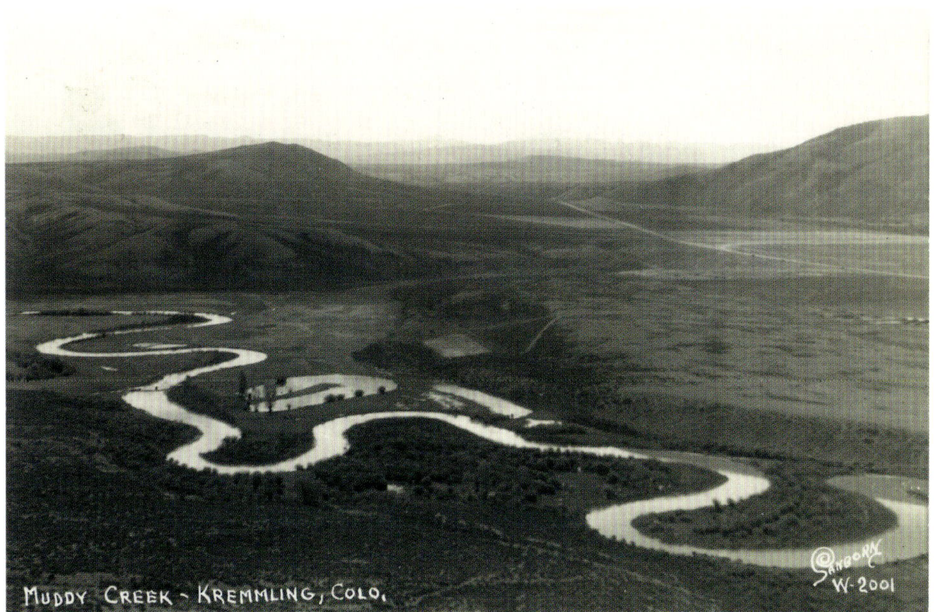

Figure 22a. Postcard, Muddy Creek, Kremmling, Colorado, c. 1930s.

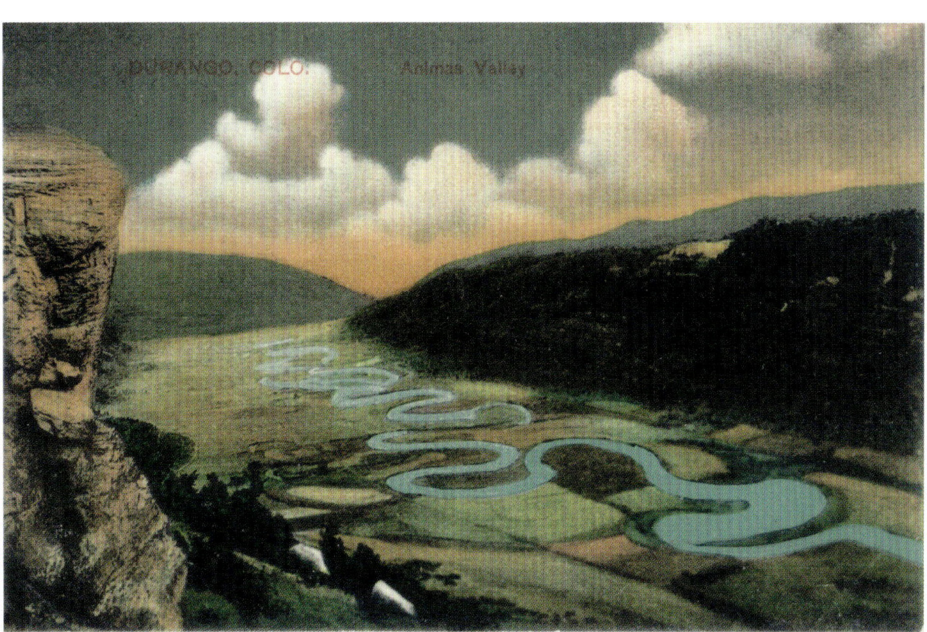

Figure 22b. Postcard, Animas Valley, Durango, Colorado, c. 1920s.

postcards that represent them, are short-lived objects that barely exist in this generation's memory. For example, only in these photographs can you see Coney Island's Parachute Drop as an operational attraction rather than a static edifice. We may have a dim recollection of pictures showing a biplane or zeppelin that was once the greatest innovation in flight, or a roller coaster or Ferris wheel that boasted excitement and speed. These all become arcane bits of

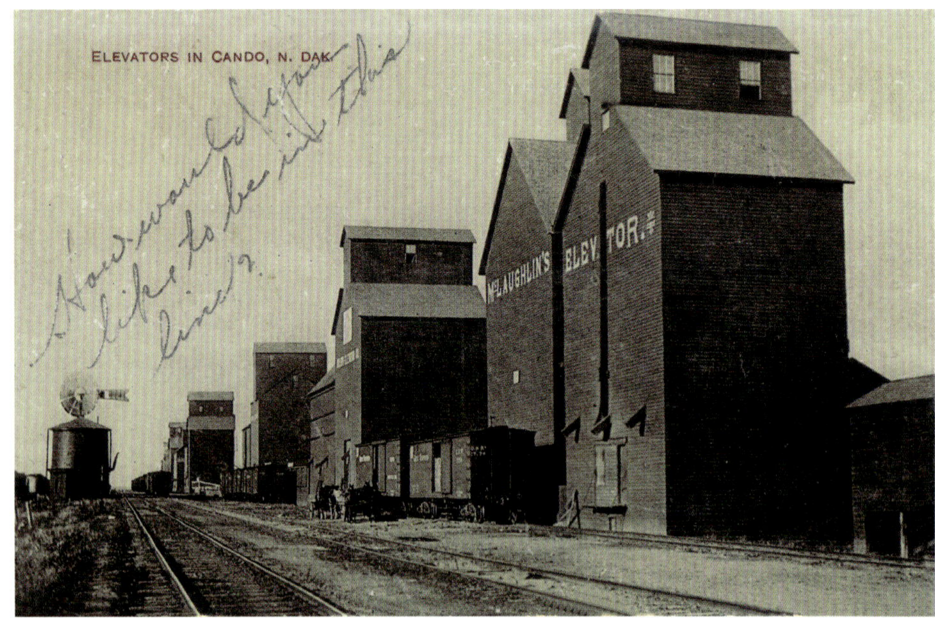

Figure 22c. Postcard, Elevators in Cando, North Dakota. Postmarked 1909.

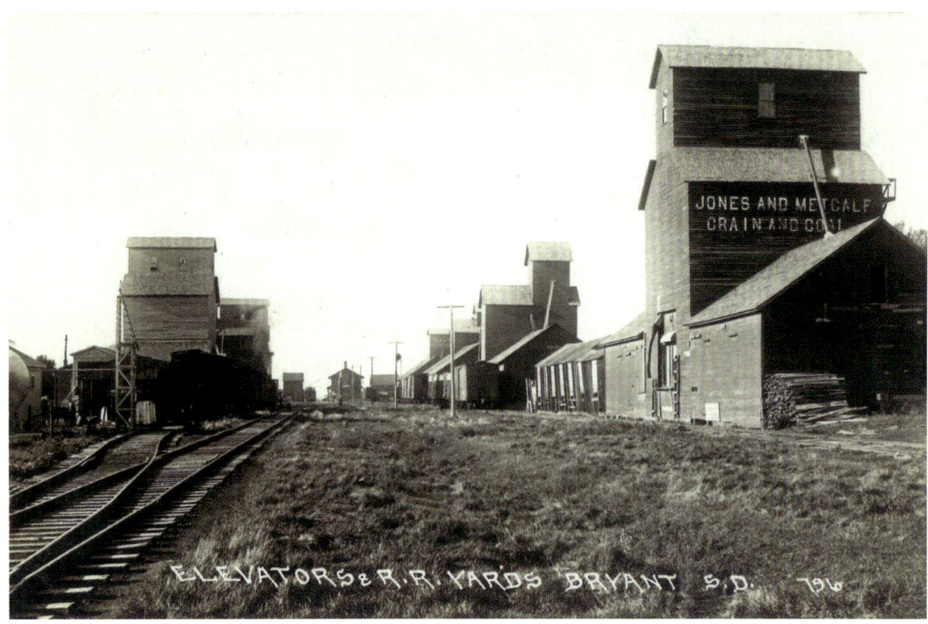

Figure 22d. Postcard, Elevators & R.R. Yards, Bryant, South Dakota. Postmarked 1919.

history, which in Steiger's mind are ripe for resurrection. The artist has stated: "...the paintings come to be about memory and what becomes detail in memory."

Steiger regularly scours postcard and ephemera fairs, thrift shops, and antique stores collecting (along with old copies of *Fortune*) postcards, anonymous photographs, and an assortment of manufacturer's catalogs and manuals from the early twentieth century. The discoveries reside in his studio; Steiger draws upon this material regularly in creating

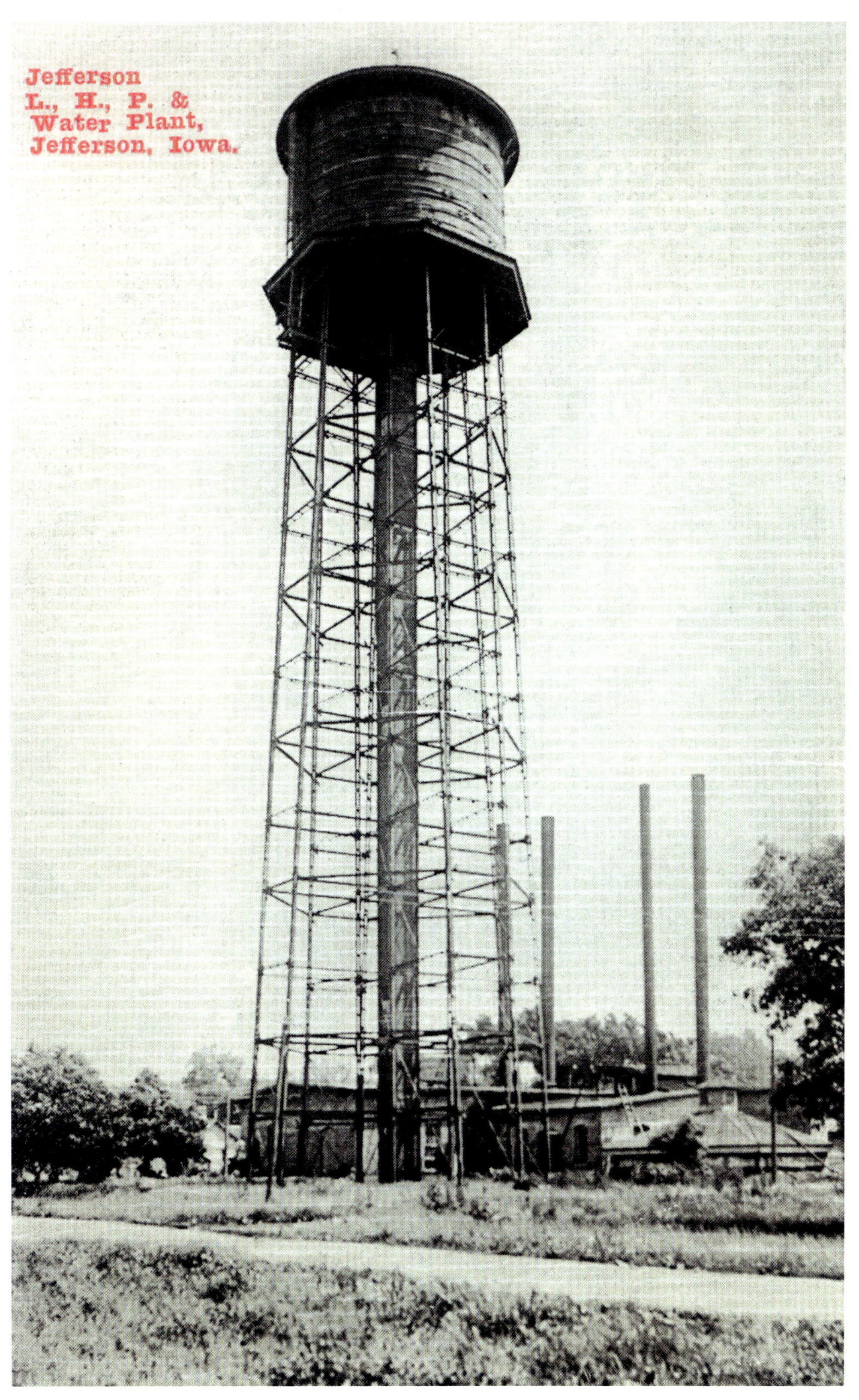

Figure 22e. Postcard, Jefferson L.H.P. & Waterplant, Jefferson, Iowa. Postmarked 1911.

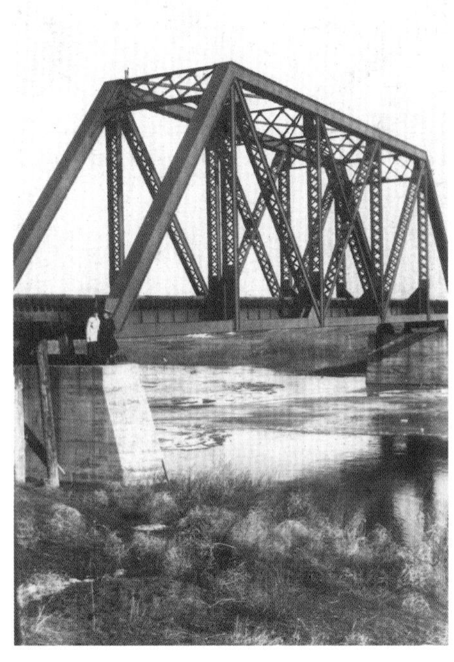

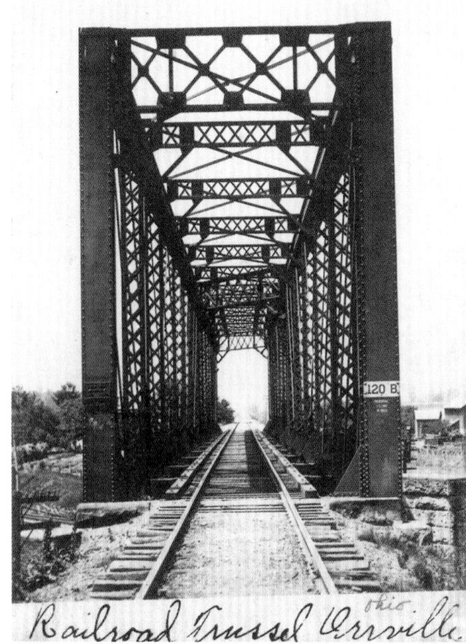

Figure 22f. Postcard, Bridge, unknown location, c. 1910.

Figure 22g. Postcard, Railroad Trestle, Orrville, Ohio. Postmarked 1907.

his compositions. The drawings and paintings are surprisingly different from the sources they reference in that color is often introduced, details emphasized or removed entirely, and nature abbreviated. The structures depicted are haunted remains of a forgotten world. Neil MacGregor, director of the British Museum, has said that the museum seeks "to enable you to understand the world you live in by exploring the world you don't live in." It is perhaps this same objective that drew Steiger away from the plein-air painting he had enjoyed in California and into the studio, where he would cull imagery using ephemeral source material, memory, and invention.

In 2009, The Metropolitan Museum of Art in New York held an exhibition of postcards gifted by the photographer Walker Evans. Built over his lifetime, the collection consists of more than 9,000 cards and was a passion that lent insight and influence to Evans's own photographs. The majority of the cards he collected date from the early twentieth century and precede some of his own most important pictures; in fact, he was working toward being a writer rather than a photographer when he began to collect. In his essay for the exhibition catalogue, Jeff L. Rosenheim writes, "...Evans matured in the peak years of the classic postcard era and was deeply influenced by what he called 'those honest, direct, little pictures that once flooded the mails.'" He even went so far as printing postcard-size format photographs of his own work for personal use. Discussing artists-as-collectors, Rosenheim muses "[Artists] collect for pleasure and instruction, to recover their lost youth, to build archives of material upon which to construct their own personas. For some, collections provide source material for their art, as did the 'working library' of textiles kept by Henri Matisse. For others, the act of collecting offers a necessary escape, a distraction from the burden of creation."

The disappearance of early-twentieth-century industrial America is mirrored in the paucity of photographic imagery and postcards (and thus historical materials) recording it; Steiger has realized the necessity to save, collect, and preserve these items and in turn he has pulled out of it imagery that excites his imagination. In his seminal book, *Prints and People*, A. Hyatt Mayor discusses ephemera similar to postcards. Citing eighteenth-century playbills (of which there were purported to be more than one million impressions), he could not find one to illustrate his book. He writes, "The commonest print always becomes the scarcest. Anybody can buy a Whistler etching, but try to find a Victorian matchbook. In the long run, pictures survive best on a material that withstands fire and burial and is not worth reusing, like the clay of Athenian pottery."

Reaching beyond his industrial subject matter, where the natural world is reduced to geometrical forms, if it is shown at all, Steiger began a series of paintings depicting rivers wending their way through tilled fields. The initial inspiration for the *River Bend* series derives from his previous aviation imagery, but this time the view is from inside the airplane looking down. The series also betrays a small debt to one of the earliest paintings to influence Steiger's recent work: Thomas Cole's breathtaking *View from Mount Holyoke, Northampton, Massachusetts, after a Thunderstorm—The Oxbow* (fig. 23). Of magnificent scale and great visual drama, the painting demonstrates Cole's use of a high perspective to achieve a

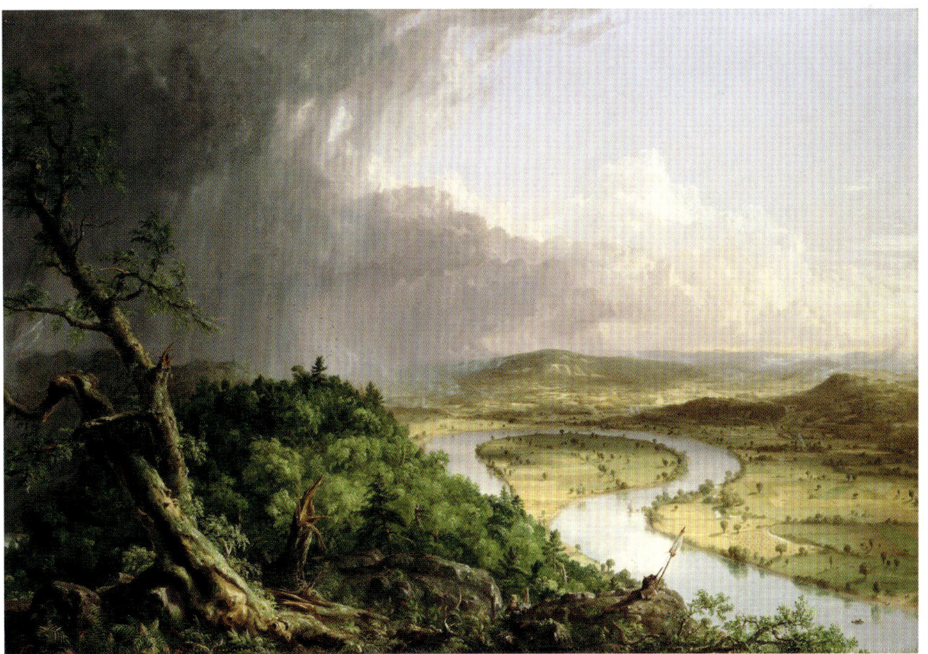

Figure 23. Thomas Cole, *View from Mount Holyoke, Northampton, Massachusetts, after a Thunderstorm—The Oxbow*, 1836, oil on canvas, 51½ x 76 inches. © The Metropolitan Museum of Art, New York, NY. Gift of Mrs. Russell Sage, 1908 (08.228).

vertiginous and powerful emotion. The same is true of the rivers Steiger paints from this aerial view, wherein clumps of trees are reduced to small dots and crops are depicted as planes of lush color. As in Cole's painting, there is an awestruck quality and a sense of grandeur in the flow and bend of the river; it is simultaneously essential to the landscape and its own entity. Steiger, though, further elevates the perspective and tilts it slightly, delivering a more contemporary view, as though seen in flight. The stillness is less that of Cole's tranquility in nature and more the massive size and stillness of the earth when seen from a distance. Colors are heightened and land patterns are rendered geometric to the point of being surreal. Rather than anchoring himself to a specific scene, the artist is capturing his—and our—collective memories of what is seen from any and every airplane window.

The artist–dealer relationship is often crucial to the encouragement and development of any artist's career. Steiger currently works with several dealers including ones in Atlanta, Chicago, Dallas, and South Korea, but his primary gallery since 1999 has been Margaret Thatcher Projects in Manhattan. Thatcher knew of Steiger's work from the mid-1990s, when he was showing at Condeso/Lawler Gallery, and subsequently asked him to join her program—an interesting addition to the gallery, as the work Thatcher showed at the time was by artists working solely in abstraction. During this period, he has used his previous subjects and ephemeral imagery as a point of departure in developing new bodies of work, and it is reasonable to surmise that the strictly minimalist aesthetic of many of Thatcher's artists have had an influence. Grain elevators from abandoned farmlands are pared down to shapes of color that form roofs, windows, and shadows; some walls are only implied within the negative space. Train signals that appear in the background of found photographs become the focal point, blown up and centralized in the picture. The artist's interest in aerial transportation has evolved as well, with unoccupied cable cars suspended in mid-air, their wires extending off the canvas and giving no sense of how they are securely tethered. To demonstrate how influential this artist–dealer relationship can be, Steiger has said that being with Margaret Thatcher Projects has made him a better artist. He has very high expectations for his own work but an additional constant—the opinion of someone whose eye he respects, who has watched the work develop over time—further elevates the standards to which he holds himself.

In addition to paintings and drawings, Steiger has added printmaking to his artistic output. Although he had made a handful of lithographs in Santa Cruz and learned etching from Orlando Condeso while he was showing with Condeso/Lawler, it was when he began working with Pace Prints in New York that Steiger became intrigued with what new perspective the challenges of printmaking could add to his work. He found that aquatint could enrich the depth of shadows in his buildings and embolden the lines of the Wonder Wheel. Another elevator building, this time executed in screenprint, becomes even more abstract, more reliant on areas of color as signifiers. The flat and even surfaces of reduction

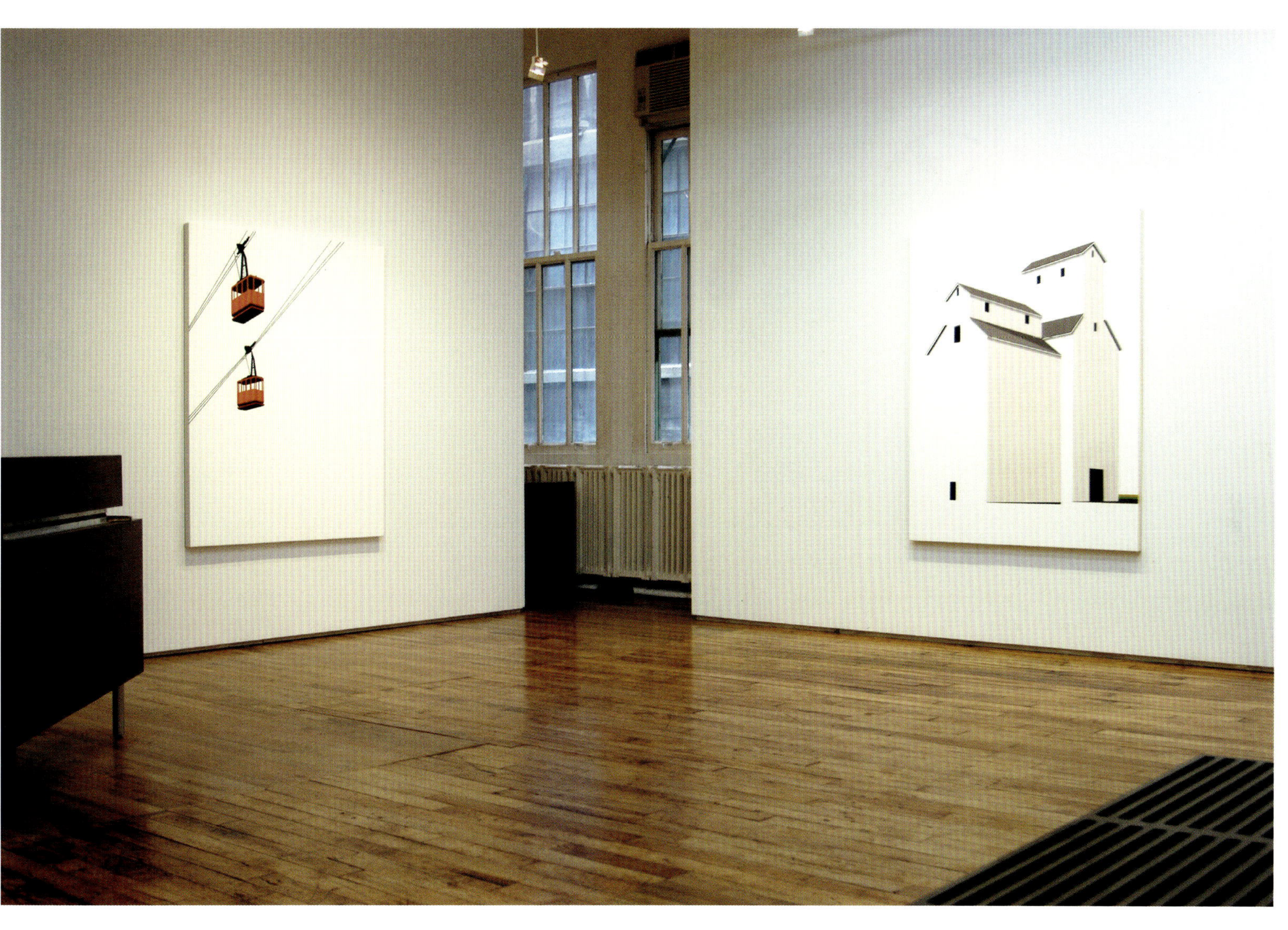

Figure 24. Exhibition, *Landmark*, Margaret Thatcher Projects, 2008.

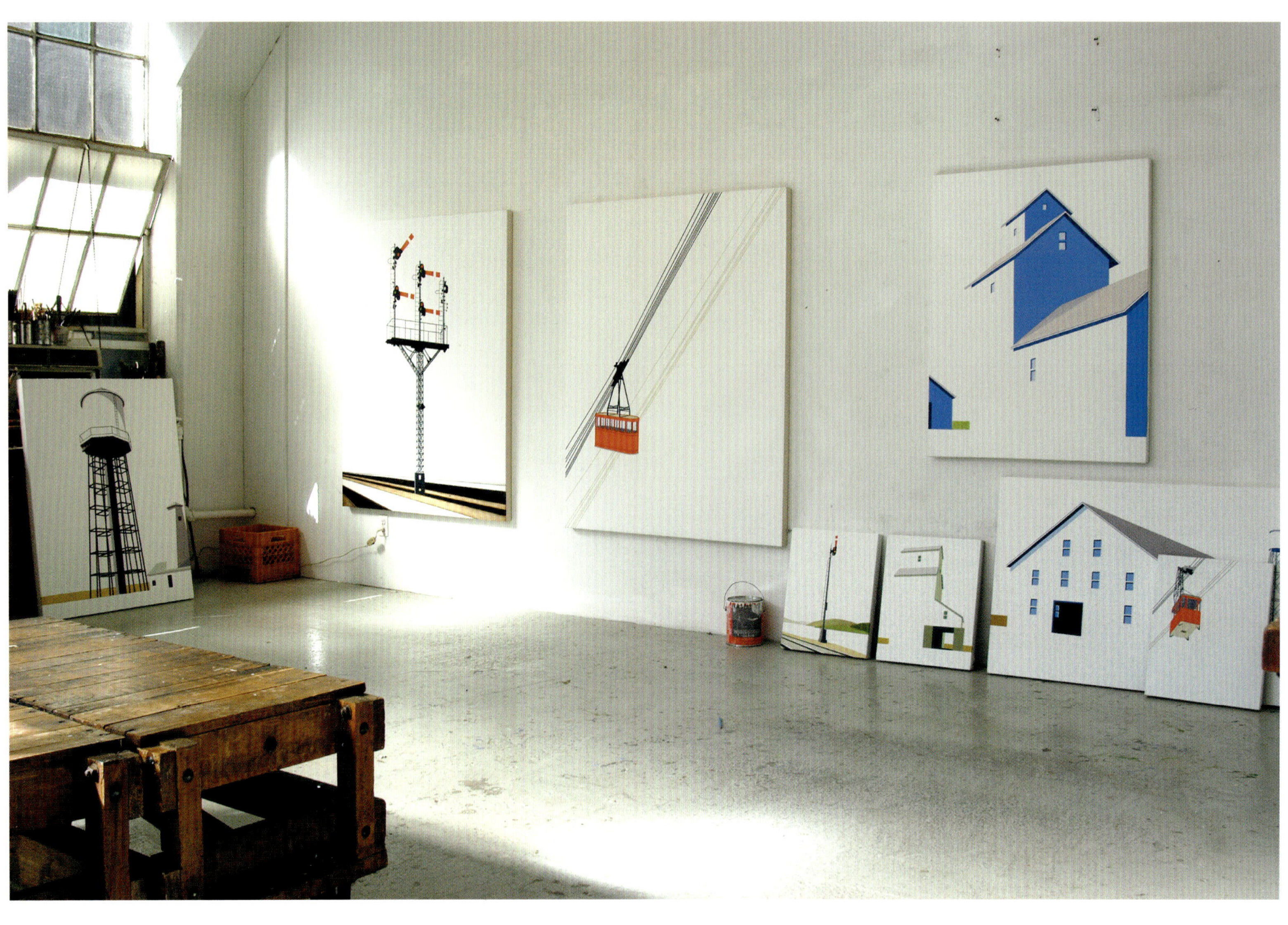

Figure 25. **Studio**, 508 West 26th Street, New York City, 2007.

linocut give the land in his *River Bends* an uninterrupted surface of pigment. Steiger says "the printers at Pace love to figure out 'how' when approaching a project—they are fearless of introducing a technique to an image and making them work together."

Steiger has constantly embraced evolution within his work, but he has remained devoted to landscape painting, even as his vistas often became devoid of visible land. The early, lush colors gave way to simple monochromes; then color reappeared in unexpected palettes and tinted canvases. Within these progressions and experimentations, one common thread has been subjects whose function precedes the study of their form. They all first existed to serve a purpose, be it a bridge or a plane, a silo to hold grain or a tower to hold water, a train (or just the signal to direct a train), a ride up a mountain in a tram or a circular ride at the amusement park. While not initially created with aesthetic objectives, Steiger visualizes these objects and reexamines their lines, shapes, and shadows; suddenly their design is very much in focus, as if that were always the intent. By zooming in on a passenger car dangling from a Ferris wheel or showing how light illuminates the roof of a grain elevator, the scenes eliminate references to time and place. We are effectively transported to both another time and frame of mind as we watch Steiger chart his future course.

WILLIAM STEIGER
TRANSPORT

IF IT CAN BE SAID that learning is the process of making the strange into something familiar, then one might be tempted to think that taking something as familiar as industrial bridges and viewing them through a strangely unfamiliar lens might be the process of un-learning. It is exactly this kind of ambiguity that is employed in the paintings of William Steiger. Such equivocation requires multiple readings. A bridge placed in the landscape in a distant view connects two shores. It *becomes* the landscape, occupies the horizon, interrupts the horizon and "becomes an object."

Steiger looks for the opportunity to slightly alter and transform our expectations of predictability. The sparseness of visual matter on these canvases makes the choice of view or the placement of the viewer in the picture plane much more critical. The slightest shift in any one direction dramatically changes our understanding of reality. As we approach the bridge and reach its proximity, the most startling transformation takes place. We are able to occupy this skeletal form and understand its spatial construct. The power of a line, drawn in steel against the whiteness of a bleak sky, heightens our peripheral vision and in turn allows us to inhabit its cathedral-like space. Just as our mind is capable of connecting dots to imply lines, we are able to connect an array of lines to imply surfaces and thus volumes.

The bridges, perhaps more than any other subject, allow for the widest array of cinematic moments, each of which completely transforms what these wonderfully unsheathed iron beasts are about. Intrinsic to their character, the structures depicted in these paintings reside in our memories, evoking movement toward, around, through, and under. It is these multiple depictions that straddle the ambiguous edge of perception and become transformative. It is remarkable that these bridges, with a simple twist and turn, are capable of evoking such a fundamental shift in our understanding. The series takes us on a journey as a detached observer of a slightly unfamiliar world, to the relative familiarity of a world we might actually inhabit, and finally back to the unfamiliar world of an unexpected view.

BRIDGE
TURAN DUDA

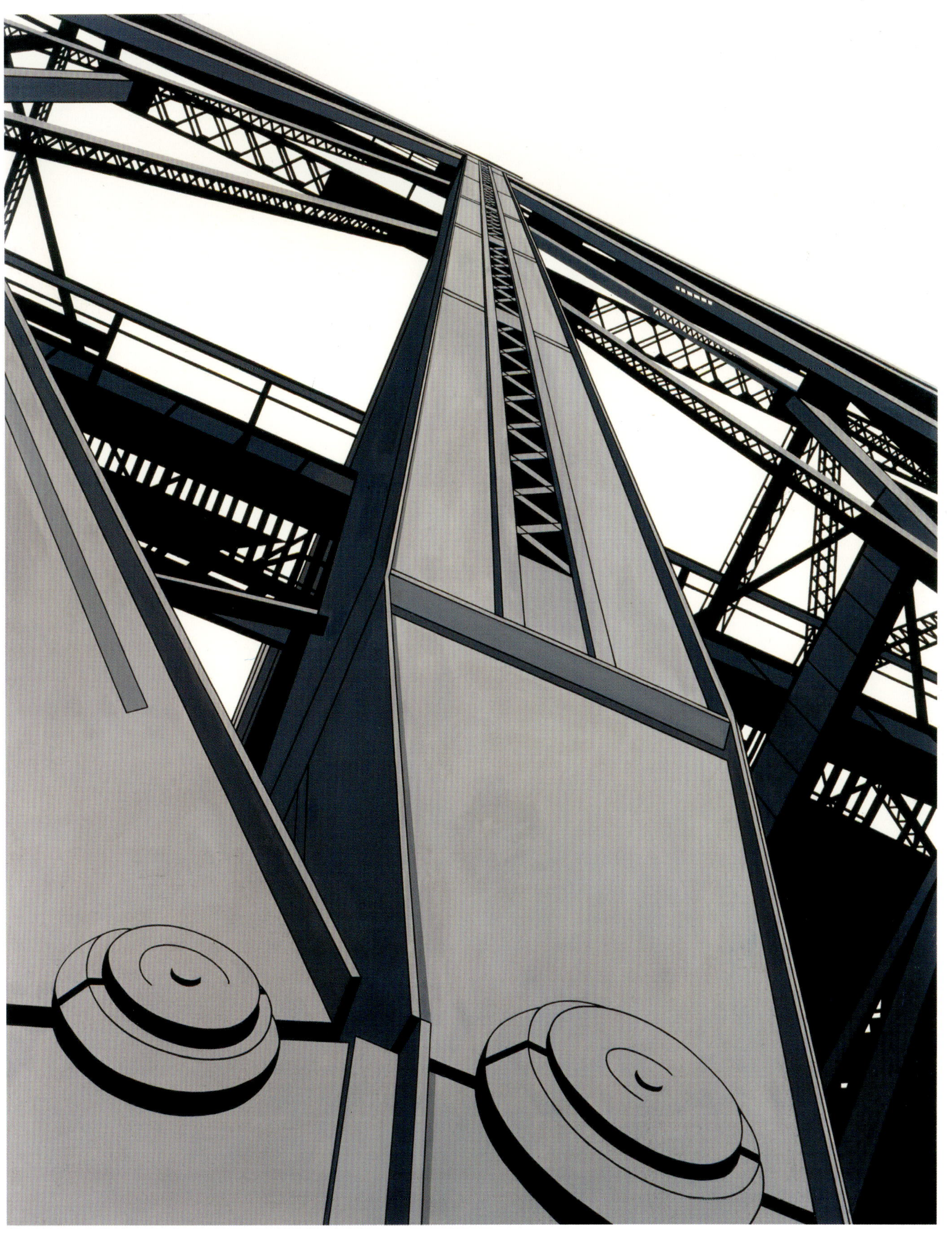

Plate 1. **Centerspan**, 2001, oil on canvas, 60 x 48 inches. Collection of artist.

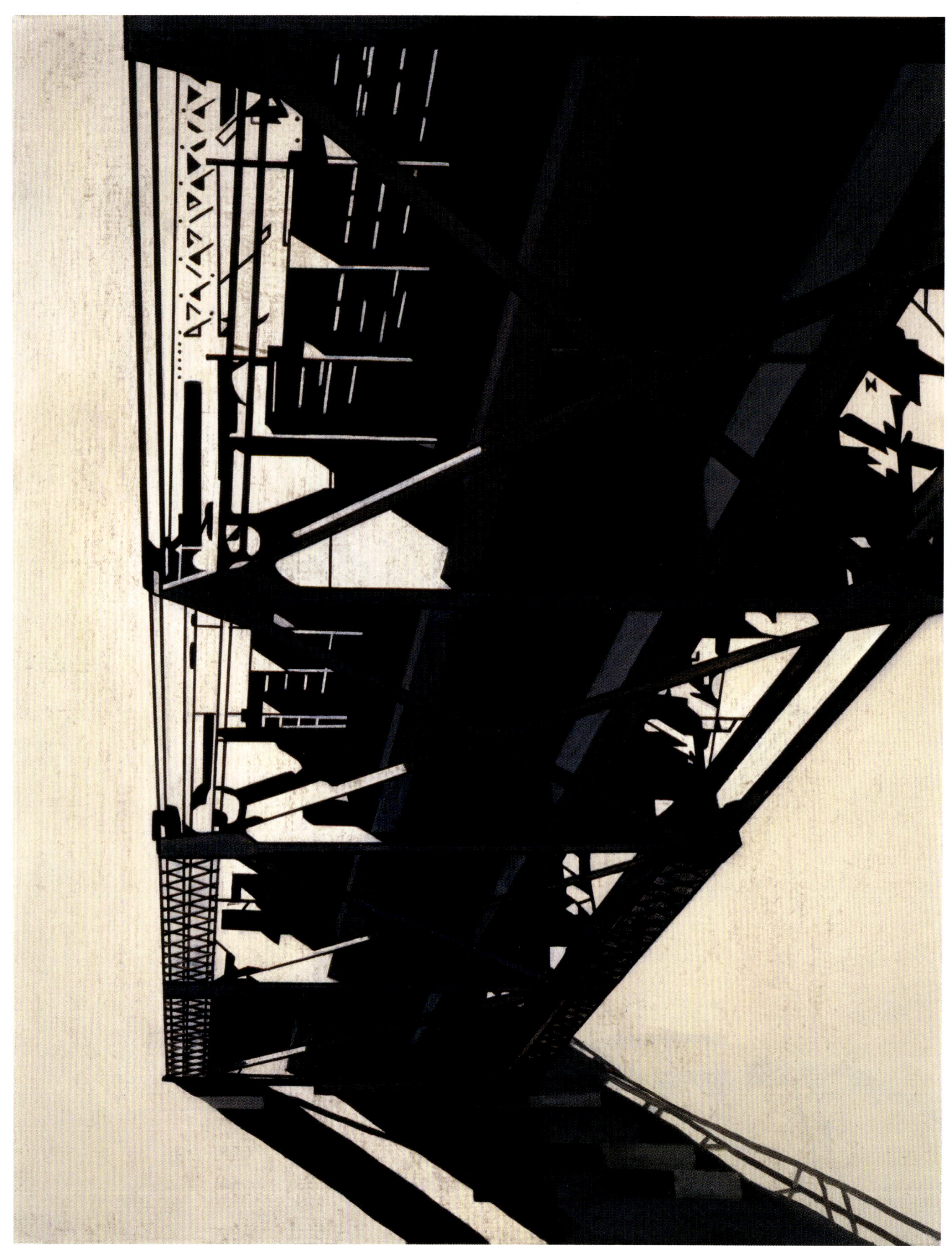

Plate 2. **Minisink I**, 1995, oil on canvas, 20 x 16 inches. Collection of artist.

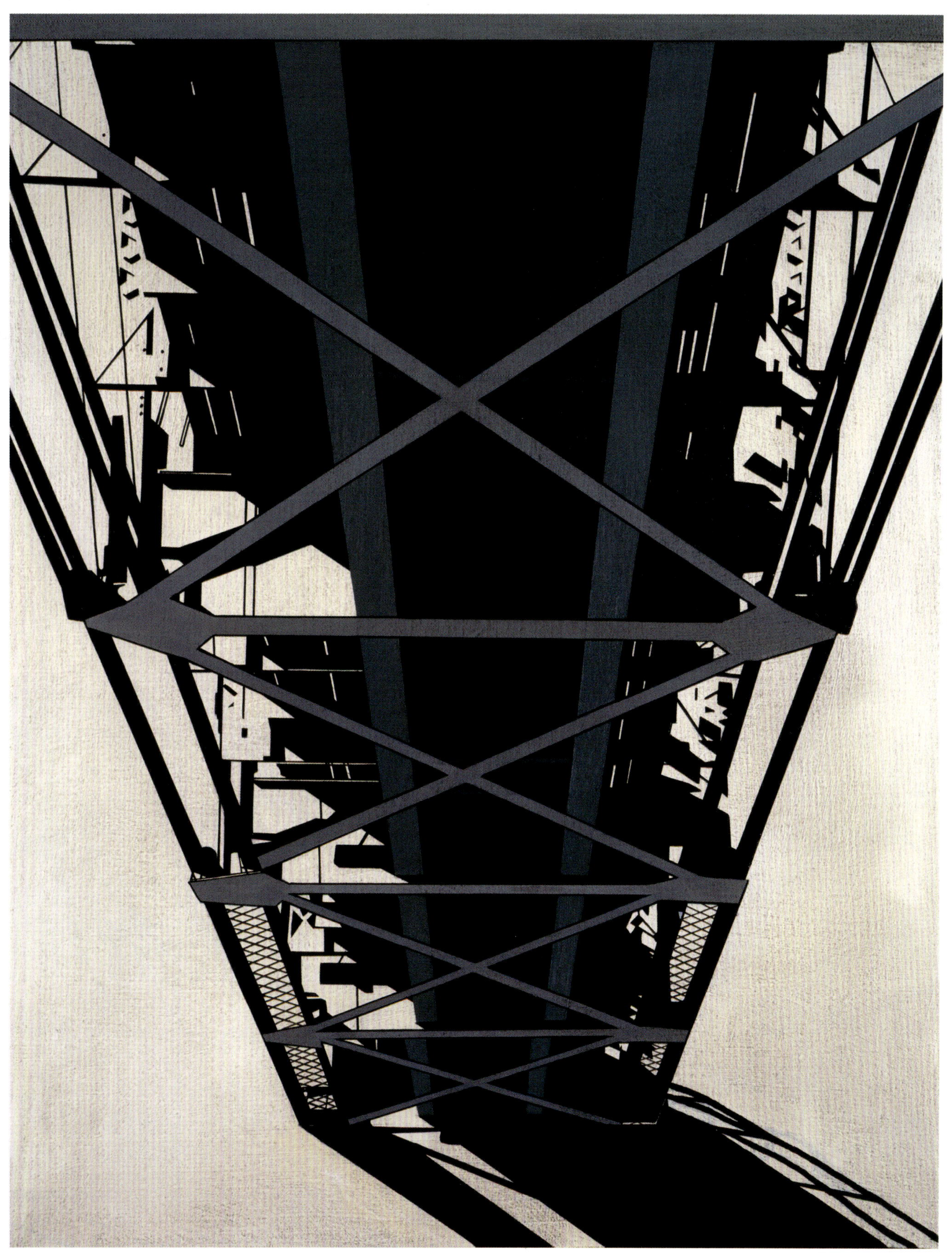

Plate 3. **Minisink II,** 1995, oil on canvas, 30 x 24 inches. Private collection.

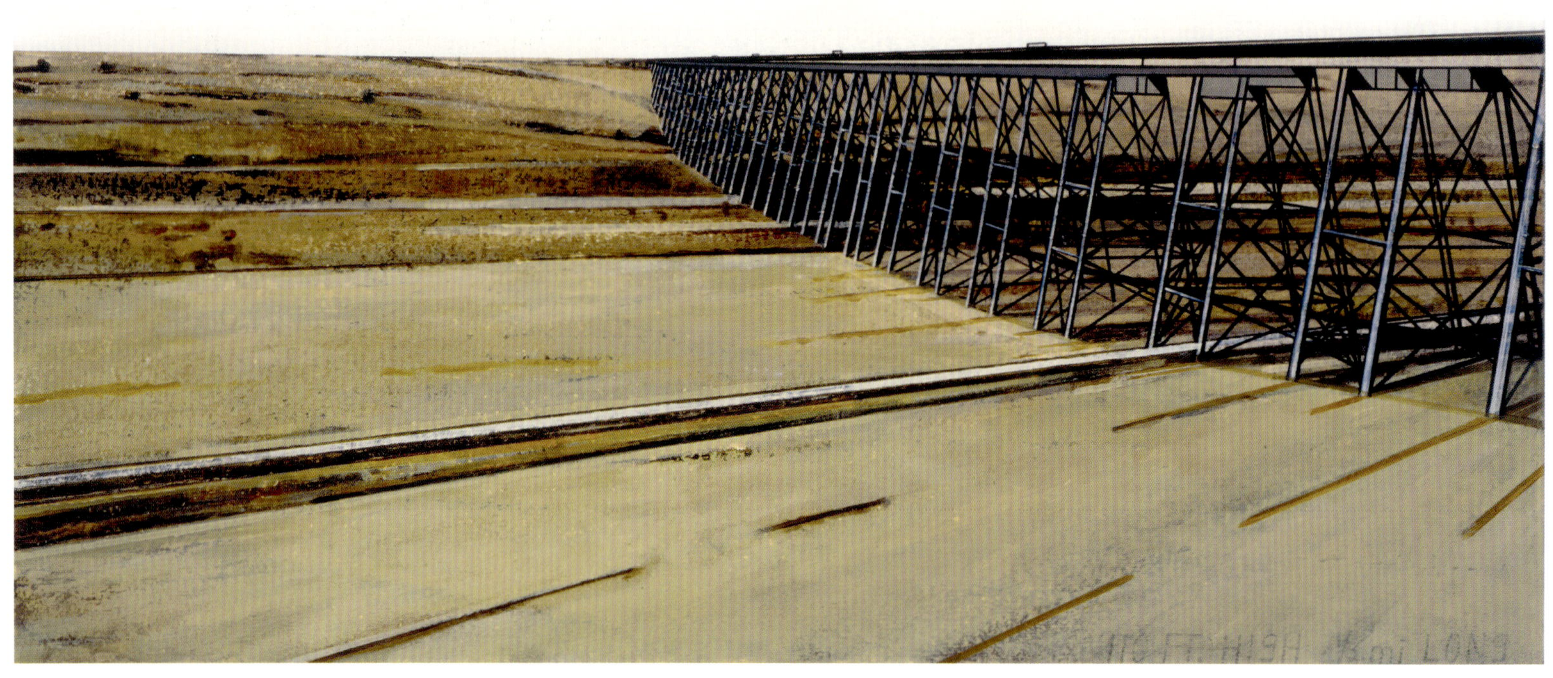

Plate 4. **110 ft. High, 1/2 Mile Long II**, 1996, oil on canvas, 17½ x 27½ inches. Private collection.

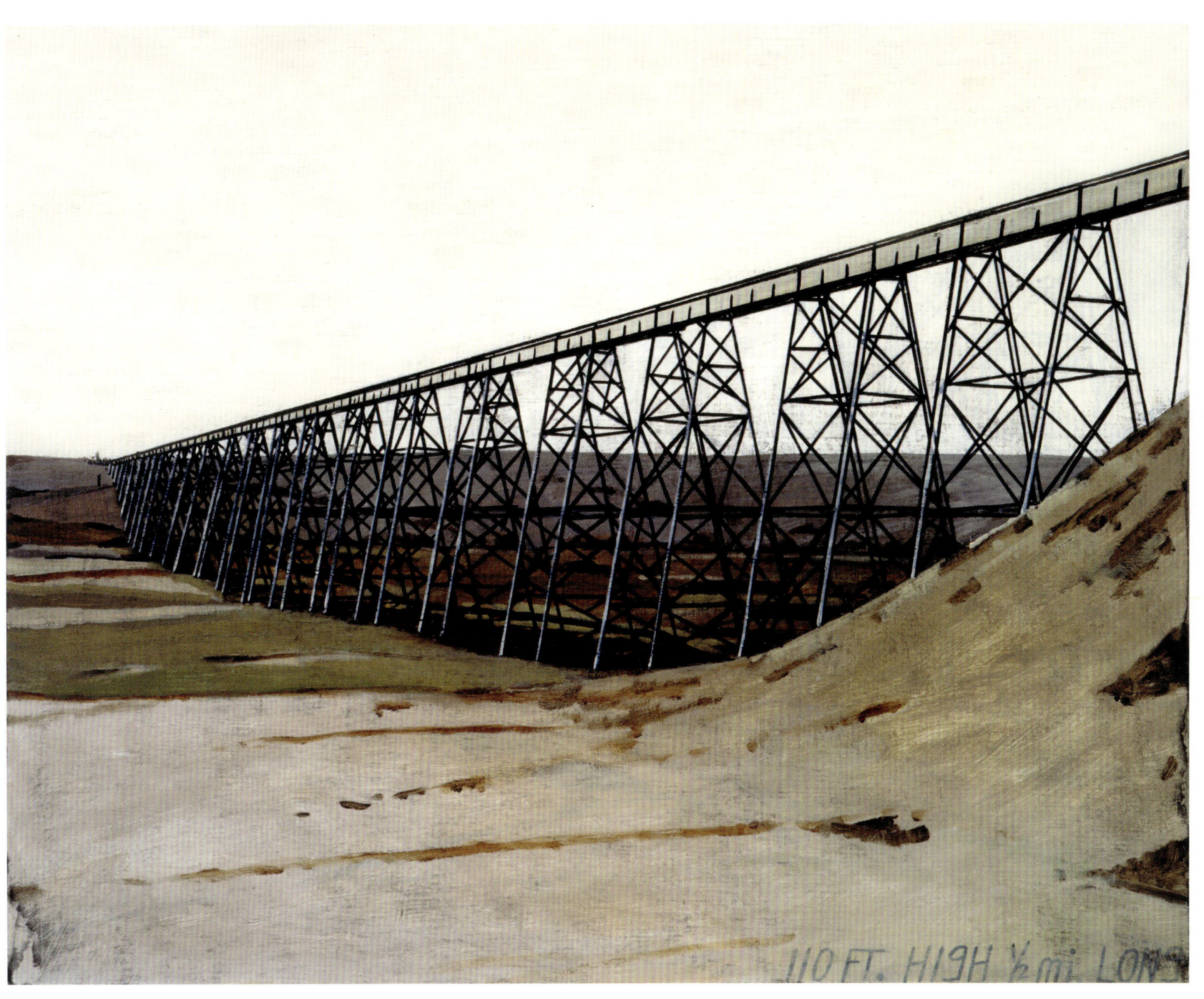

Plate 5. **110 ft. High, 1/2 Mile Long I**, 1996, oil on canvas, 16 x 20 inches. Private collection.

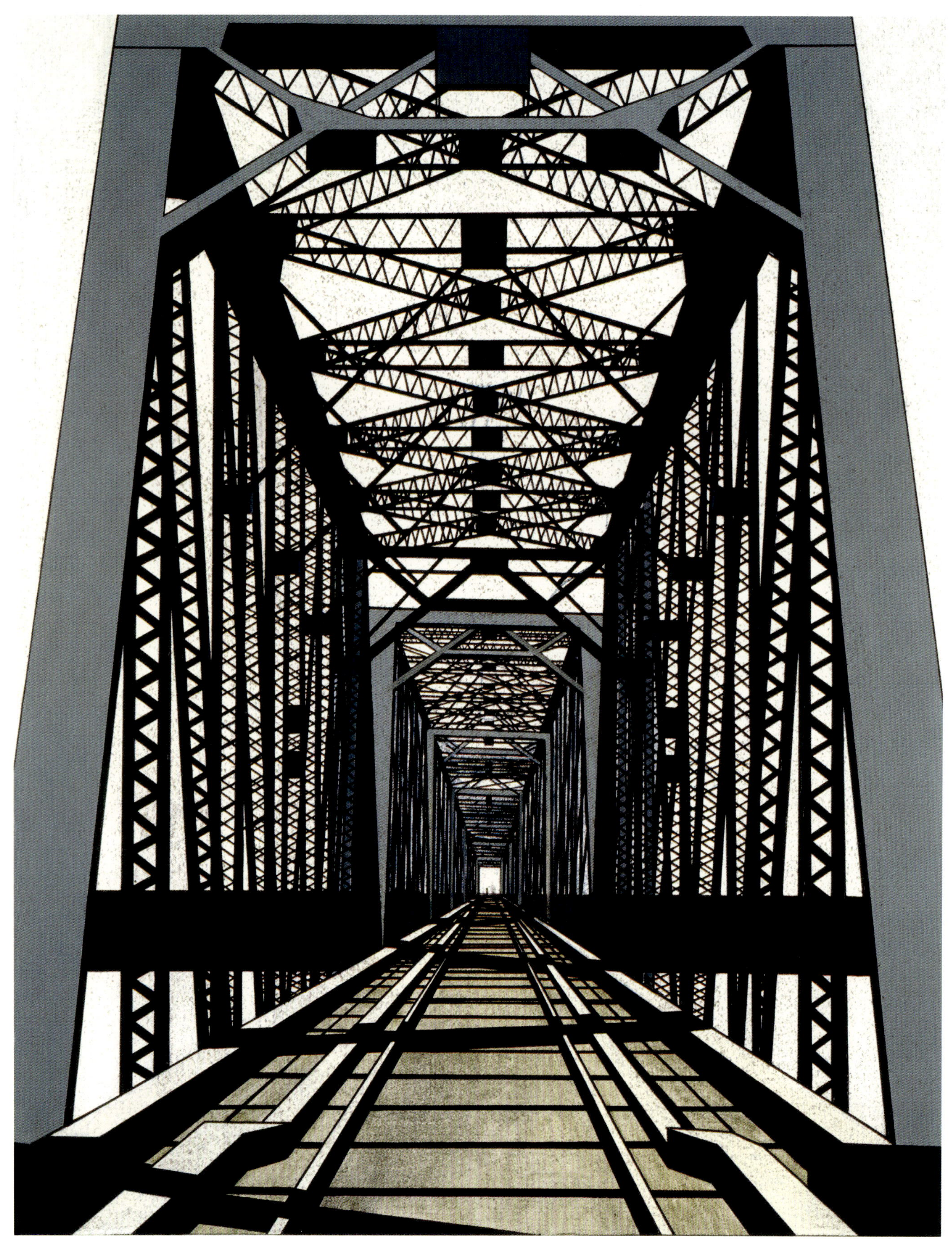

Plate 6. **Lehigh**, 1996, oil on canvas, 30 x 24 inches. Collection of artist.

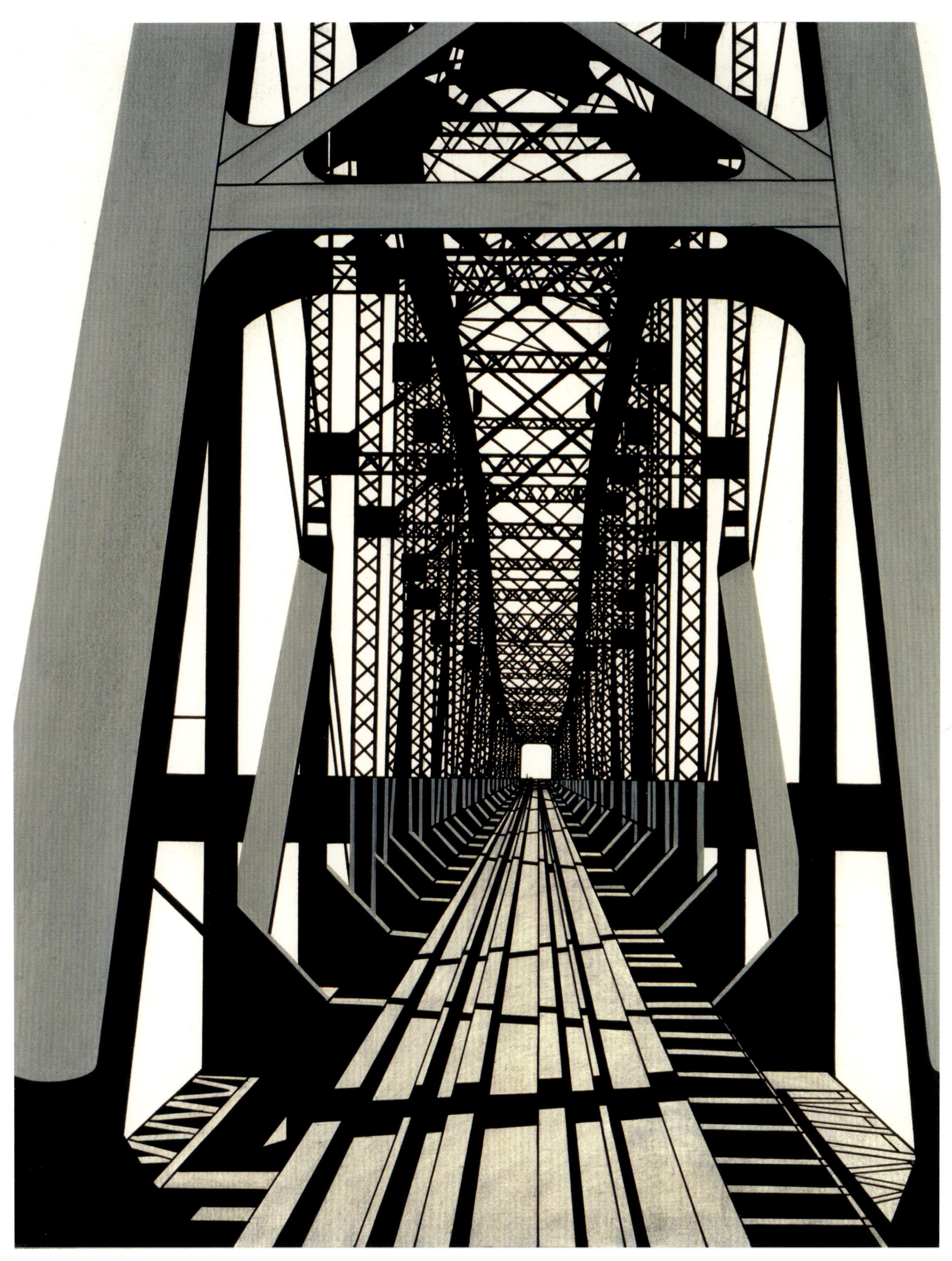

Plate 7. **Pontis**, 1998, oil on canvas, 44 x 35 inches. Collection of artist.

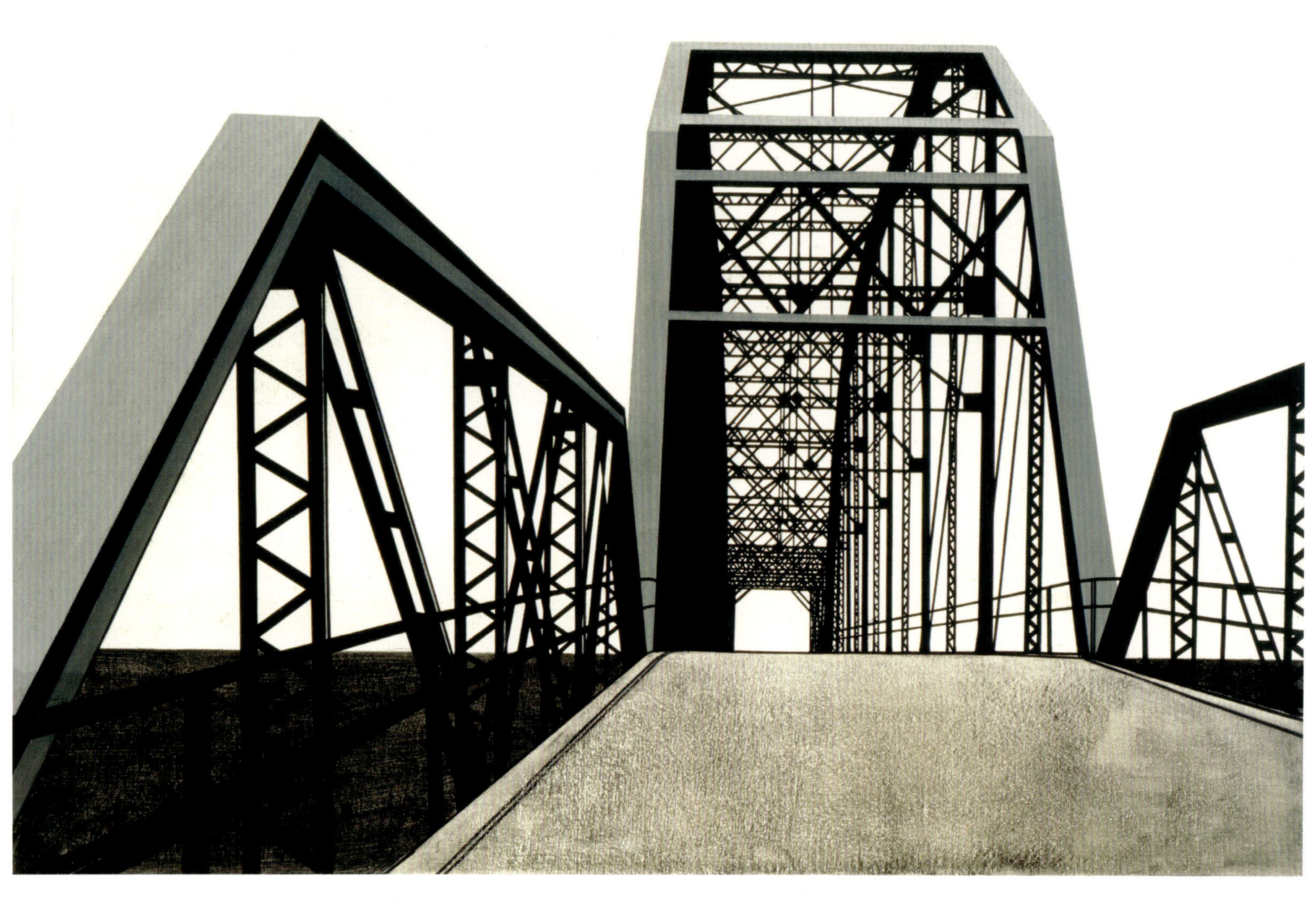

 Plate 8. **600 ft. in Length**, 1998, oil on canvas, 30 x 45 inches. Collection of artist.

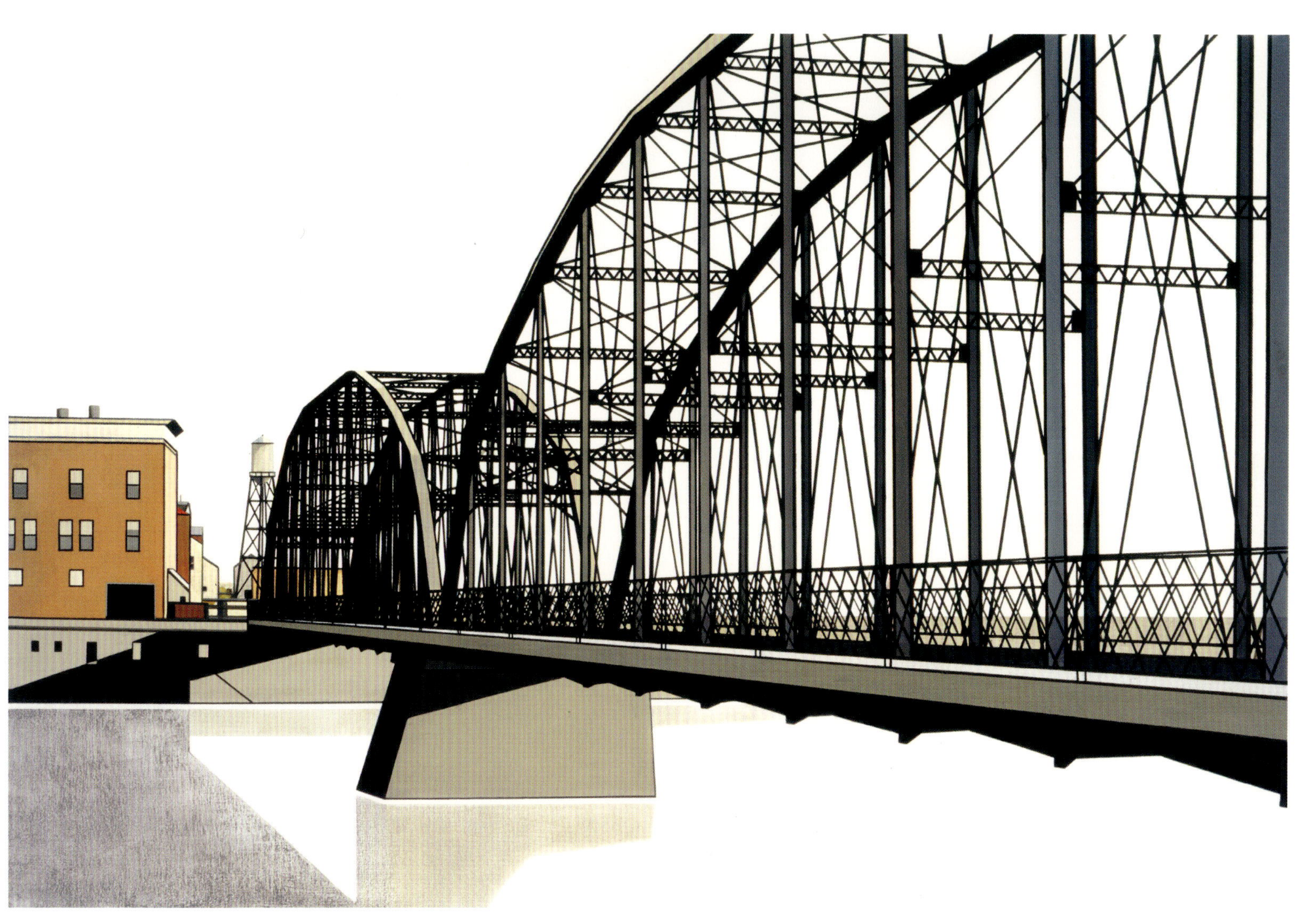

Plate 9. **Grand Ave. Bridge**, 2000, oil on canvas, 30 x 45 inches. Collection of Gerald and Dianna Peterson.

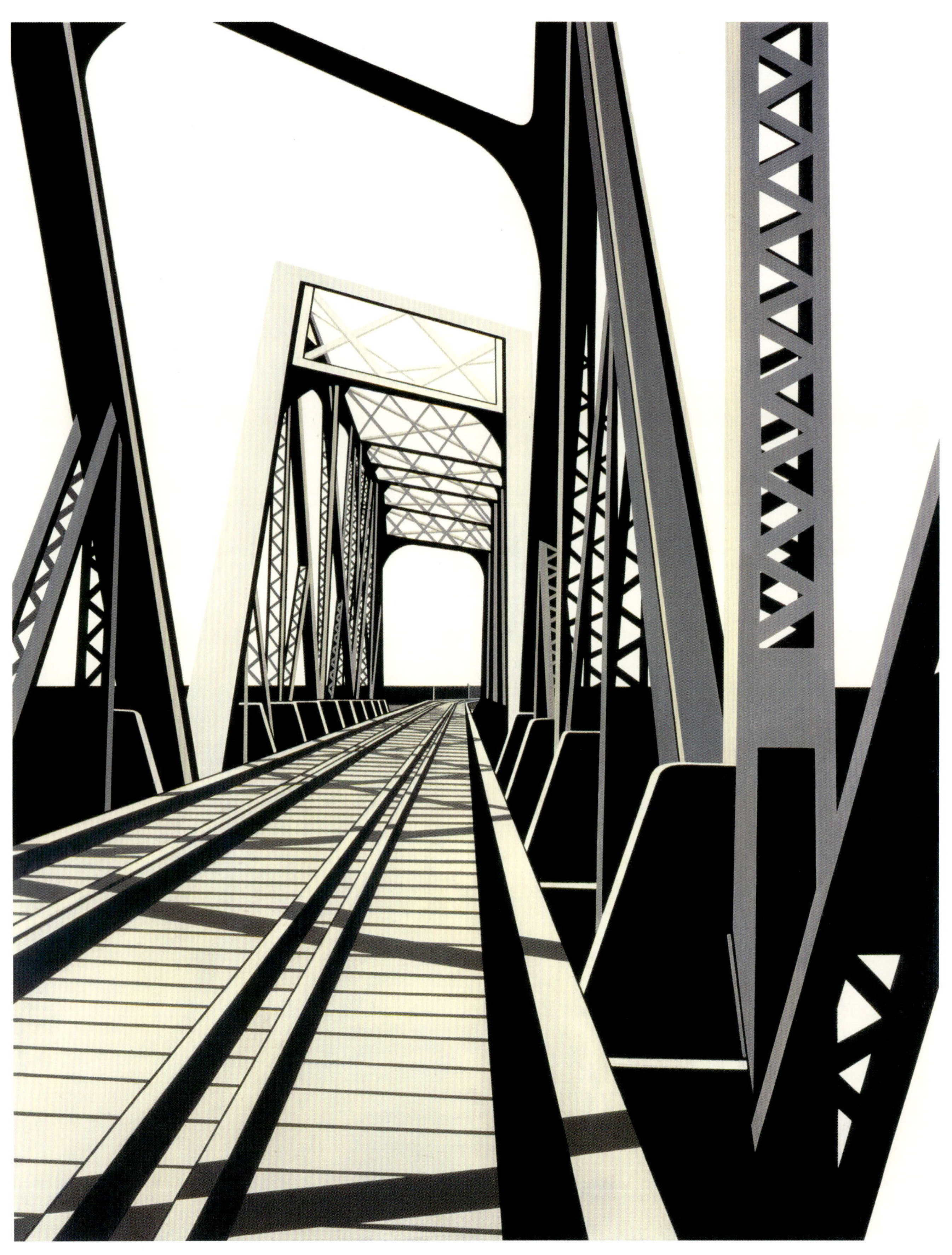

Plate 10. **NP Railroad Bridge**, 2000, oil on canvas, 60 x 48 inches. Collection of Charles Wall.

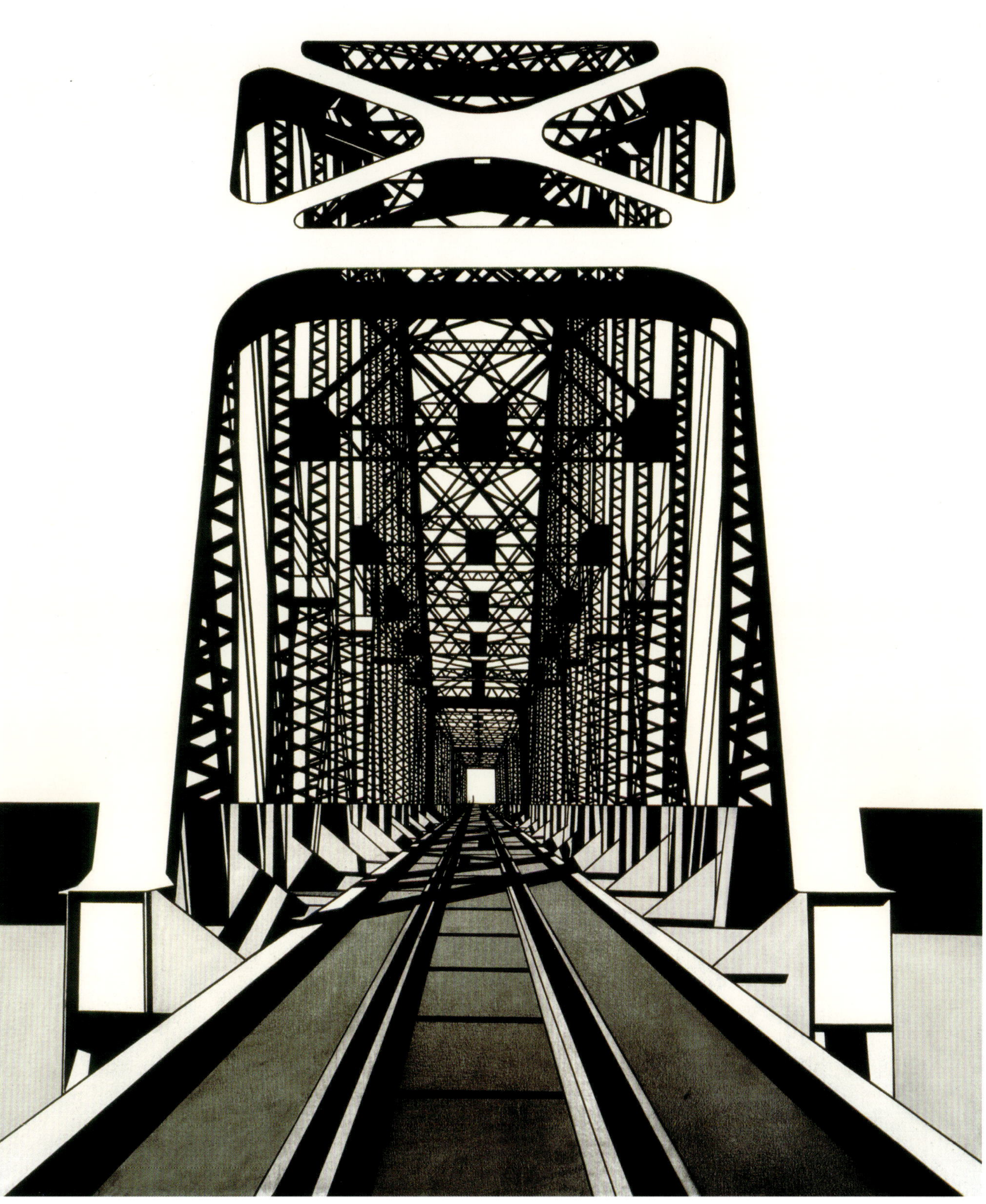

Plate 11. **NP Bridge**, 1997, oil on canvas, 44 x 35 inches. Collection of Keith and Kathleen Krolak.

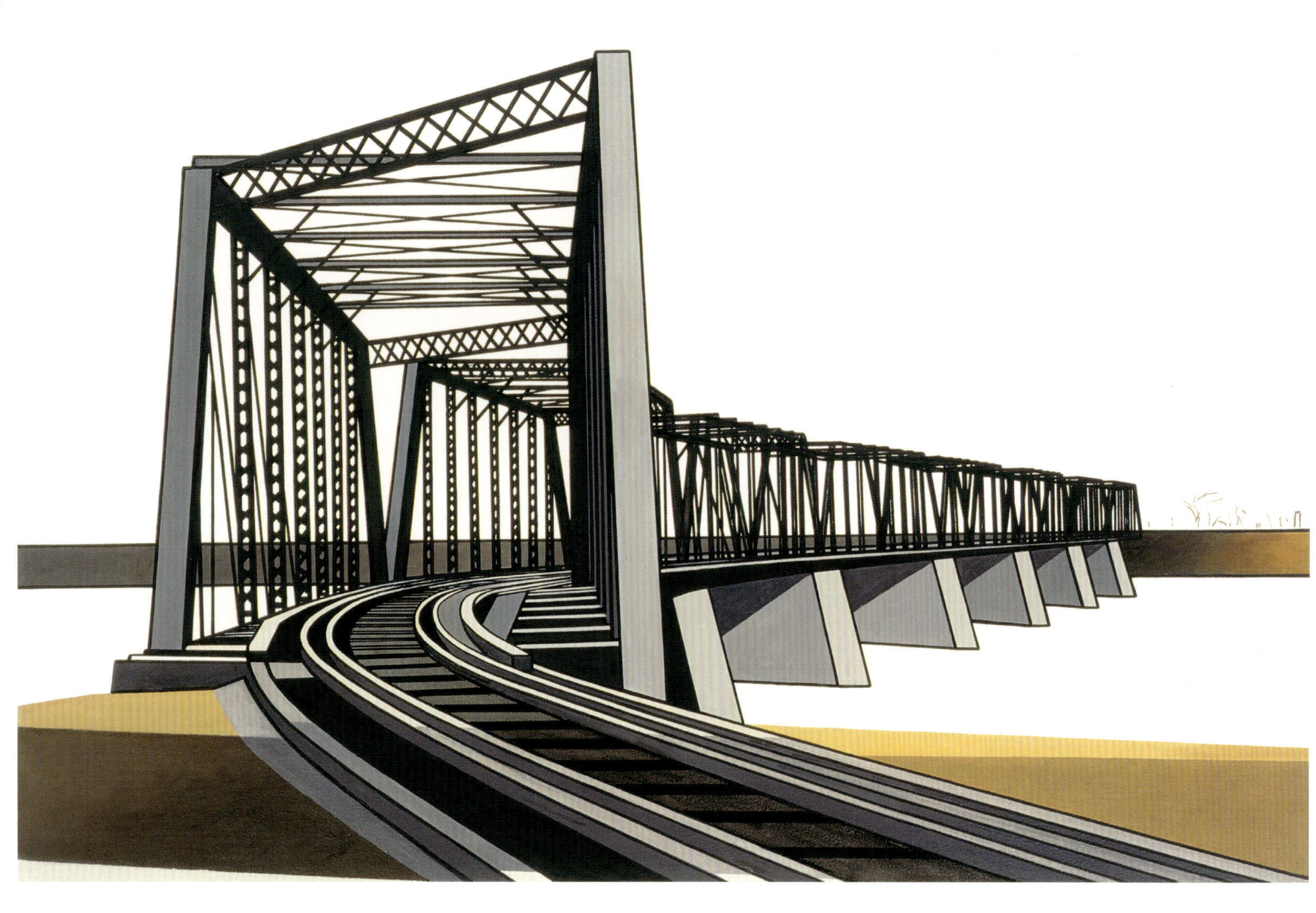

56   Plate 12. **Railroad Bridge**, 2001, oil on canvas, 30 x 45 inches. Collection of Eric Lorberfeld.

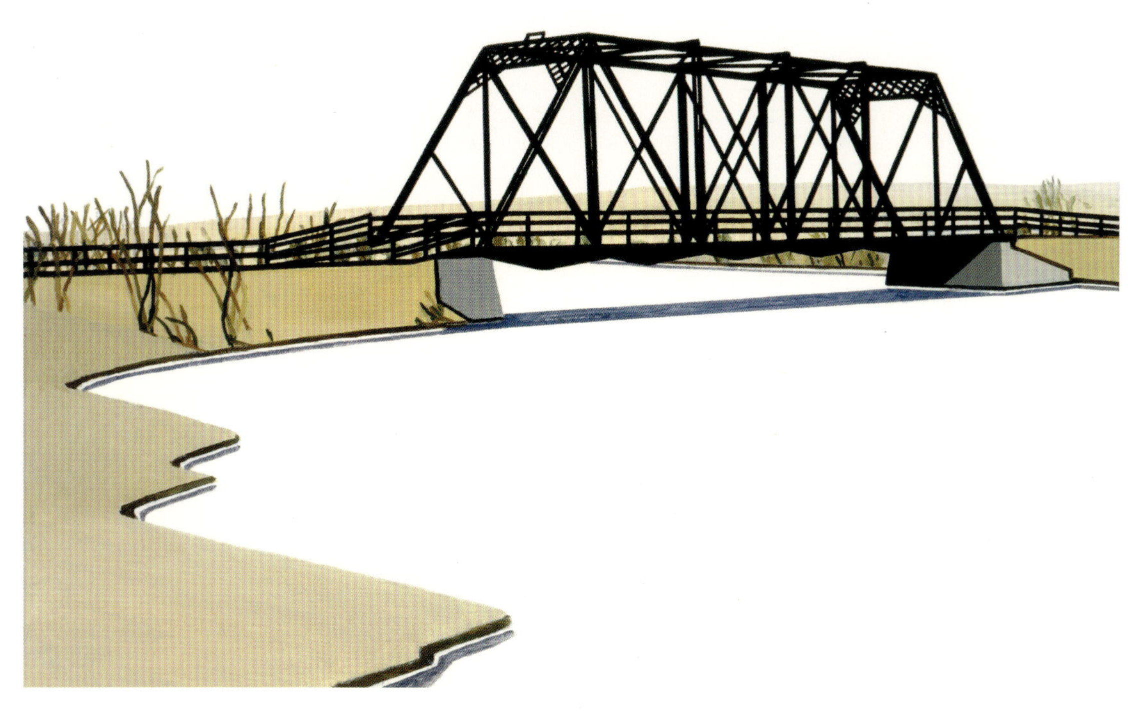

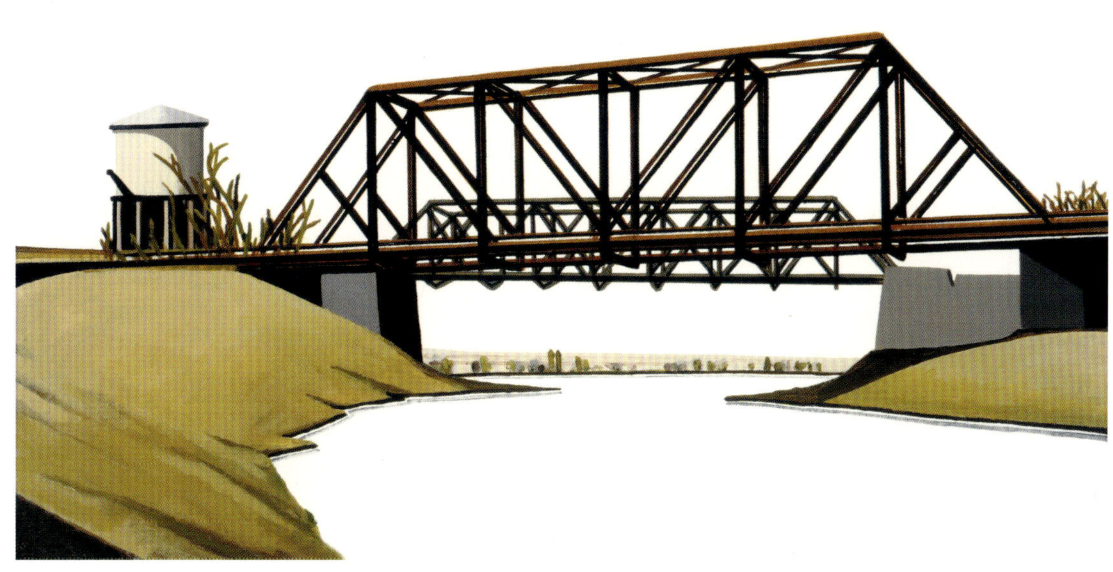

Plate 13. **Rock River Bridge**, 2001, oil on linen, 12 x 16 inches. Collection of Susanna Lawler.

Plate 14. **North Fork Crossings**, 2001, oil on linen, 12 x 16 inches. Collection of Rita and Chris Wulke.

WILLIAM STEIGER'S RENDERINGS of vintage propeller planes and dirigibles are immaculately spare; elegant visual testaments to the artist's fascination with the past. We are immediately drawn to the delicate graphic element and marvel at the discipline of an artist who allows himself so few lines. There is nothing self-indulgent about these paintings, no dramatic flourishes or decadent details to distract the viewer from the simple beauty of these early flying machines.

Airborne and *Record 50 Mile* are graceful little paintings of traditional aircraft executed in a simple palette of black and white—especially appropriate when one considers the vintage photographs that serve as Steiger's inspiration. The white represents sky, expansive and unknown, while the areas of black delicately communicate the craft's structural ingenuity and, simultaneously, its vulnerability. The artist portrays the planes at rest and in flight, and he even imagines the aftermath of a plane's falling from the sky. Yet the "accident" pictures are hardly tragic; the aircraft rest in comically unnatural states, curiously erect and minimally damaged, suddenly awkward seeming with their noses bent into the ground.

The dirigibles, or zeppelins, are studied in detail and from various angles; their girth implies immense weight and yet they appear graceful. Steiger's aptly titled 1998 painting *Emergence* depicts a newly completed vessel emerging from a hangar for its maiden voyage. The craft is evocative of a bullet, the desolate landscape reminiscent of the shadowy rural factories that produced armaments during the First and Second World Wars. Upon takeoff, the dirigibles seem almost pilotless, soaring through a sky bound by no horizon, with only a series of beams and wires suspending them in midair.

Steiger has studied mechanical rendering carefully and understands the purpose of each element of construction. The minutiae of detail are sometimes revealed, but what is always present is the artist's perpetual sense of awe at early aviation technology and the wonder of flight.

FLIGHT

BETTINA PRENTICE

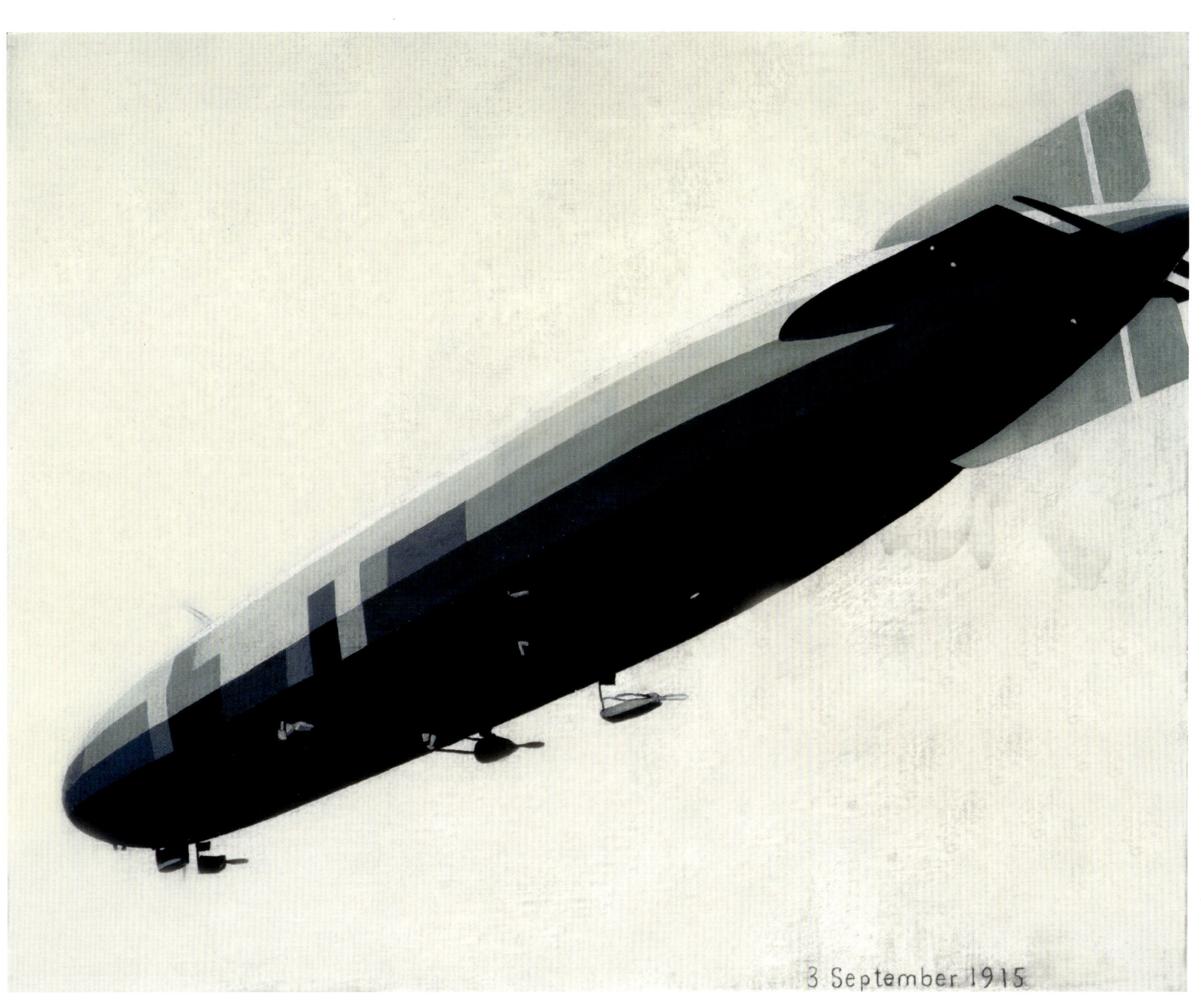

Plate 15. **3 September 1915**, 1995, oil on canvas, 16 x 20 inches. Private collection.

Plate 16. **Flight II**, 1996, oil on canvas, 16 x 20 inches. Collection of Carla Westcott.

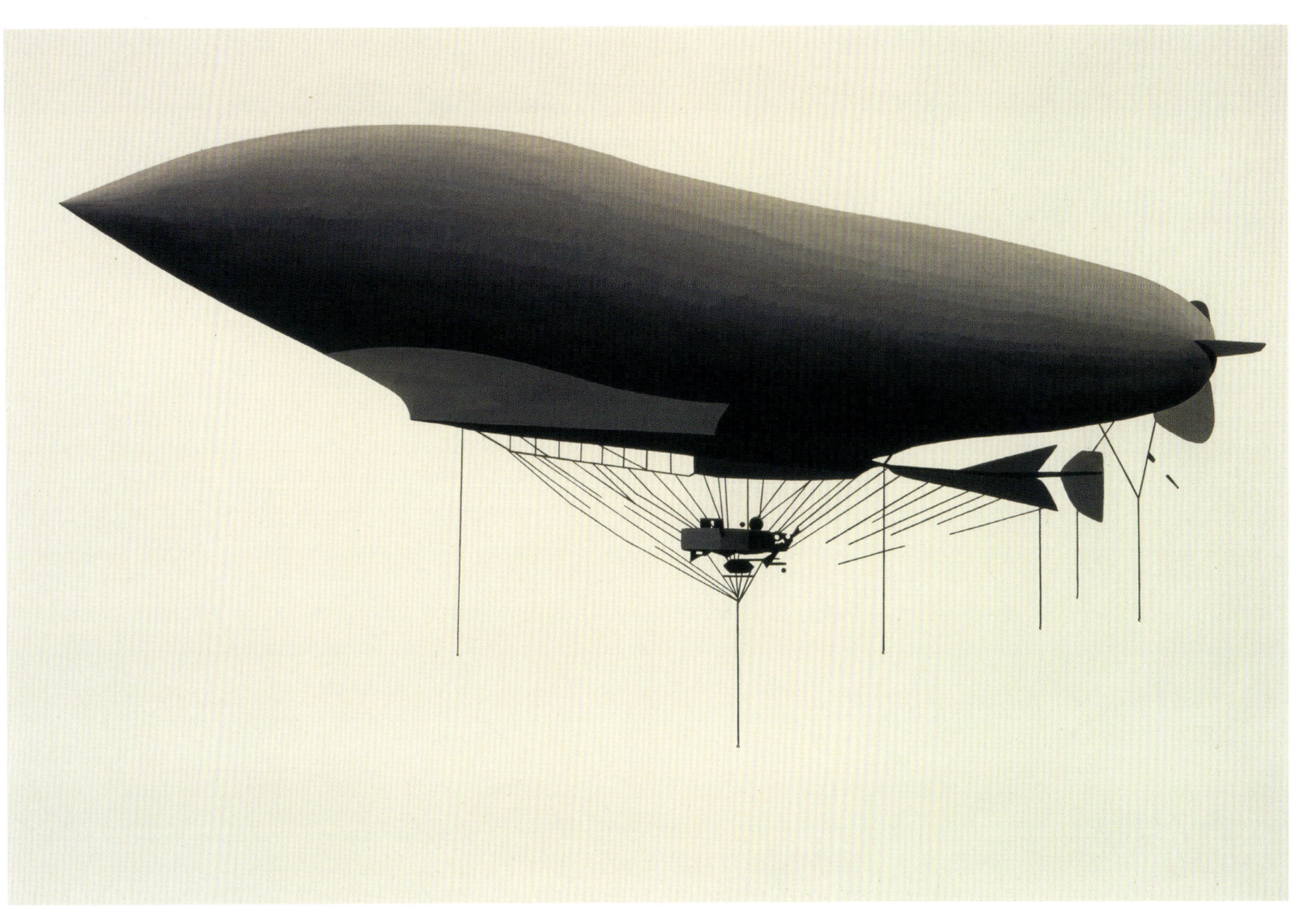

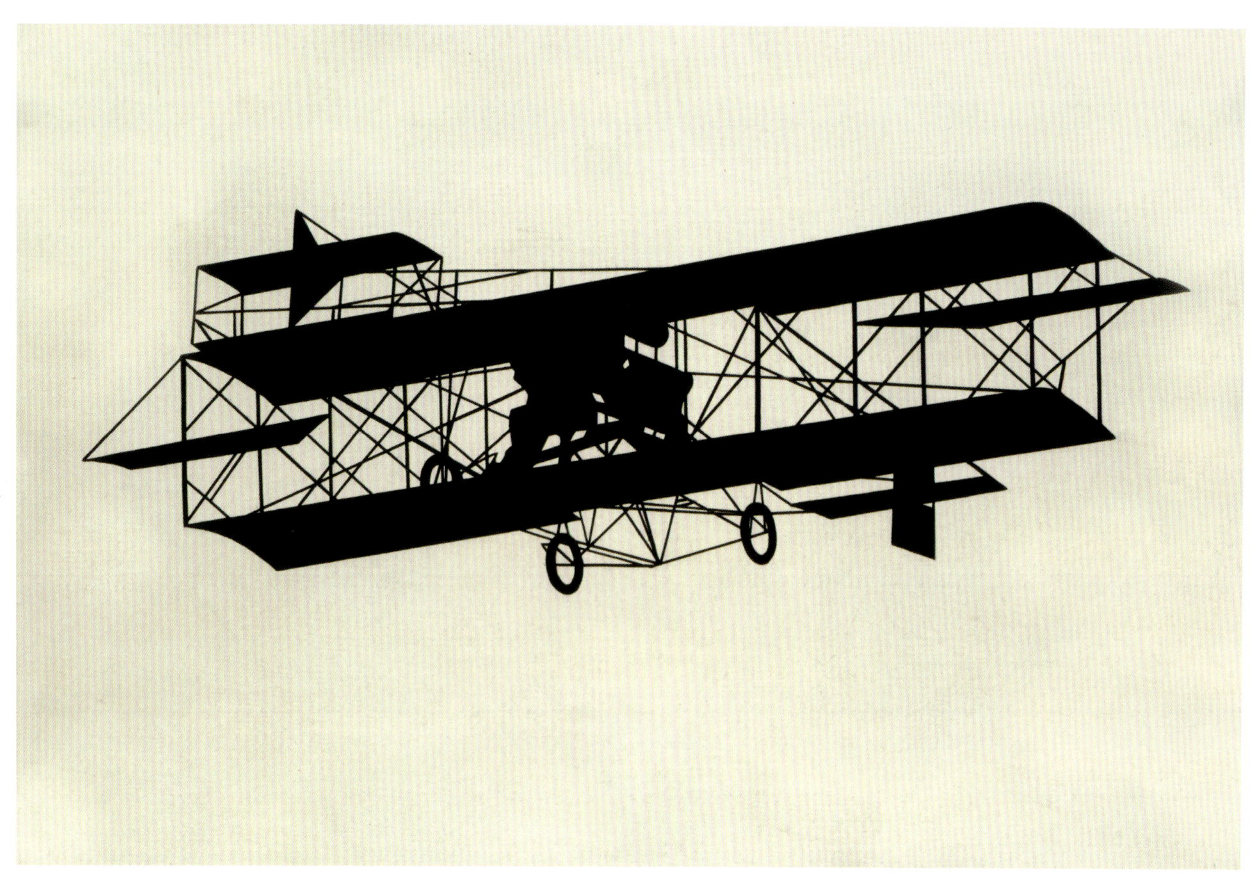

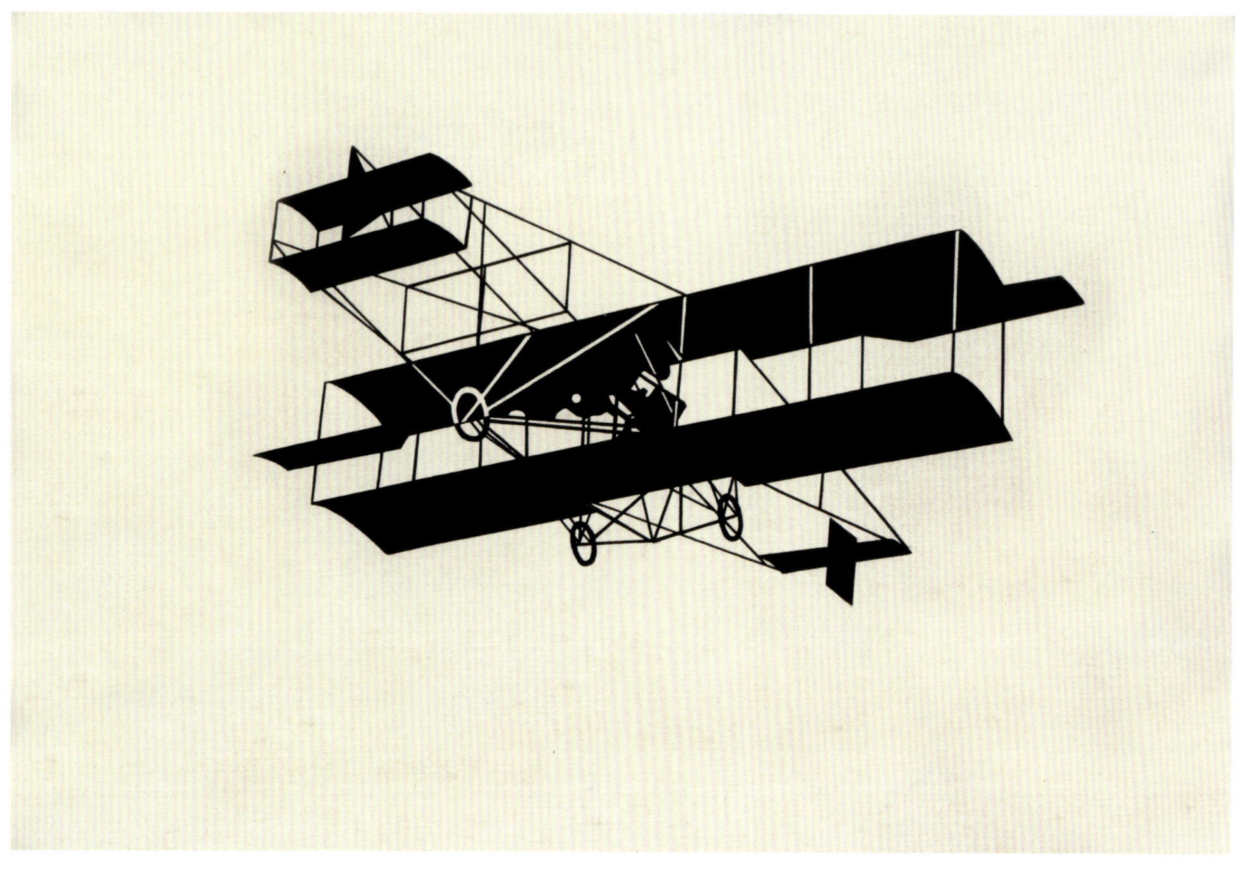

Plate 18. **Record 50 Mile Flight**, 1998, oil on canvas, 20 x 30 inches. Collection of artist.

Plate 19. **Catching Updraft**, 1998, oil on canvas, 20 x 30 inches. Collection of artist.

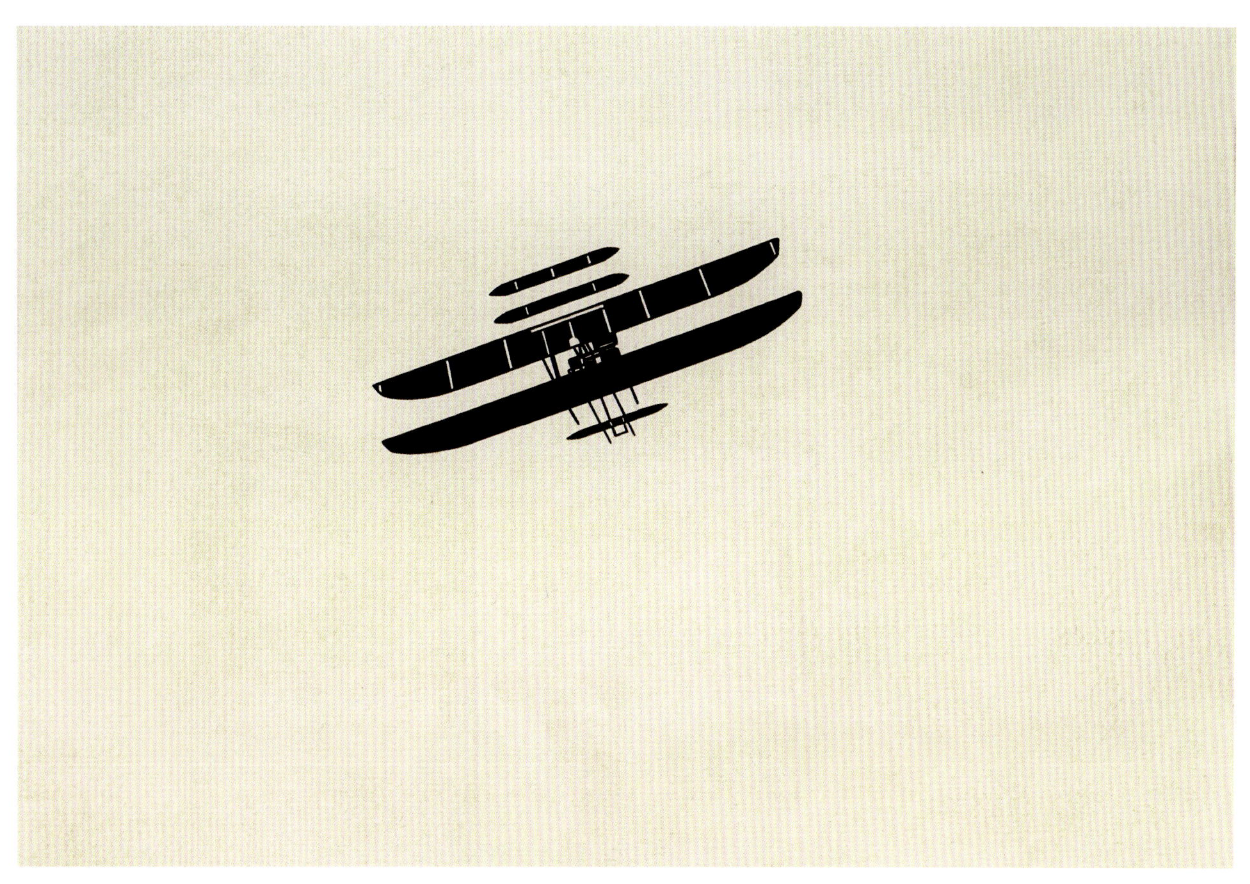

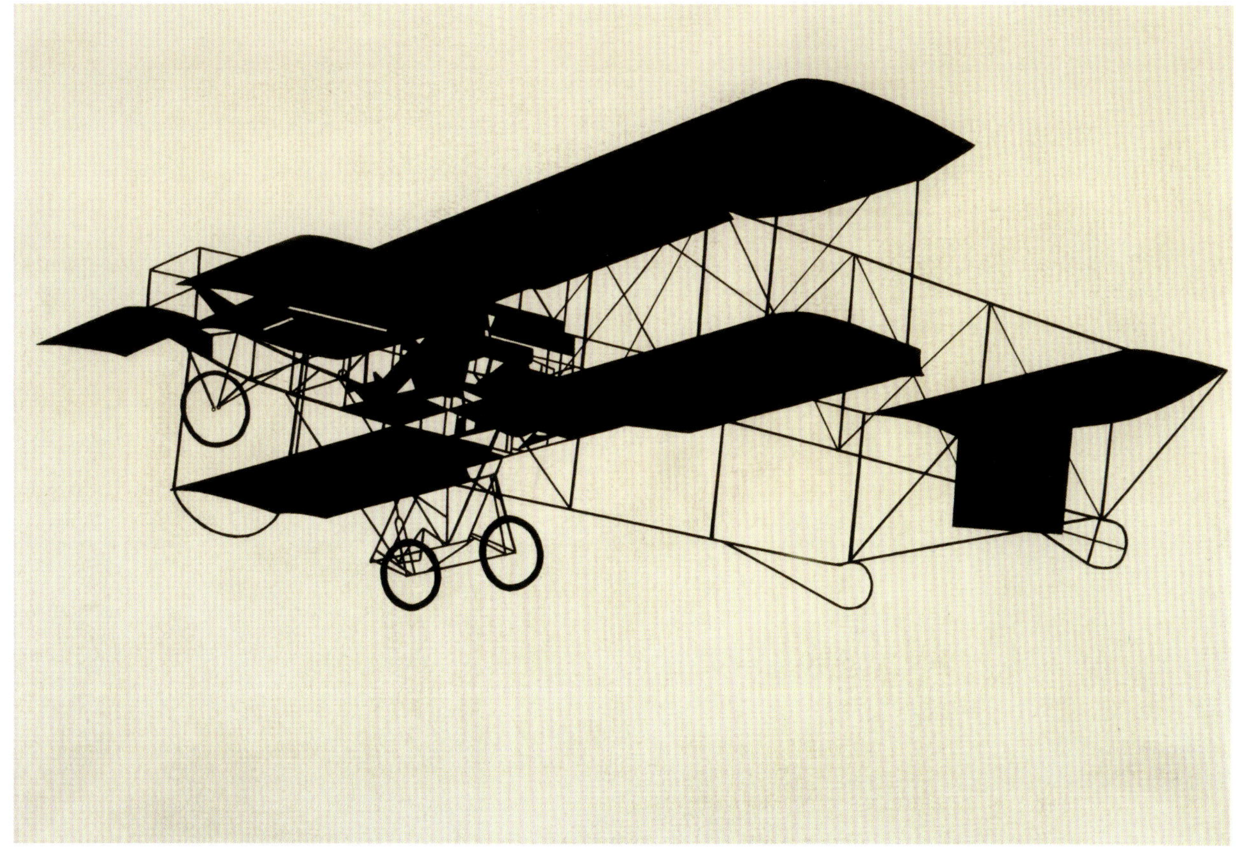

Plate 20. **Machine in Midair**, 1998, oil on canvas, 20 x 30 inches. Collection of artist.

Plate 21. **L'Aviation**, 1998, oil on linen, 20 x 30 inches. Collection of artist.

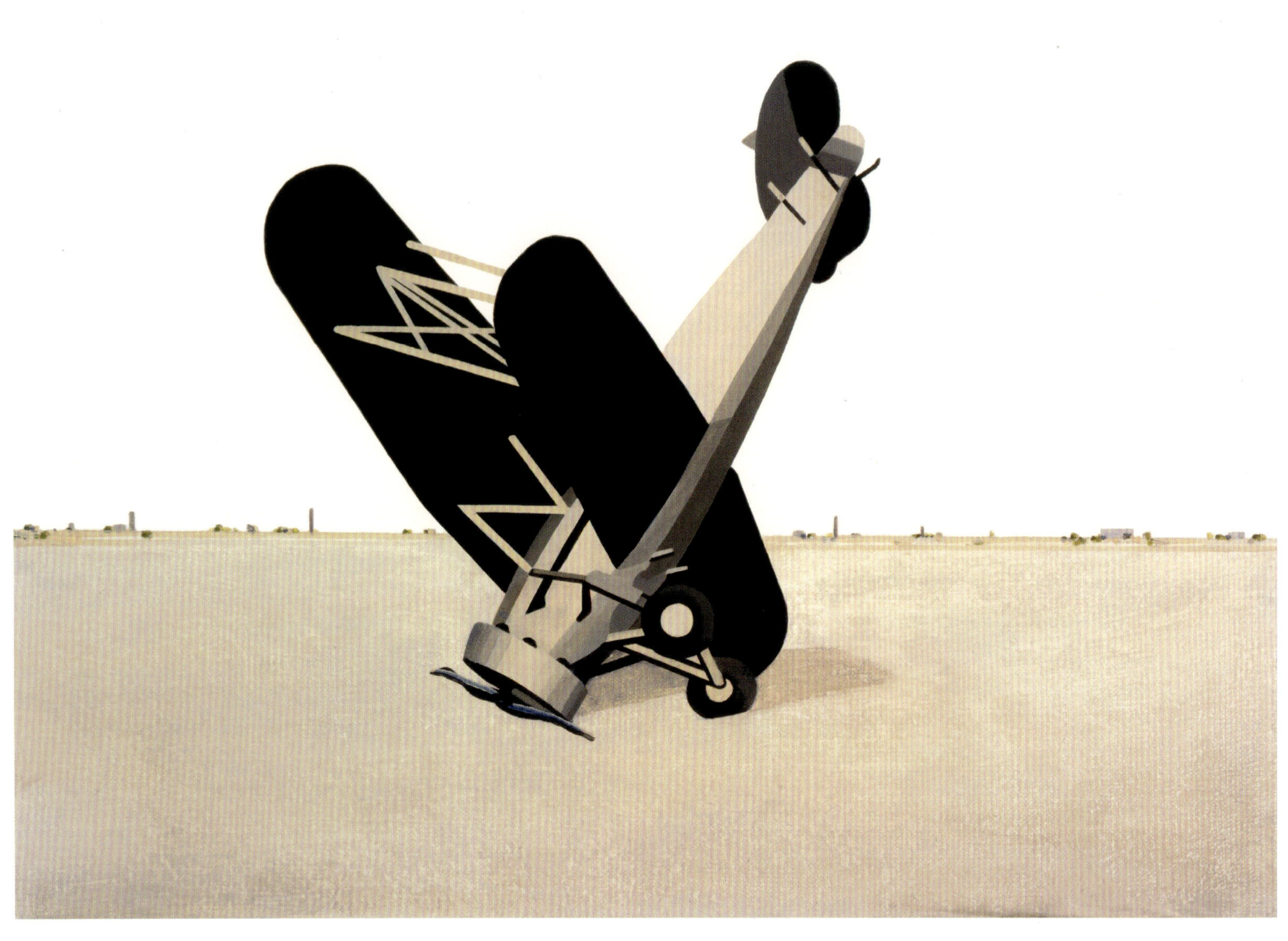

Plate 22. **Accident #1**, 2000, oil on linen, 12 x 16 inches. Collection of Charles Wall.

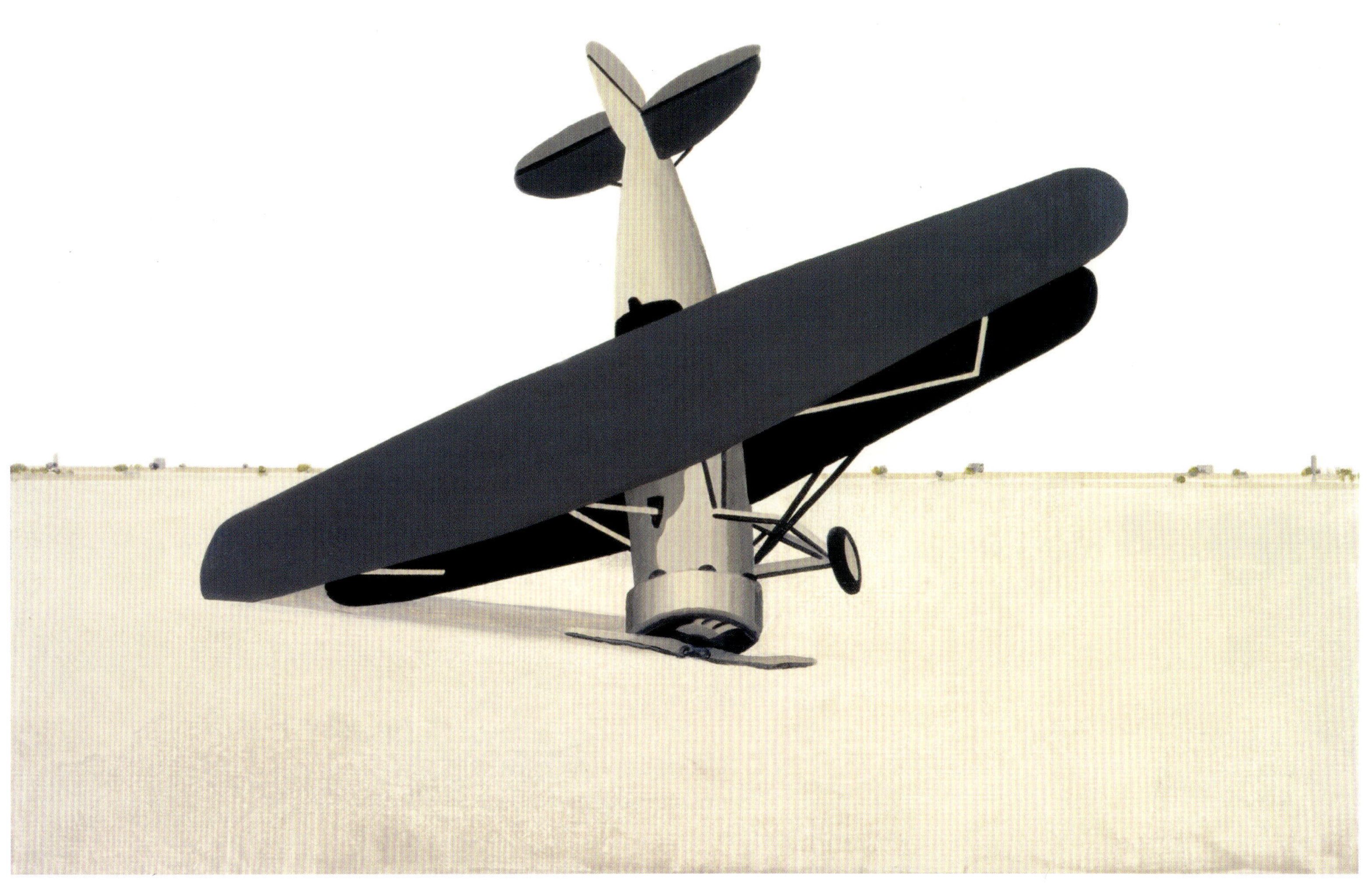

Plate 23. **Accident #2**, 2000, oil on linen, 12 x 16 inches. Collection of Charles Wall.

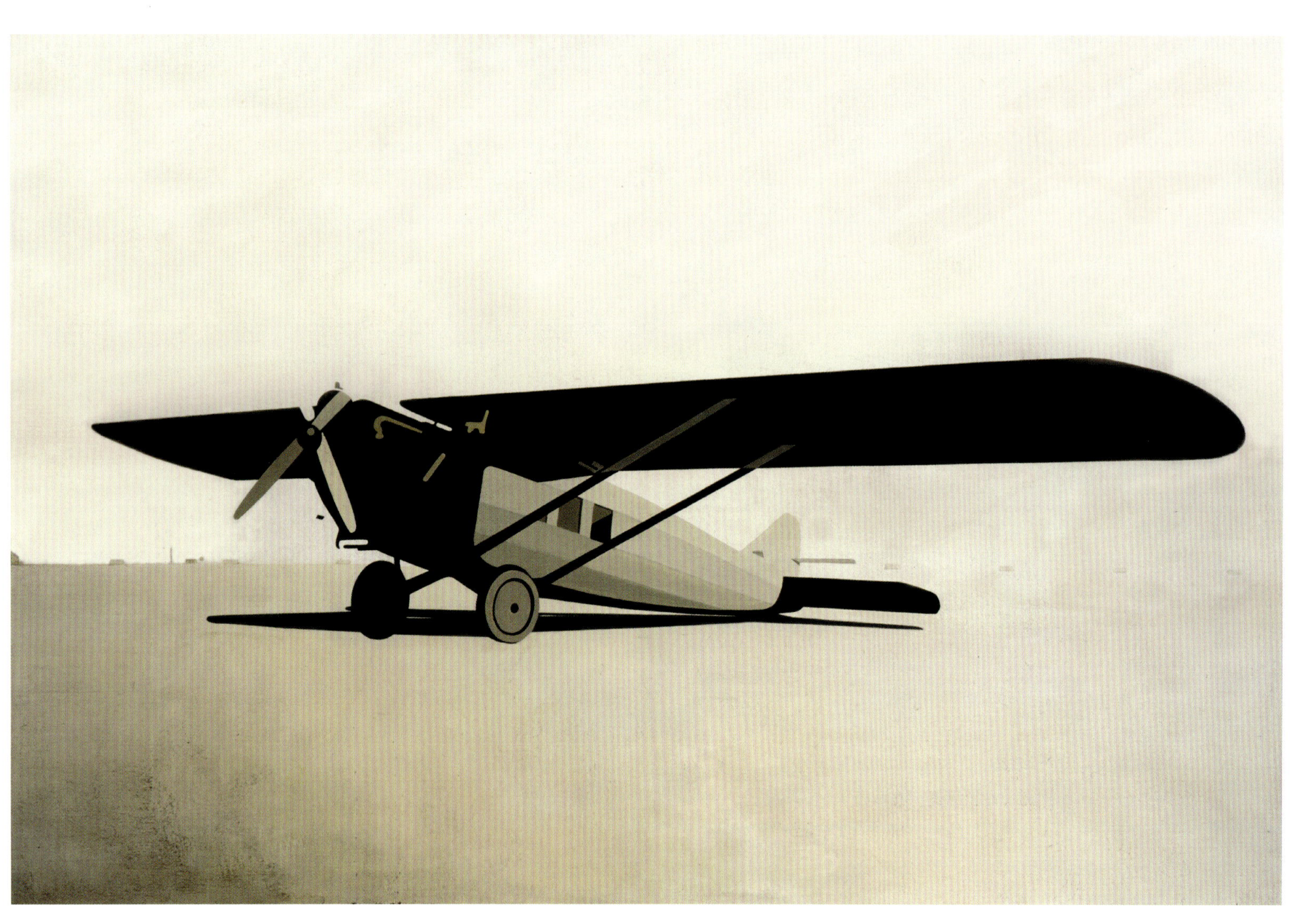

Plate 24. **At the Flight Grounds**, 1997, oil on canvas, 30 x 45 inches. Collection of Charles Wall.

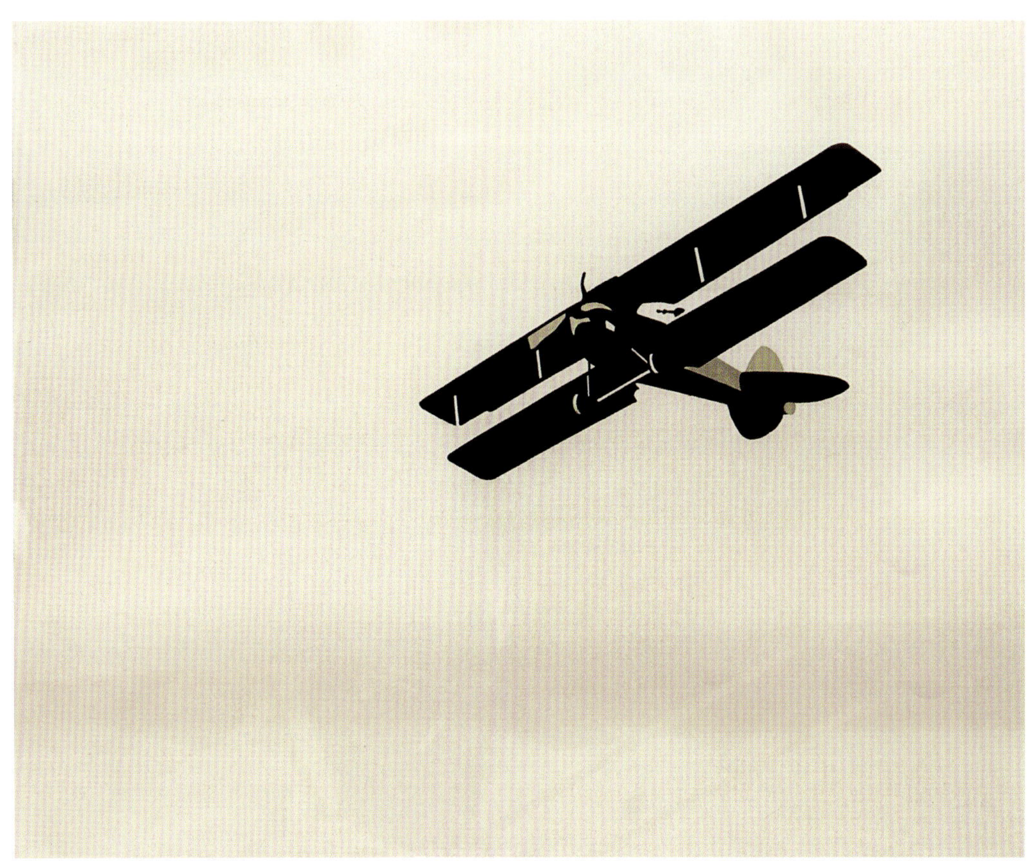

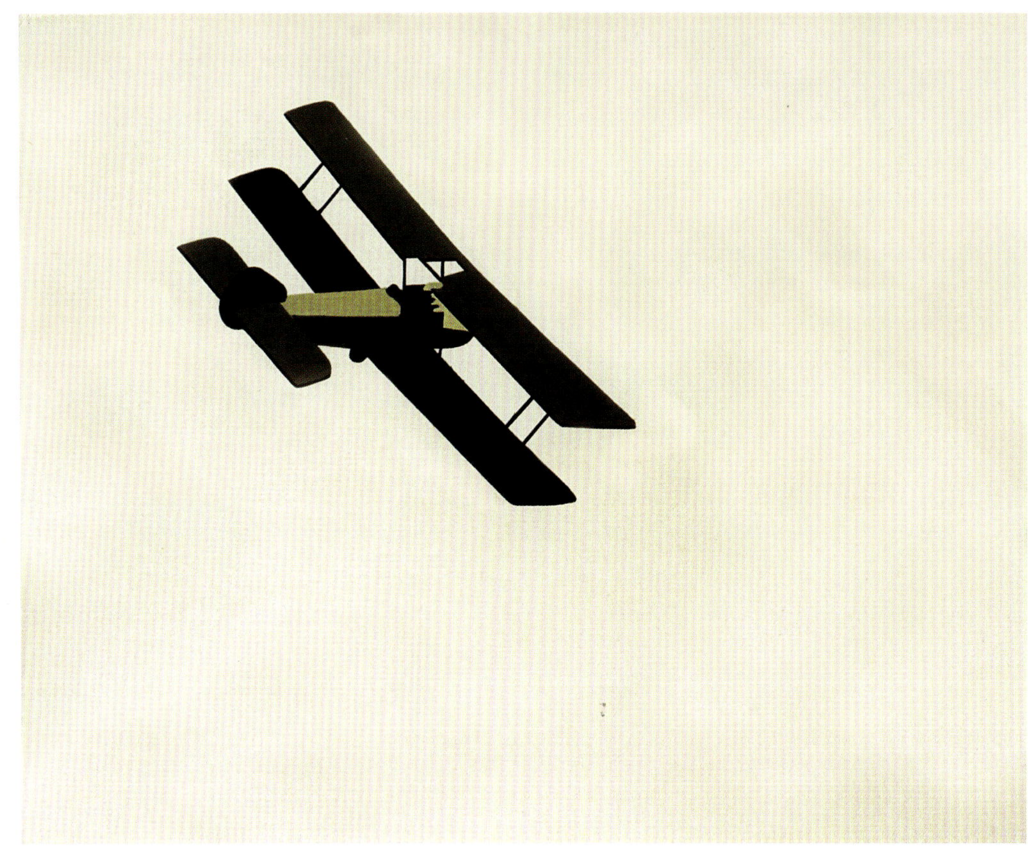

Plate 25. **Airborne**, 1999, oil on canvas, 16 x 20 inches. Private collection.

Plate 26. **Flyby**, 2001, oil on canvas, 16 x 20 inches. Private collection.

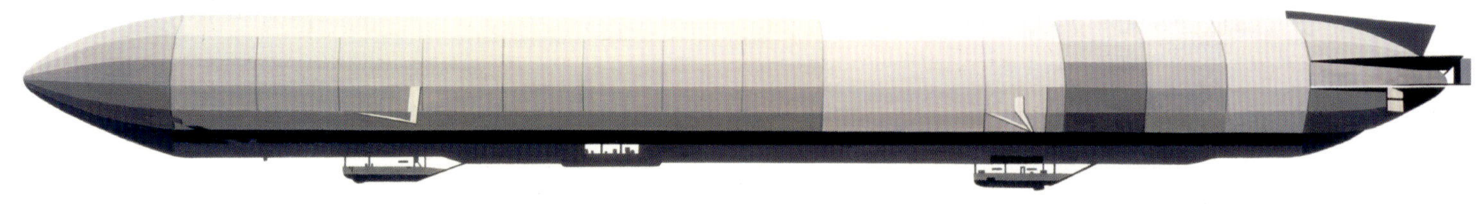

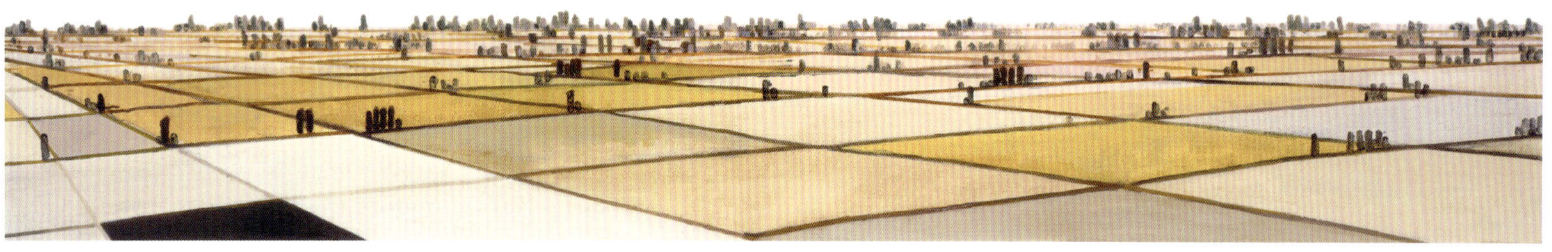

 Plate 27. **5 Sept 10**, 2000, oil on canvas, 24 x 48 inches. Private collection.

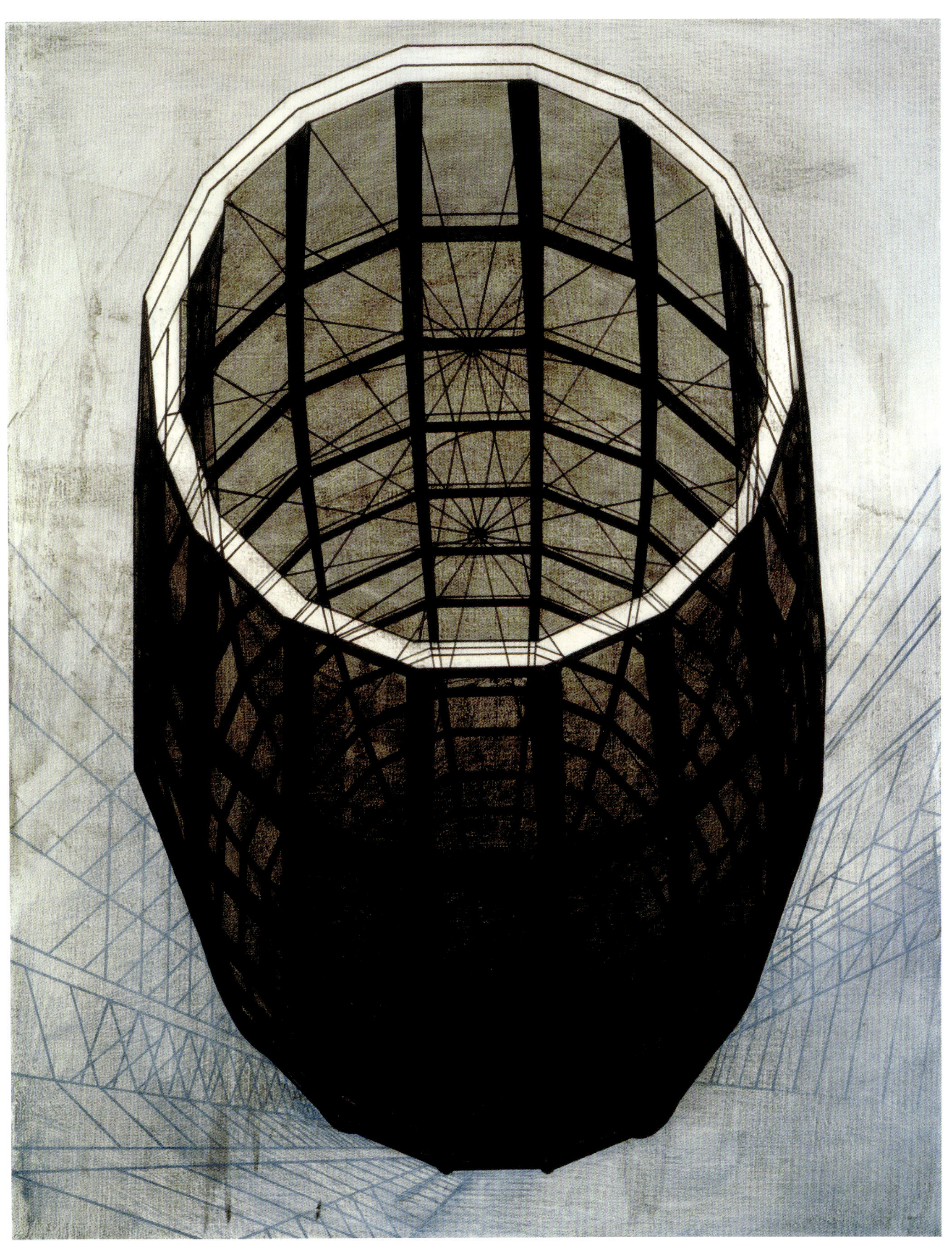

Plate 28. **Dirigible Frame I**, 1996, oil on canvas, 30 x 24 inches. Private collection.

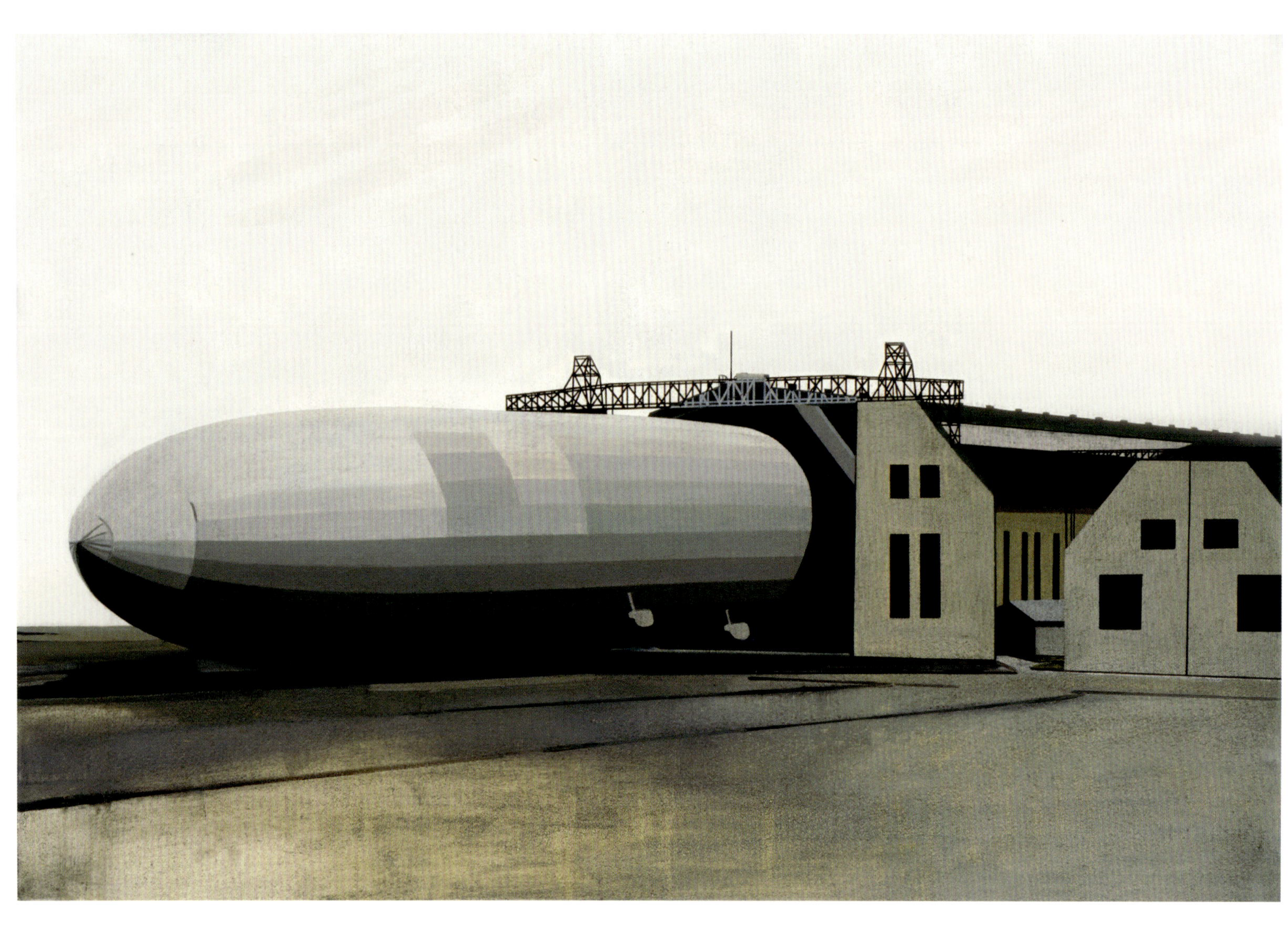

Plate 29. **Emergence**, 1998, oil on canvas, 30 x 45 inches. Collection of Noel Kirnon.

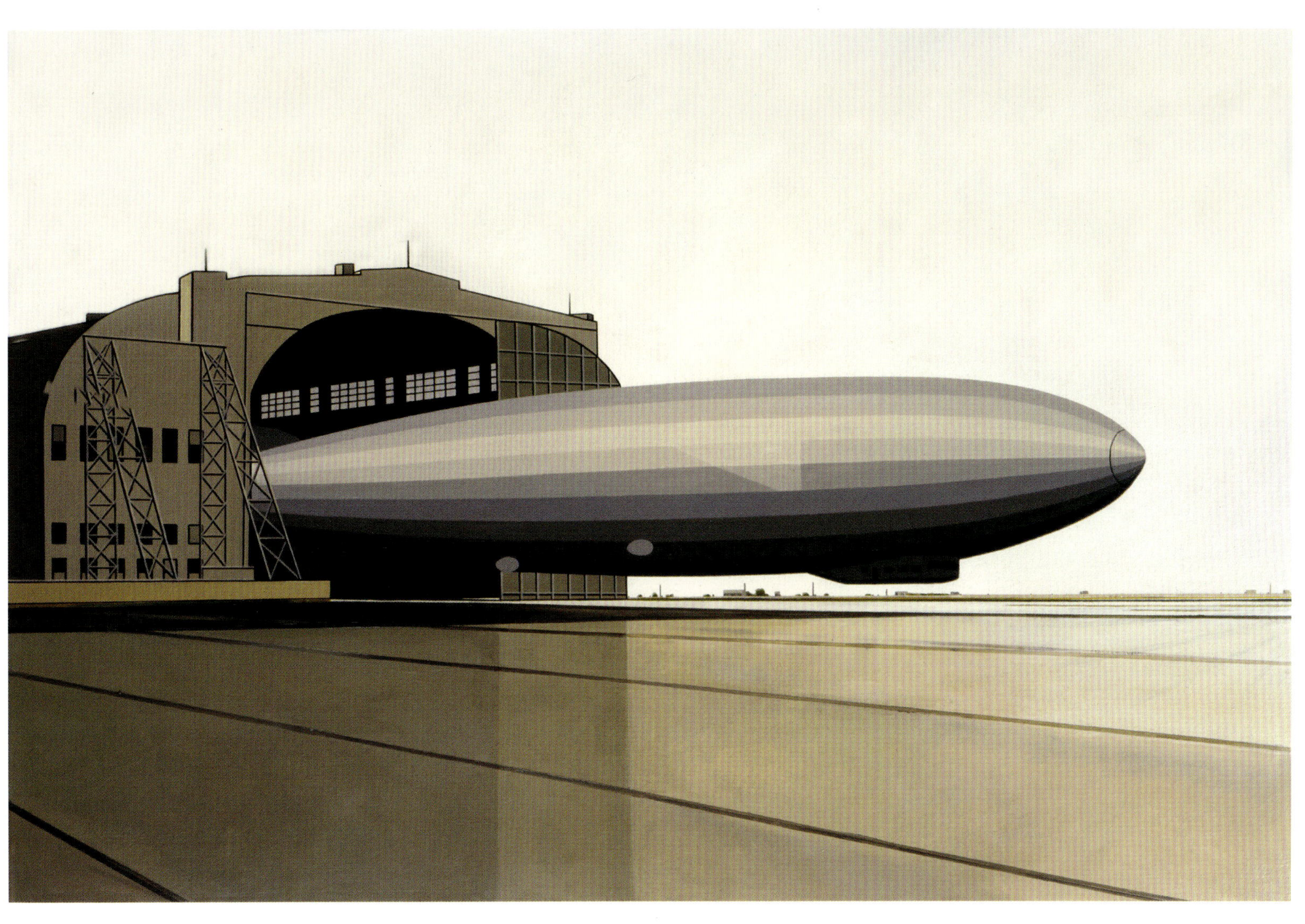

Plate 30. **Untitled (dirigible)**, 2001, oil on canvas, 30 x 45 inches. Collection of Evan Lobel.

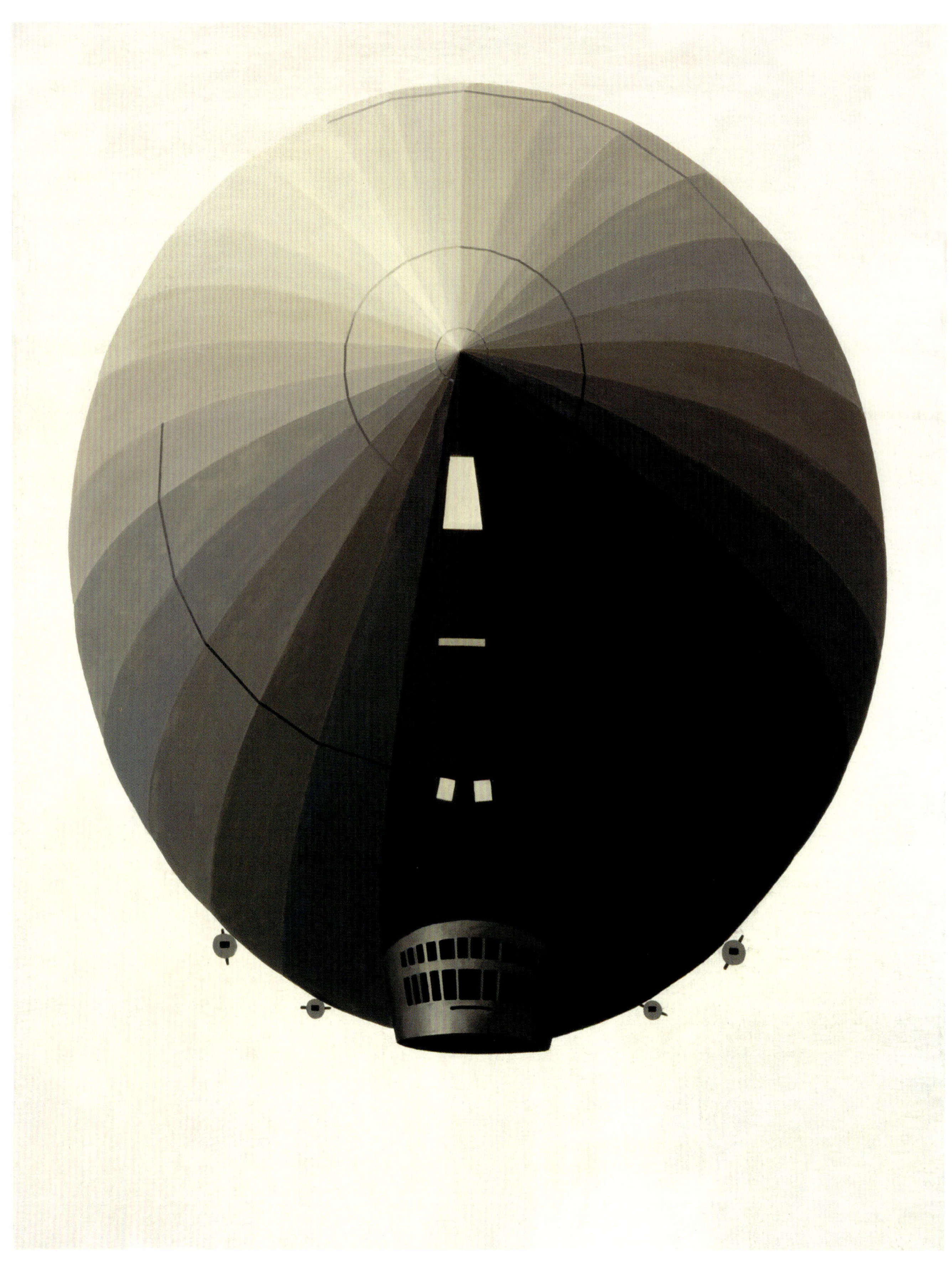

 Plate 31. **Lift**, 2000, oil on canvas, 30 x 24 inches. Collection of Christopher Mangum.

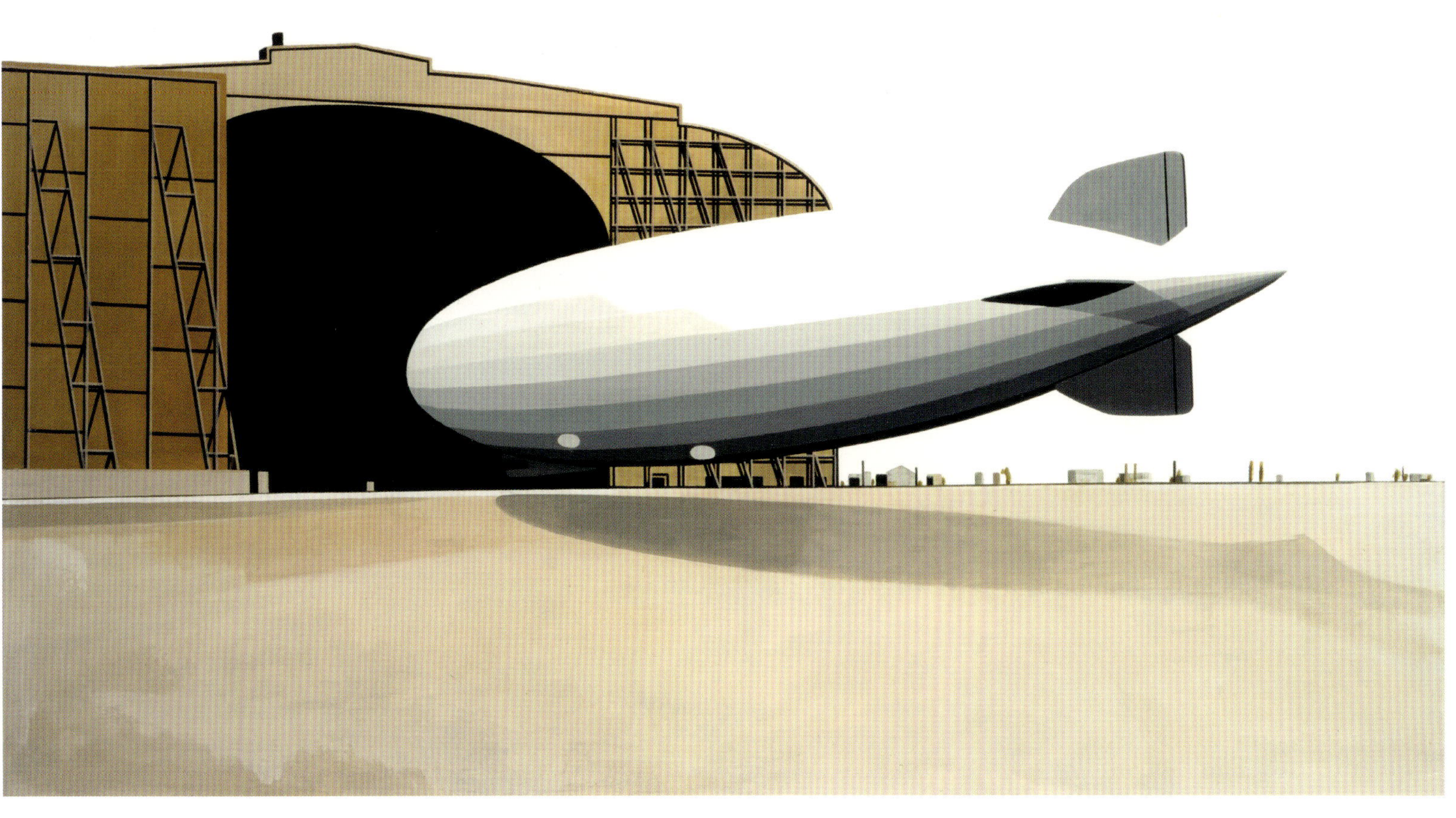

Plate 32. **Lakehurst**, 2002, oil on canvas, 30 x 45 inches. Collection of artist.

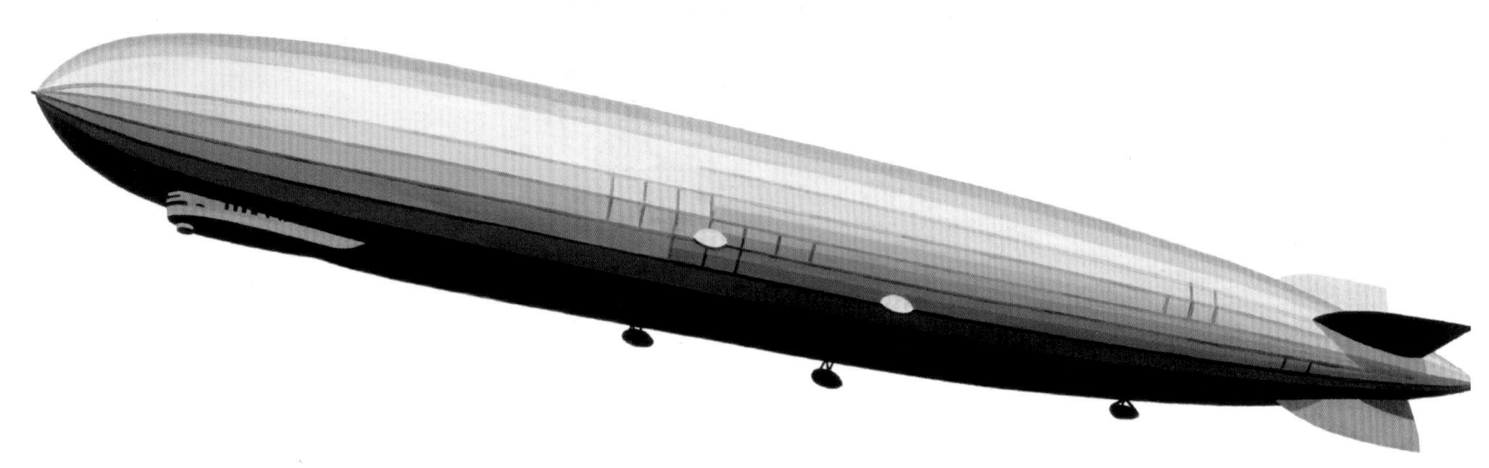

  Plate 33. **Dirigible**, 1997, oil on canvas, 20 x 30 inches. Courtesy Roy Boyd Gallery.

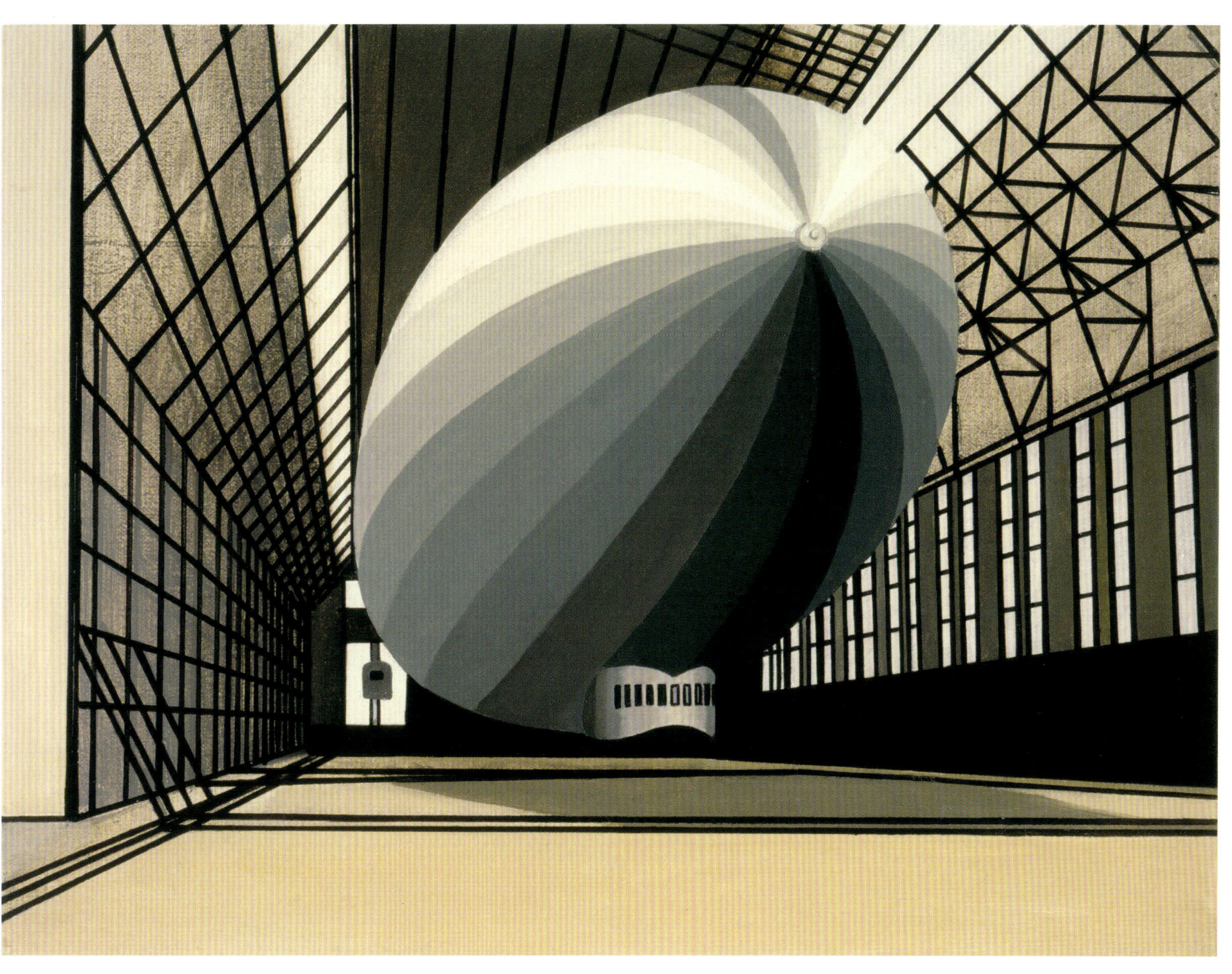

Plate 34. **Dirigible in Hanger**, 2001, oil on linen, 12 x 16 inches. Collection of Thomas Werner.

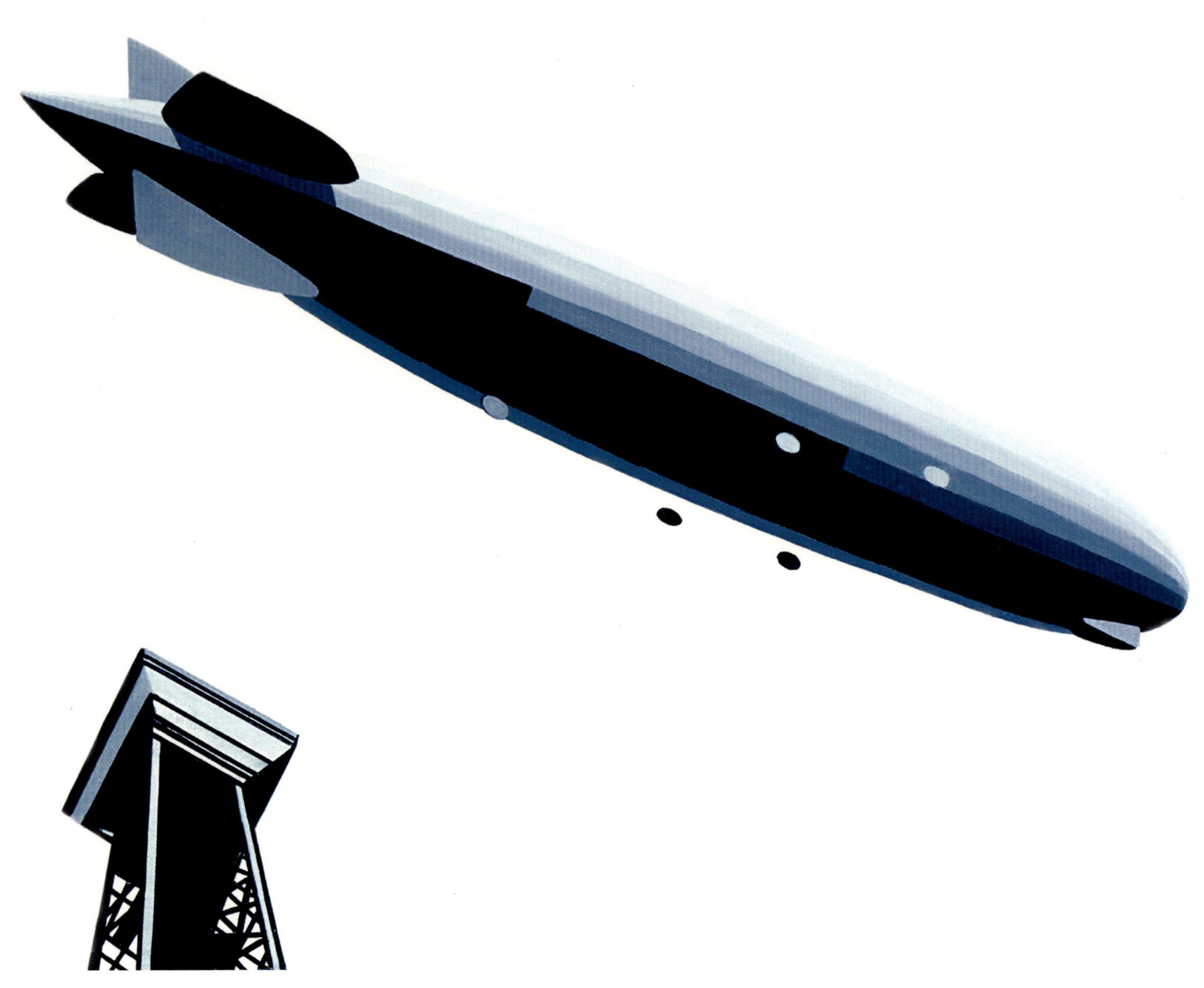

Plate 35. **Dirigible over Tower**, 2007, oil on linen, 12 x 16 inches. Collection of John R. Eckel, Jr. Estate.

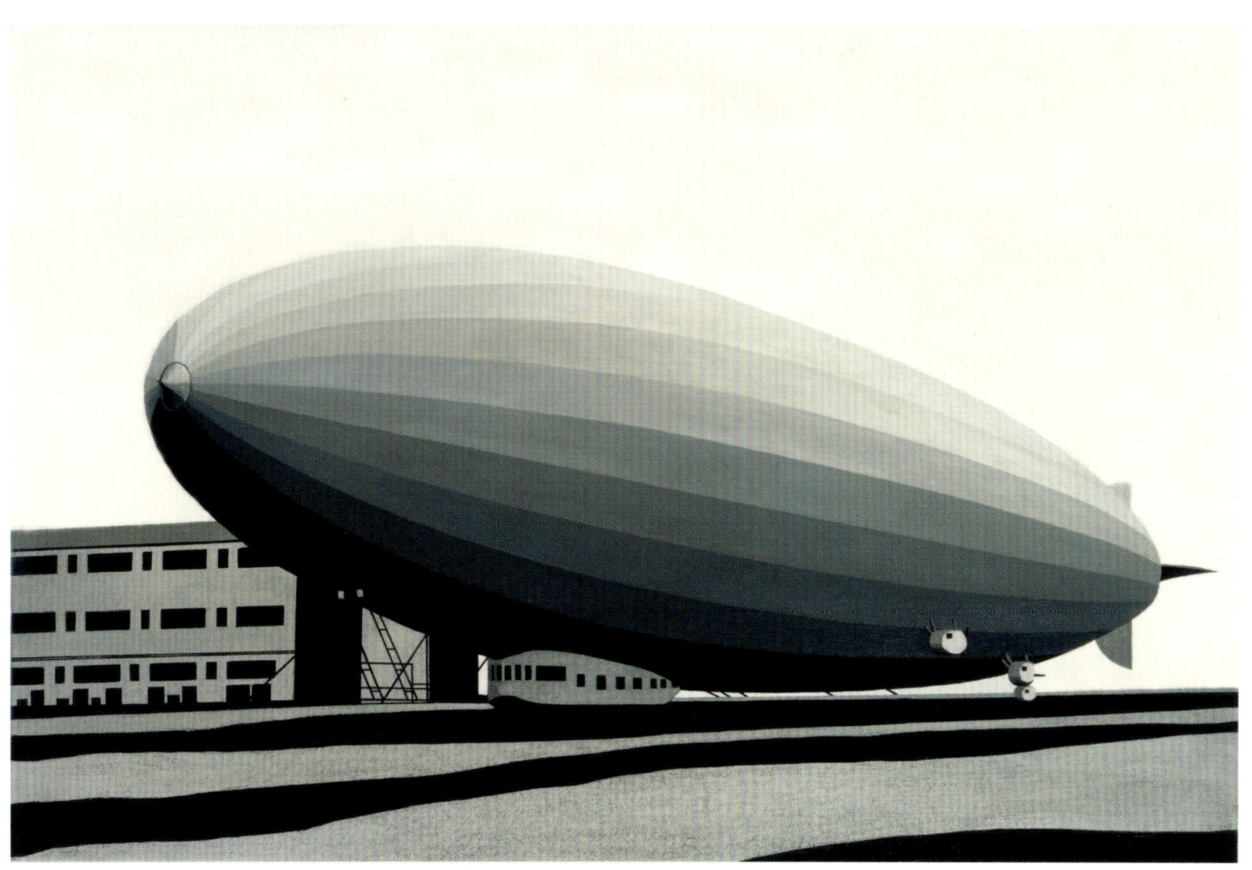

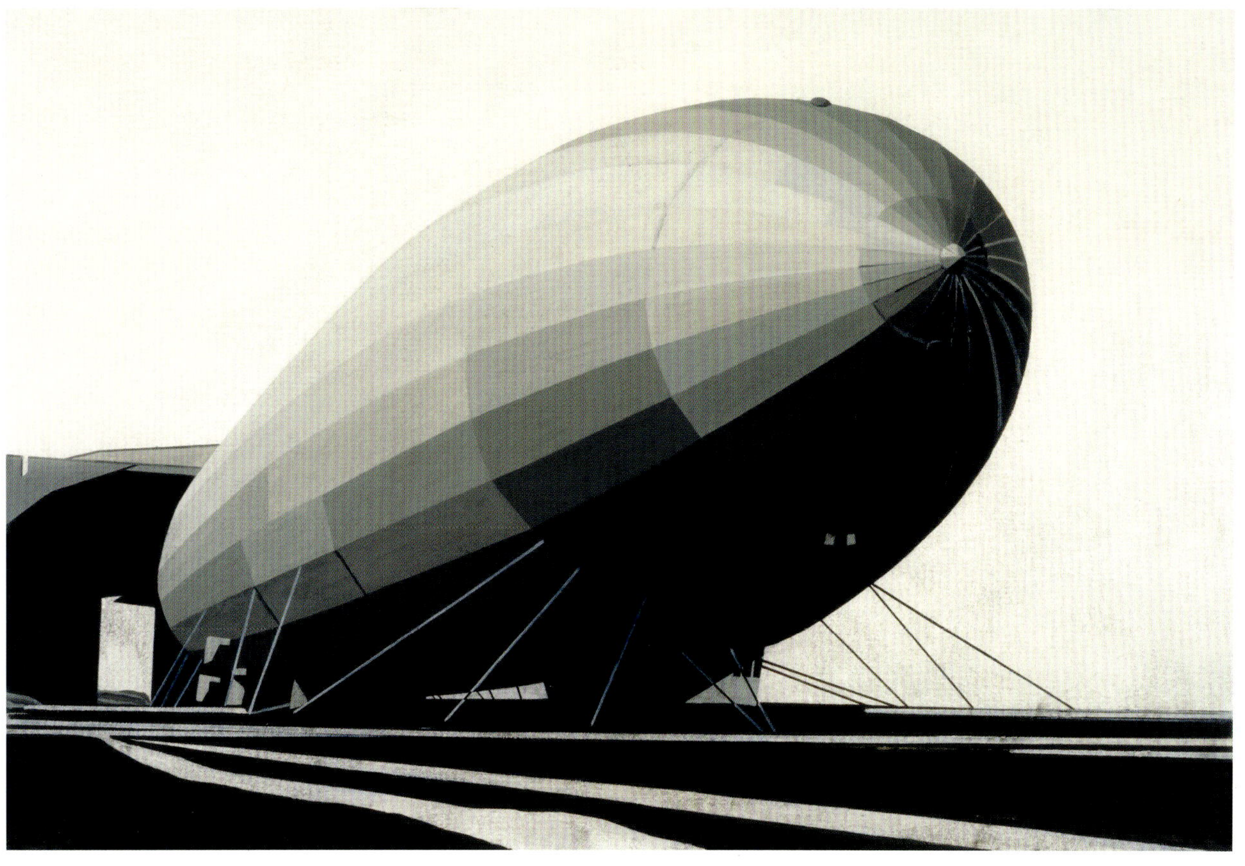

Plate 36. **Test Flight**, 1997, oil on canvas, 20 x 30 inches. Collection of artist.

Plate 37. **Launch**, 1997, oil on canvas, 20 x 30 inches. Courtesy Roy Boyd Gallery.

WILLIAM STEIGER'S WATER TOWERS give heroic stature to an often overlooked engineering icon. Water tanks are hardly a recent innovation, having been in use for centuries, yet Steiger's paintings renew our attention to these practical constructs by rendering each of them with individuality while also emphasizing their structural resilience and timelessness. With their pervasive sense of purpose rather than nostalgia, the *Water Tower* paintings reveal Steiger's fascination with architecture reinterpreted as art.

Architects are devoted to the principle that form follows function and in like manner the austere style of Steiger's paintings aims to preserve the truth through the subject's form. The circles, triangles, and squares that Steiger uses to define his water tanks build volume (that holds volume) on a flat plane. Often rendered in a modern color palette of ochre, greens, and reds, the antiquated tanks remain ageless. His bold black lines delineate the balanced diagonals in the tower's body, turning the design into dizzying geometric patterns as well as structural support. Even the slight use of shadows and the stark white background dominant in all of Steiger's work underscores his straightforward approach to painting; the concentration is on a singular object occupying the greater part of the canvas with monumental spirit.

Not just scenic examples of the American landscape, the water towers suggest a significant relationship between nature and the built environment. These tall, confident-seeming architectural forms define an oasis in a vast, empty landscape. The industrial/agricultural building punctuates the horizon like an inverted exclamation point, perhaps signifying an exciting conquest of man over nature. The looming, top-heavy structures are alone and isolated, but with a commanding presence.

WATER TOWER

ALLISON PETERS QUINN

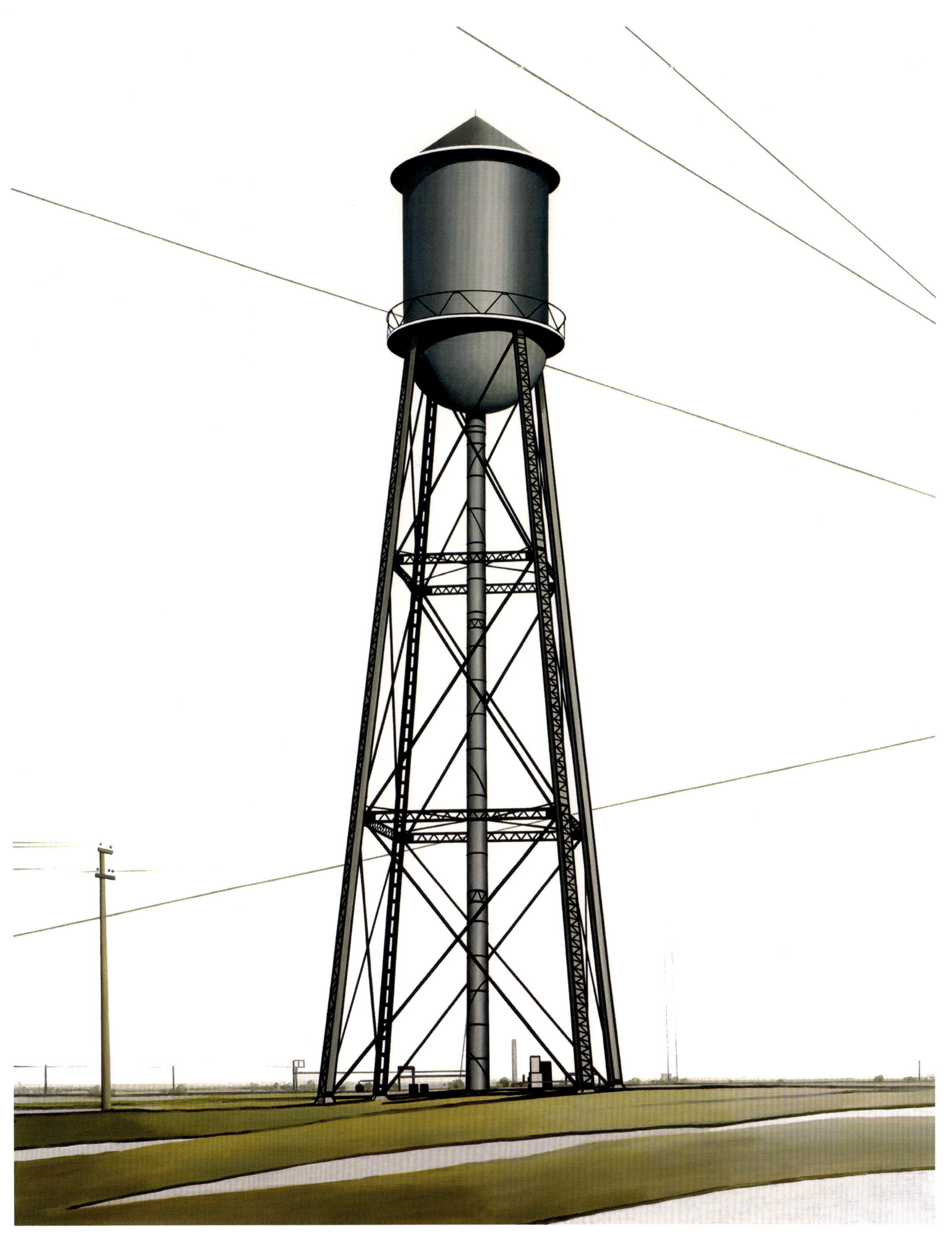

Plate 38. **Coldwater**, 1999, oil on canvas, 60 x 48 inches. Collection of artist.

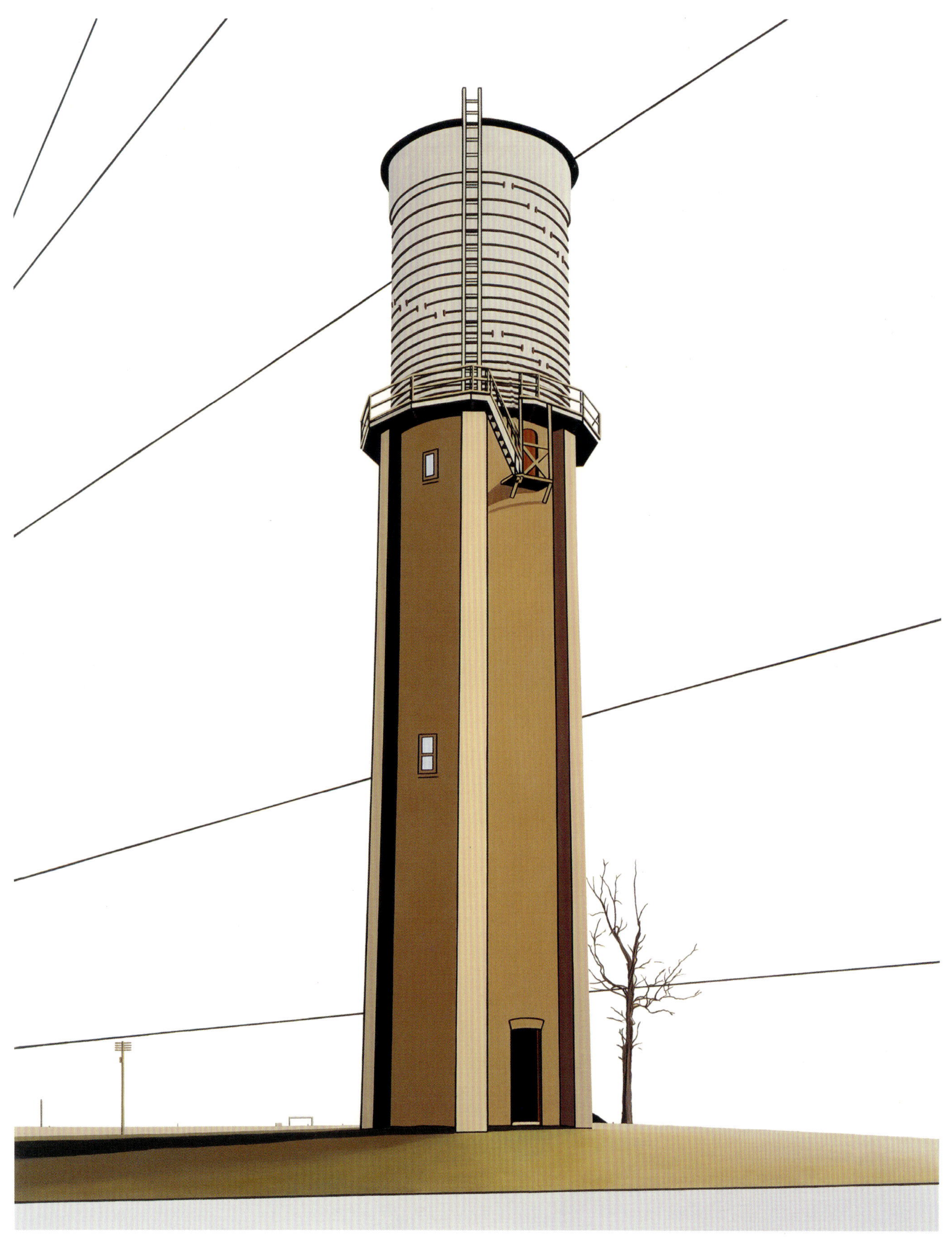

Plate 39. **Height to Top of Tank 92 ft.**, 2002, oil on canvas, 60 x 48 inches. Courtesy Roy Boyd Gallery.

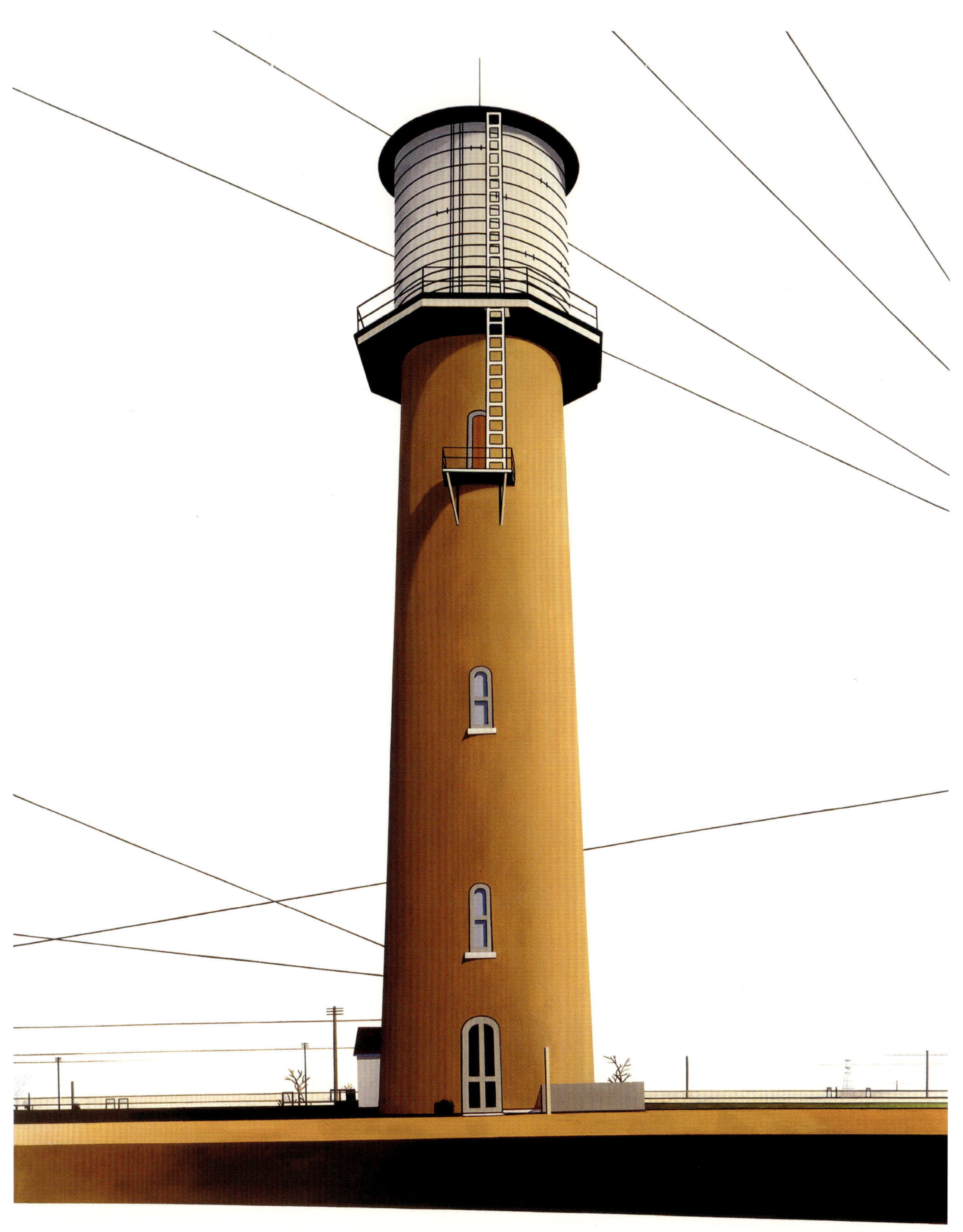

Plate 40. **Watertower 130 ft. High**, 2000, oil on canvas, 60 x 48 inches. Private collection.

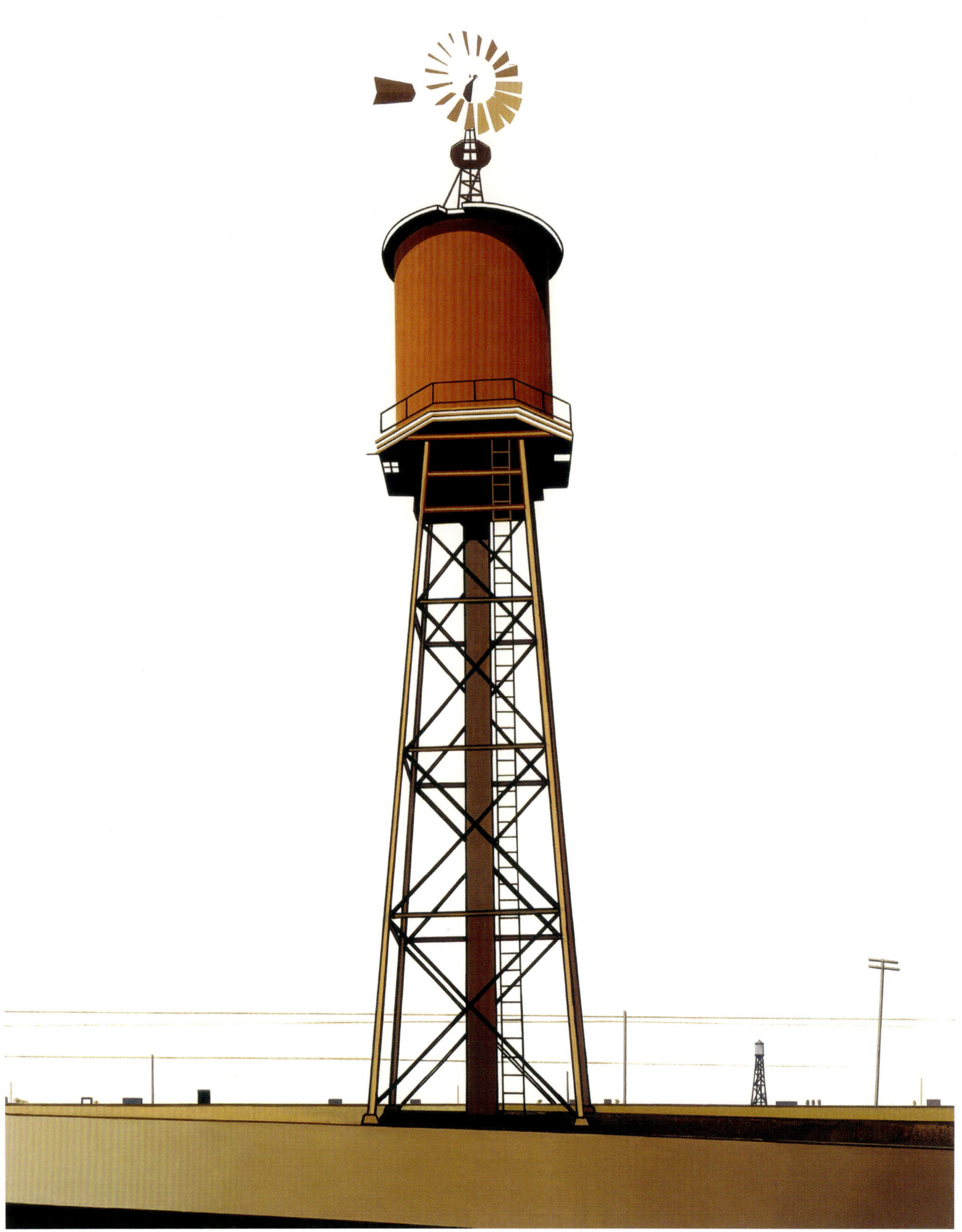

  Plate 41. **Windmill-Watertower**, 2003, oil on canvas, 44 x 35 inches. Private collection.

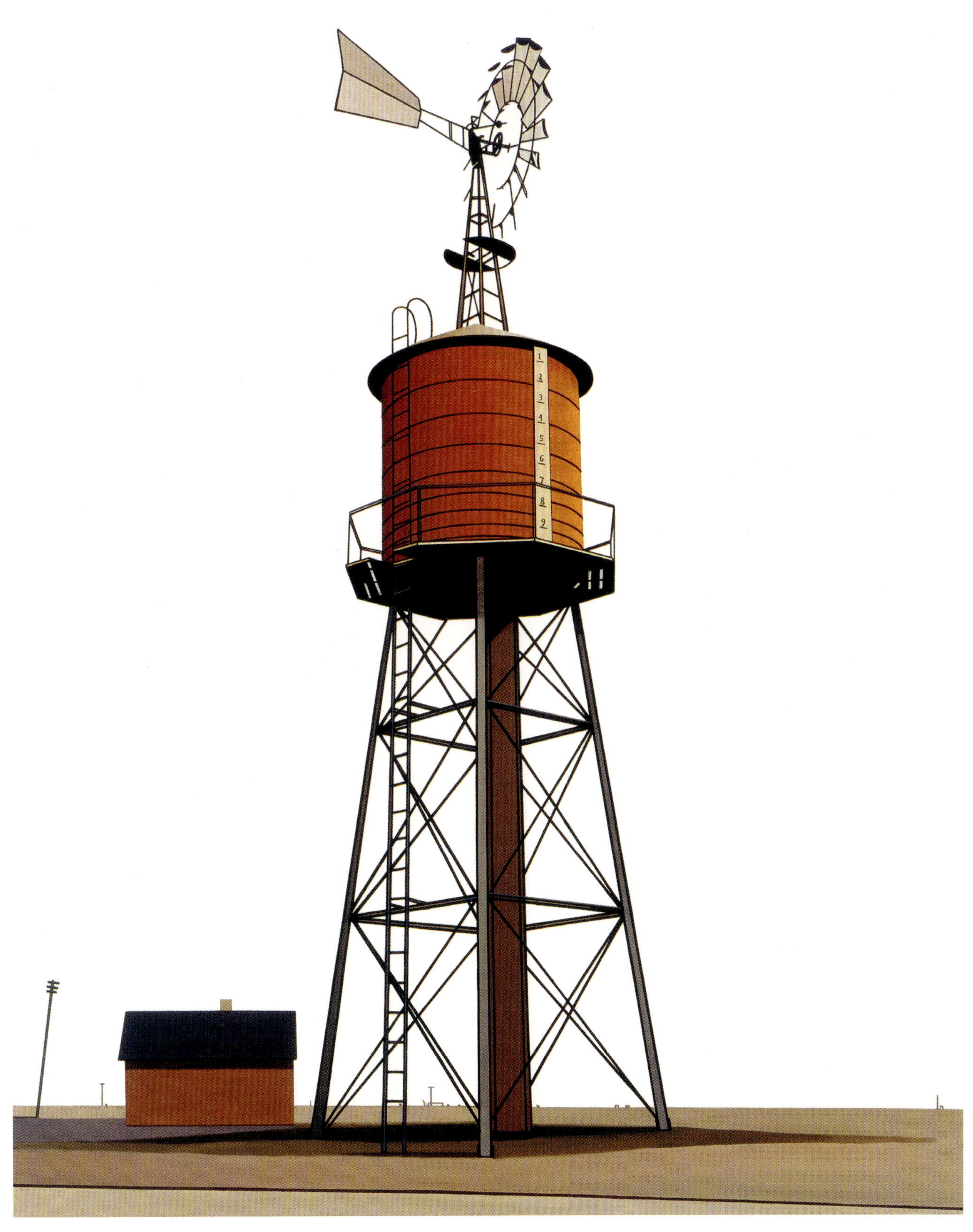

Plate 42. **Watertank/Windmill**, 2003, oil on canvas, 44 x 35 inches. Private collection.

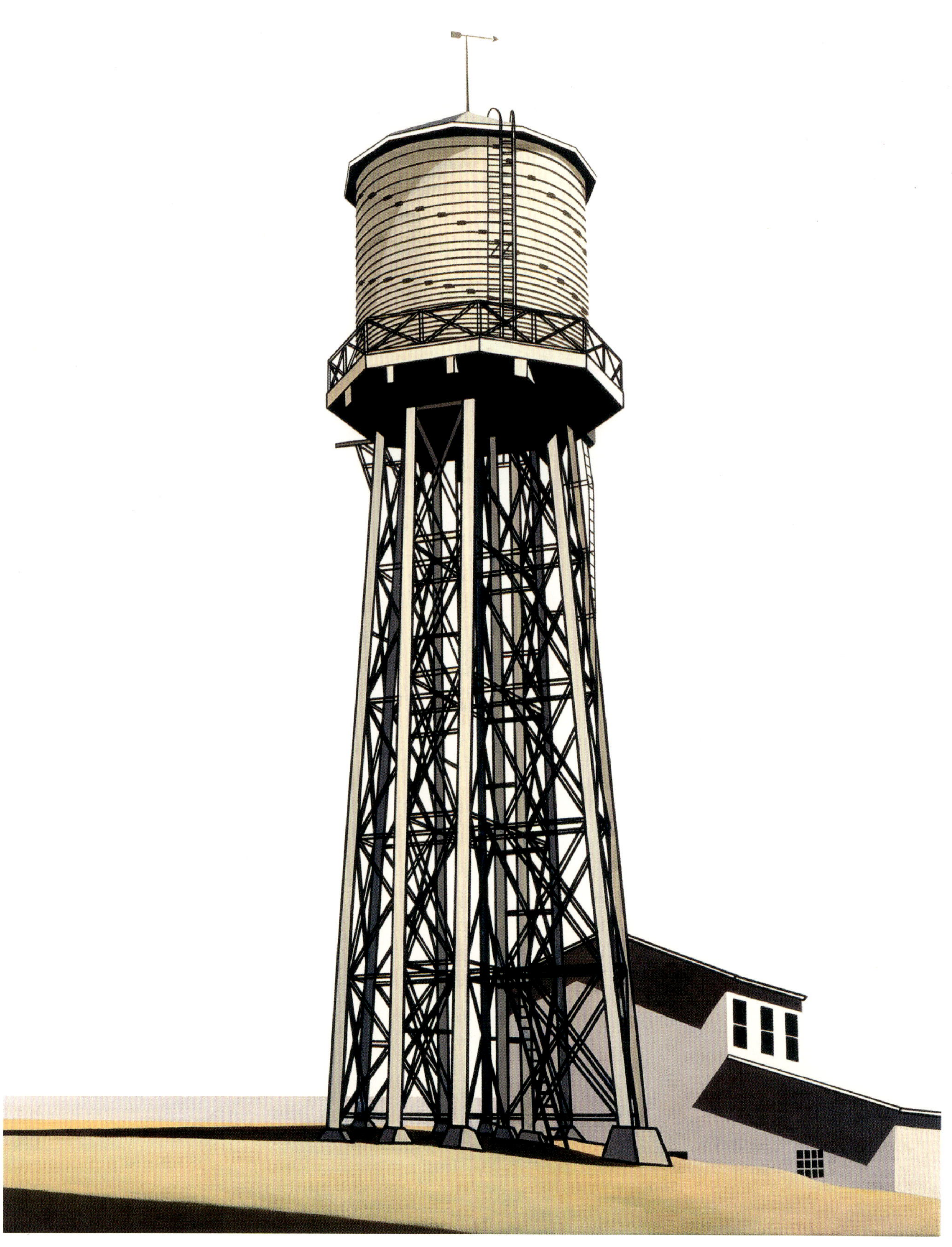

Plate 43. **Watertower, 87 ft. High, 65 thou. Gal.**, 2001, oil on canvas, 44 x 35 inches. Private collection.

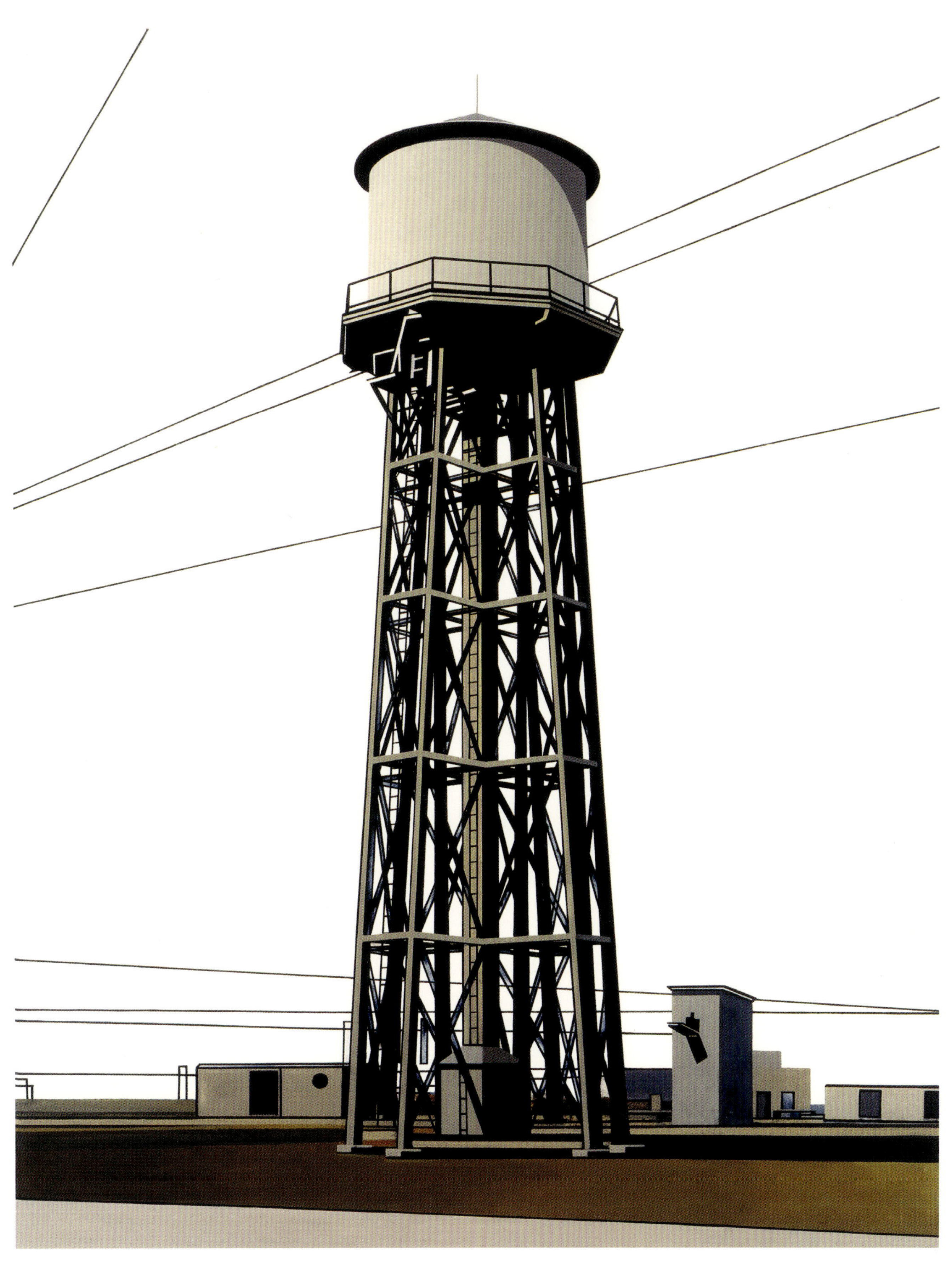

Plate 44. **Watertank Capacity 3200 bbl.**, 2002, oil on canvas, 44 x 35 inches. Private collection.

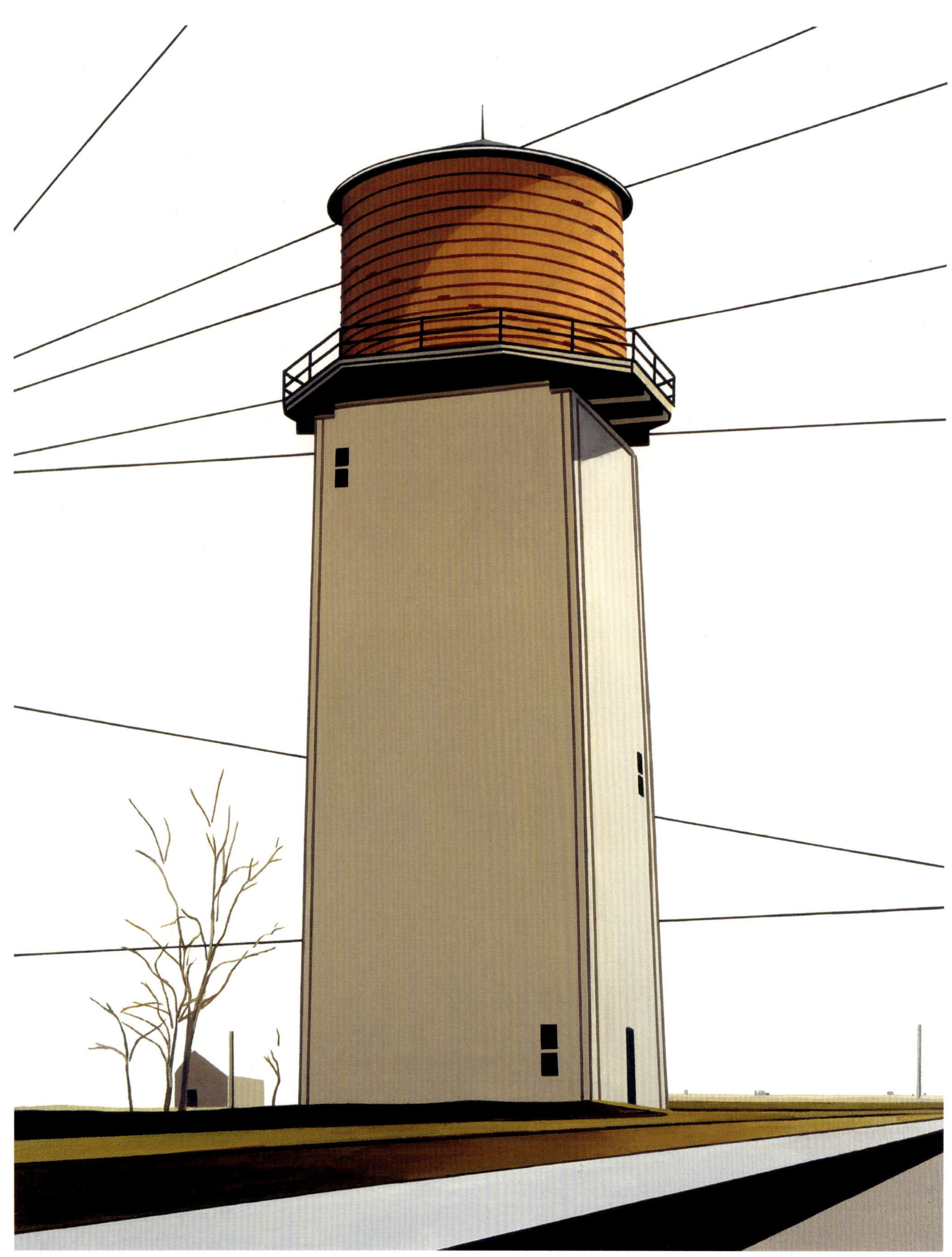

Plate 45. **Waterdepot**, 2003, oil on canvas, 30 x 24 inches. Collection of artist.

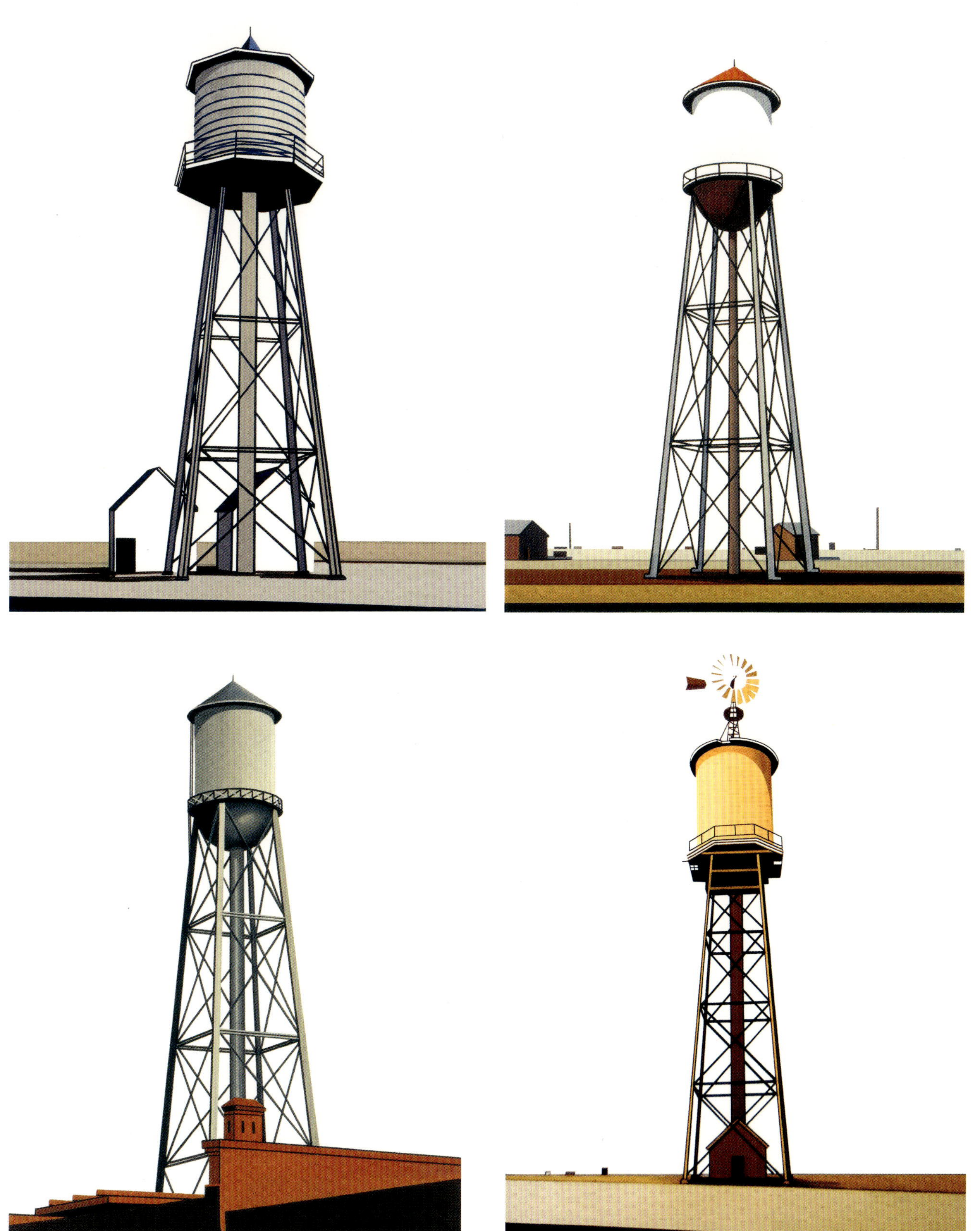

Plate 46. **Blue Watertank**, 2002, oil on linen, 20 x 16 inches. Private collection.

Plate 47. **105 ft. in Height**, 2003, oil on linen, 20 x 16 inches. Collection of artist.

Plate 48. **Watertower Durham**, 2001, oil on canvas, 20 x 16 inches. Private collection.

Plate 49. **Windmill/Watertank**, 2003, oil on canvas, 44 x 35 inches. Collection of Jeffrey and Patricia Paine.

EVERY MORNING FOR THE PAST FOURTEEN YEARS I have gazed at one of Will Steiger's river-bends—a stunning mosaic of parceled farmland marked by abstracted trees and a curving white river against a blank horizon. The picture is a powerful drama about ingenuity and dominance. The natural world has been reduced to geometry, yet the geometry cannot hold back a river's mighty force. Abstraction and realism are so precisely balanced that they work on me almost hypnotically, transporting my mind to real and imaginary places. I soar above the Midwest in a single-engine plane. I am in a novel about the anxiety of dislocation such as *Winesburg, Ohio* or *Sister Carrie*.

Timeless and evocative, unpopulated yet overwhelmingly human, Steiger's depiction of the clash of nature and man never ceases to move me. Looking at it now, I feel lonely and inspired.

RIVER BEND

MELISSA MILGROM

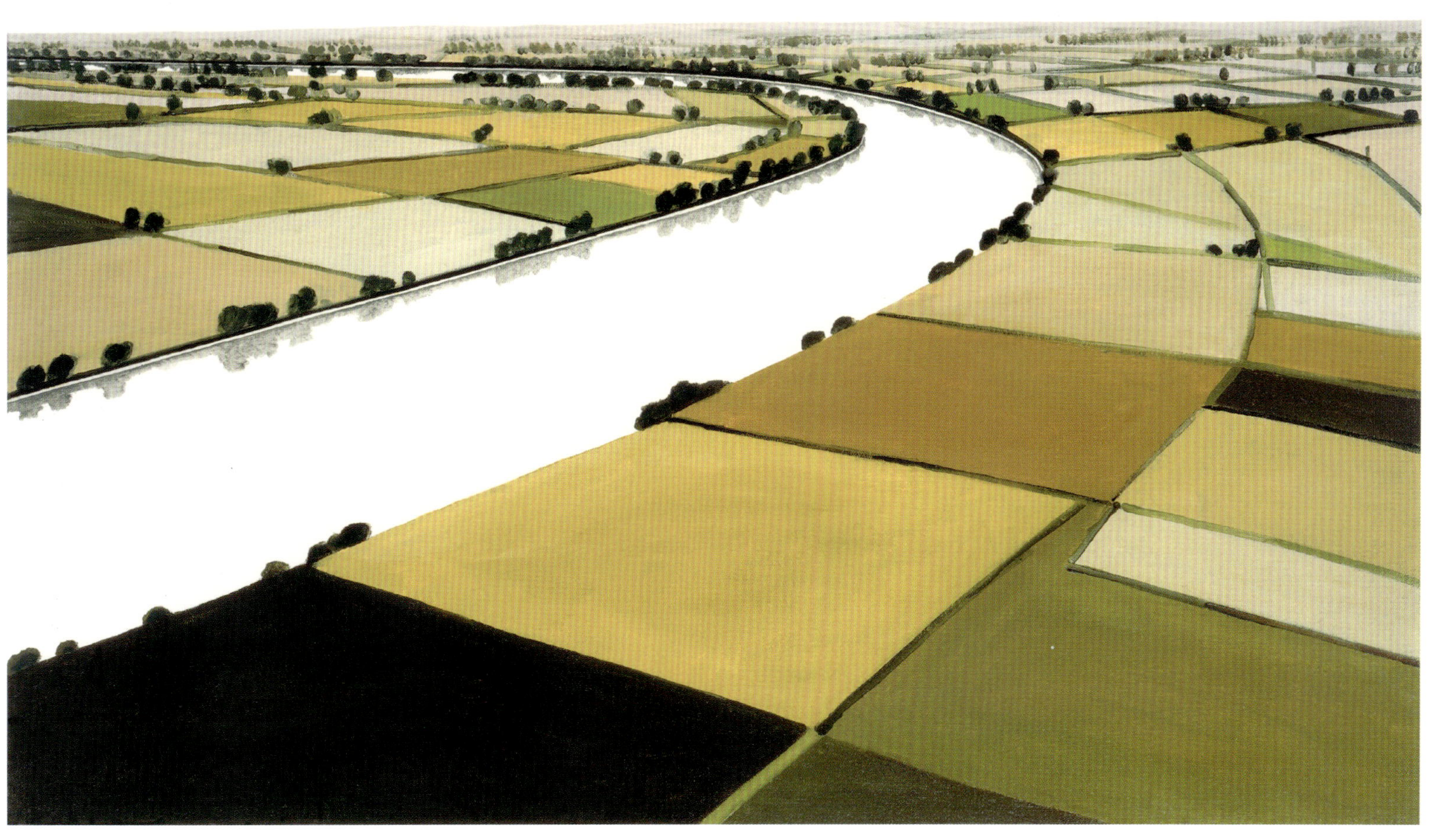

Plate 50. **Bend in the River,** 1999–2001, oil on canvas, 20 x 30 inches. Private collection.

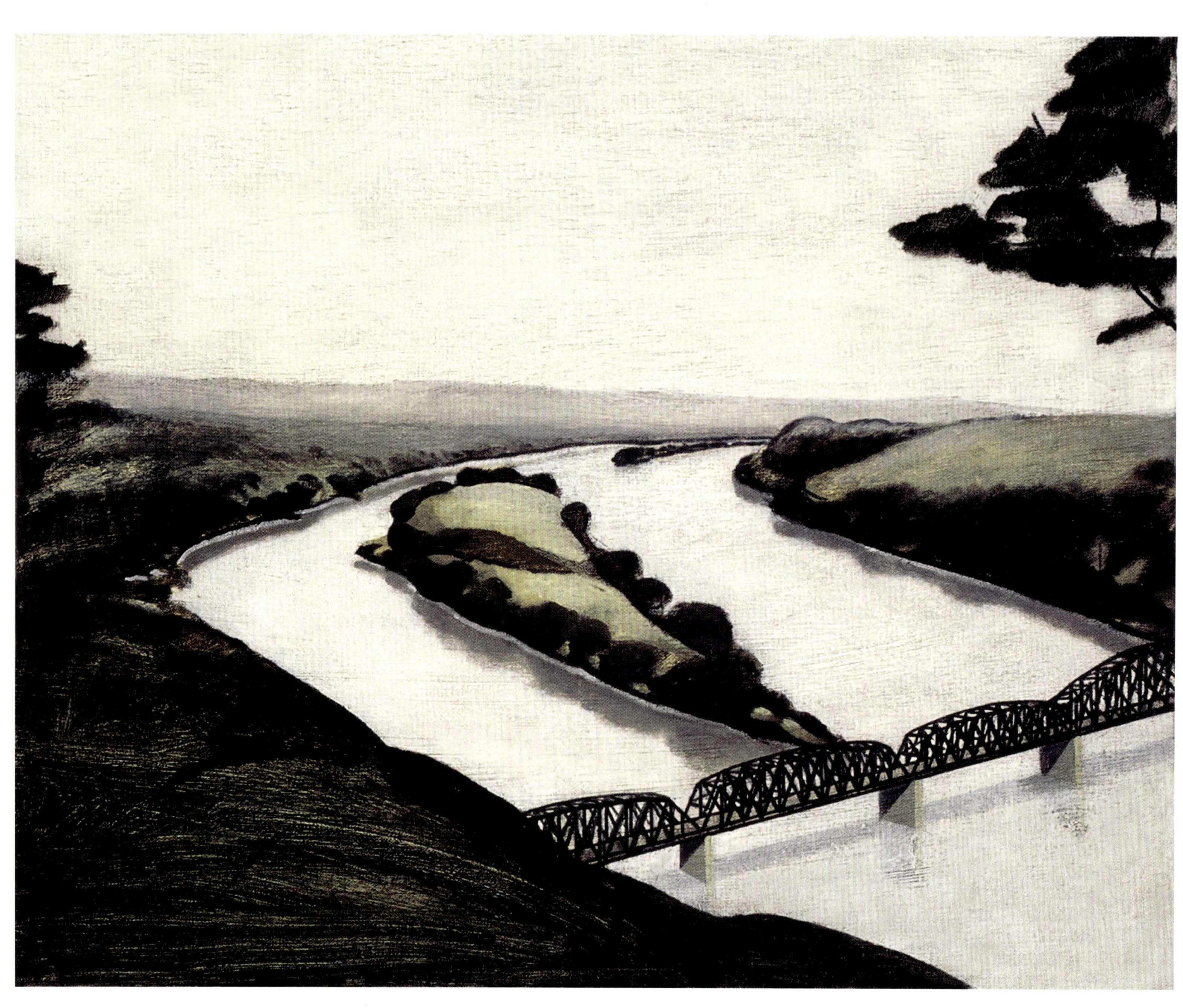

Plate 51. **The River Near Our Town**, 1995, oil on canvas, 16 x 20 inches. Collection of Susanna Lawler.

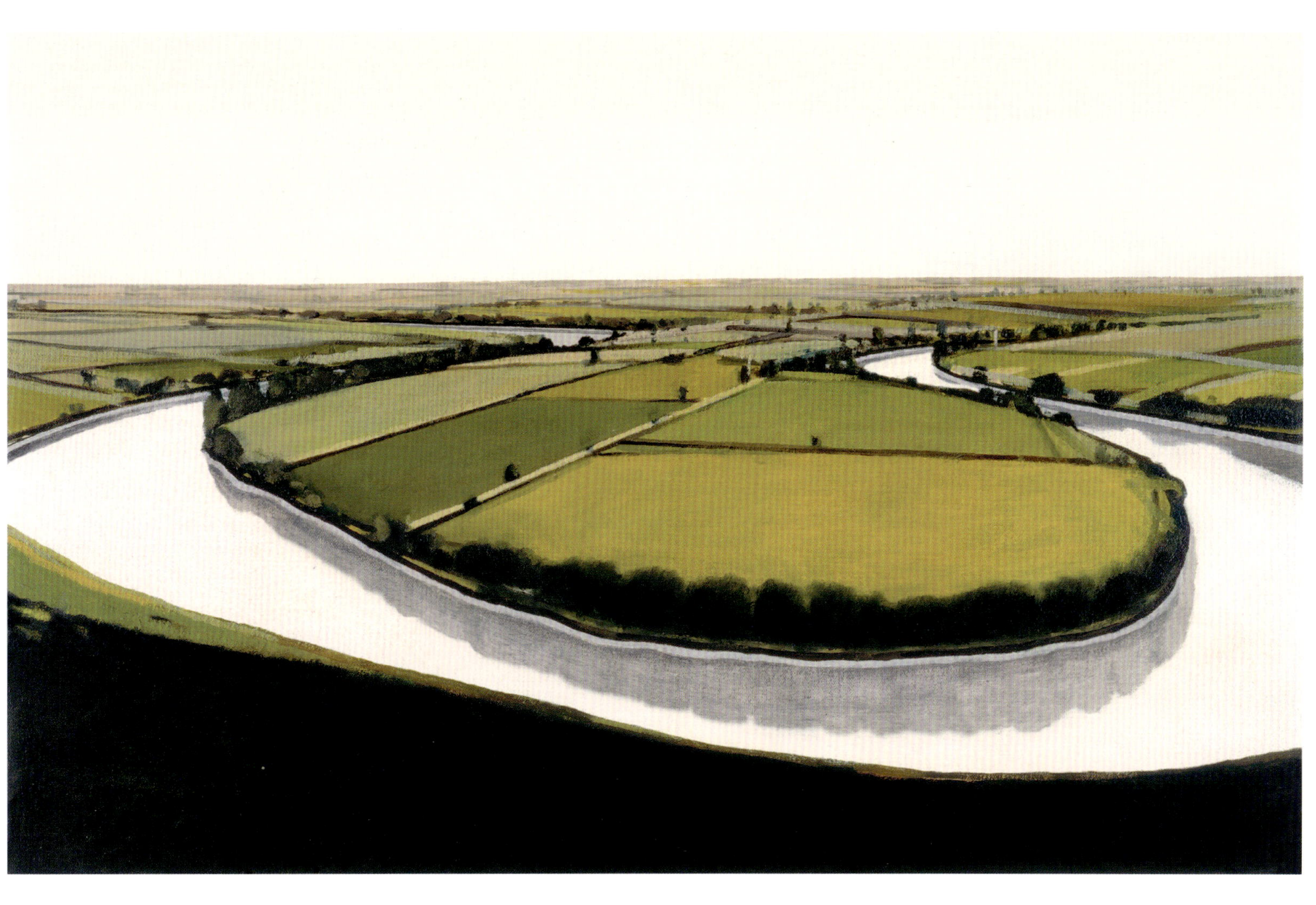

Plate 52. **Schuylkill**, 1997, oil on canvas, 17 ½ x 27 ½ inches. Private collection.

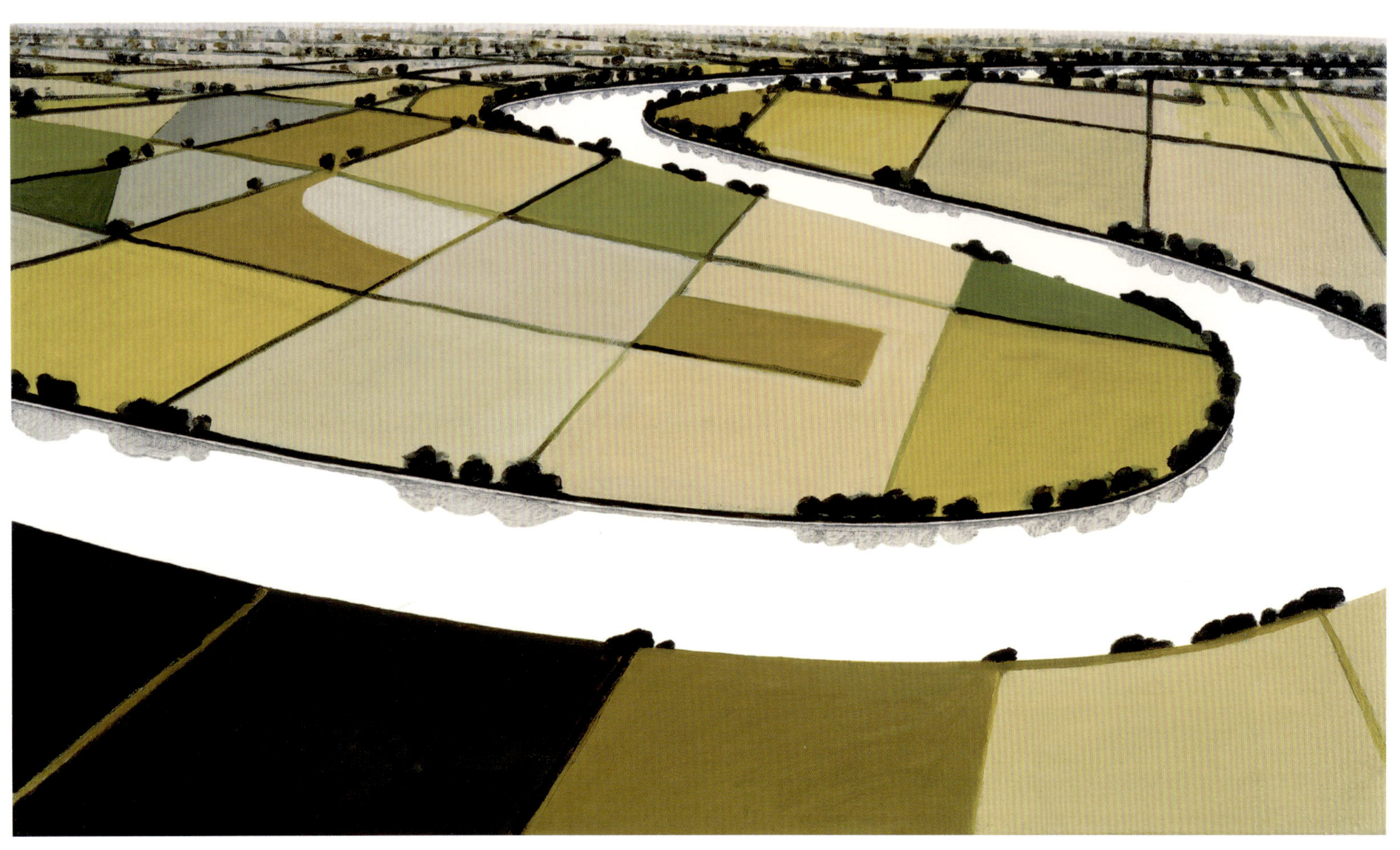

    Plate 53. **Ess Bend**, 2002, oil on canvas, 20 x 30 inches. Collection of Steven Nothern.

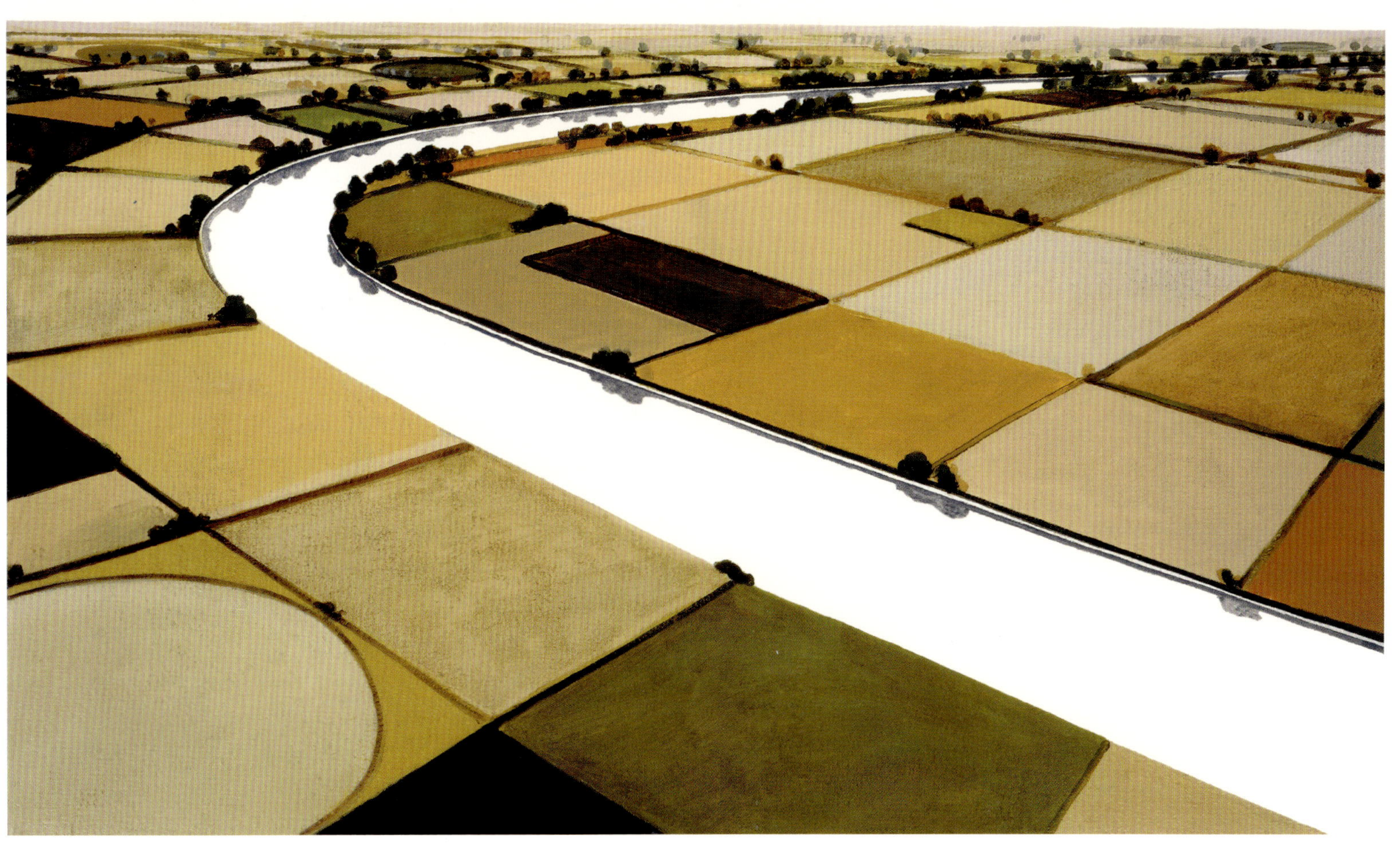

Plate 54. **Riverbend**, 2000, oil on canvas, 20 x 30 inches. Collection of Joy and Michael Millette.

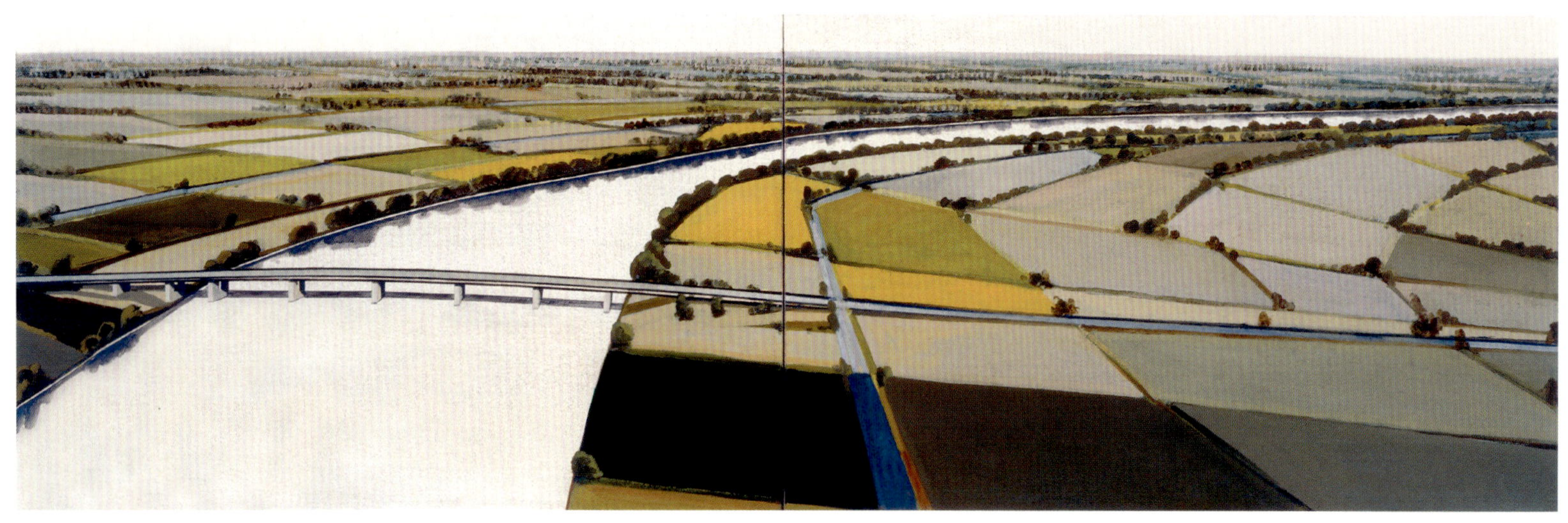

 Plate 55. **Riverbend with Bridge**, 1998, oil on canvas, 17 ½ x 55 inches (two panels). Private collection.

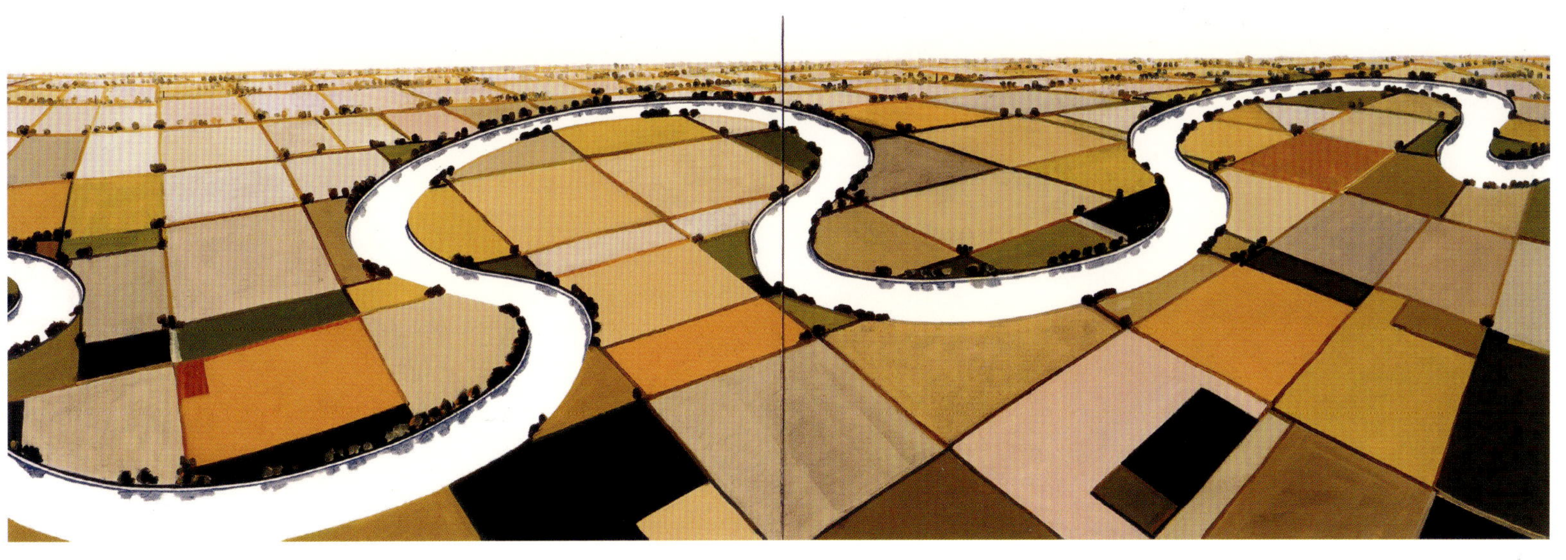

Plate 56. **Watercourse**, 2001, oil on canvas, 20 x 60 inches (two panels). Collection of Linda and Turan Duda.

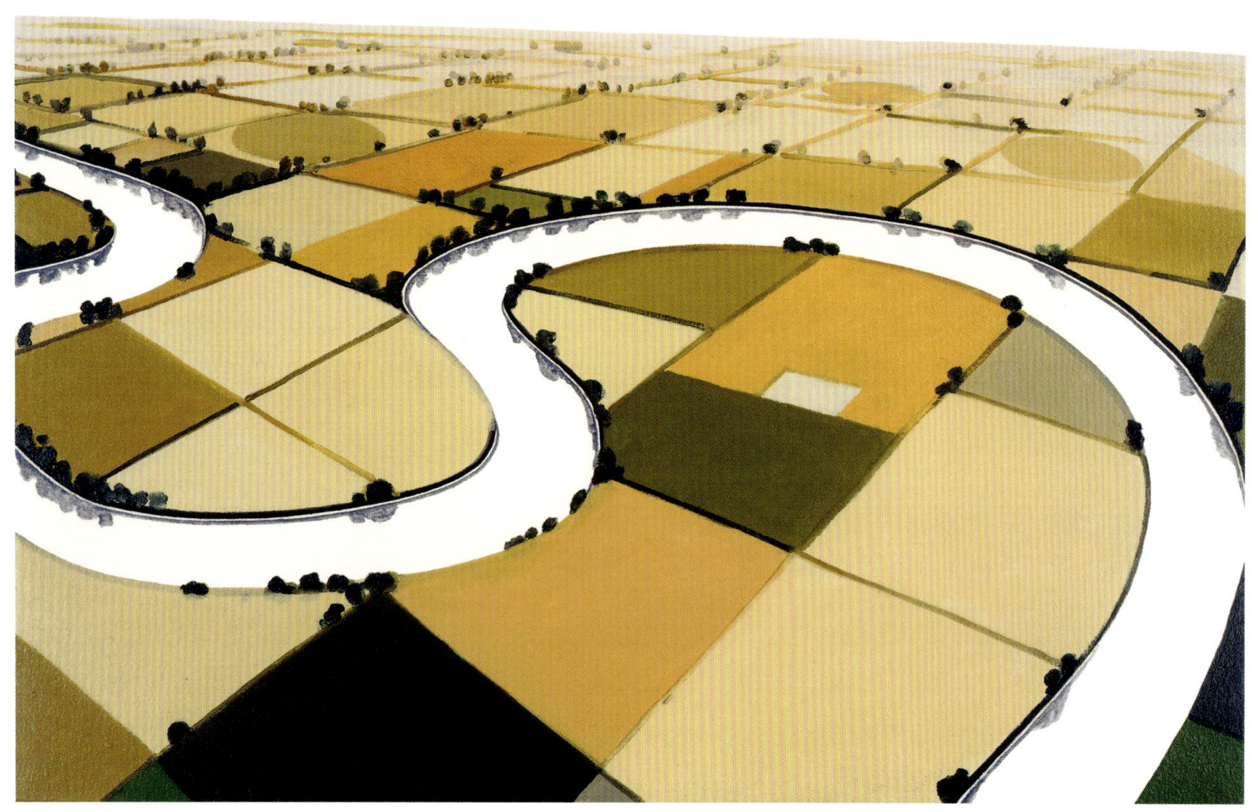

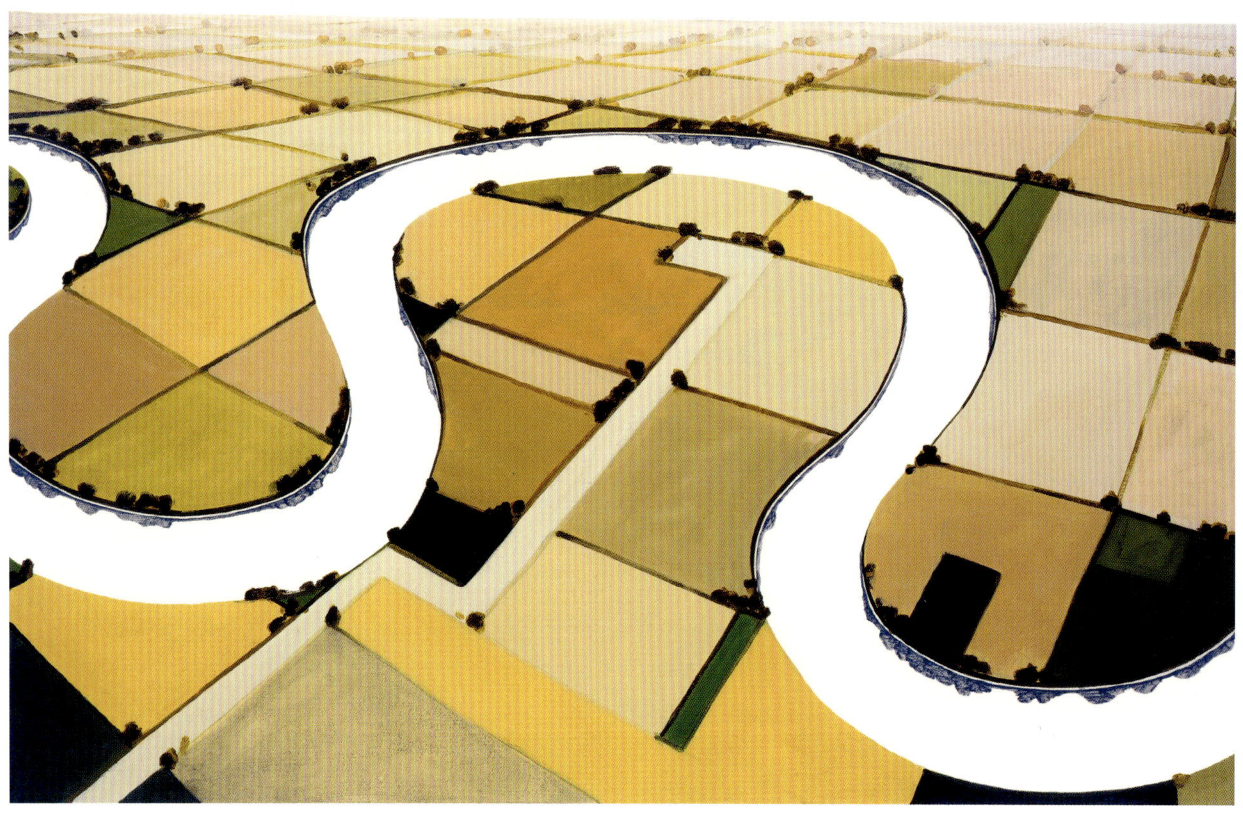

Plate 57. **Doubleturn**, 1999, oil on canvas, 20 x 30 inches. Collection of Dr. H. Elliott Albers.

Plate 58. **Winding River**, 2000, oil on canvas, 20 x 30 inches. Pfizer Collection.

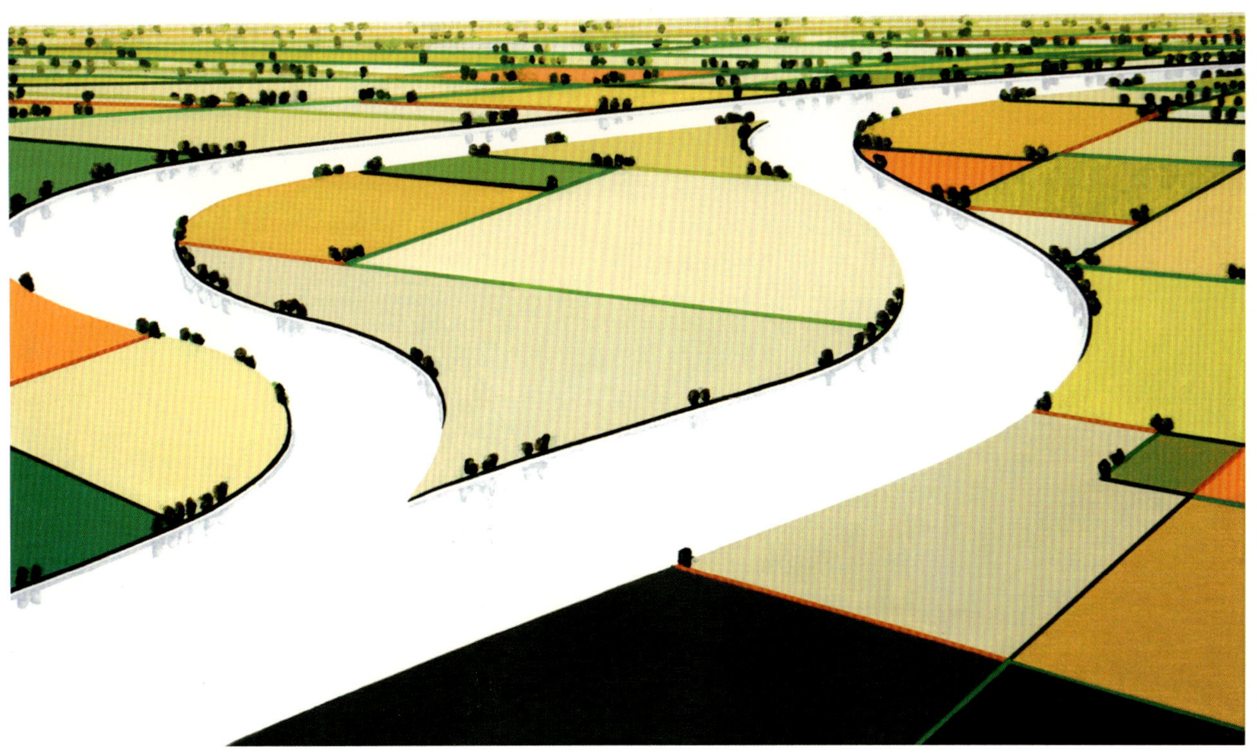

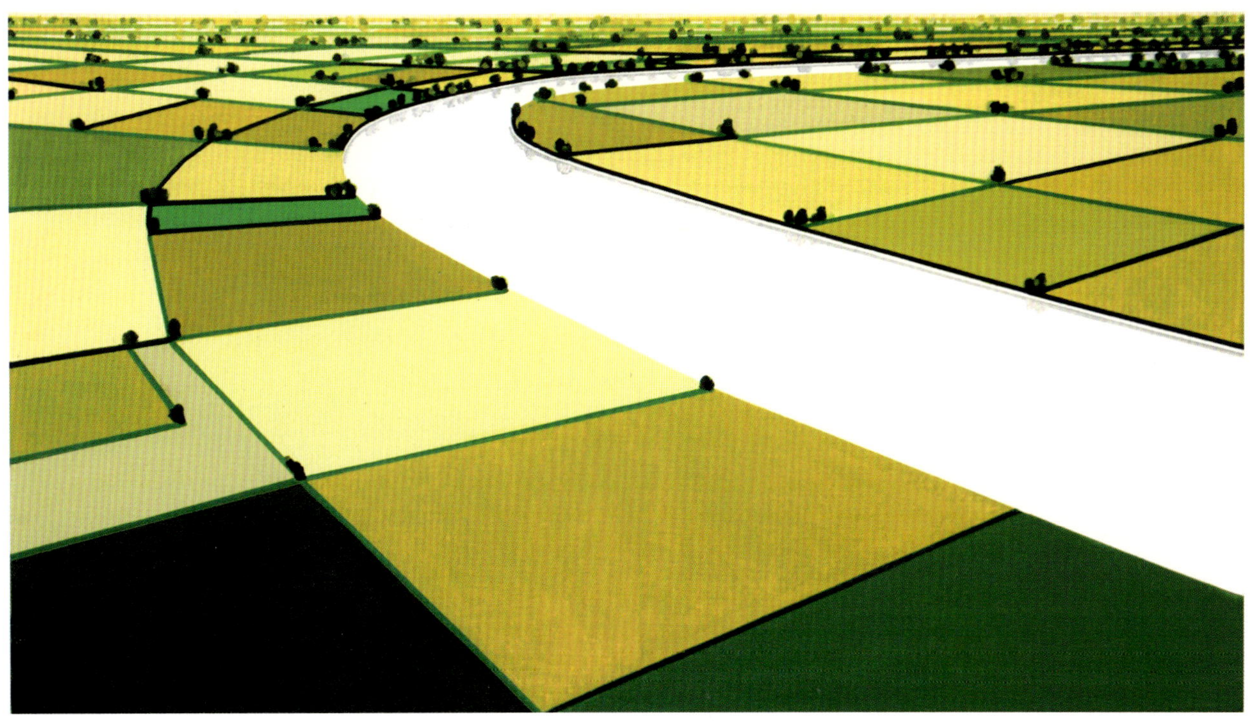

Plate 59. **Riverbend-Island**, 2006, oil on linen, 20 x 30 inches. Collection of Hana Bank.

Plate 60. **Green Riverbend**, 2005, oil on linen, 17½ x 27½ inches. Collection of Richard Smolin.

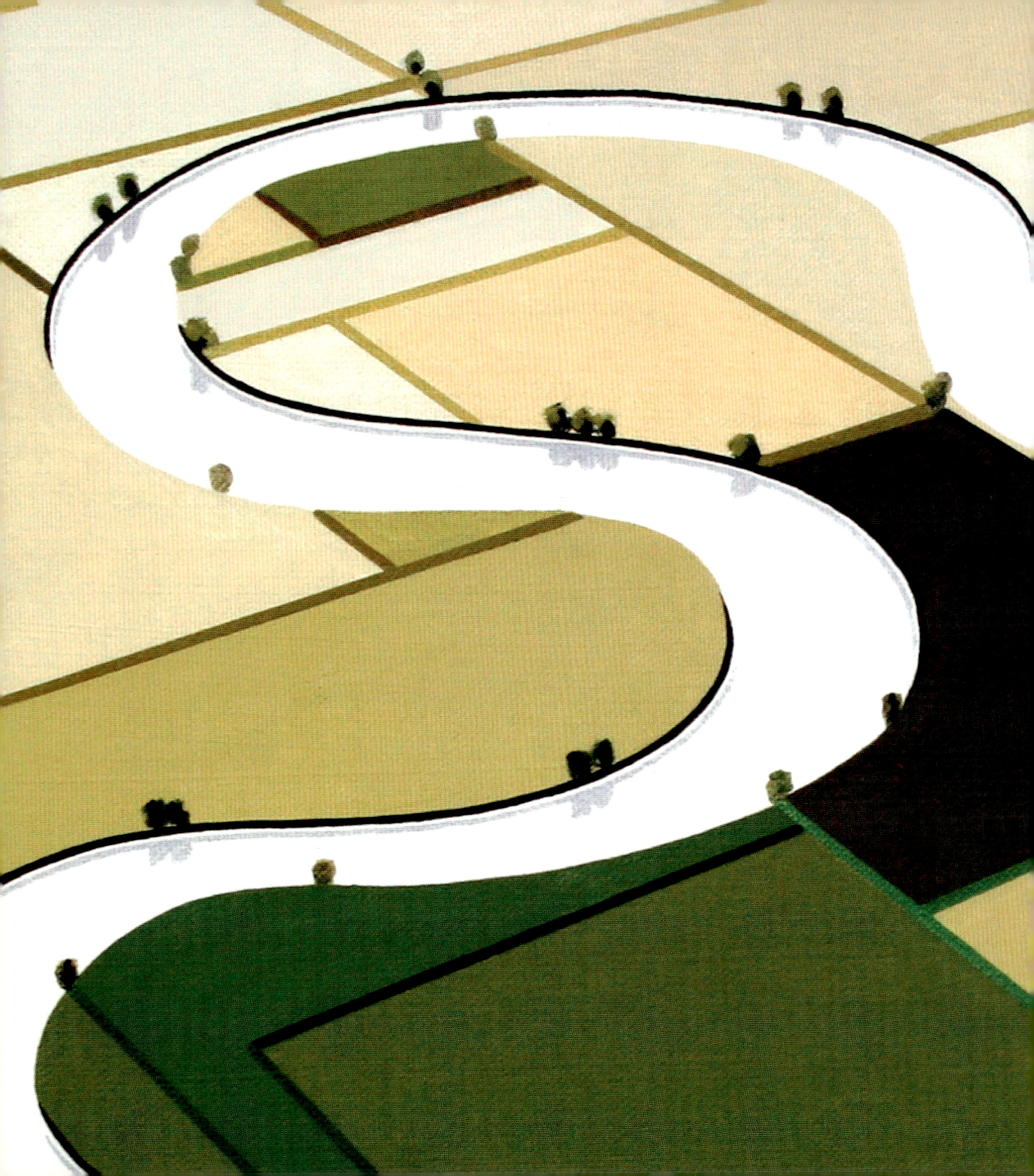

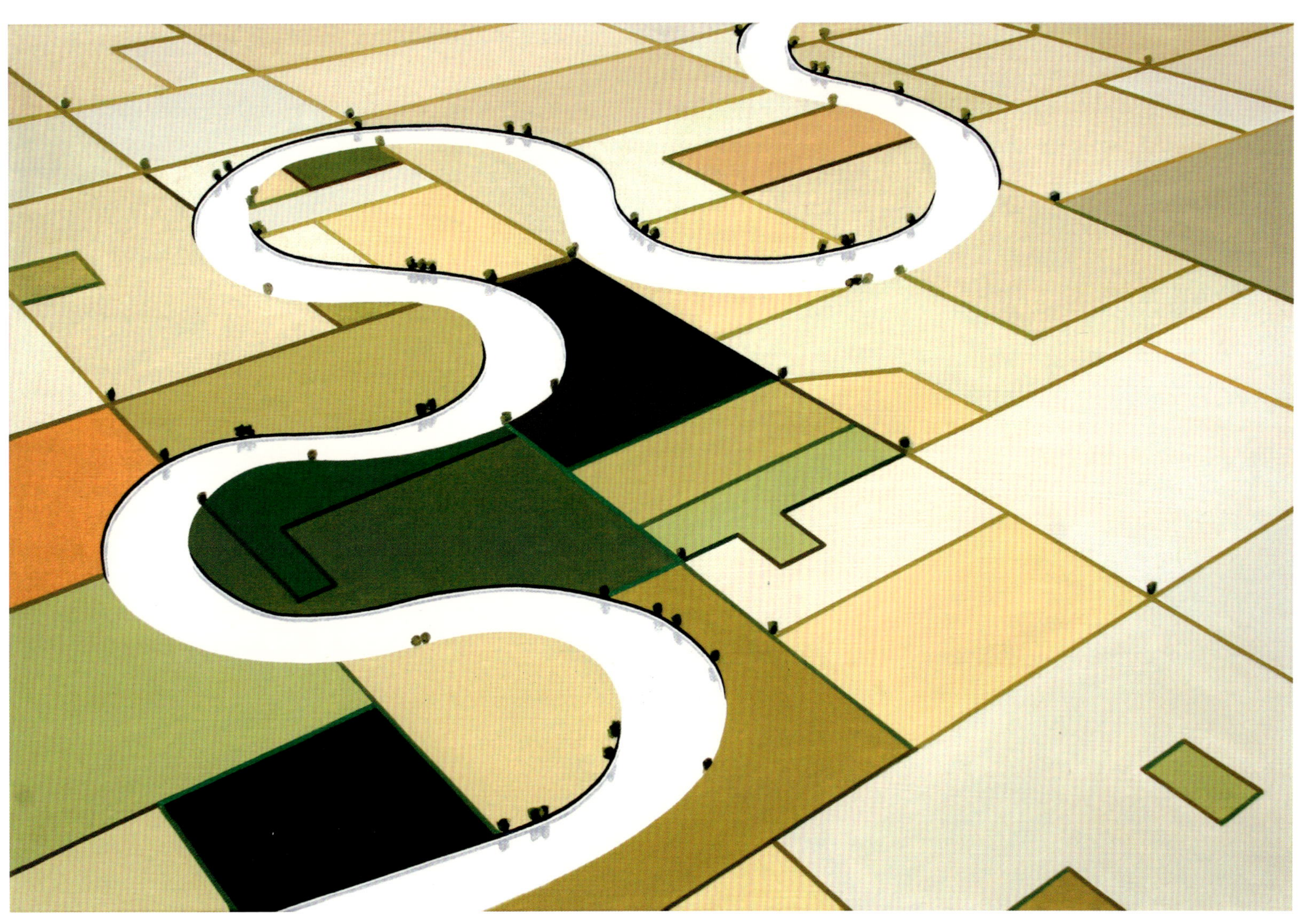

Plate 61. **Switchback**, 2009, oil on linen, 20 x 30 inches. Courtesy Marcia Wood Gallery.

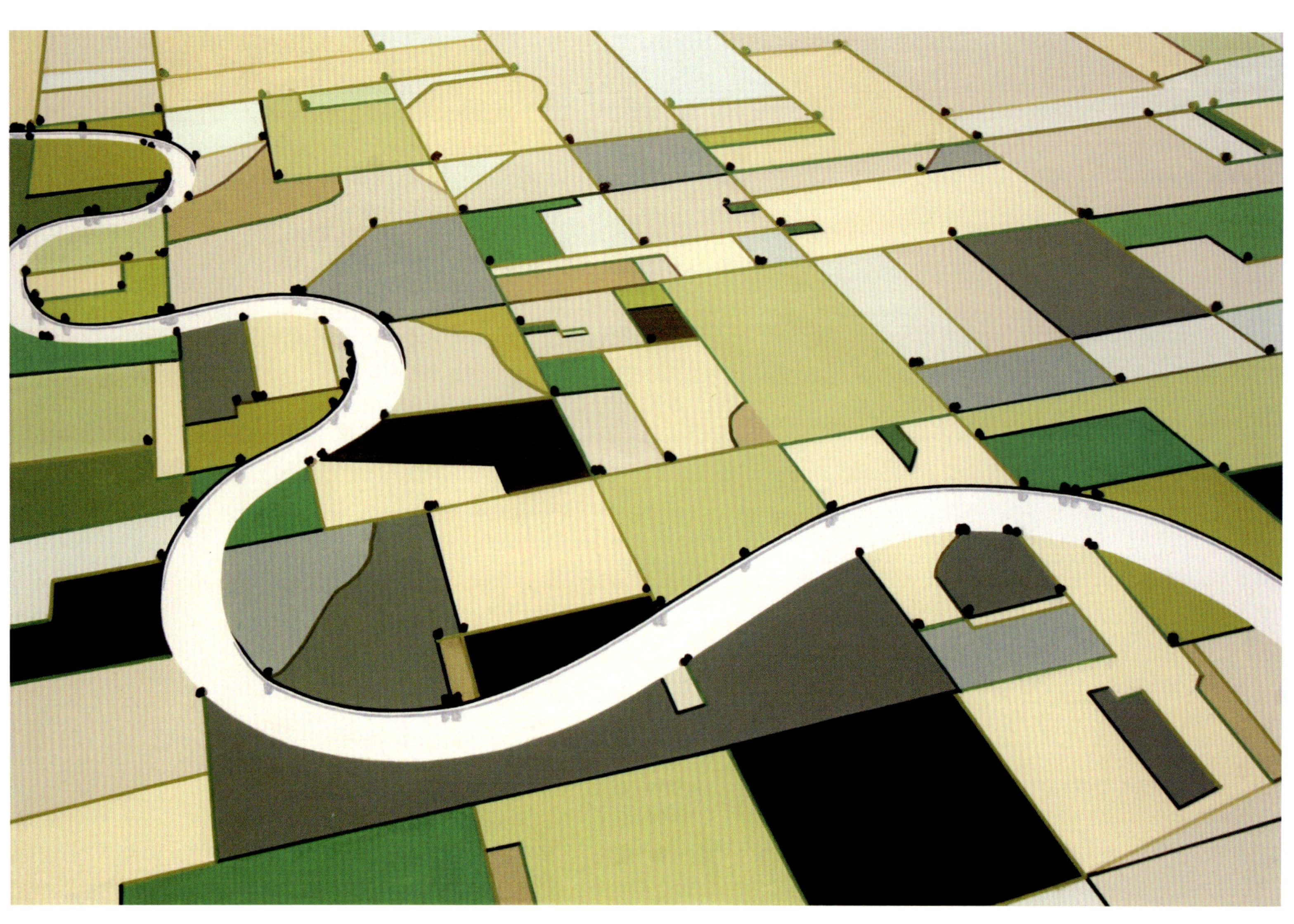

Plate 62. **Ramble**, 2008, oil on linen, 20 x 30 inches. Courtesy Margaret Thatcher Projects.

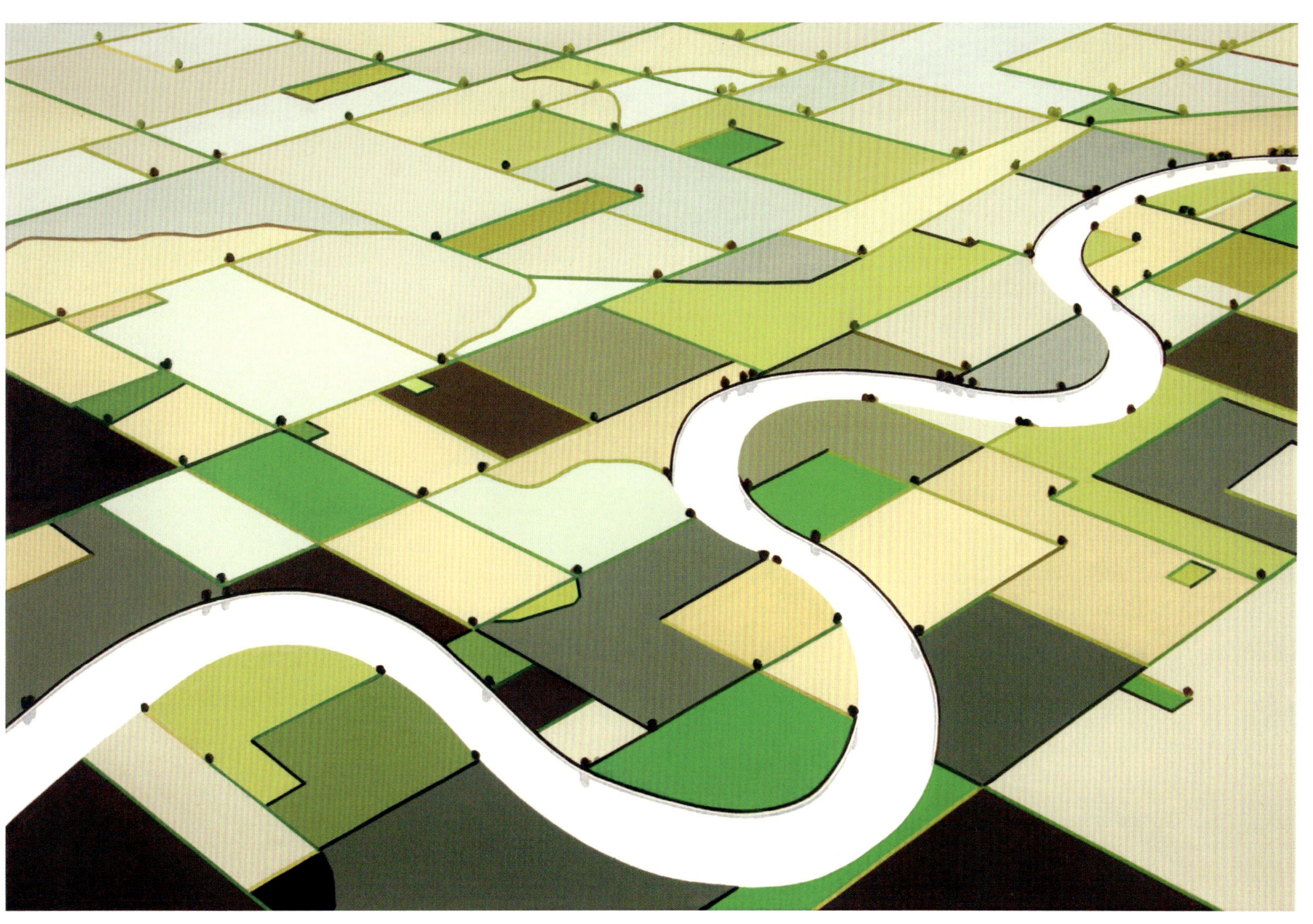

THRUST FRONT AND CENTER in a variety of stark, sweeping landscapes, William Steiger's *Signal* and *Semaphore* towers command the eye with their quirky surfaces and startling forms. These mechanical and odd, yet elegant and poignant structures, often ignored in real life, become the sole focus in Steiger's minimal paintings. All other unique elements of the surrounding landscape have been stripped away, leaving a full frontal portrait of another, more industrial age. In Steiger's precise and careful renditions, these towers fully occupy the space while being conceptually and physically isolated in their design obsolescence.

As a contemporary painter working in a computerized age, Steiger is fascinated by and cognizant of the tensions between the old world and the new, embodied by these familiar, semi-industrial forms. Visually, Steiger knits these two eras together by interpreting the heavy train tracks as more tactile wires or cabling, speeding our eye towards an infinite vanishing point. As a deft counterpoint, Steiger inserts these distinctive towers into this timeless field of vision, directing our focus towards something interesting, unique, and rather unexpected. Upright, vertical construction, lacy, decorative latticework, heavy bases and delicate ladders serve to accent both their function and aesthetic. Even though Steiger has eliminated all traces of actual people, human presence is felt on every level with his rational spacing, grid work, and drawn perspective lines cutting through the vast expanse. Time, change, even history are uncertain in Steiger's paintings. There is nothing but the eternal present as embodied by these strange hybrid structures trying to communicate something in a coded language. As physical objects, they are a deft combination of whimsy, utility, and versatility. These funny towers with their spots of high color and their Rockette-like precision of jutting armatures tend to stop us in our tracks.

SIGNAL

LISA HATCHADOORIAN

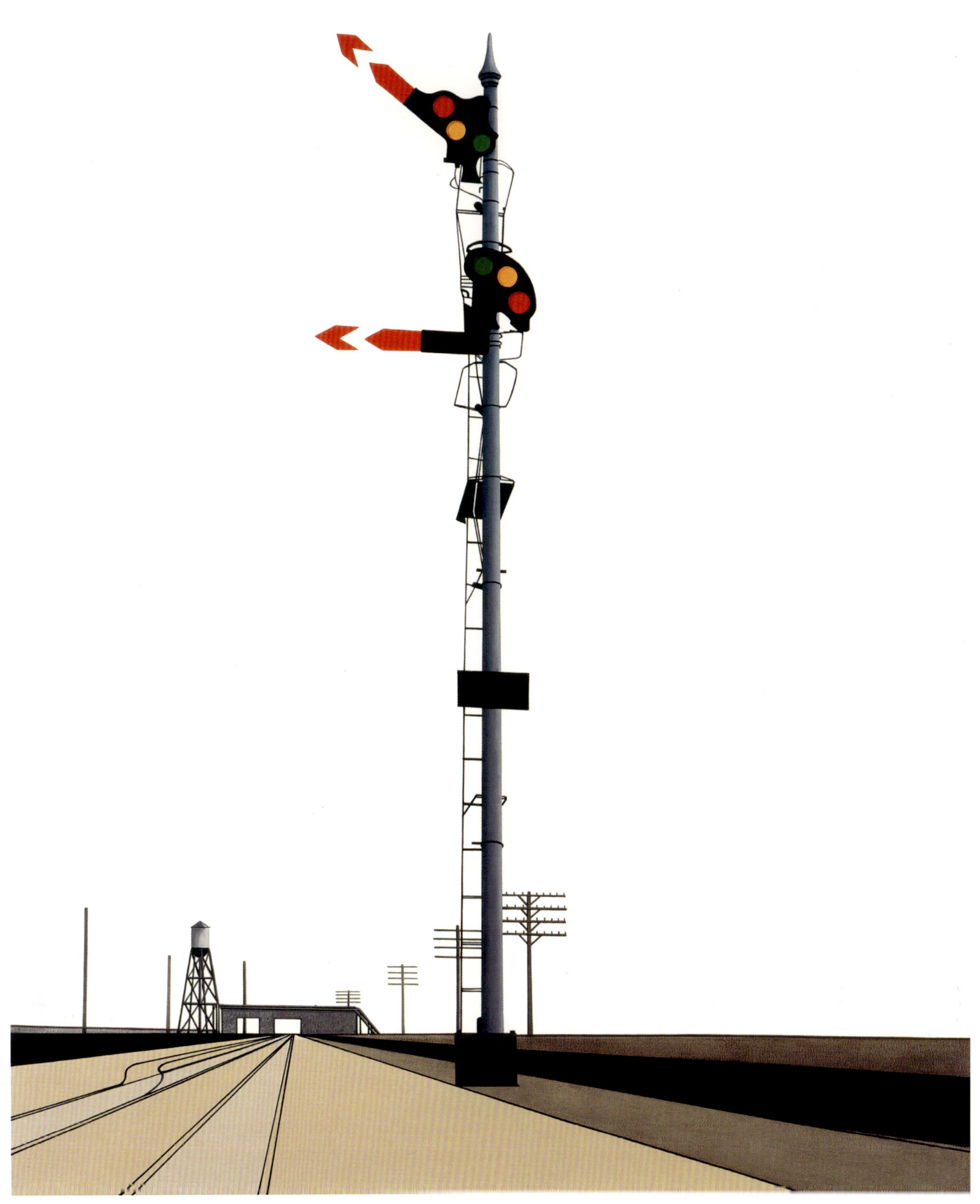

Plate 64. **Semaphore II**, 2002, oil on canvas, 60 x 48 inches. Collection of Charles Wall.

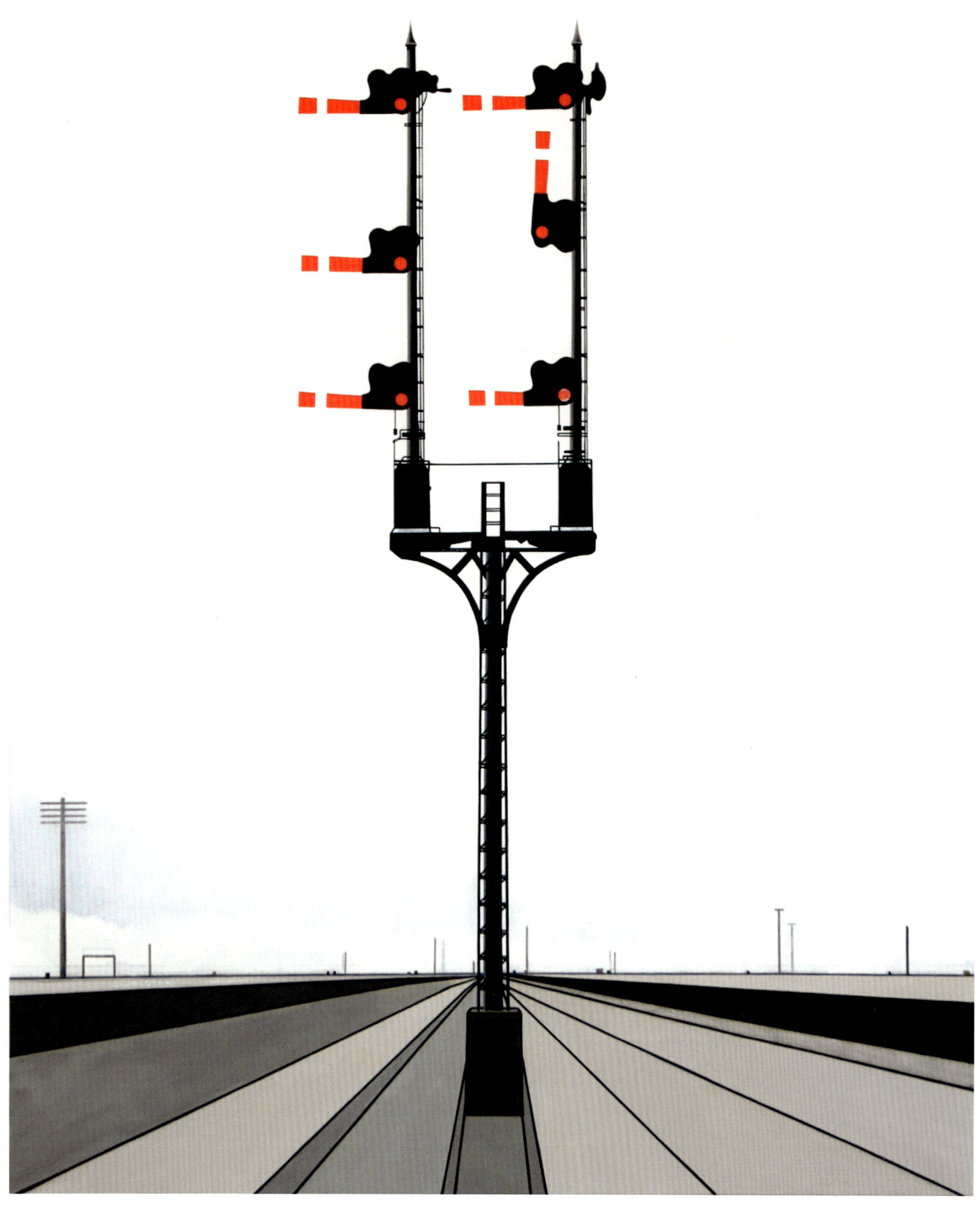

Plate 65. **Semaphore III**, 2003, oil on canvas, 60 x 48 inches. Collection of artist.

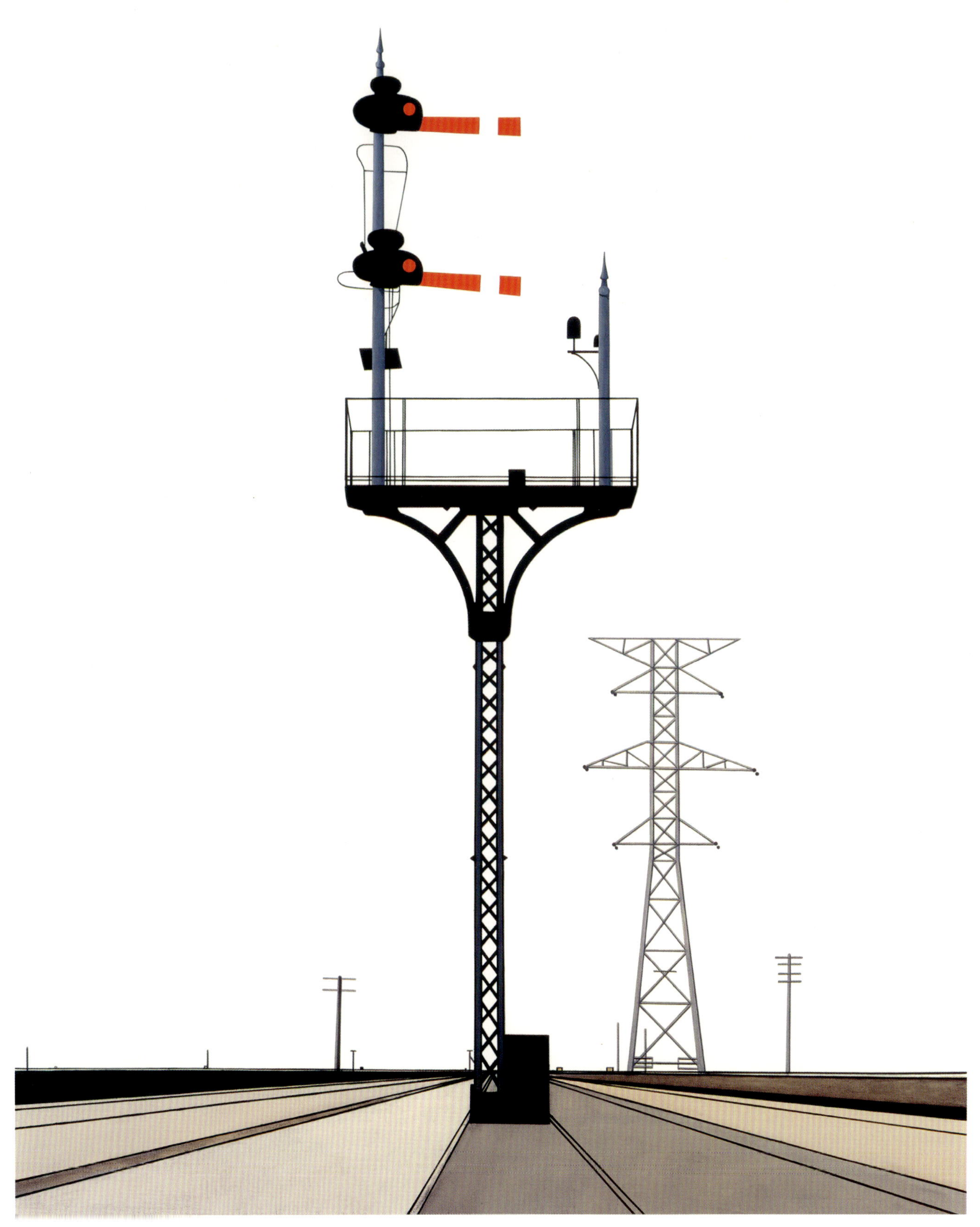

Plate 66. **Semaphore I**, 2002, oil on canvas, 60 x 48 inches. Private collection.

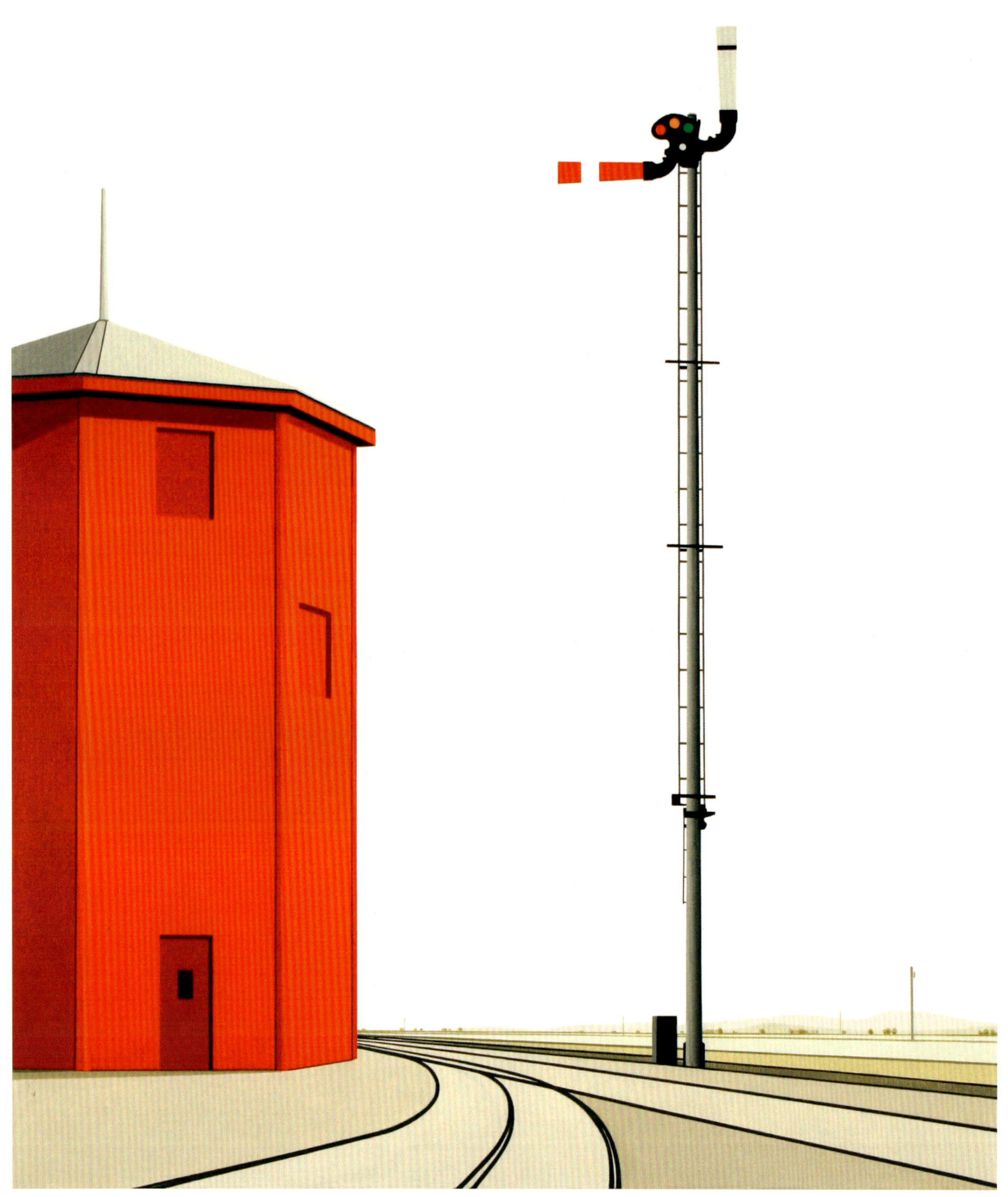

Plate 67. **Junction**, 2007, oil on linen, 44 x 35 inches. Courtesy Roy Boyd Gallery.

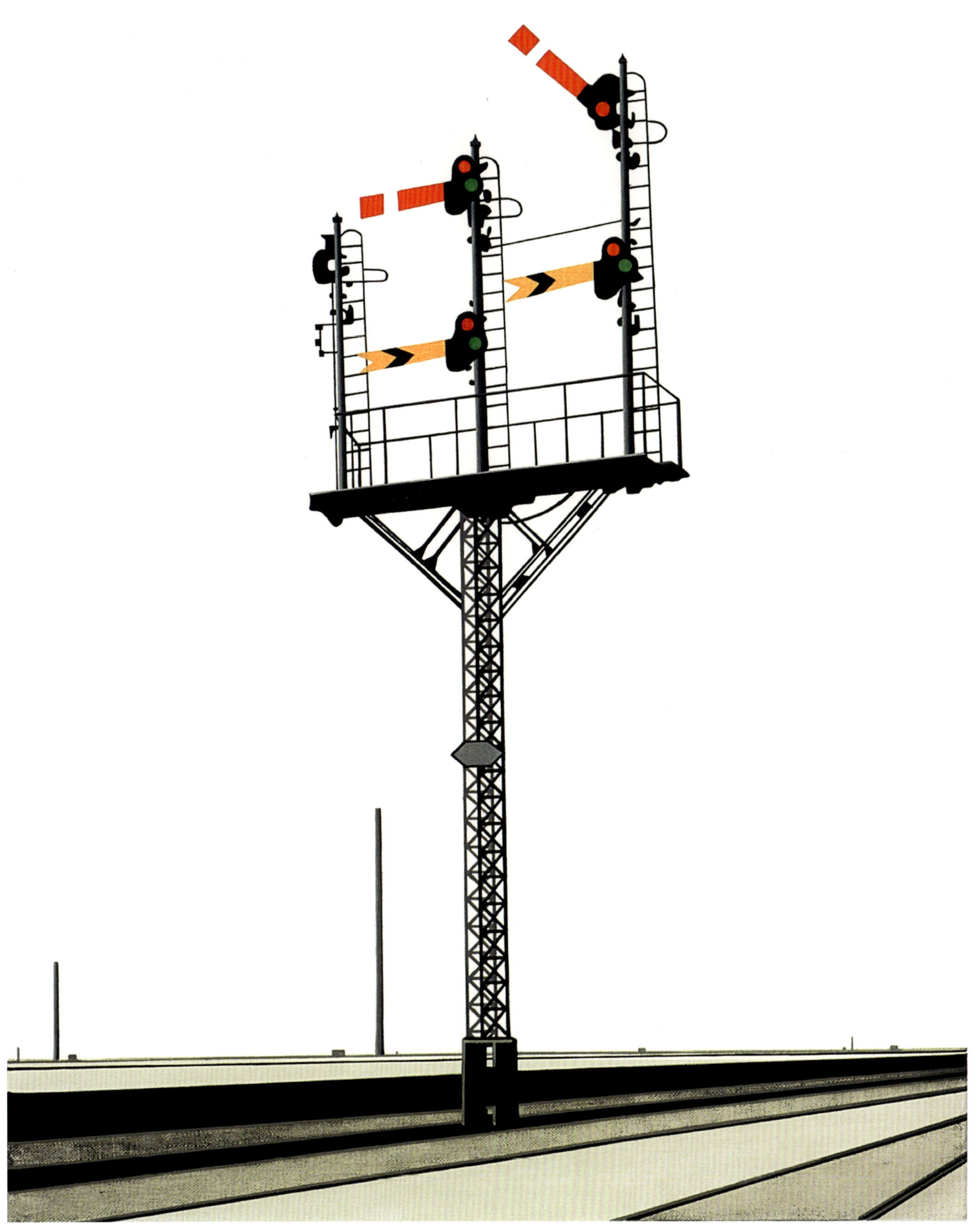

Plate 68. **Proceed with Caution**, 2003, oil on canvas, 30 x 24 inches. Collection of Ted and Mary Shasta.

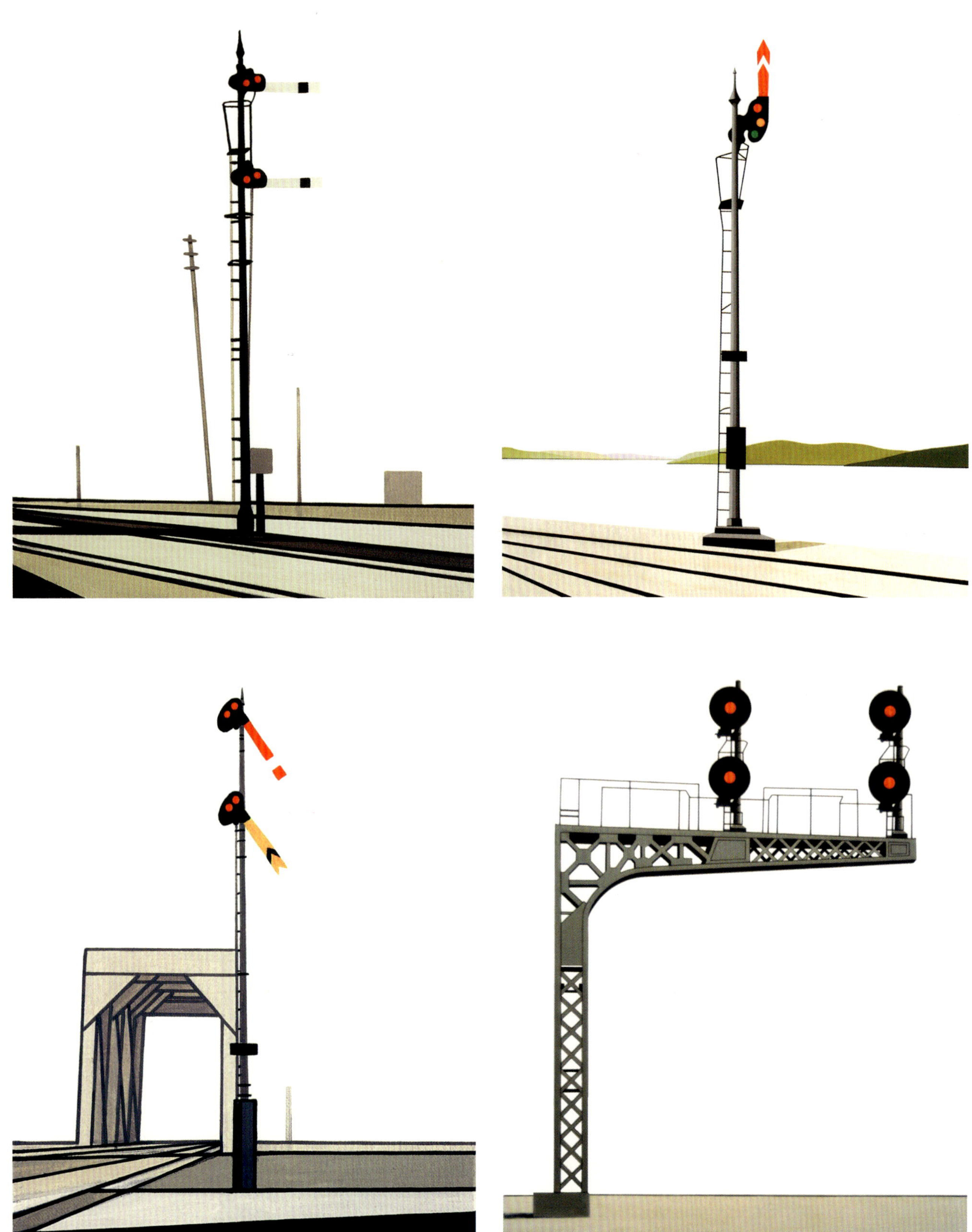

Plate 69. **Semaphore #10**, 2002, oil on linen, 10 x 8 inches. Collection of Anne and Steven Price.

Plate 70. **Semaphore Lakeside**, 2005, oil on linen, 30 x 24 inches. Courtesy Marcia Wood Gallery.

Plate 71. **Semaphore #7**, 2002, oil on linen, 10 x 8 inches. Private collection.

Plate 72. **Signals**, 2004, oil on canvas, 60 x 48 inches. Collection of John R. Eckel, Jr. Estate.

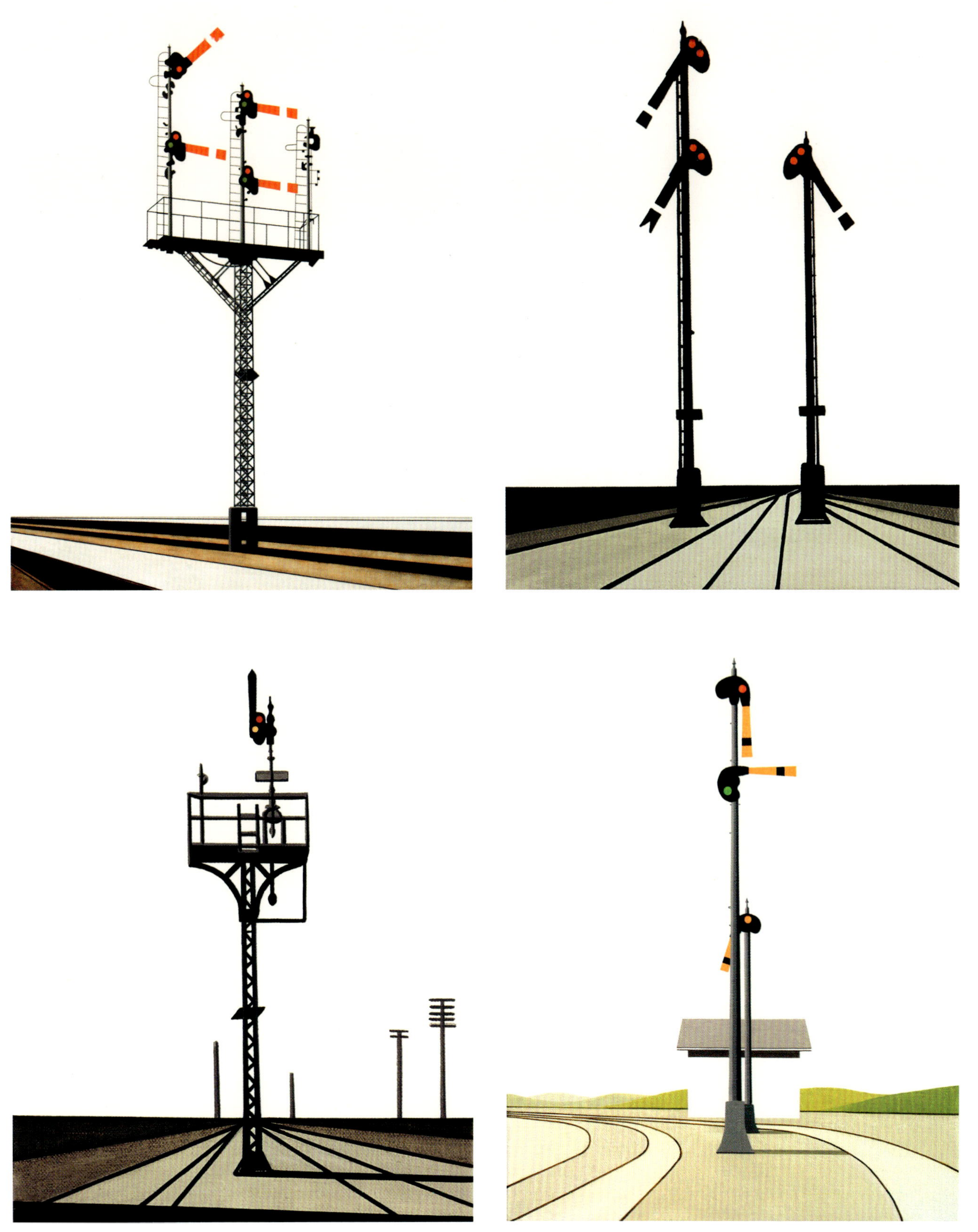

Plate 73. **Signal**, 2006, oil on canvas, 60 x 48 inches. Private collection.

Plate 74. **Semaphore #12**, 2002, oil on linen, 10 x 8 inches. Private collection.

Plate 75. **Semaphore #8**, 2002, oil on linen, 10 x 8 inches. Private collection.

Plate 76. **Signal #2**, 2005, oil on linen, 20 x 16 inches. Collection of Noel Kirnon.

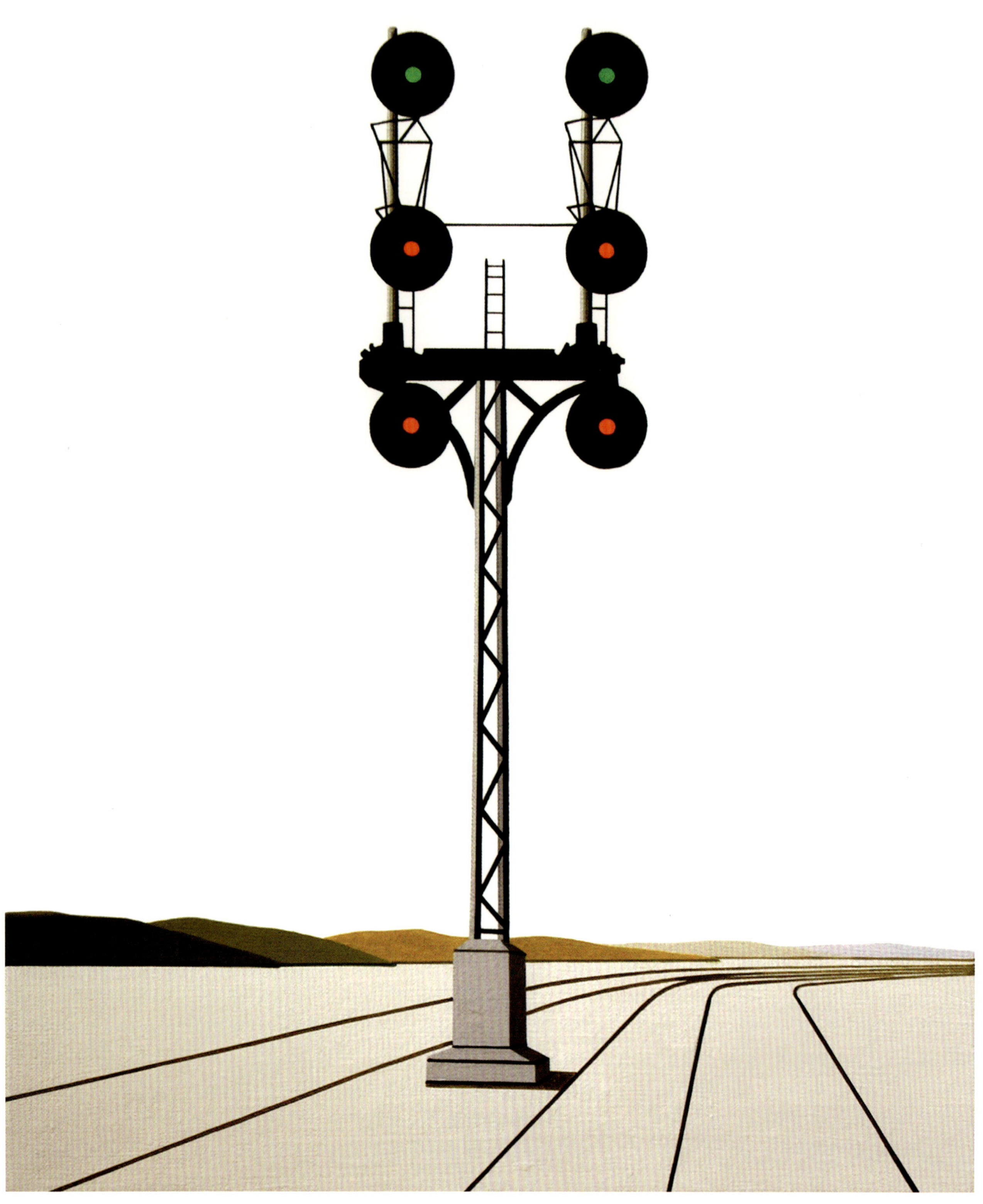

Plate 77. **Electric Signal**, 2005, oil on linen, 20 x 16 inches. Courtesy Marcia Wood Gallery.

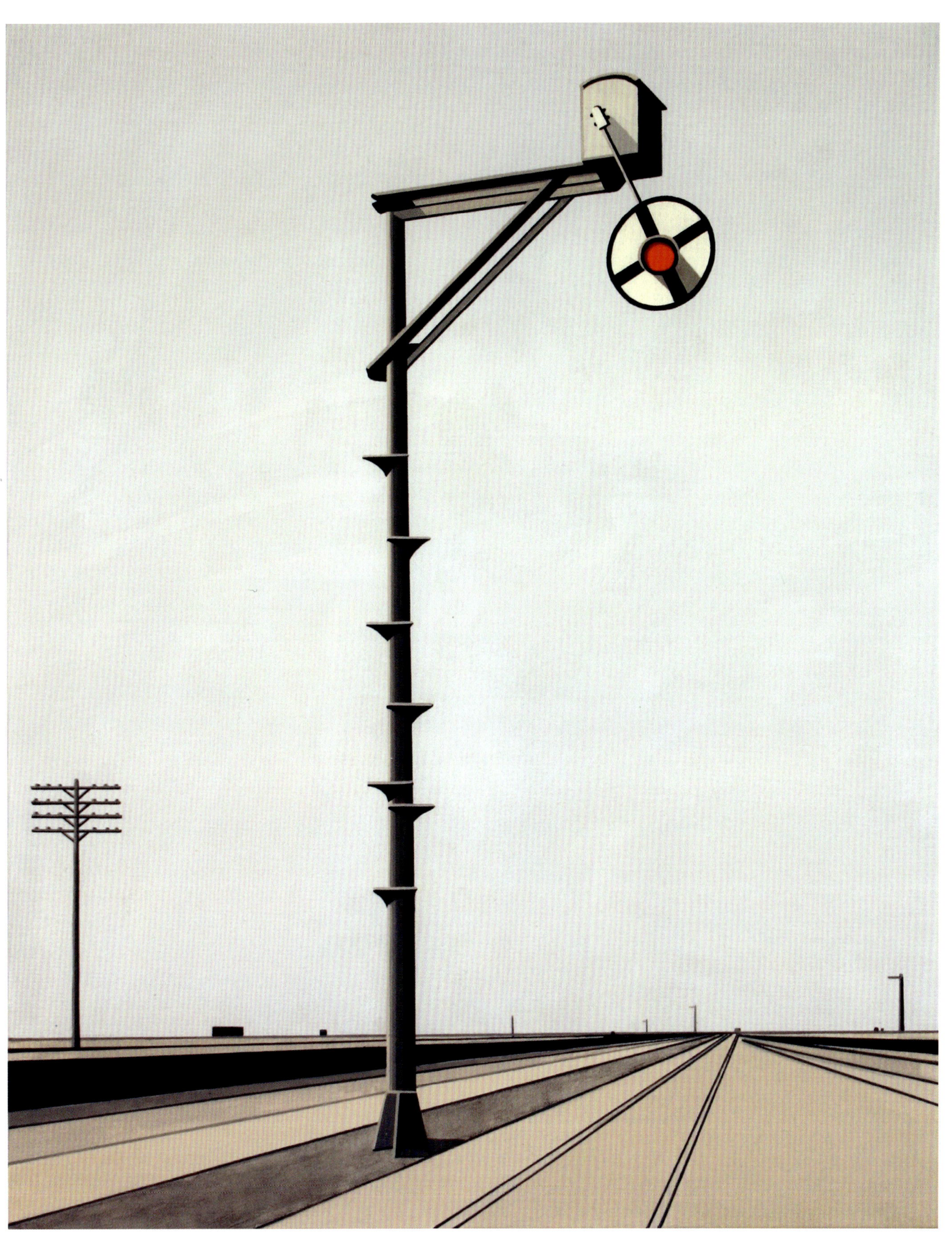

Plate 78. **Wigwag**, 2004, oil on canvas, 30 x 24 inches. Courtesy Roy Boyd Gallery.

SLOW AND STEADY is the locomotive. A symbol of nineteenth-century American muscle, joining the Pacific and Atlantic coasts, the humble train now shares the horizon with the superhighway. History has been unkind to it, but the railroad still evokes expanse and possibility —and gets the job done. No longer a romantic fixture of the landscape, but still a reliable workhorse.

Of all the fleet, it's the lowly caboose and tanker car that inspire William Steiger—function over form, and one that has remained largely unchanged for more than a century. From his collection of vintage postcards, train sets, and railroad memorabilia, Steiger appropriates this Pop icon and renders it as a Minimalist graphic. Just as we focus on a train from a distance— and it's often unclear if she's coming, going, or idling—Steiger's paintings of single train cars pose a similar question: arriving or departing? Are we admiring the perfect toy train fresh from the box or the gleaming anchor of Union Pacific freight? Each composition opens a chapter of adventure and commerce, or tells a cautionary tale of a proud but retired relic. Isolated from other trains, the lone rail car becomes a metaphor for time's passing and performs a balancing act between former glory and enduring purpose.

Once synonymous with ambition and progress, Steiger's modest trains still shine. And the only hint of context—the way the wheels square at their bottom edges, suggesting track—tells us they're ready for service. Marvel of utility, the train lumbers forward into a new age, but remains forever fixed in the imagination to a different time and place.

TRAIN
LOWELL PETTIT

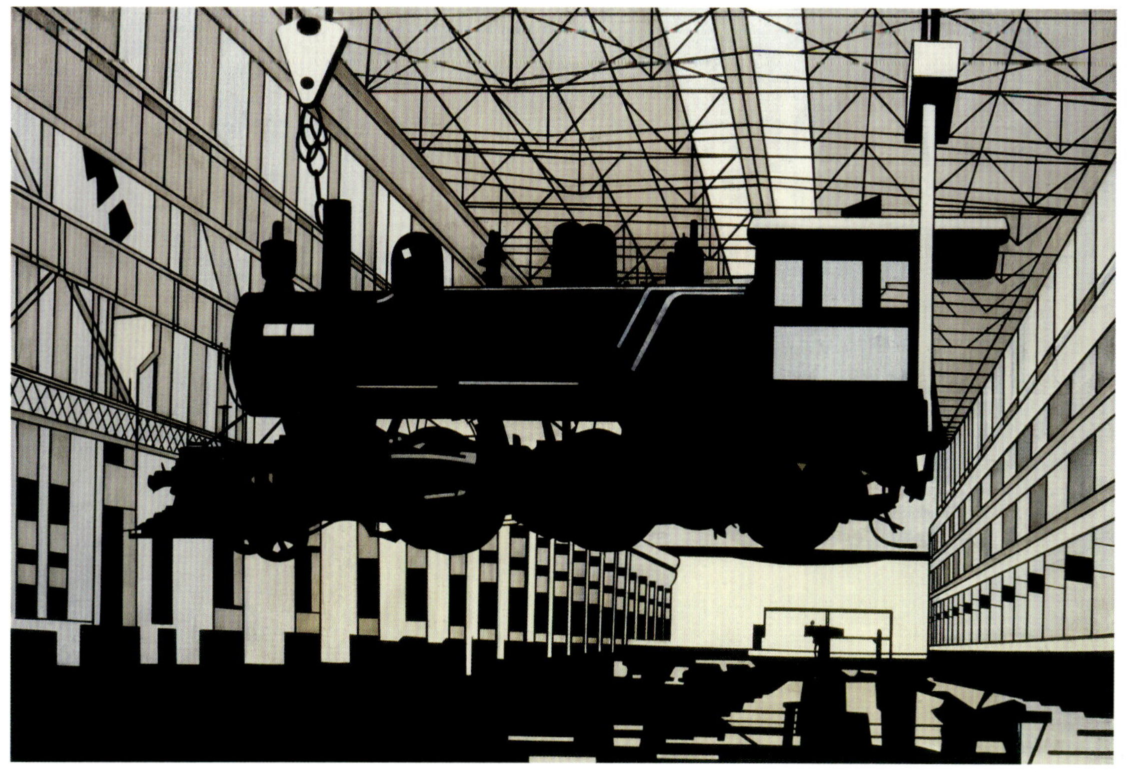

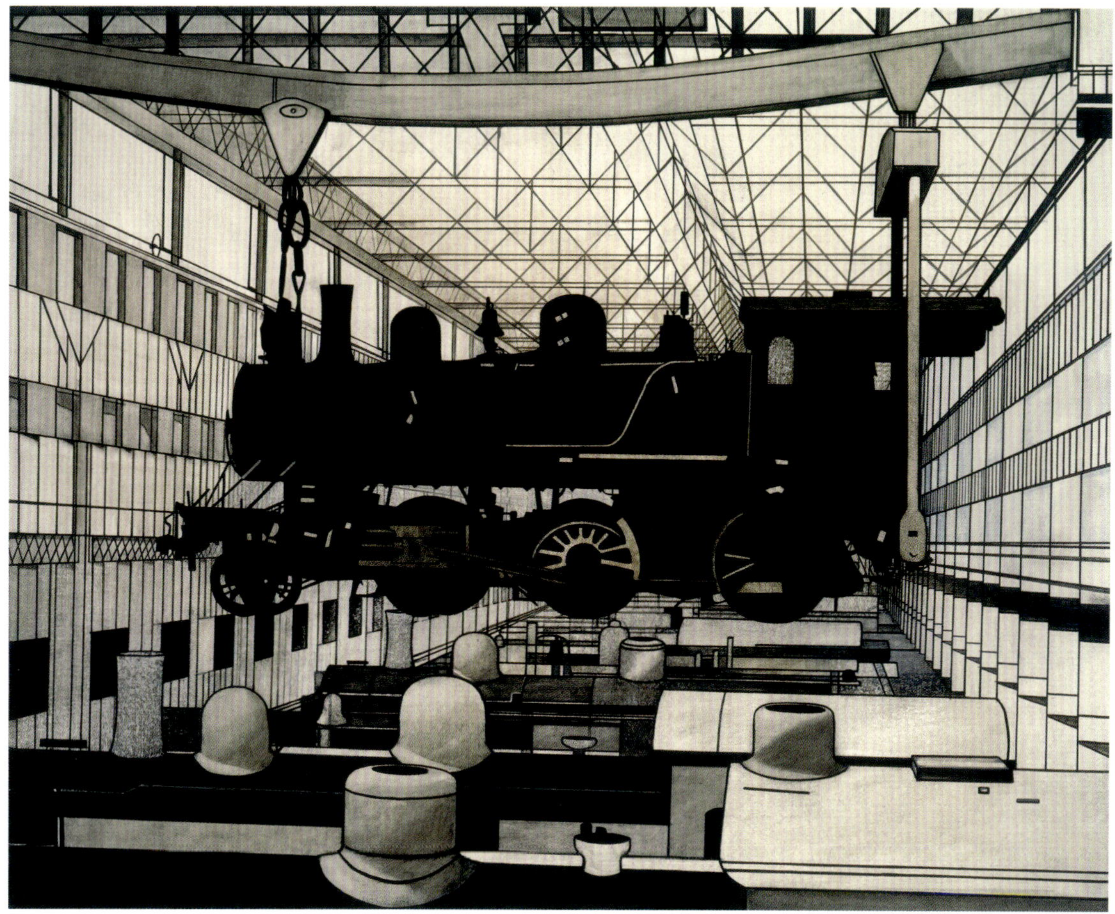

Plate 79. **Battlecreek**, 1999, oil on canvas, 30 x 45 inches. Collection of Gerald and Dianna Peterson.

Plate 80. **Hanging Train**, 1997, oil on canvas, 35 x 44 inches. Private collection.

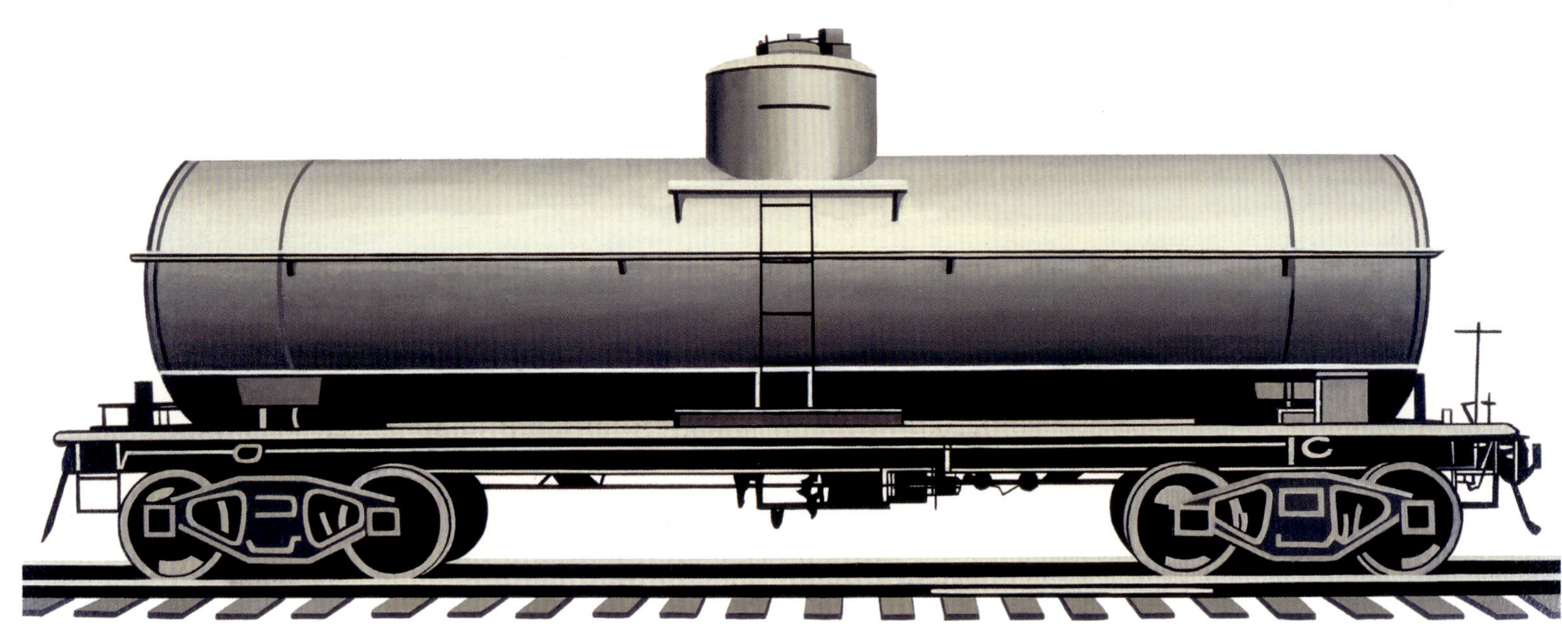

 Plate 81. **Railway Tanker**, 1999, oil on canvas, 20 x 30 inches. Private collection.

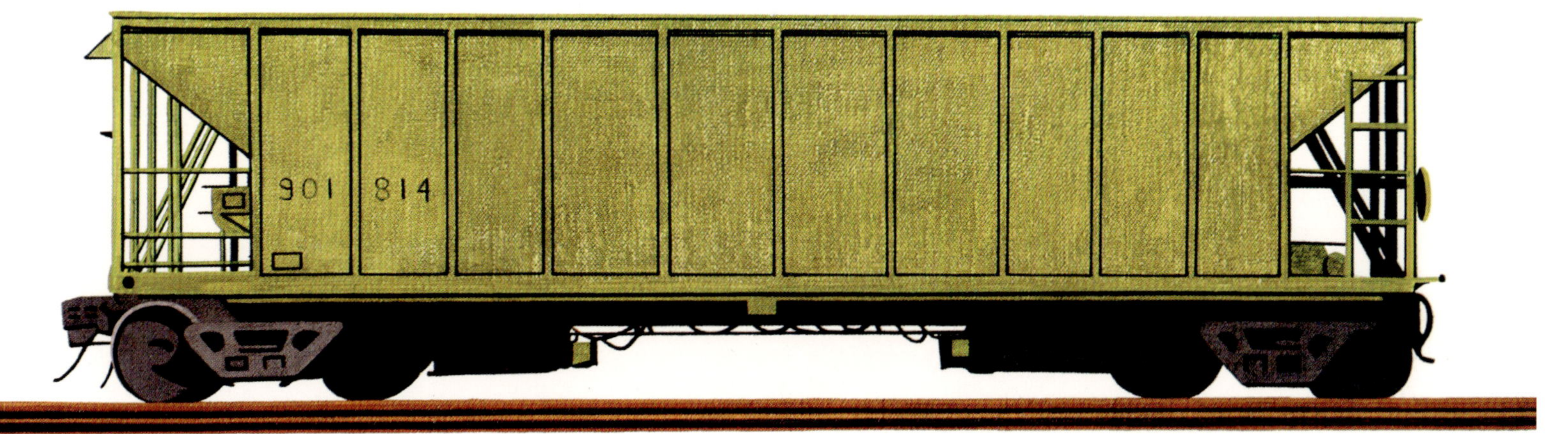

Plate 82. **Railway Car**, 2005, oil on linen, 20 x 30 inches. Collection of artist.

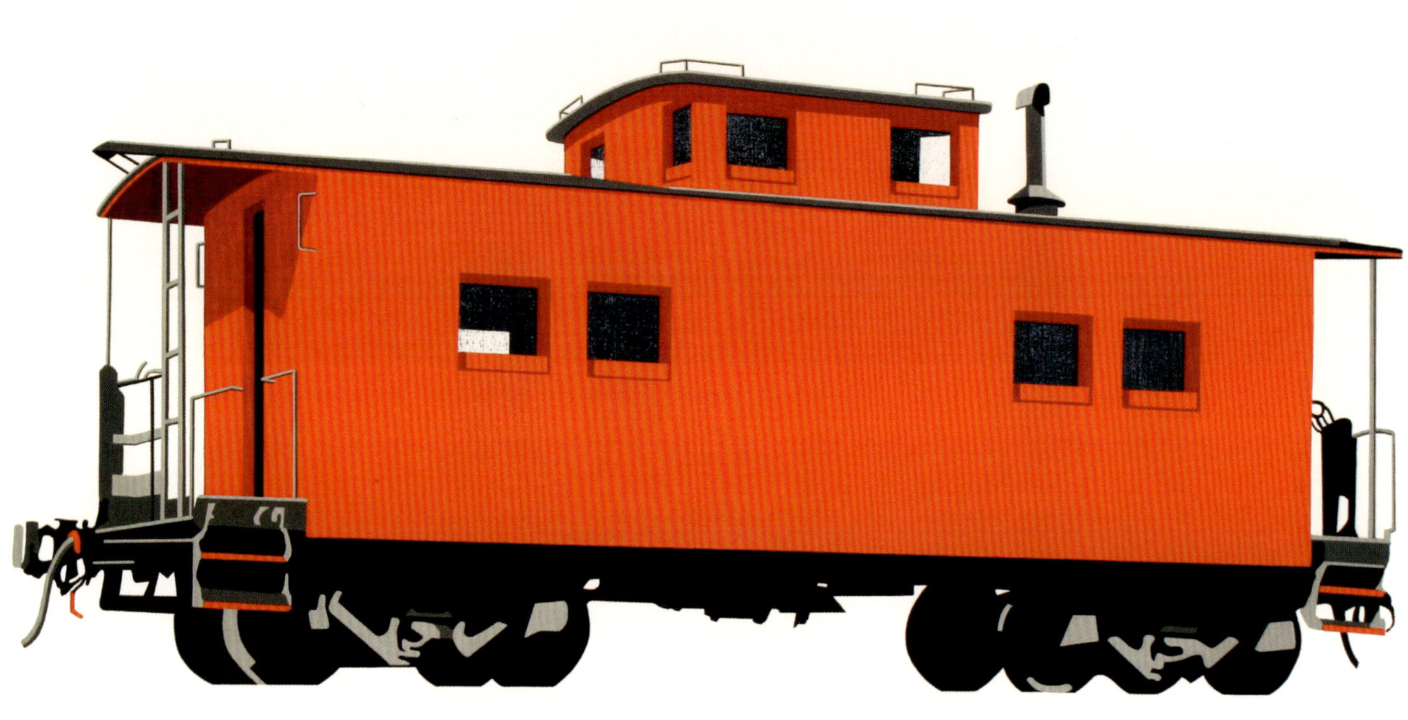

Plate 83. **Caboose**, 2006, oil on linen, 20 x 30 inches. Collection of John R. Eckel, Jr. Estate.

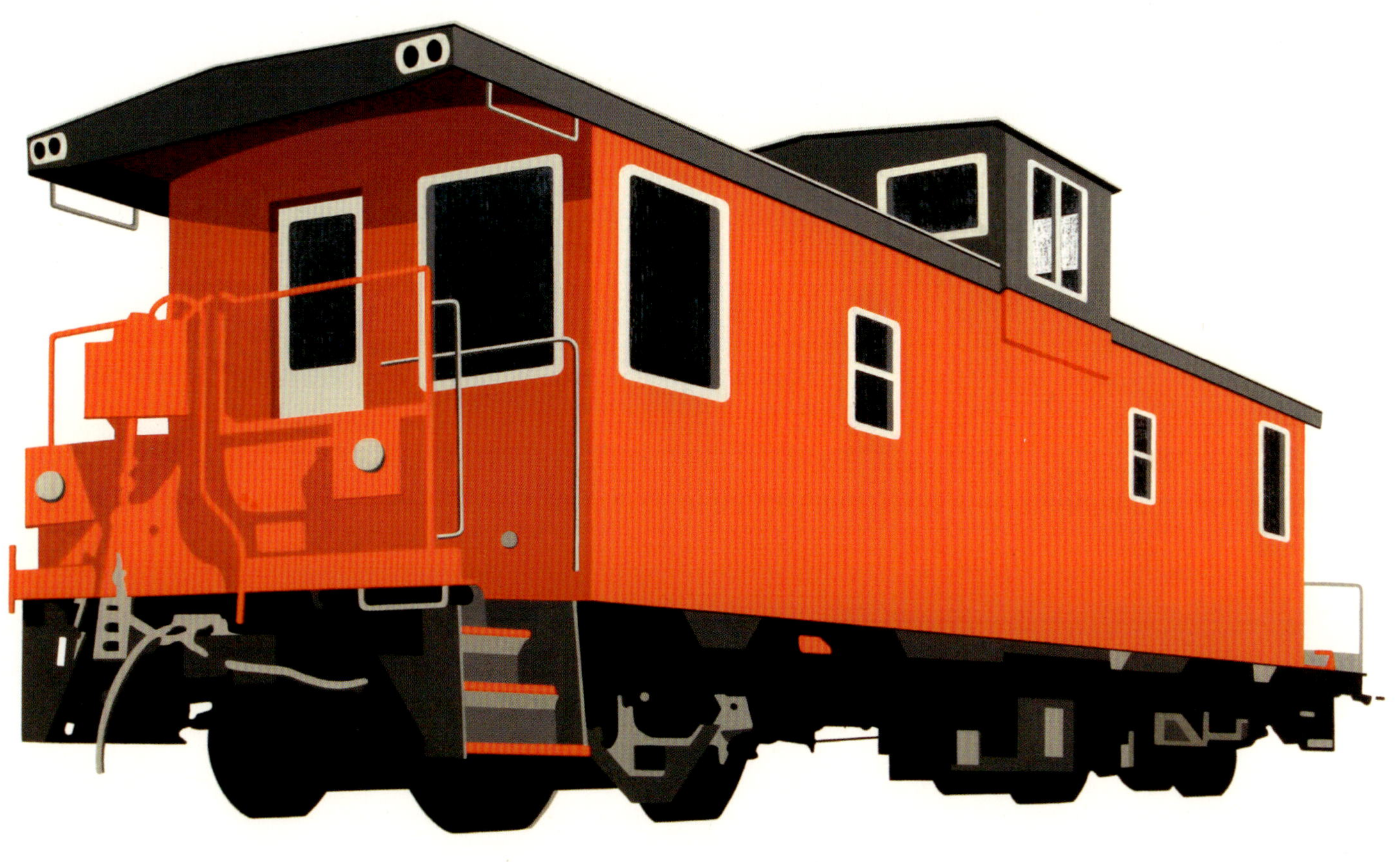

Plate 84. **Caboose #2**, 2007, oil on linen, 20 x 30 inches. Collection of Brian McConville.

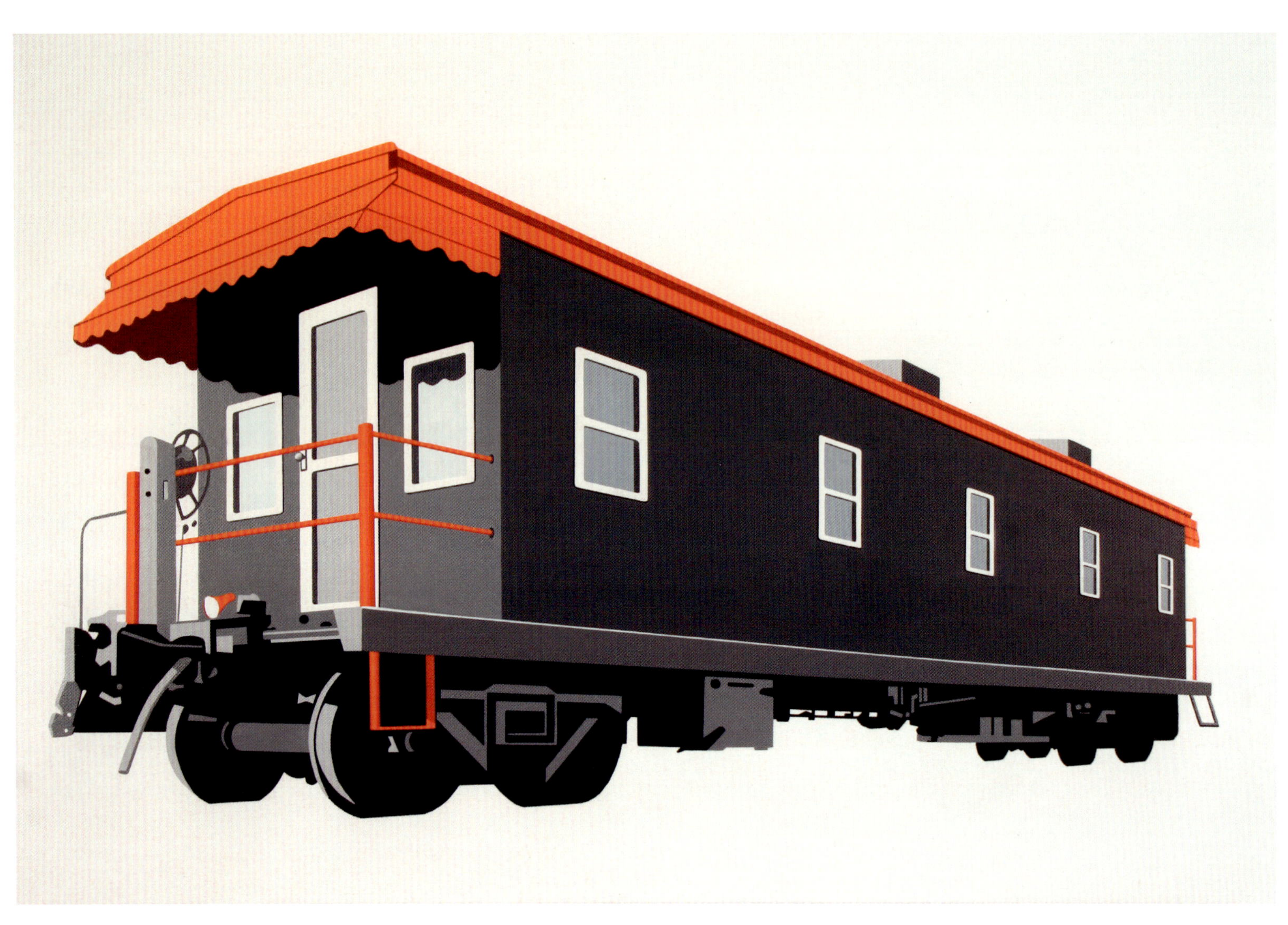

    Plate 85. **Caboose #3**, 2007, oil on linen, 20 x 30 inches. Collection of John R. Eckel, Jr. Estate.

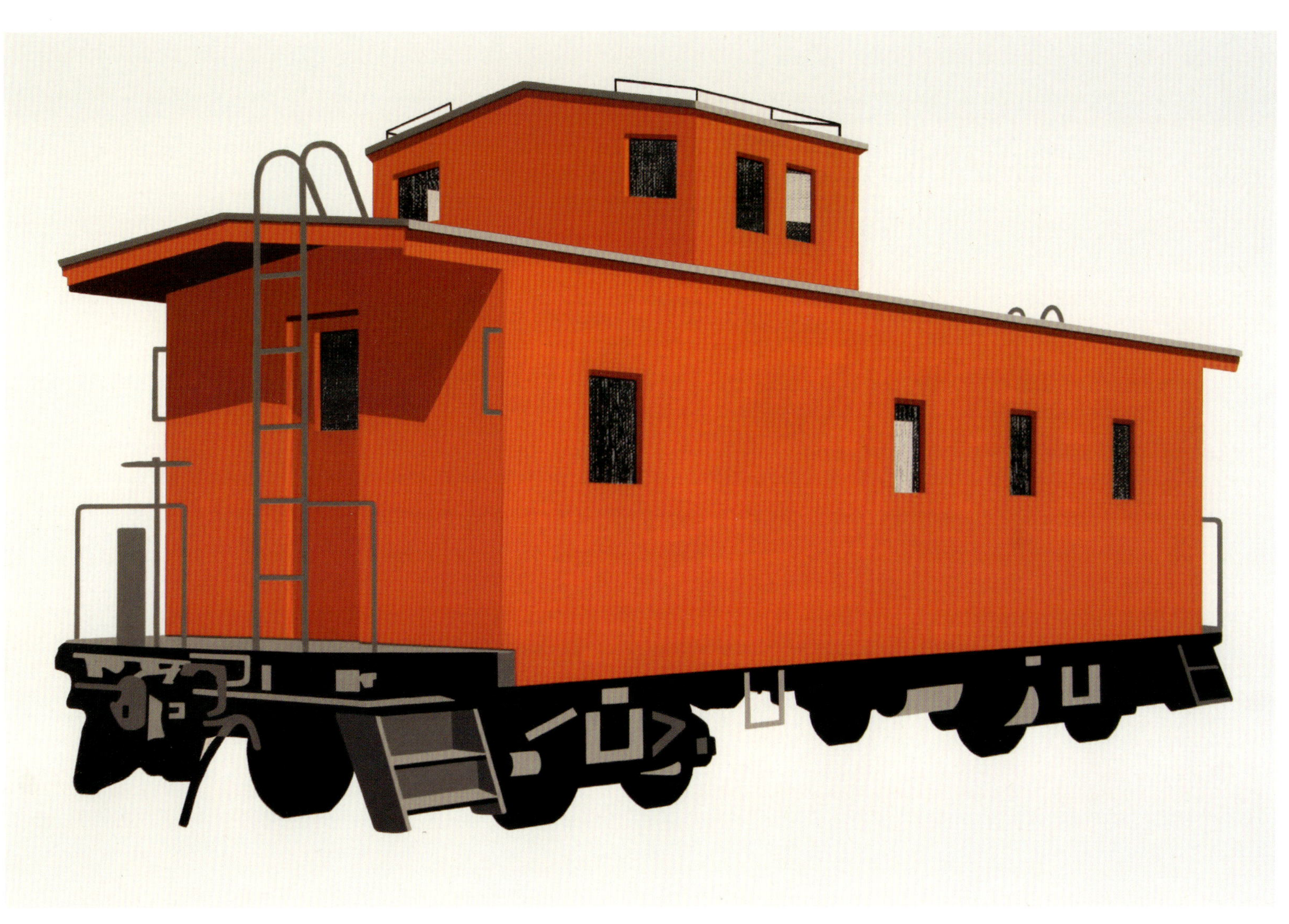

Plate 86. **Caboose #5**, 2010, oil on linen, 20 x 30 inches. Courtesy Margaret Thatcher Projects.

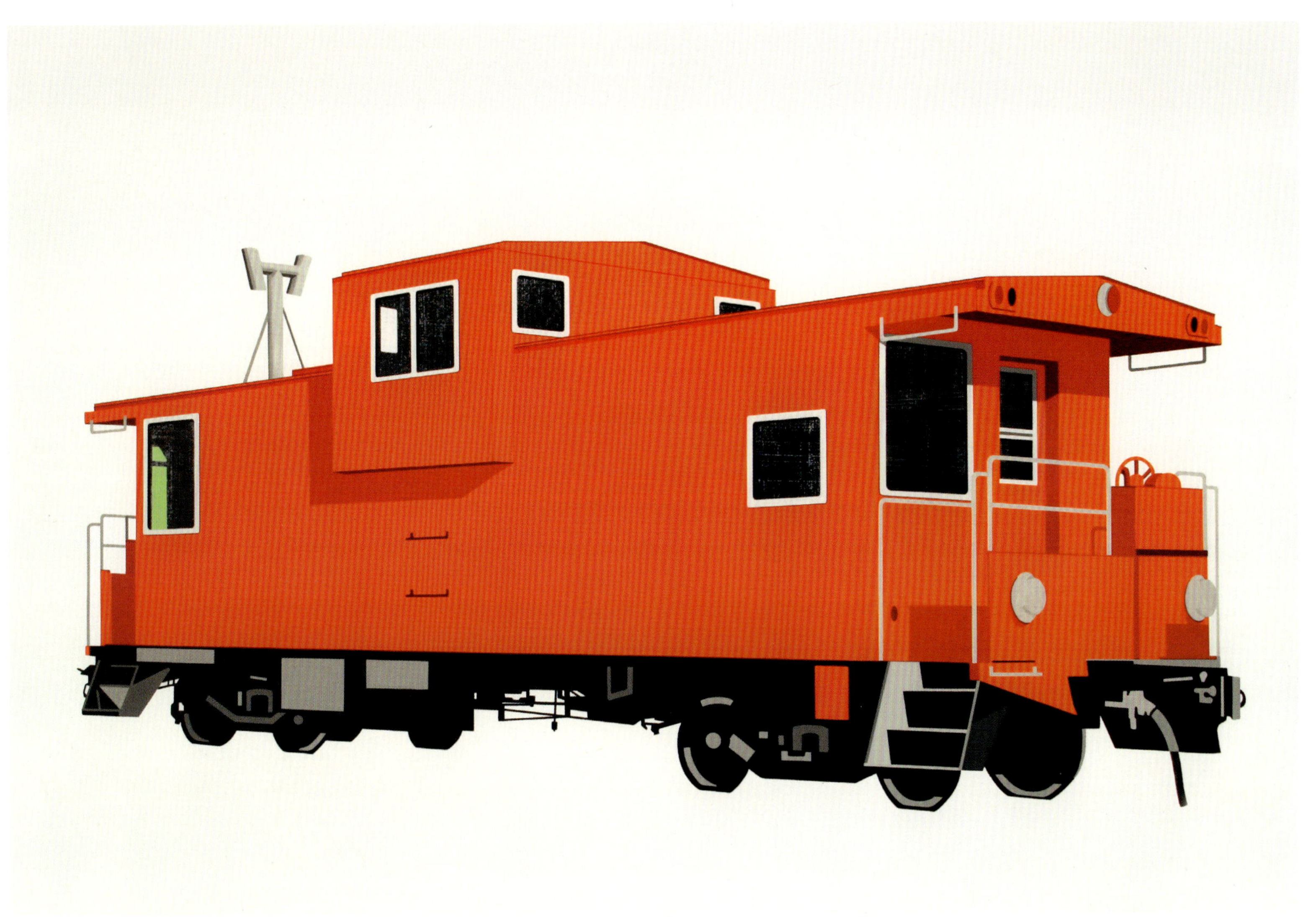

Plate 87. **Waycar II**, 2010, oil on linen, 40 x 60 inches. Courtesy Margaret Thatcher Projects.

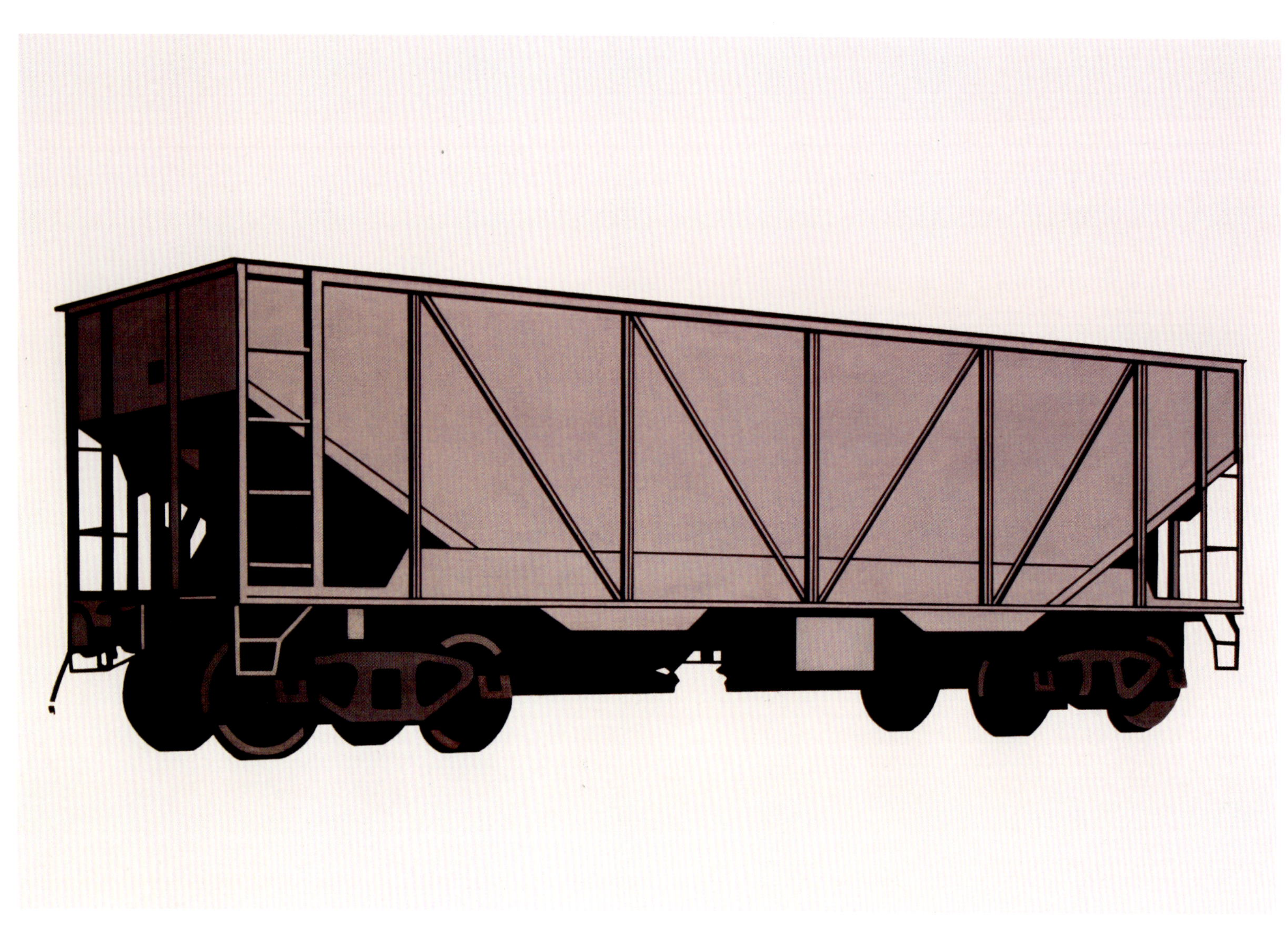

Plate 88. **Boxcar**, 2008, oil on linen, 20 x 30 inches. Courtesy Holly Johnson Gallery.

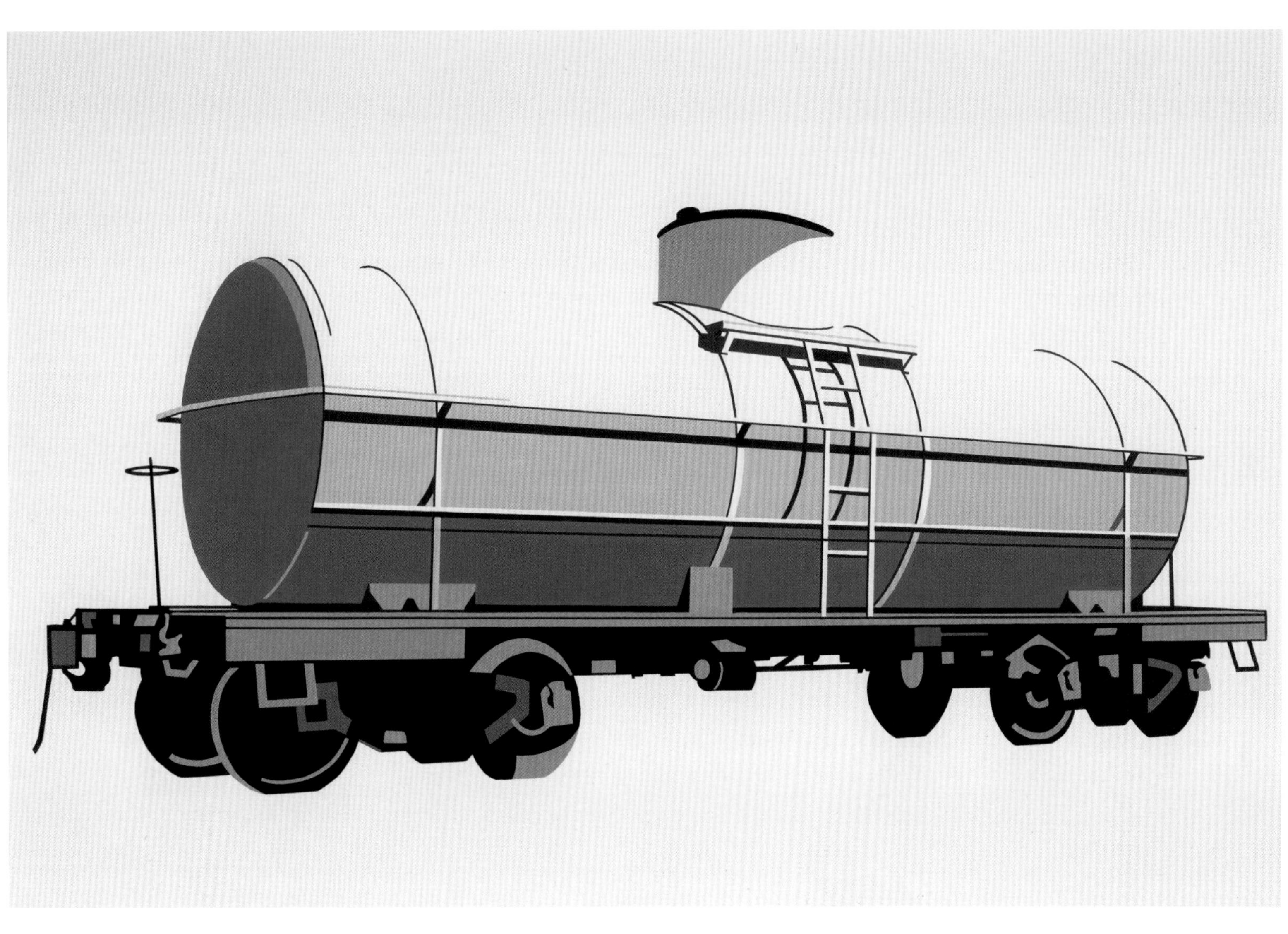

Plate 89. **Tanker Car**, 2008, oil on linen, 20 x 30 inches. Collection of John R. Eckel, Jr. Estate.

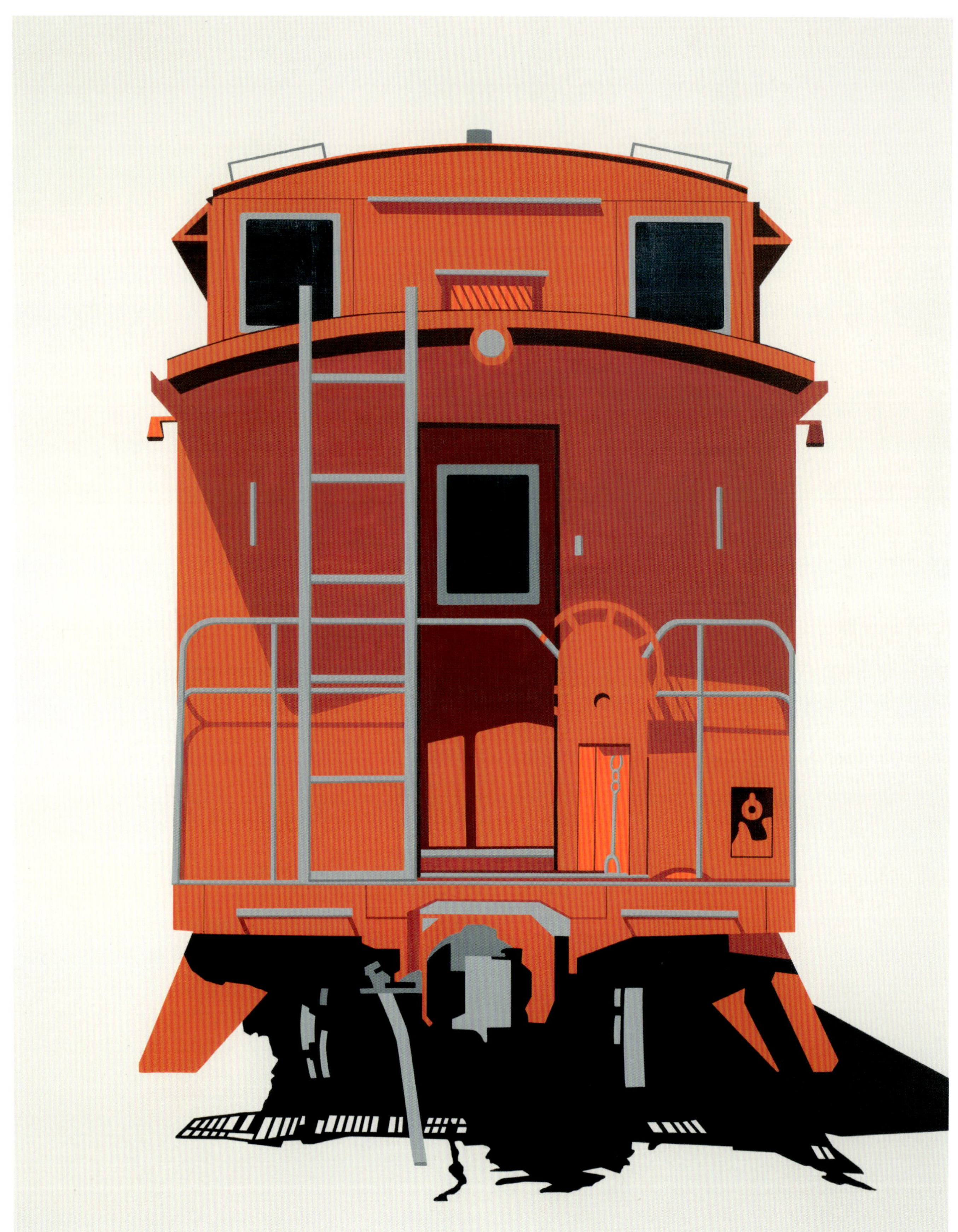

Plate 90. **Caboose End View**, 2008, oil on linen, 44 x 35 inches. Collection of Patricia Brett and Thomas Butcher.

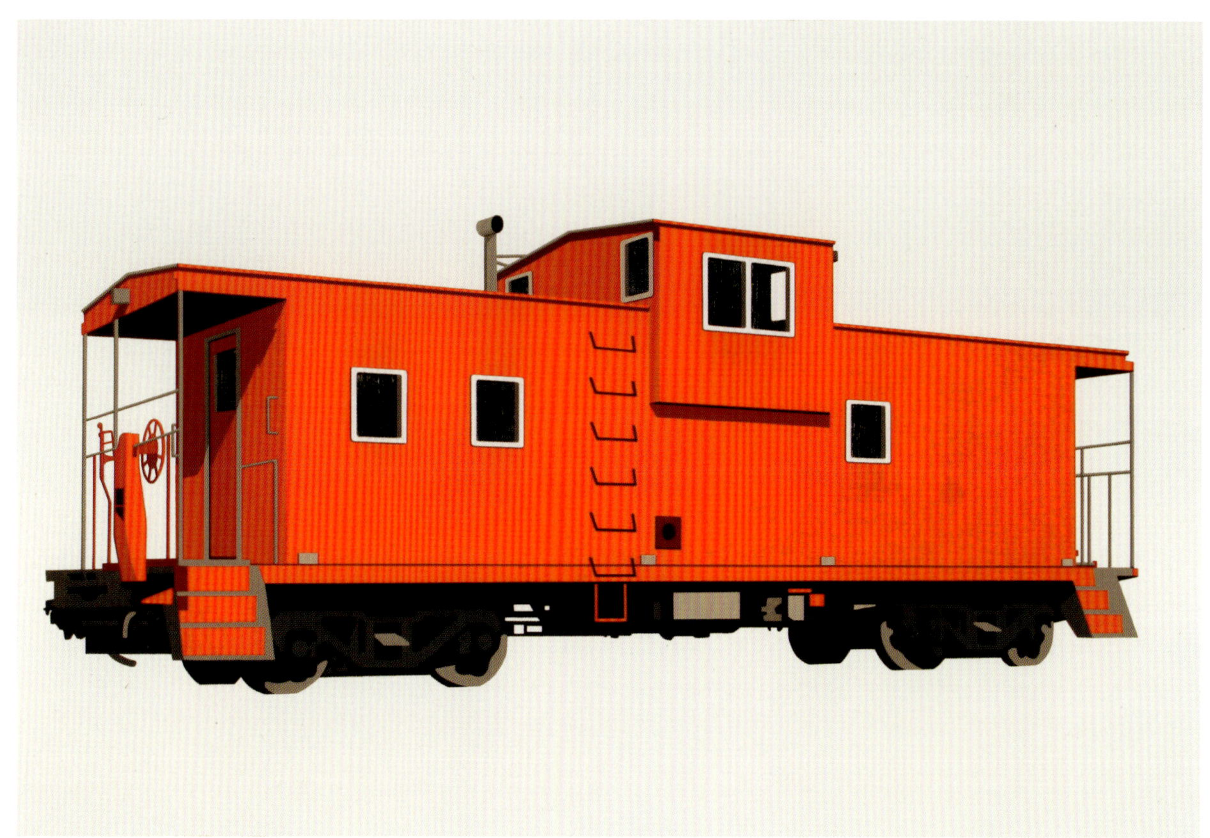

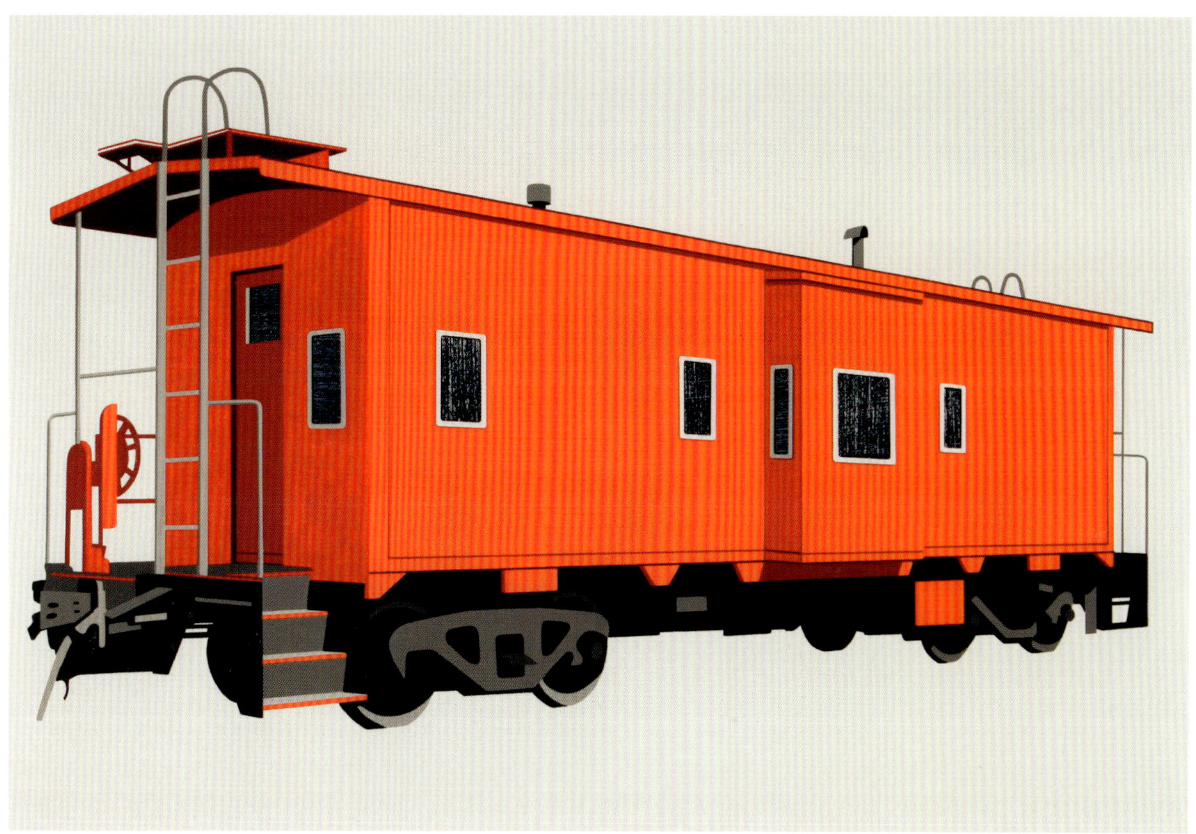

Plate 91. **Waycar**, 2009, oil on linen, 40 x 60 inches. Collection of Noel Kirnon.

Plate 92. **Caboose Bay Window**, 2009, oil on linen, 20 x 30 inches. Collection of David and Birgit McQueen.

WILLIAM STEIGER'S ELEVATOR PAINTINGS create a world imbued with psychological and existential riddles. Whether or not these buildings are inhabited or industrial is unknown, and perhaps unimportant; whatever the case, the hidden interiors remain a mystery to the viewer. The artist leaves the face of the structures the same white as the background, producing a surface that is bursting with light. Edges are defined by deep shadows, which are often richly colored and seemingly bottomless within the brightness. Softer shades serve to define only what we need to know about the subject's shape, and certain lines are omitted altogether, causing the white of the building to merge into the landscape. Because of his use of light and color, the white elevators do not seem actually to be painted, but rather painted around, which raises questions about their solidity and existence.

Steiger's panorama, as external portrait of place, is suggestive of memory and longing. I am compelled to ask, "What is its relationship to me, or mine to it?" We are teased with the dichotomy of a seductive peace and an unnerving isolation. The lack of detail, the brightness, and the sense of stillness bring to mind old faded photos with all that those imply: a private history with its own attachment of intensely personal emotions. The viewer becomes a visitor within the painting, invited into a vista that proffers no other form of life. There is not even a tree to which we may feel aligned. This produces a feeling of exposure and vulnerability to whatever experiences lie in wait. We are suspended between the blinding light and an unknown and profound darkness, between what seems an unending, sun-beaten plain and an interior conjuring our own memories. The doors appear impenetrable; the sense of our own mortality is a presence to be reckoned with. Despite the tangible loneliness the paintings evoke, there is something refreshing about the solitude and the questions of existence. It is eerie to entertain the idea that since this painting is not my own creation, I am somewhere I don't belong. Separated from the contents by my inability to enter, a truce of sorts ensues. But the interaction feels secure and I am left paralyzed with enchantment, realizing that there is eternity in Steiger's distances.

ELEVATOR
MAURA ROBINSON

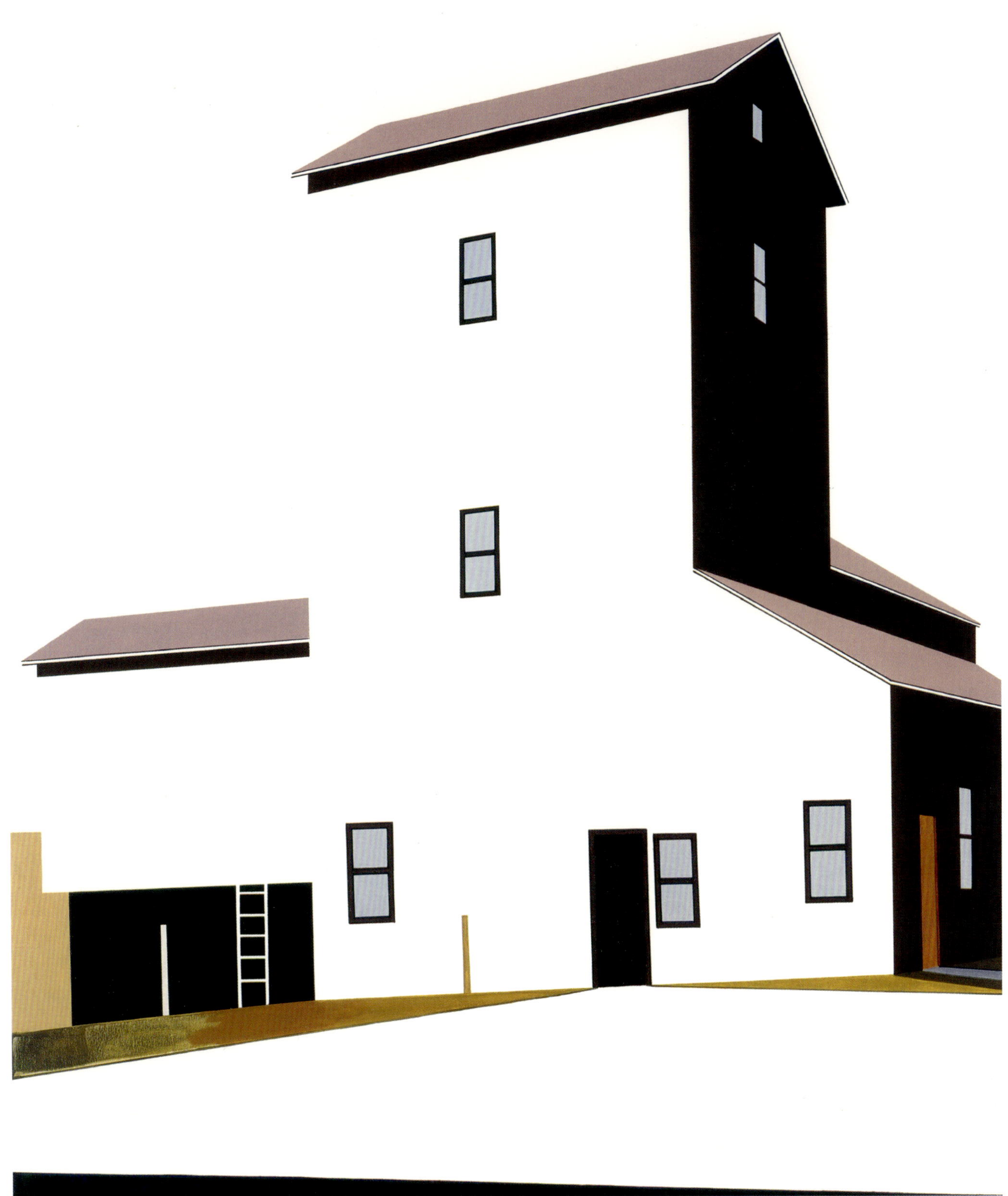

Plate 93. **Elevator I**, 2002, oil on canvas, 60 x 48 inches. Private collection.

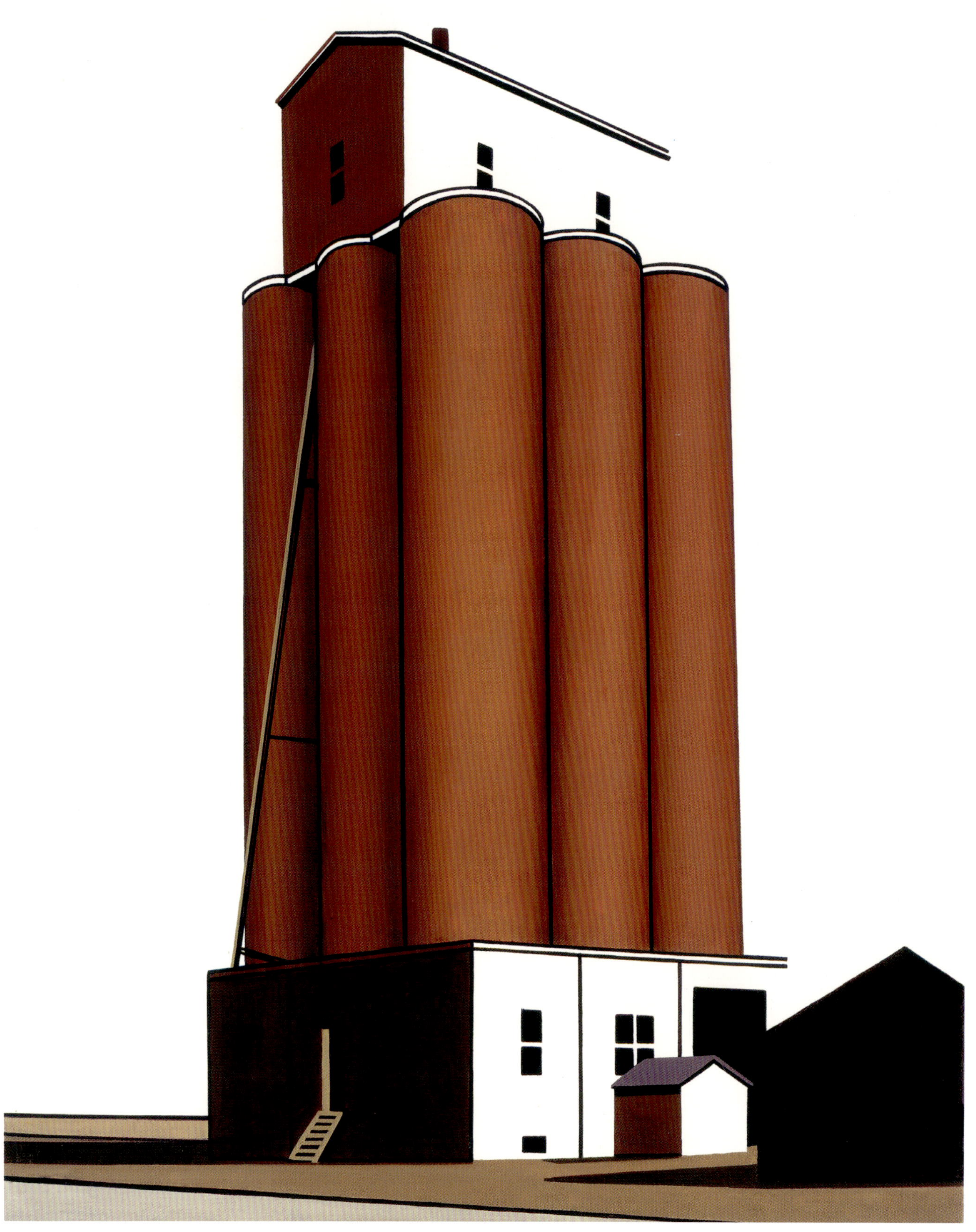

Plate 94. **Elevator Tanks**, 2002, oil on linen, 20 x 16 inches. Collection of Stacey and Rob Goergen.

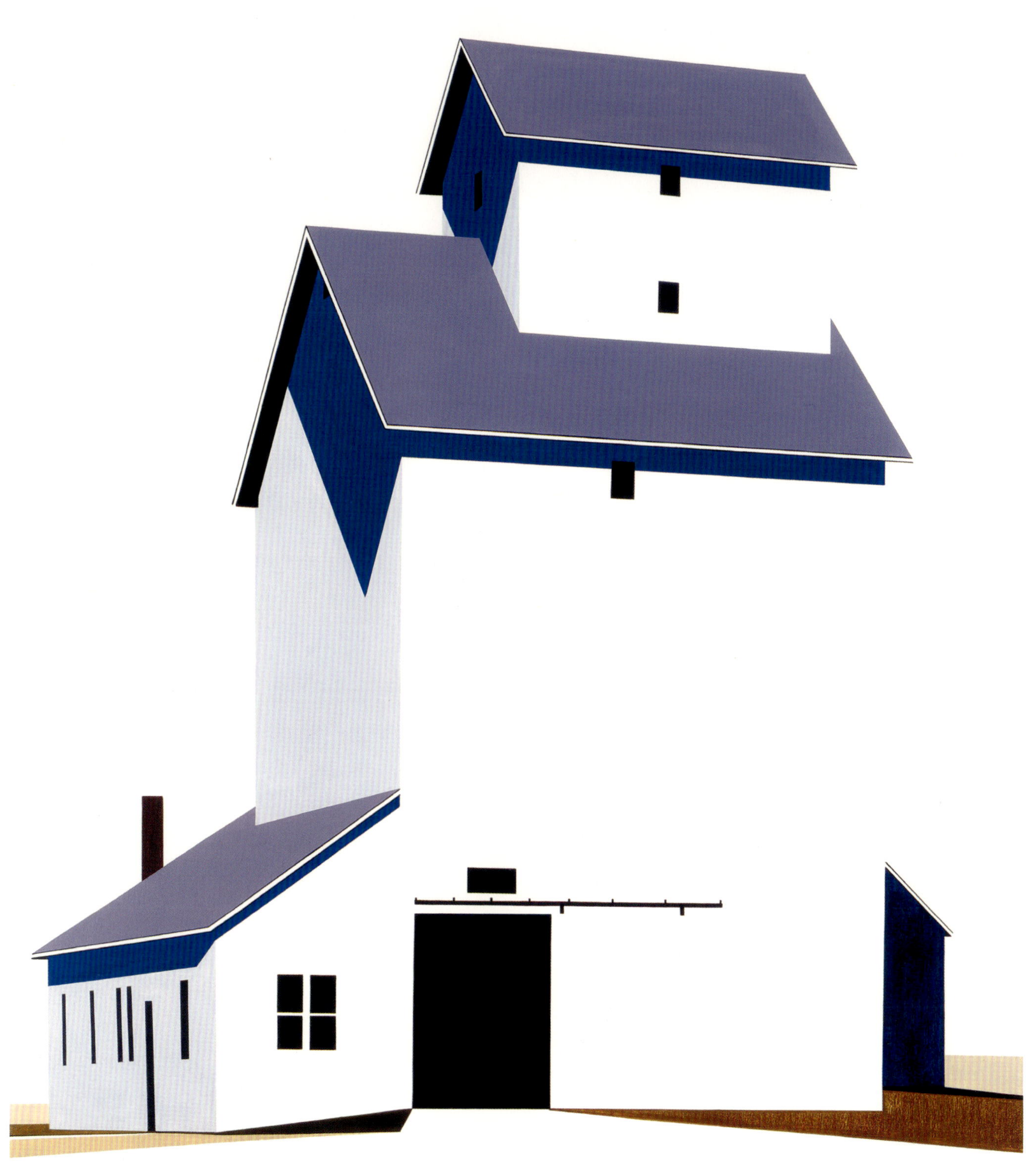

Plate 95. **Elevator II**, 2002, oil on canvas, 60 x 48 inches. Collection of Joy and Michael Millette.

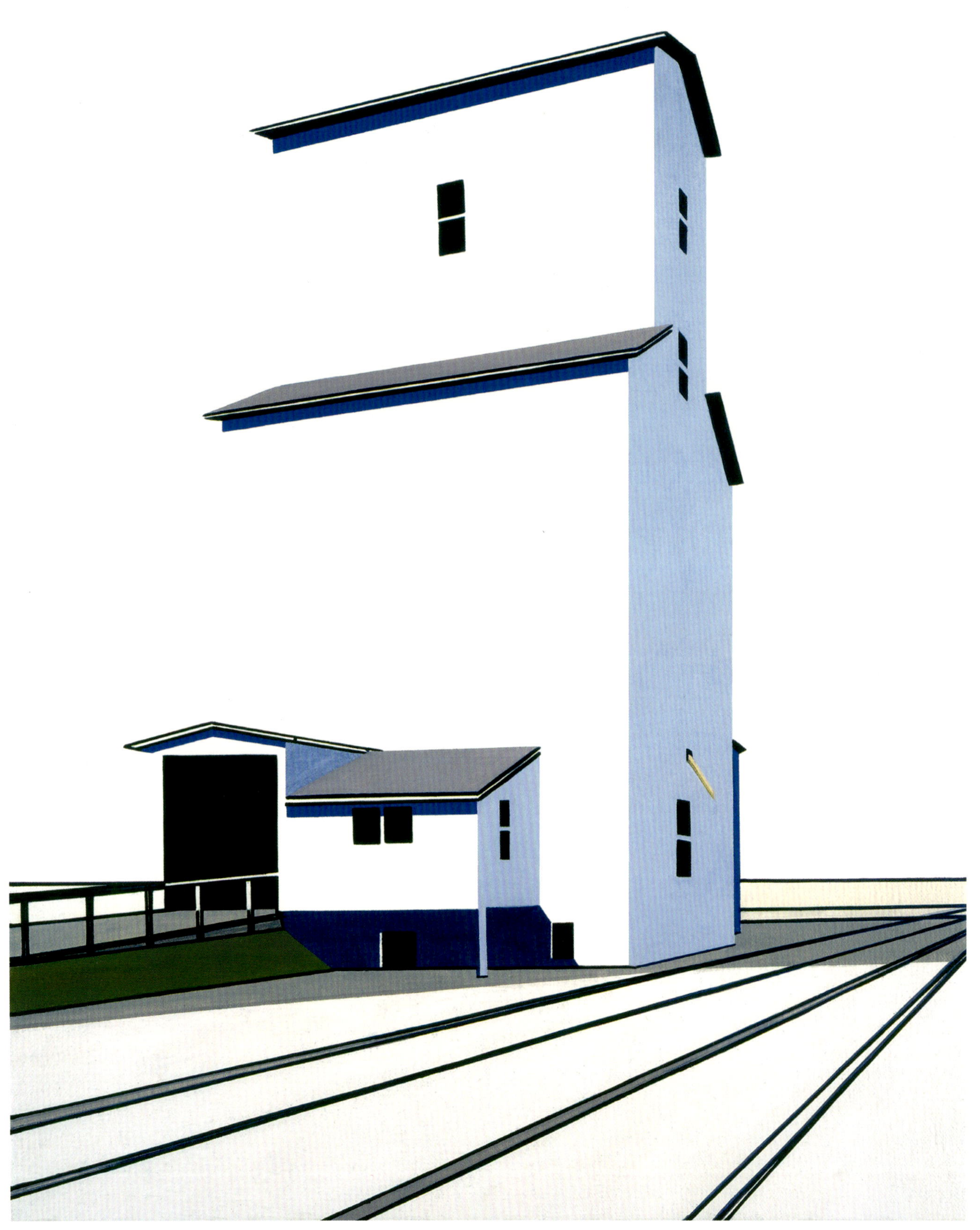

Plate 96. **Elevator #5**, 2003, oil on linen, 20 x 16 inches. Private collection.

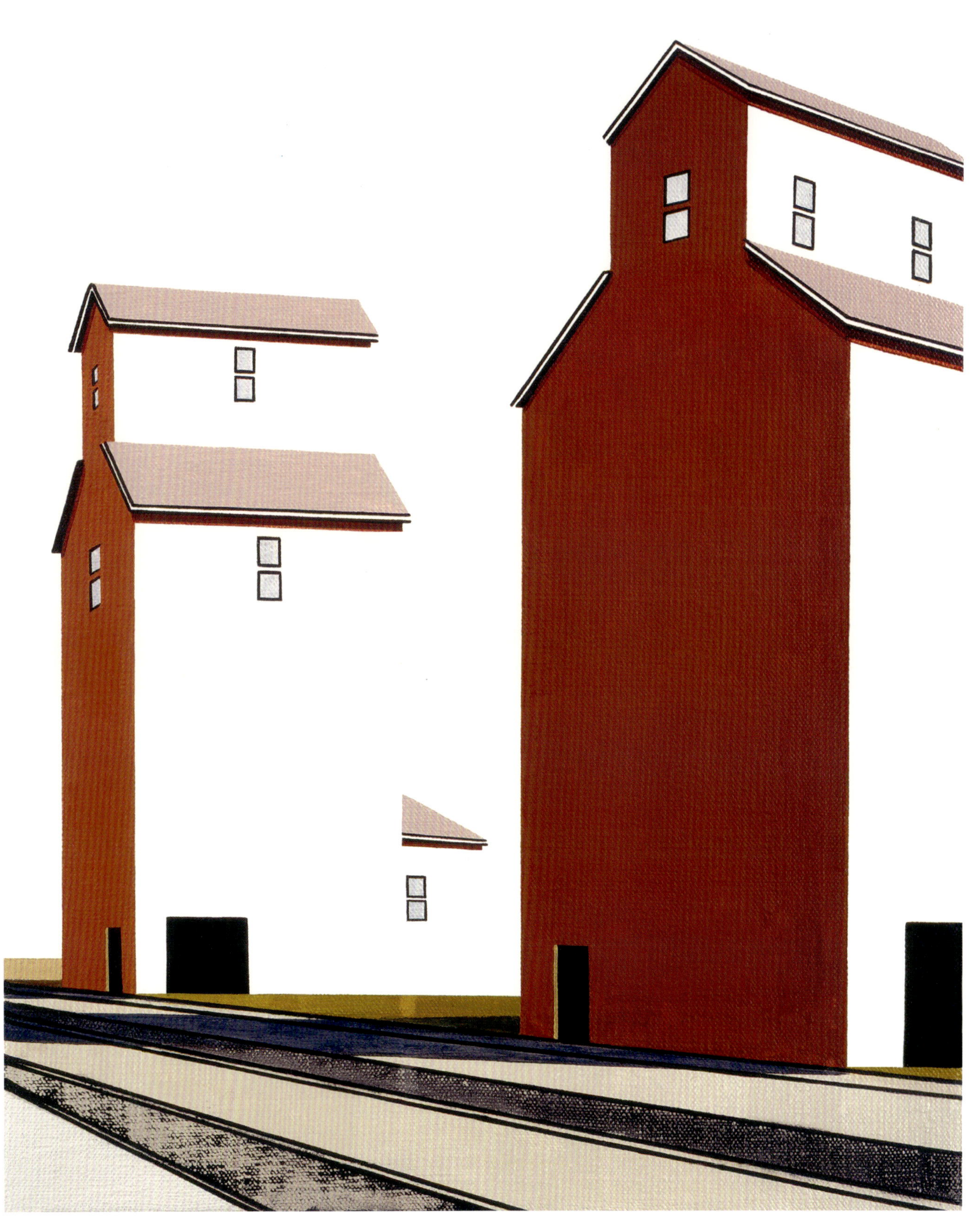

Plate 97. **Hay, Feed, & Seed**, 2003, oil on linen, 20 x 16 inches. Private collection.

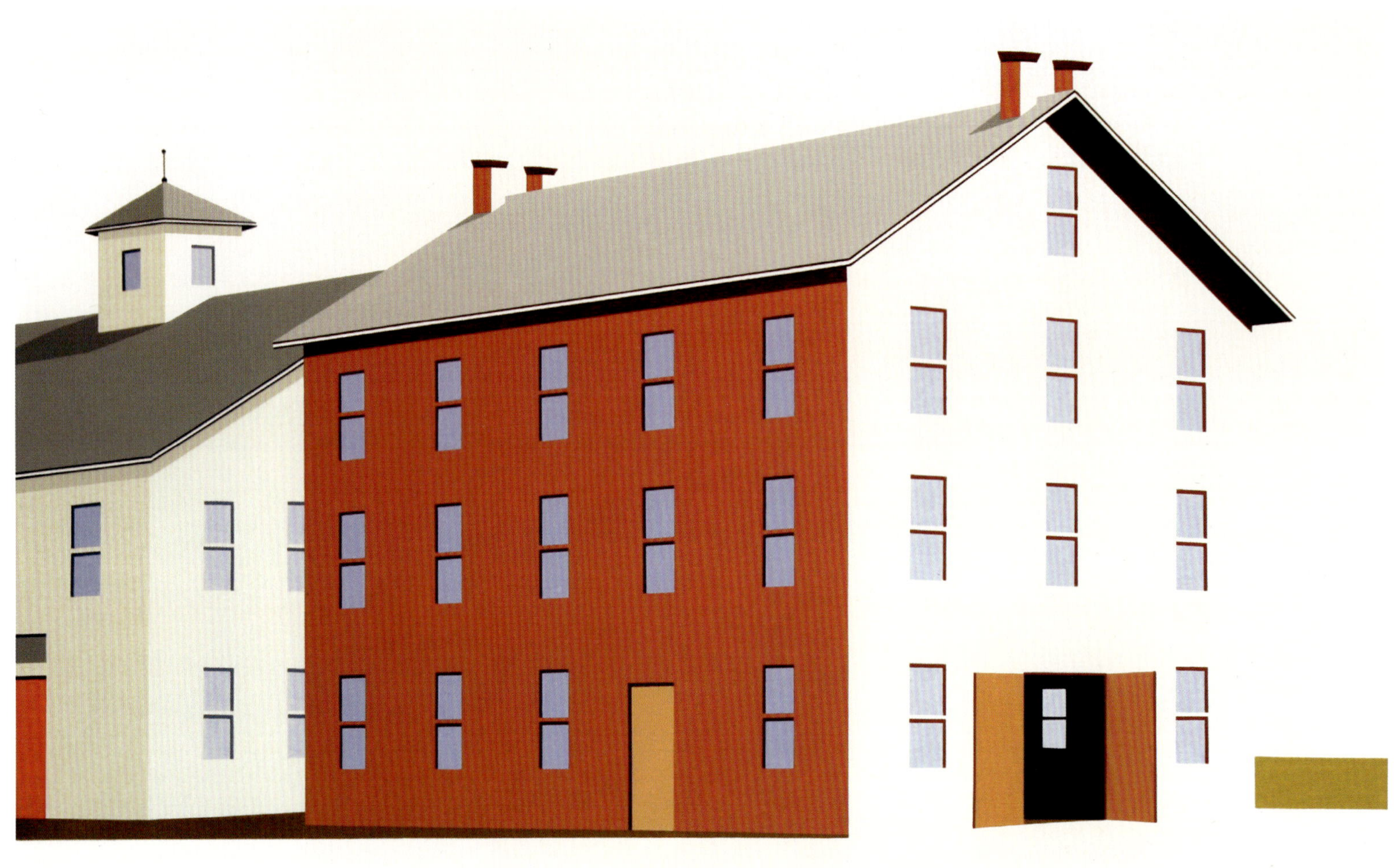

132   Plate 98. **Mill with Red Door**, *2008, oil on linen, 20 x 30 inches. Private collection.*

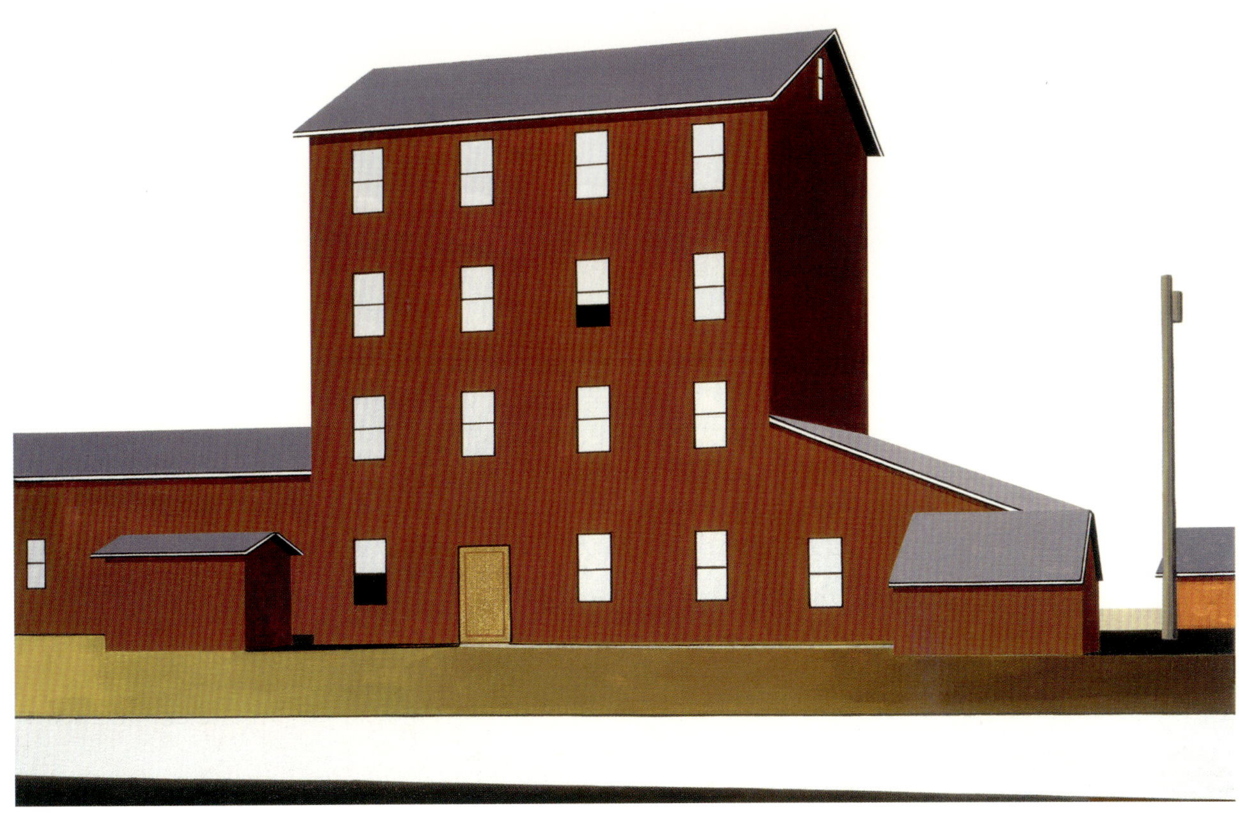

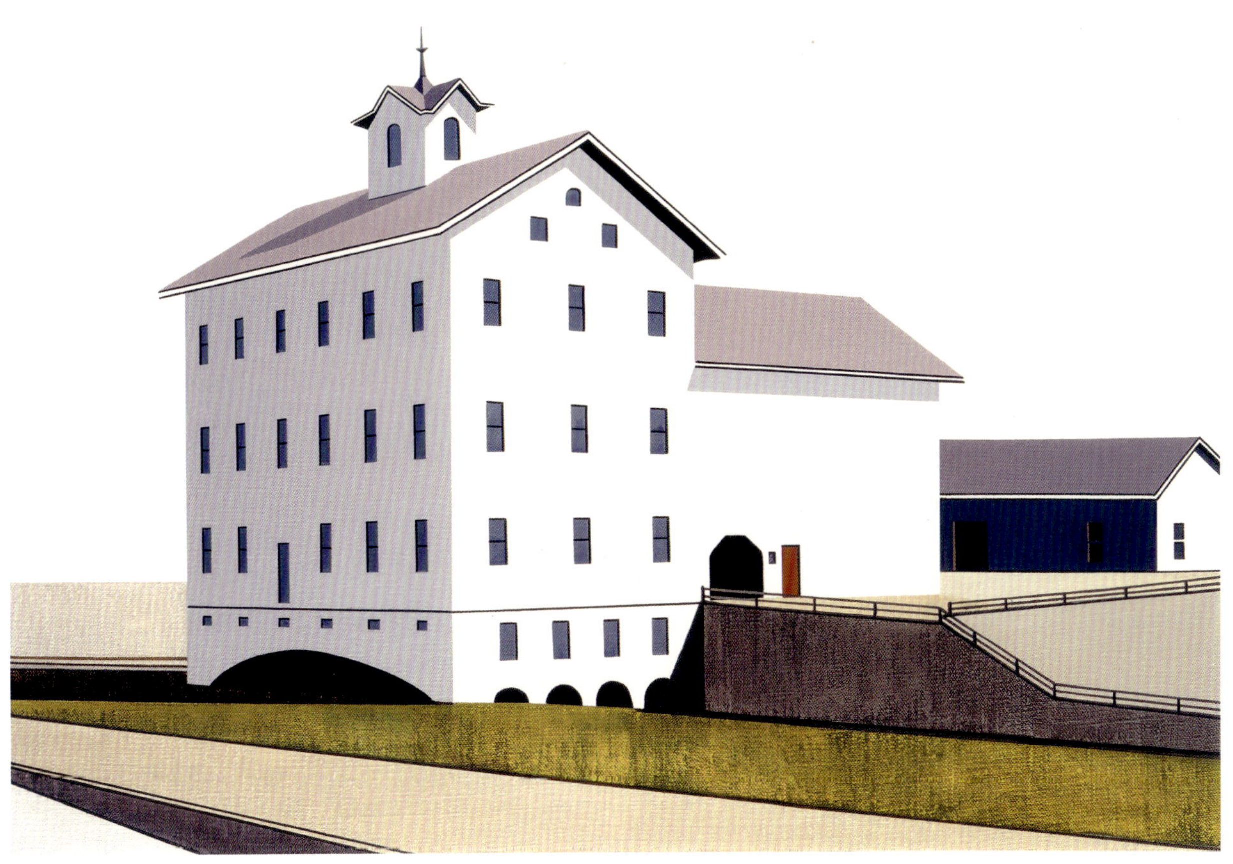

Plate 99. **The Red Mill**, 2003, oil on linen, 20 x 30 inches. Collection of Stefany and Ethan Morris.

Plate 100. **Millhouse**, 2003, oil on linen, 20 x 30 inches. Collection of Stefany and Ethan Morris.

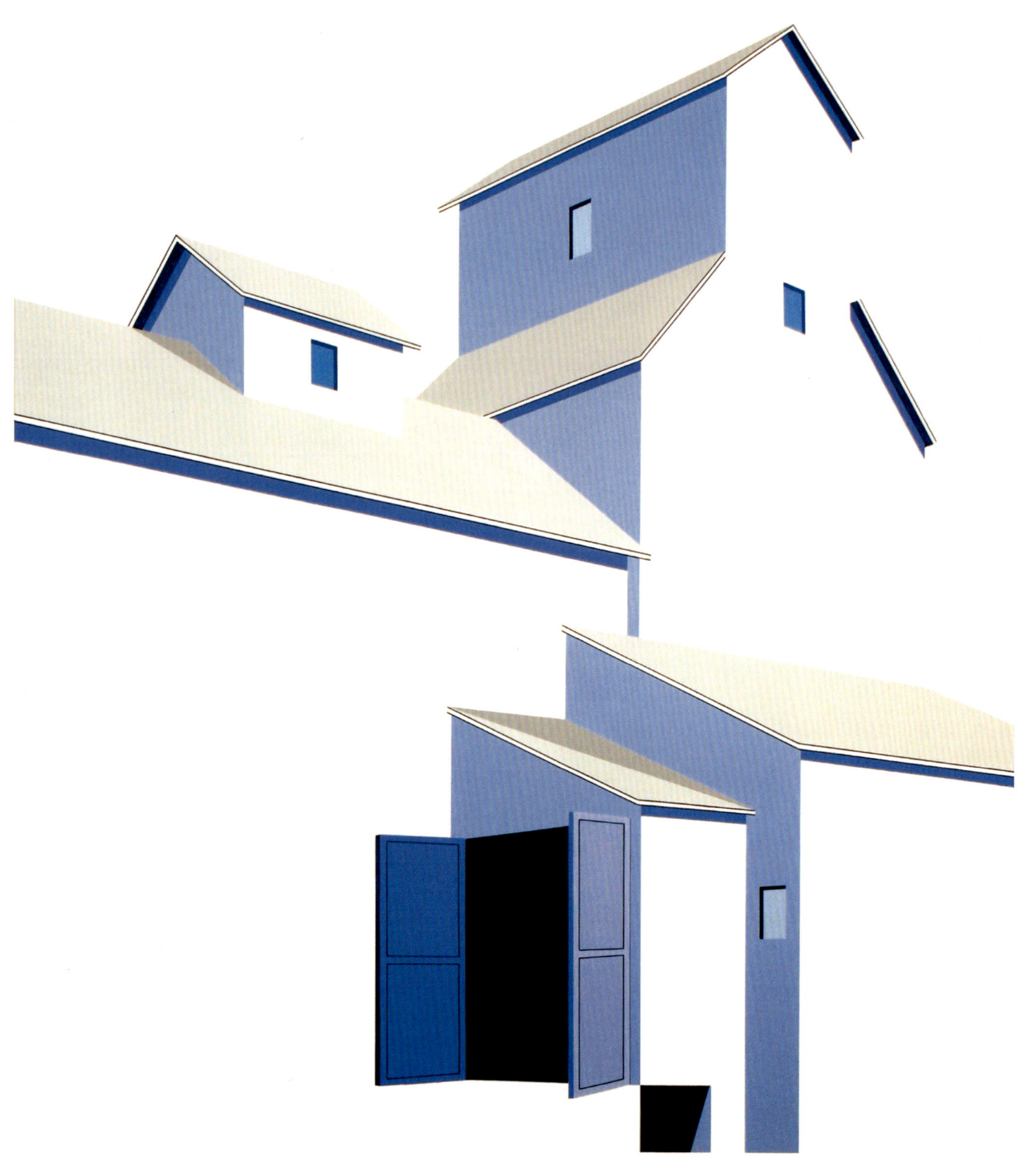

Plate 101. **Blue Elevator**, 2006, oil on canvas, 60 x 48 inches. Courtesy Margaret Thatcher Projects.

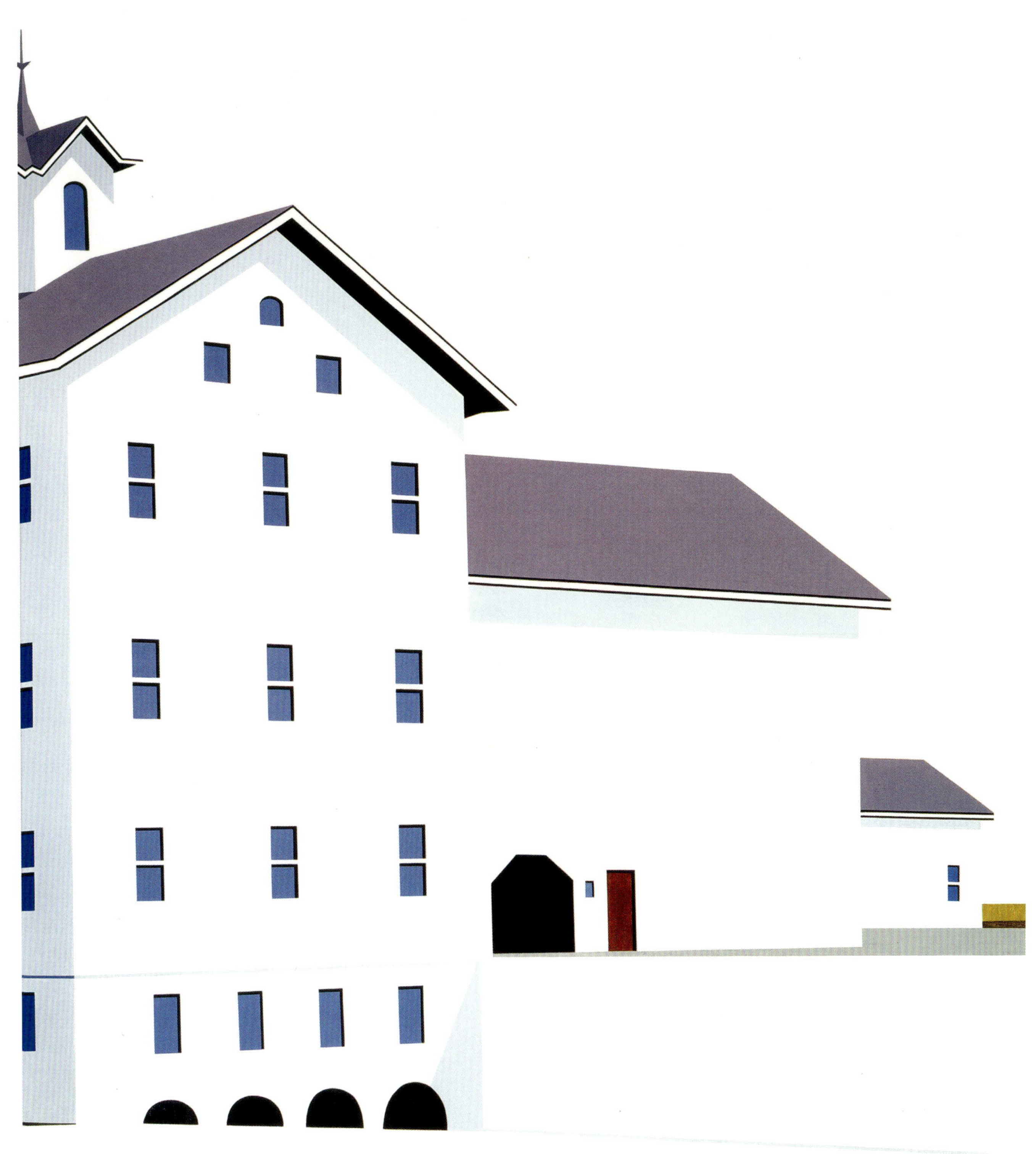

Plate 102. **Blue Mill**, *2004, oil on linen, 60 x 48 inches. Collection of John R. Eckel, Jr. Estate.*

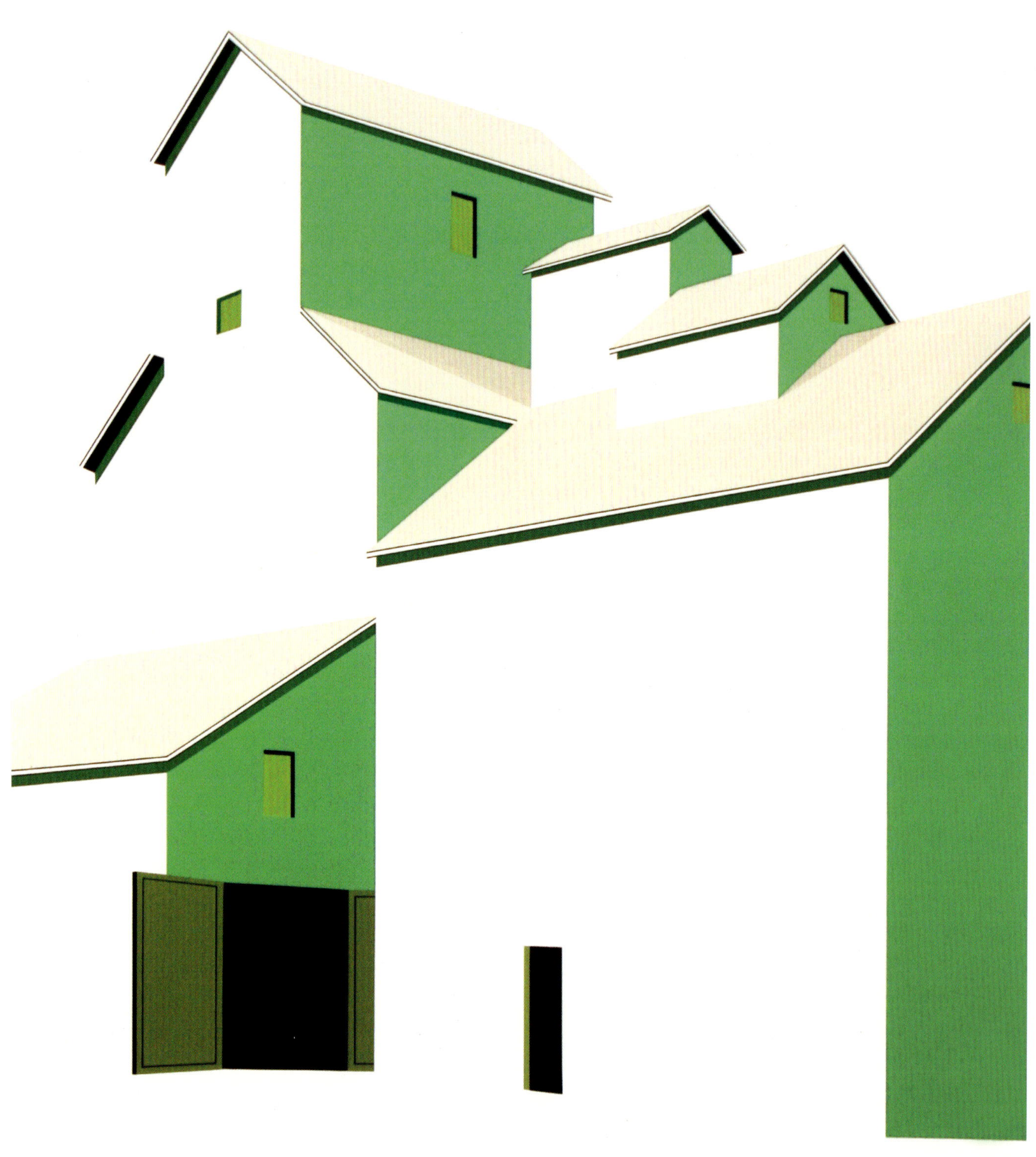

    Plate 103. **Green Elevator**, 2006, oil on canvas, 60 x 48 inches. Courtesy Margaret Thatcher Projects.

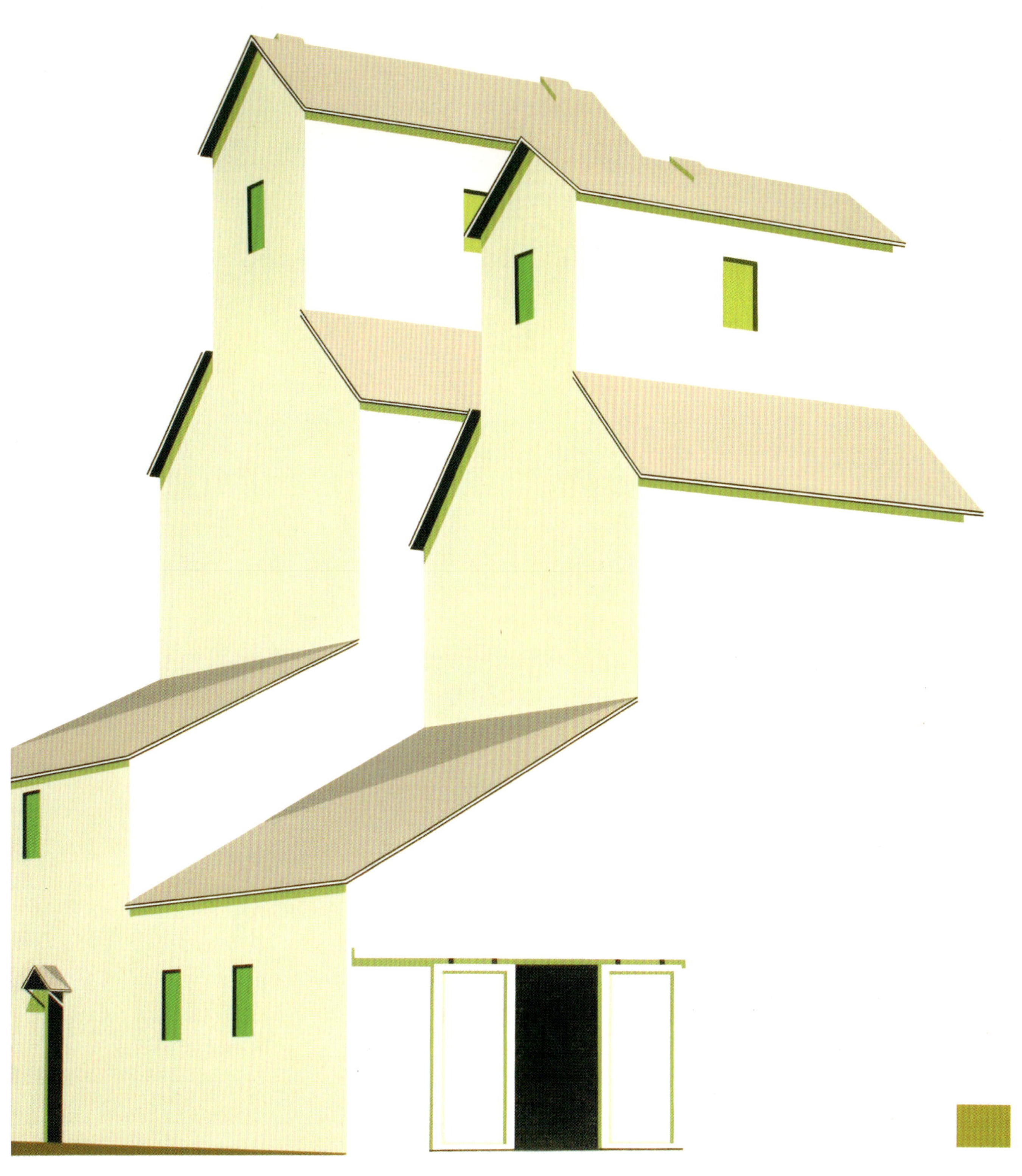

Plate 104. **Grain Elevator #6**, 2008, oil on linen, 30 x 24 inches. Private collection.

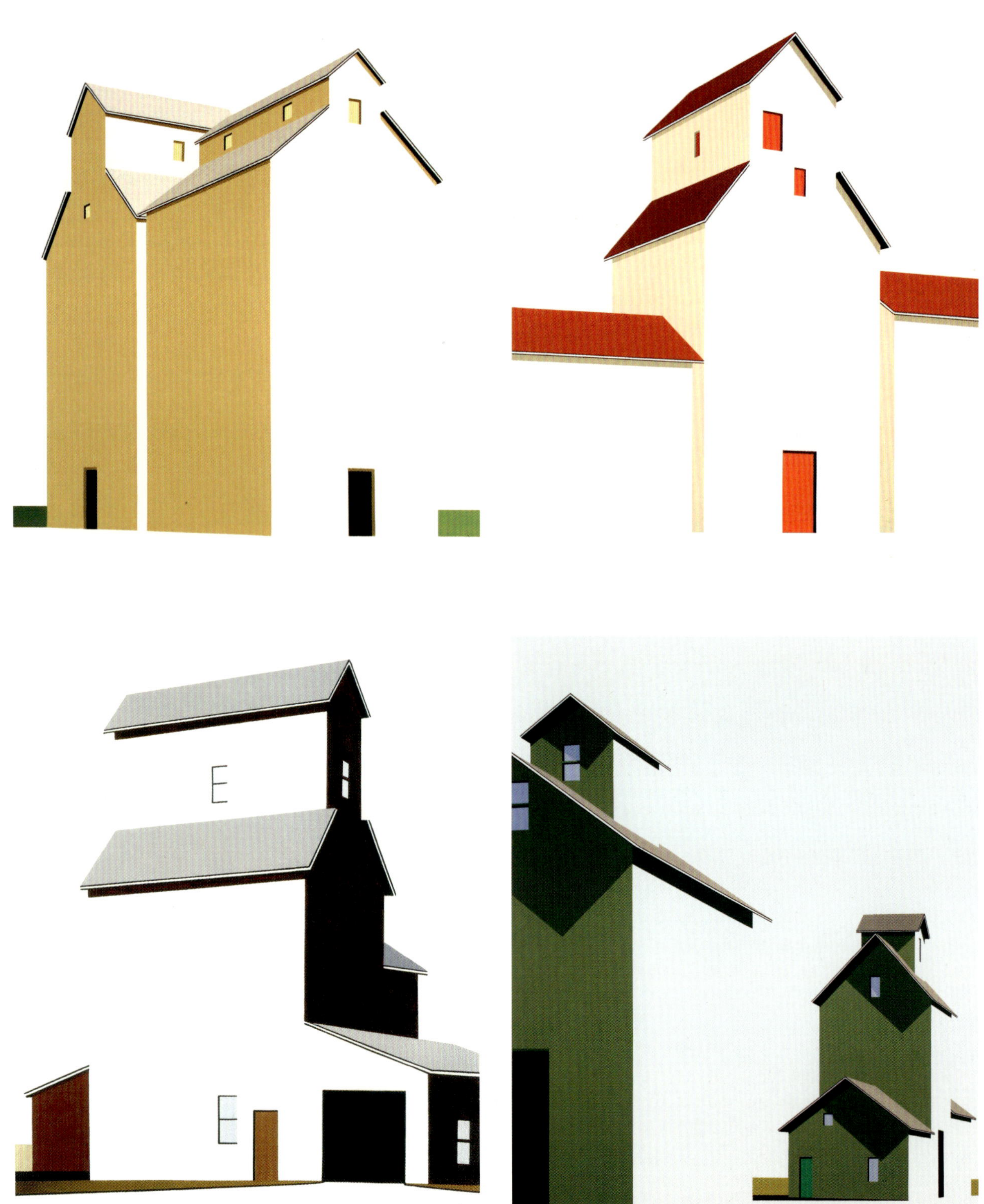

Plate 105. **Wheat Pool #D**, 2006, oil on linen, 20 x 16 inches. Collection of John Robertshaw.

Plate 106. **Wheat Pool #9**, 2008, oil on linen, 30 x 24 inches. Courtesy Marcia Wood Gallery.

Plate 107. **Elevator #11**, 2004, oil on linen, 20 x 16 inches. Collection of Diana and Ken Lewis.

Plate 108. **Grain Elevator #8**, 2008, oil on linen, 30 x 24 inches. Courtesy Holly Johnson Gallery.

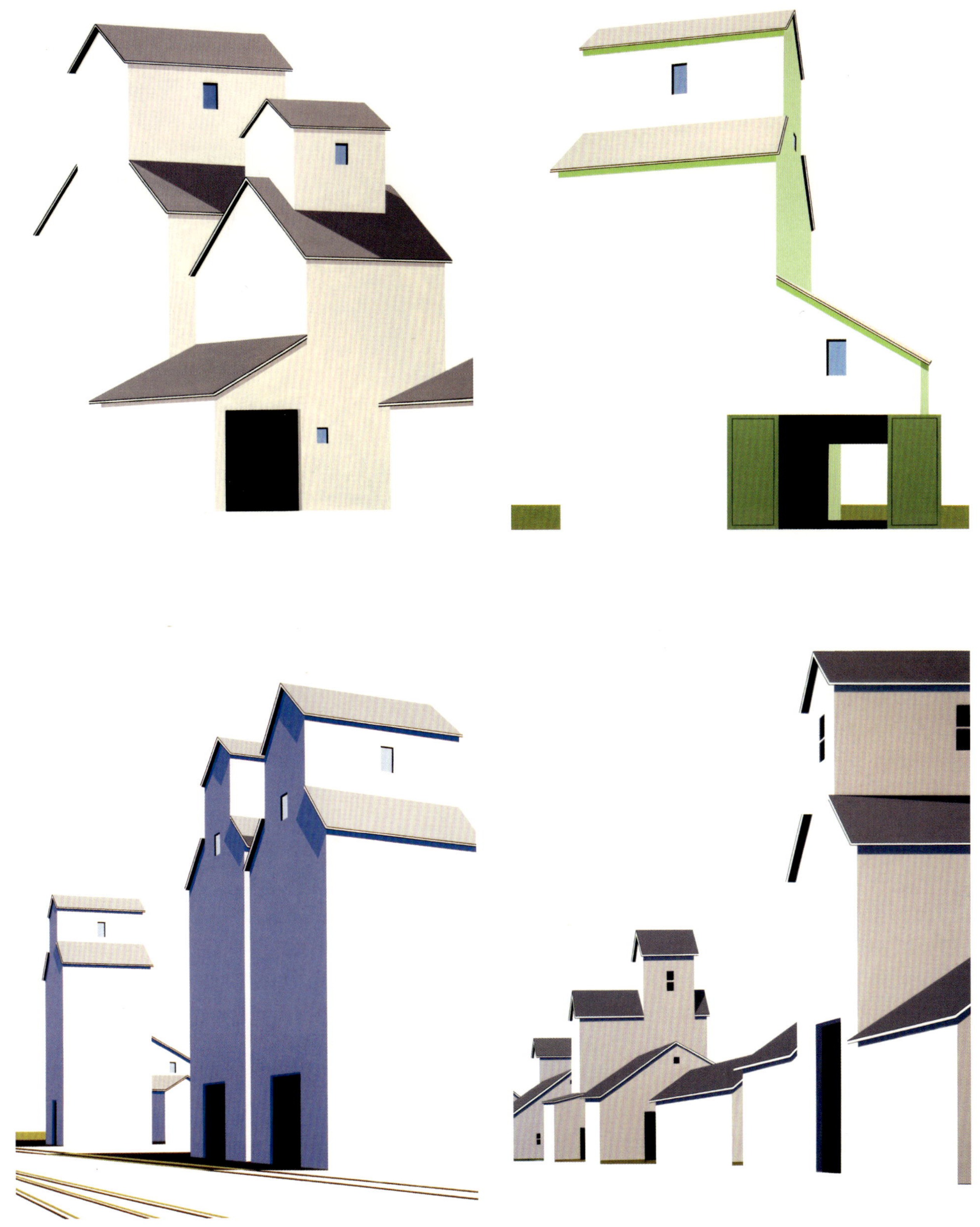

Plate 109. **Grain Elevator #2**, 2005, oil on canvas, 30 x 24 inches. Collection of Barbara Hewson.

Plate 110. **Wheat Pool #6**, 2006, oil on linen, 30 x 24 inches. Collection of Margaret Thatcher.

Plate 111. **Grain Elevator #7**, 2008, oil on linen, 30 x 24 inches. Courtesy Holly Johnson Gallery.

Plate 112. **Elevator V**, 2004, oil on canvas, 60 x 48 inches. Courtesy Marcia Wood Gallery.

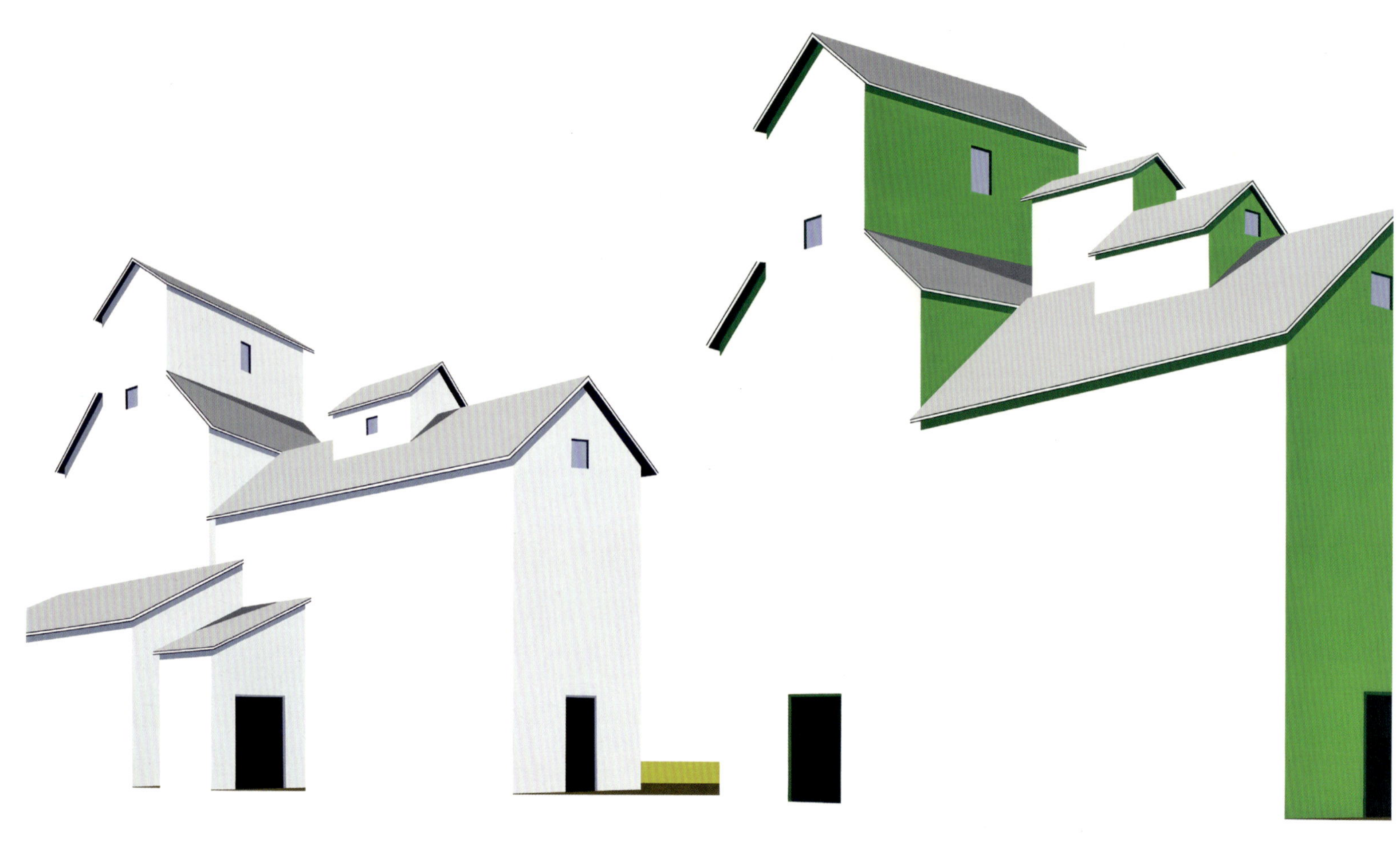

     Plate 113. **Wheat Pool II**, 2008, oil on linen, 40 x 60 inches. Courtesy Margaret Thatcher Projects.

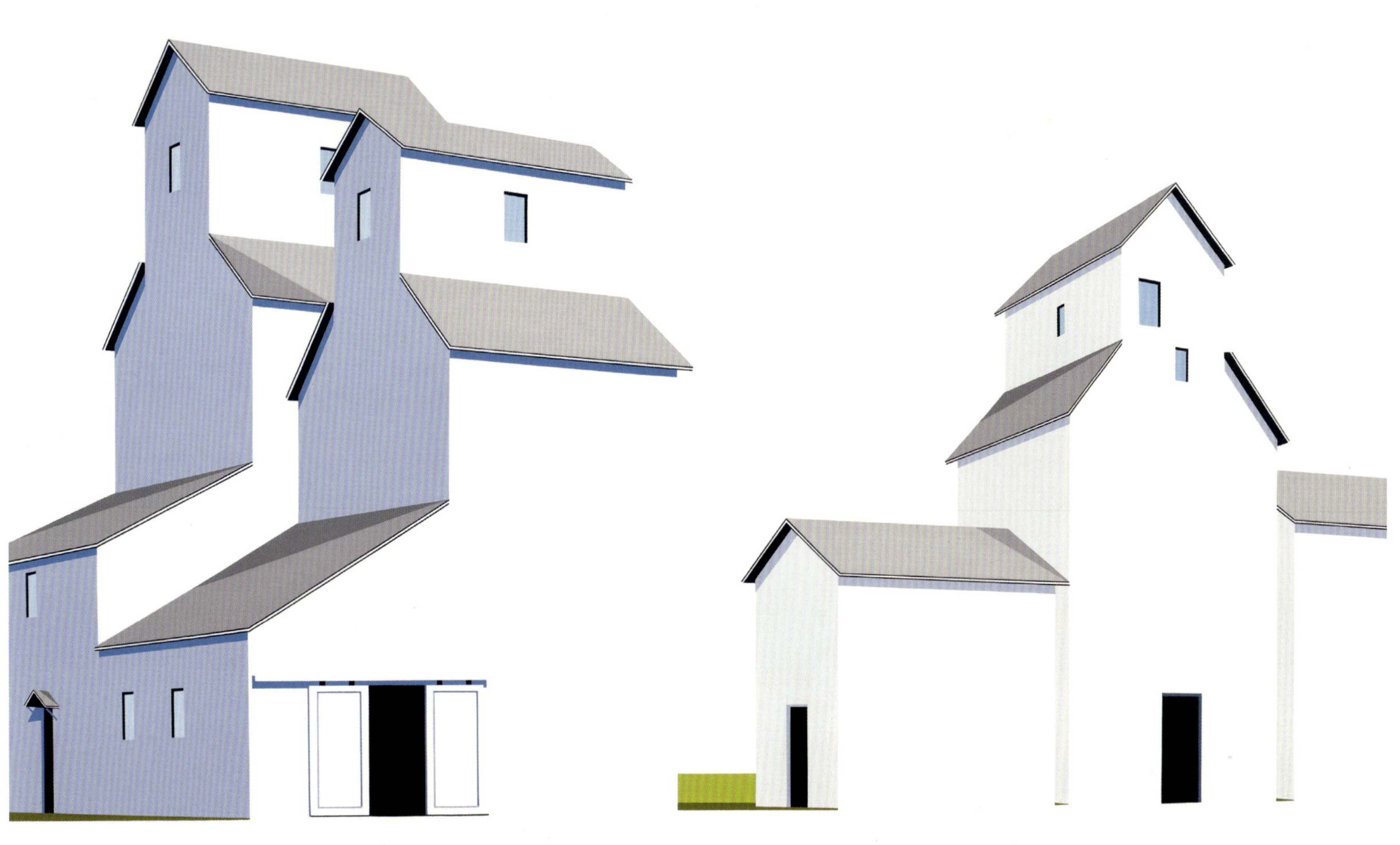

Plate 114. **Grain Growers #6**, 2008, oil on linen, 30 x 45 inches. Courtesy Margaret Thatcher Projects.

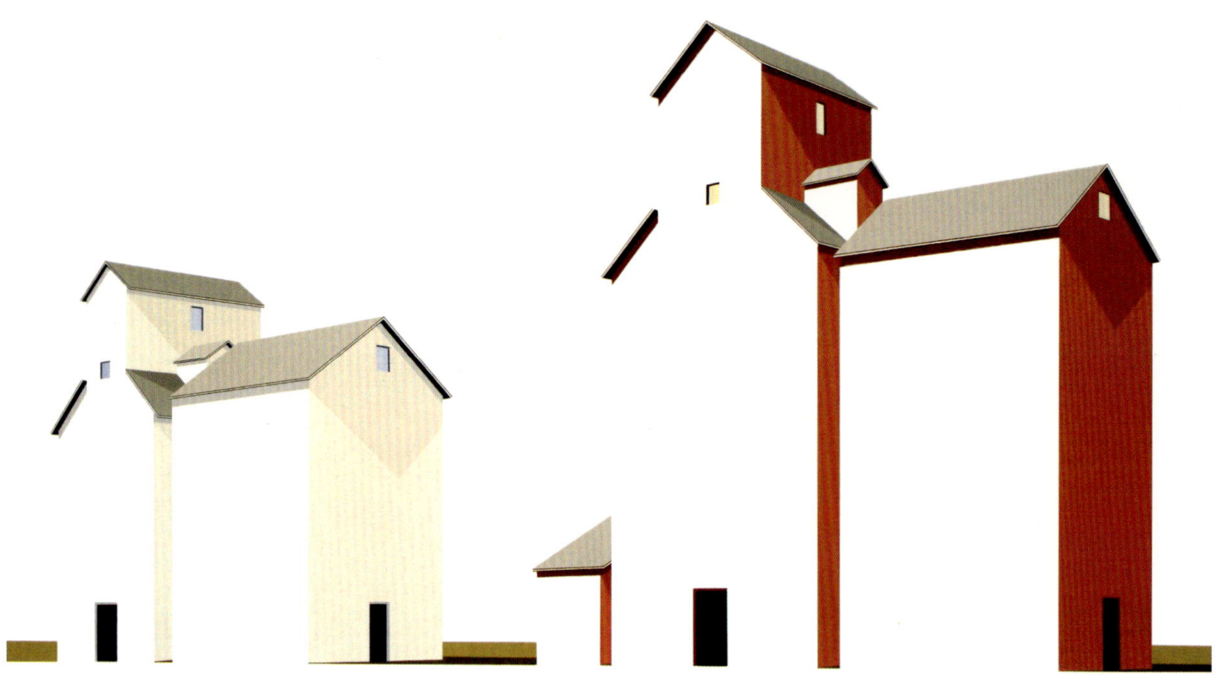

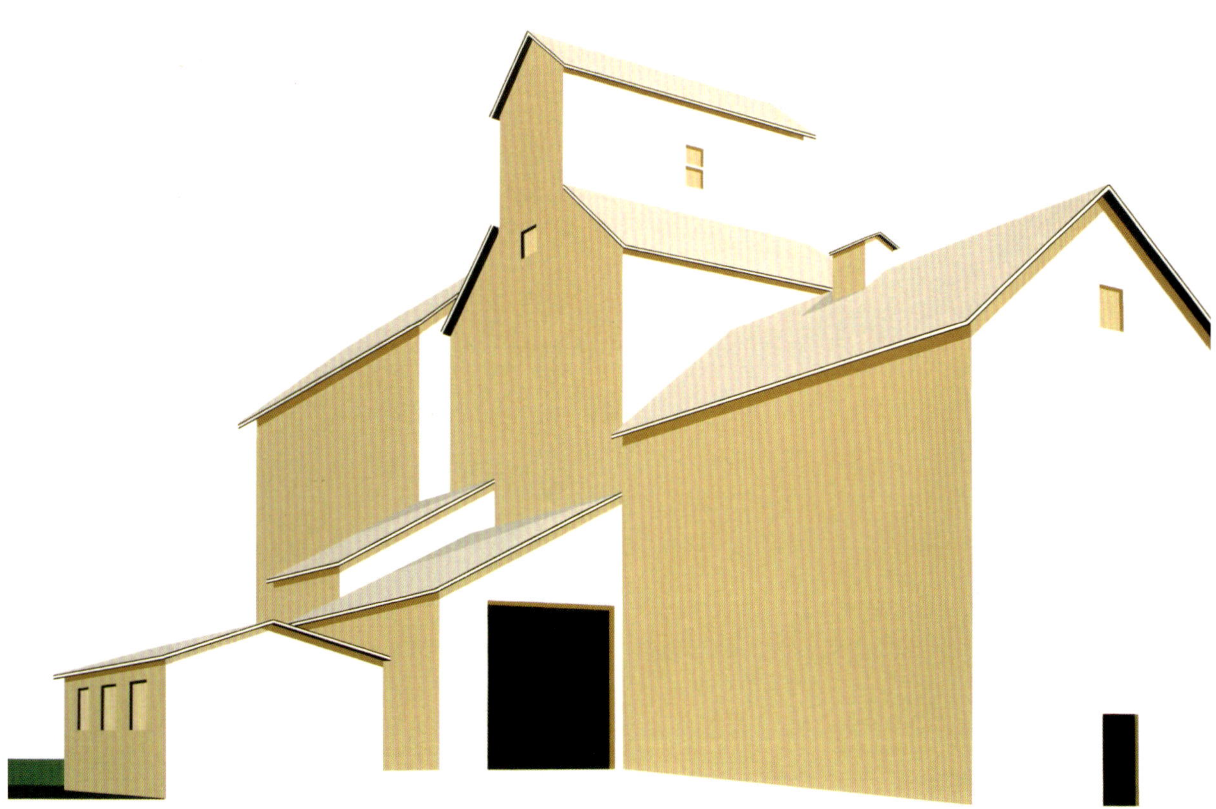

Plate 115. **Grain Growers #2**, 2008, oil on linen, 40 x 60 inches. Courtesy Marcia Wood Gallery.

Plate 116. **Grain Growers**, 2006, oil on linen, 30 x 45 inches. Collection of Lamattina and Henry Family.

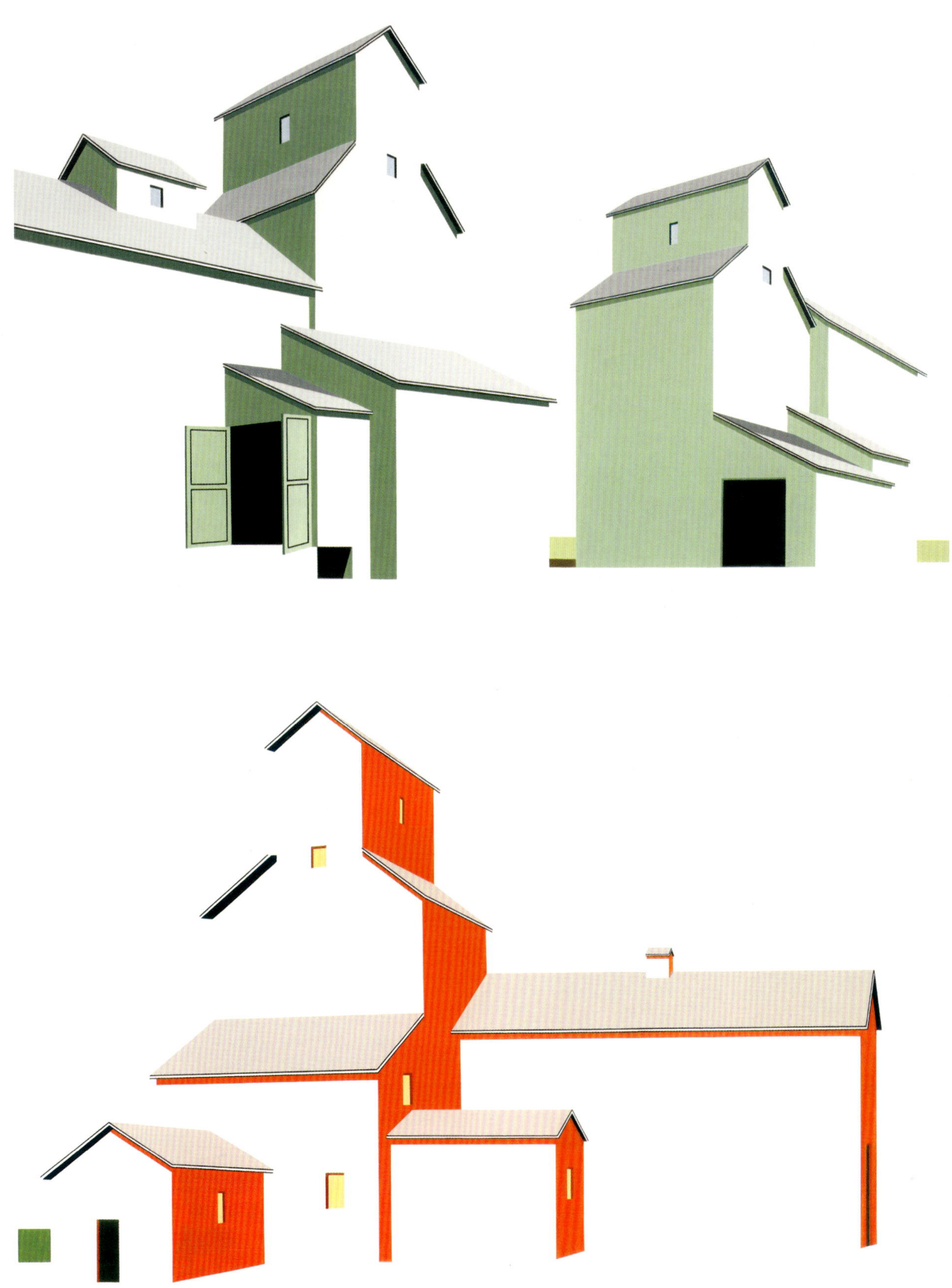

Plate 117. **Wheat Pool #12**, 2008, oil on linen, 20 x 30 inches. Courtesy Margaret Thatcher Projects.

Plate 118. **Red Barns**, 2005, oil on linen, 30 x 45 inches. Collection of Mr. and Mrs. Michael J. Figge.

THE AESTHETIC AND SYMBOLIC APPEAL of Steiger's aerial tramways holds us in their calm
wake's sway. We are poised between what we see and what we know. Steiger has chosen rel-
atively innocuous subjects—ones that we think we already understand everything about. Onto
them, however, he applies a strenuous and rigorous template of contemporary conceptual
and perceptual precision, producing a re-presentation. Because we recognize them, or think
we do, the images become like a scene from memory—unexpected, pensive sources of stored
narratives and forgotten emotions. These images, he seems to suggest, have that cultural
role to play, too, as sudden reminders of something significant—necessary, but almost lost—
and recovered now for a purpose.

Through brushwork and handwork Steiger's cable cars become imbued with a startling inti-
macy. Using highly exaggerated whites as the shining non-color par excellence, occupying
positive and negative spaces at will, Steiger paints his centralized images as though a blinding light has startled them into a trancelike state: mirages caught in a nanosecond of cogni-
tive lucidity. Their ordinariness becomes dramatic. By insisting on this moment, and pressing
on its incompleteness, Steiger poses questions about the nature of the relationship between
vision, emotion, and memory. How and why does an image stay rooted in our minds? How
does memory affect our perception of an image even while we are looking at it?

TRAMWAY

BRUCE W. FERGUSON

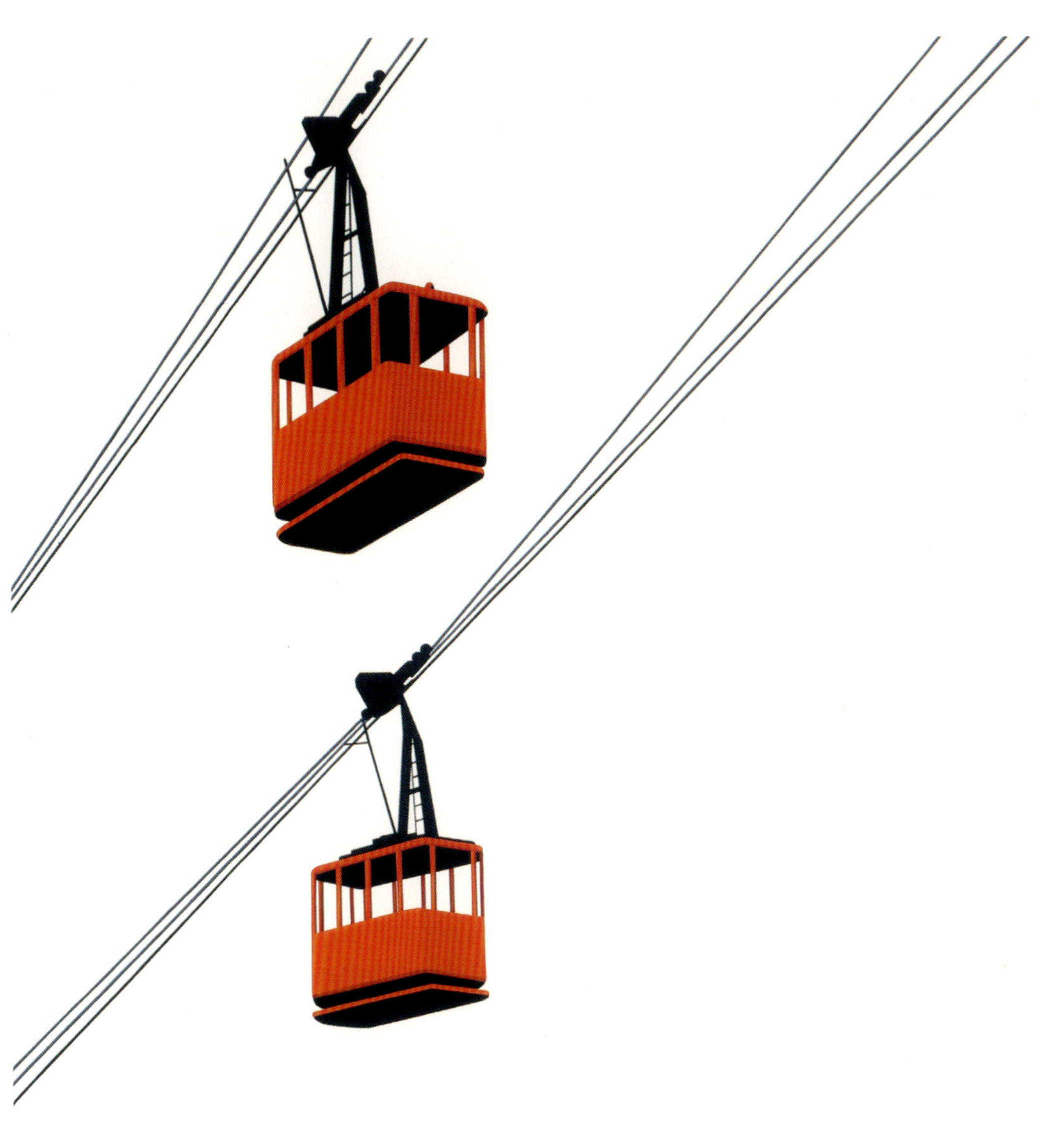

Plate 119. **Cable Cars**, 2004, oil on linen, 60 x 48 inches. Collection of Patricia Brett and Thomas Butcher.

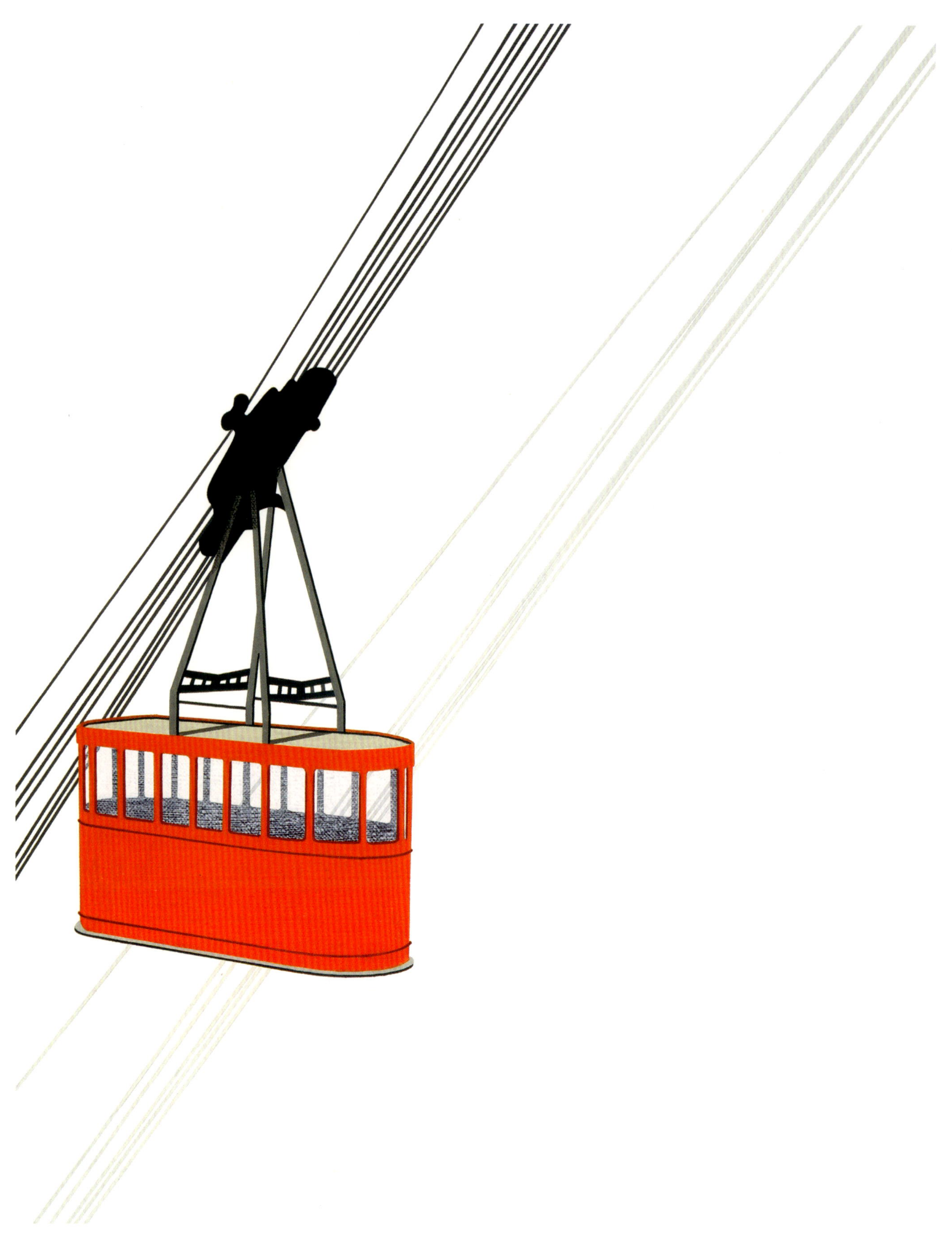

Plate 120. **Red Cable Car**, 2006, oil on linen, 25 x 20 inches. Collection of Charles Wall.

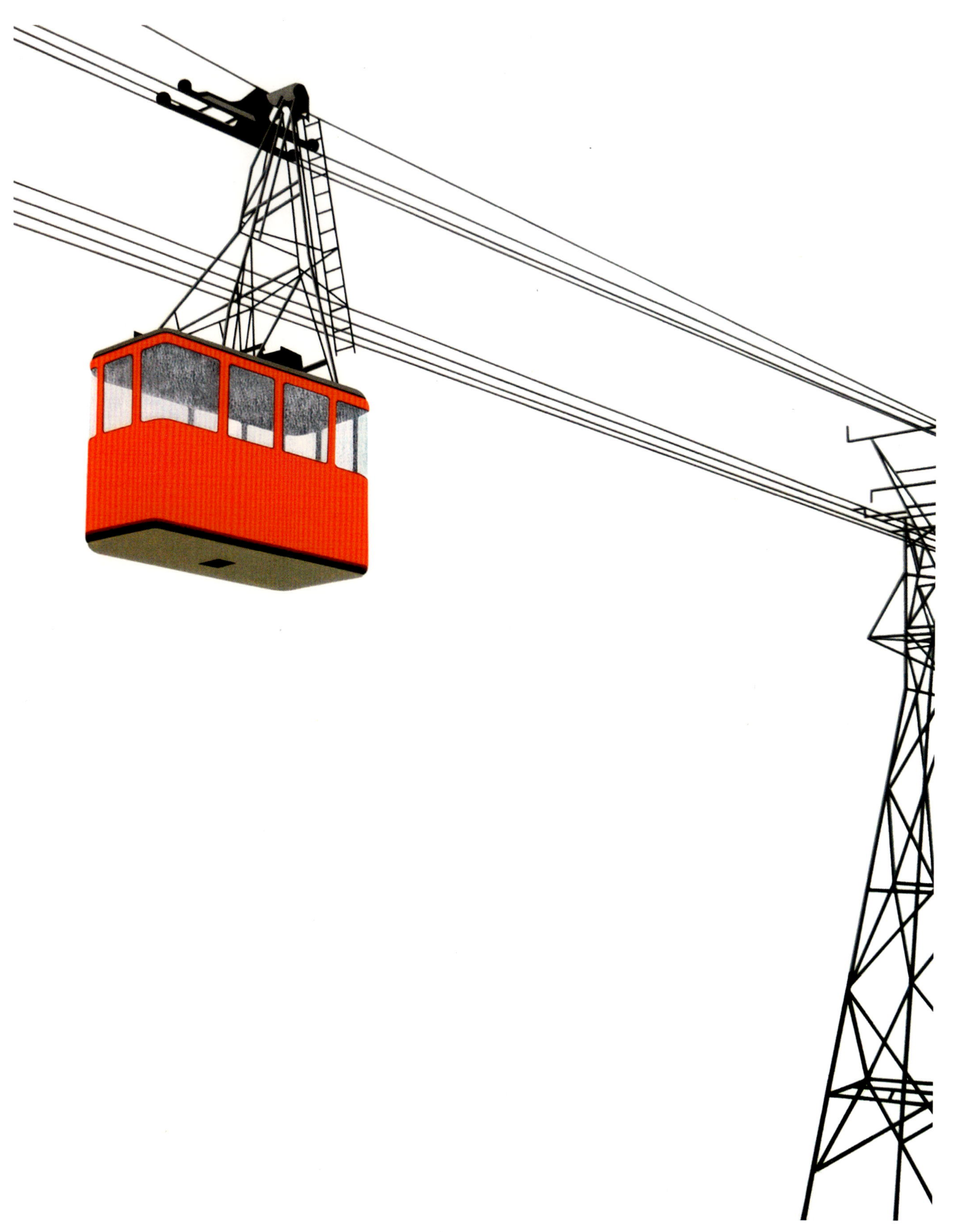

Plate 121. **Tramway**, 2005, oil on canvas, 60 x 48 inches. Courtesy Marcia Wood Gallery.

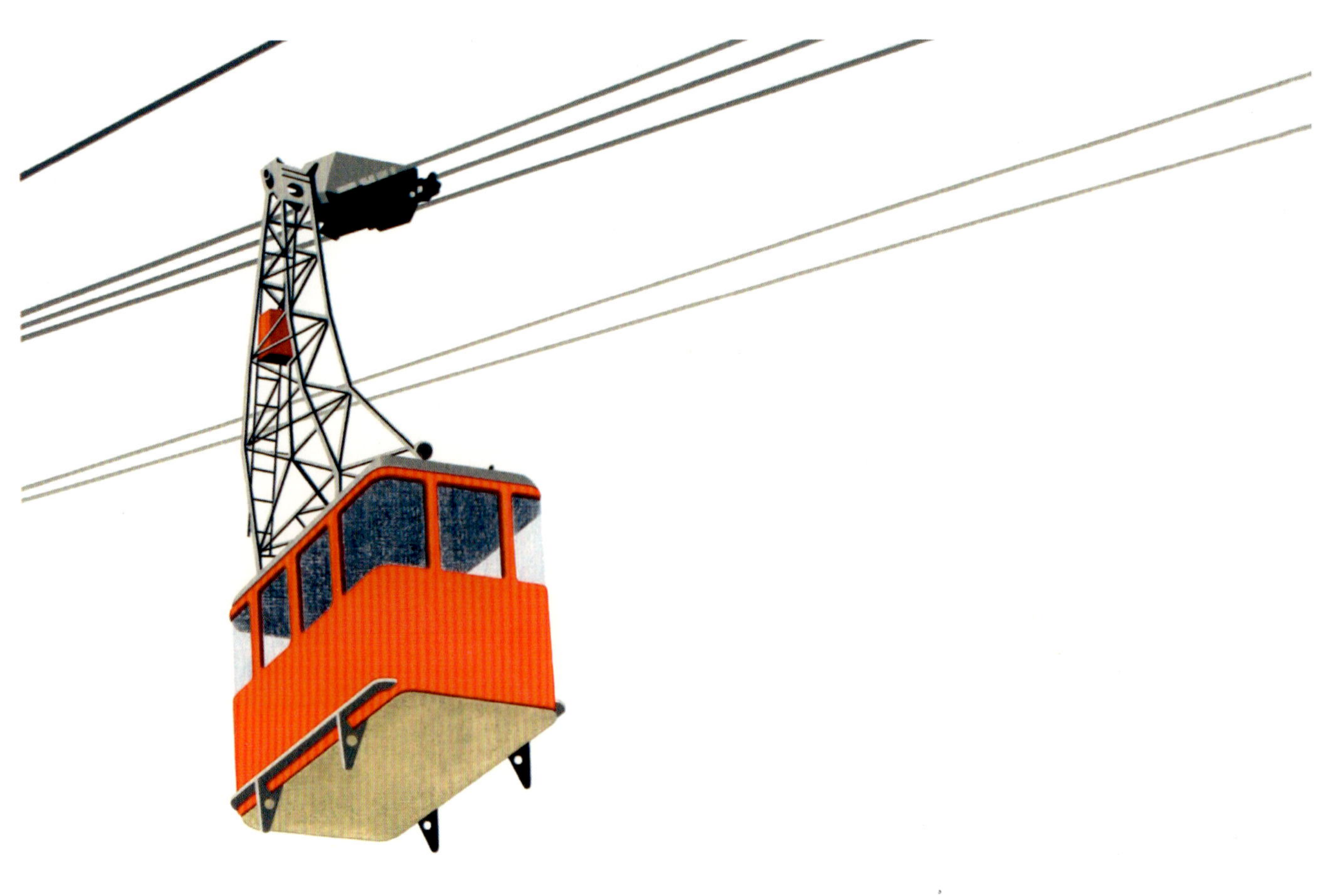

Plate 122. **Aerial Tramway**, 2007, oil on linen, 44 x 35 inches. Private collection.

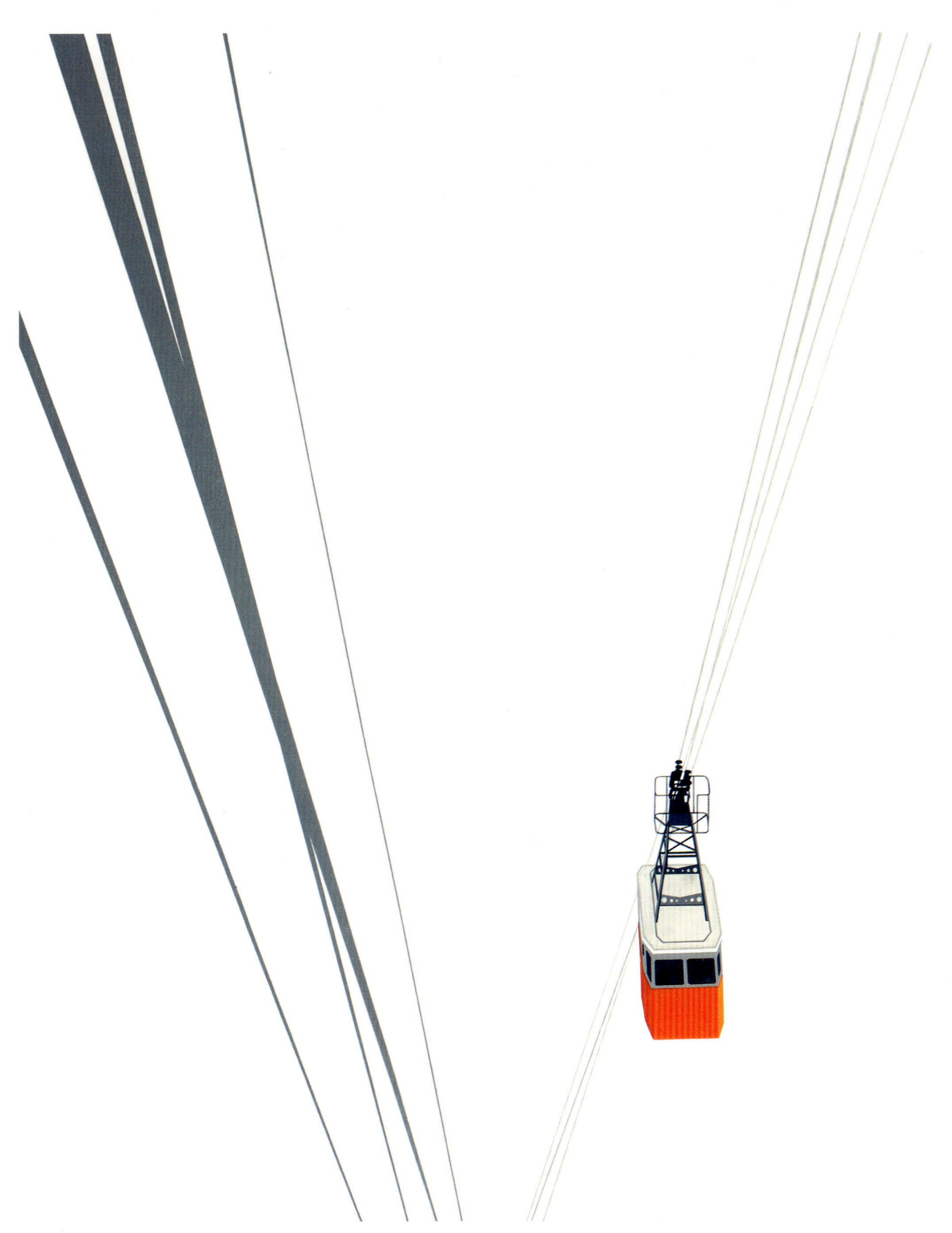

Plate 123. **Leonard's Tram**, oil on linen, 60 x 48 inches. Collection of Charles Wall.

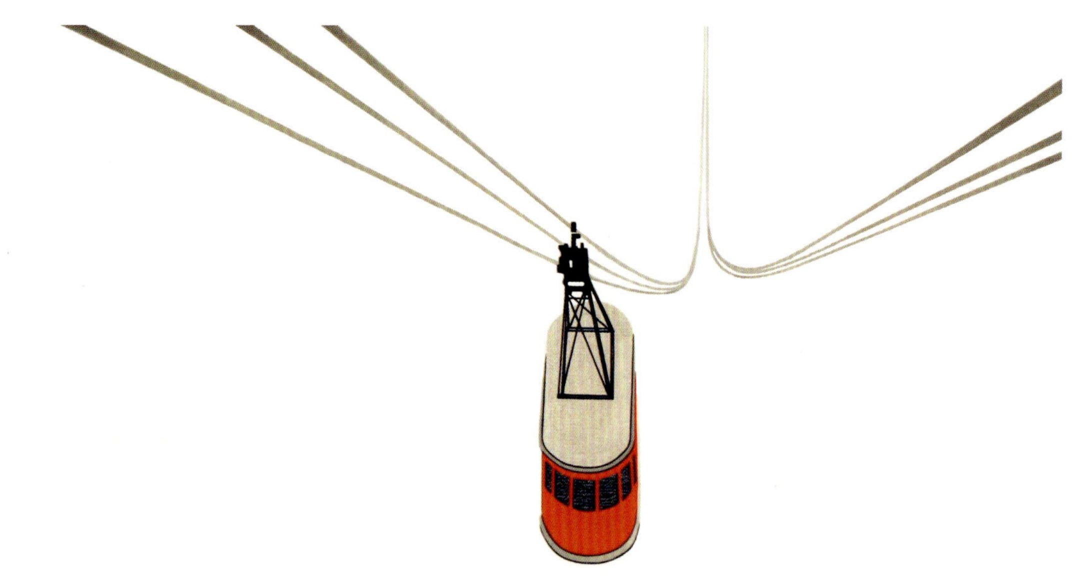

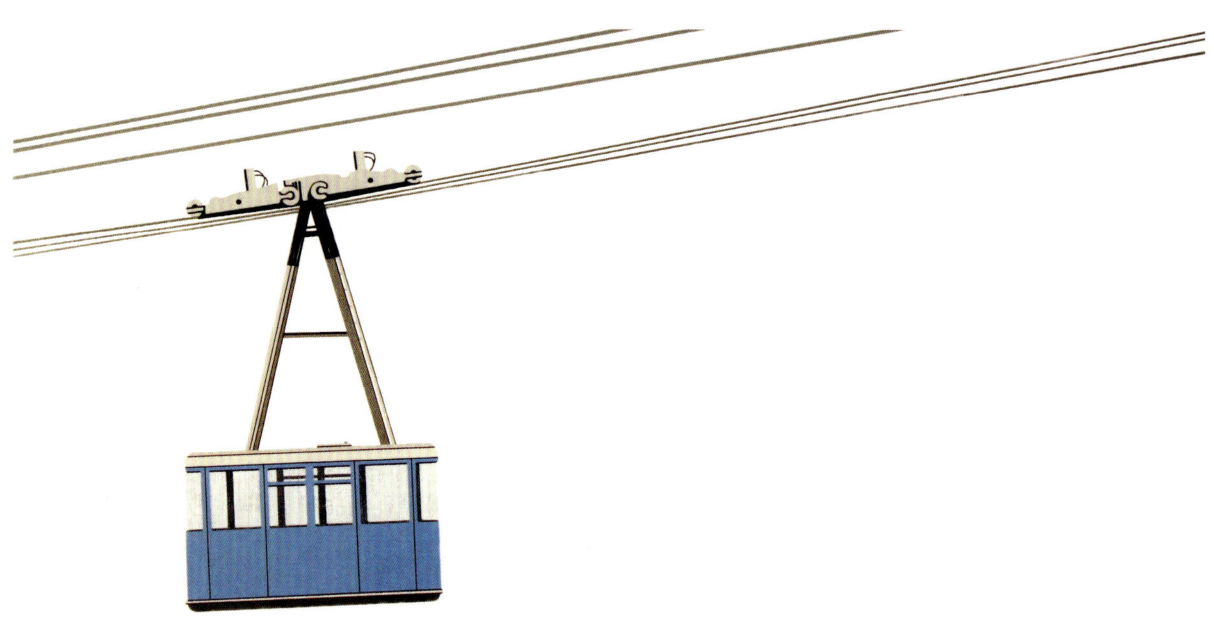

Plate 124. **Tramway from Above**, 2007, oil on linen, 20 x 30 inches. Courtesy Roy Boyd Gallery.

Plate 125. **Blue Cable Car**, 2007, oil on linen, 30 x 45 inches. Private collection.

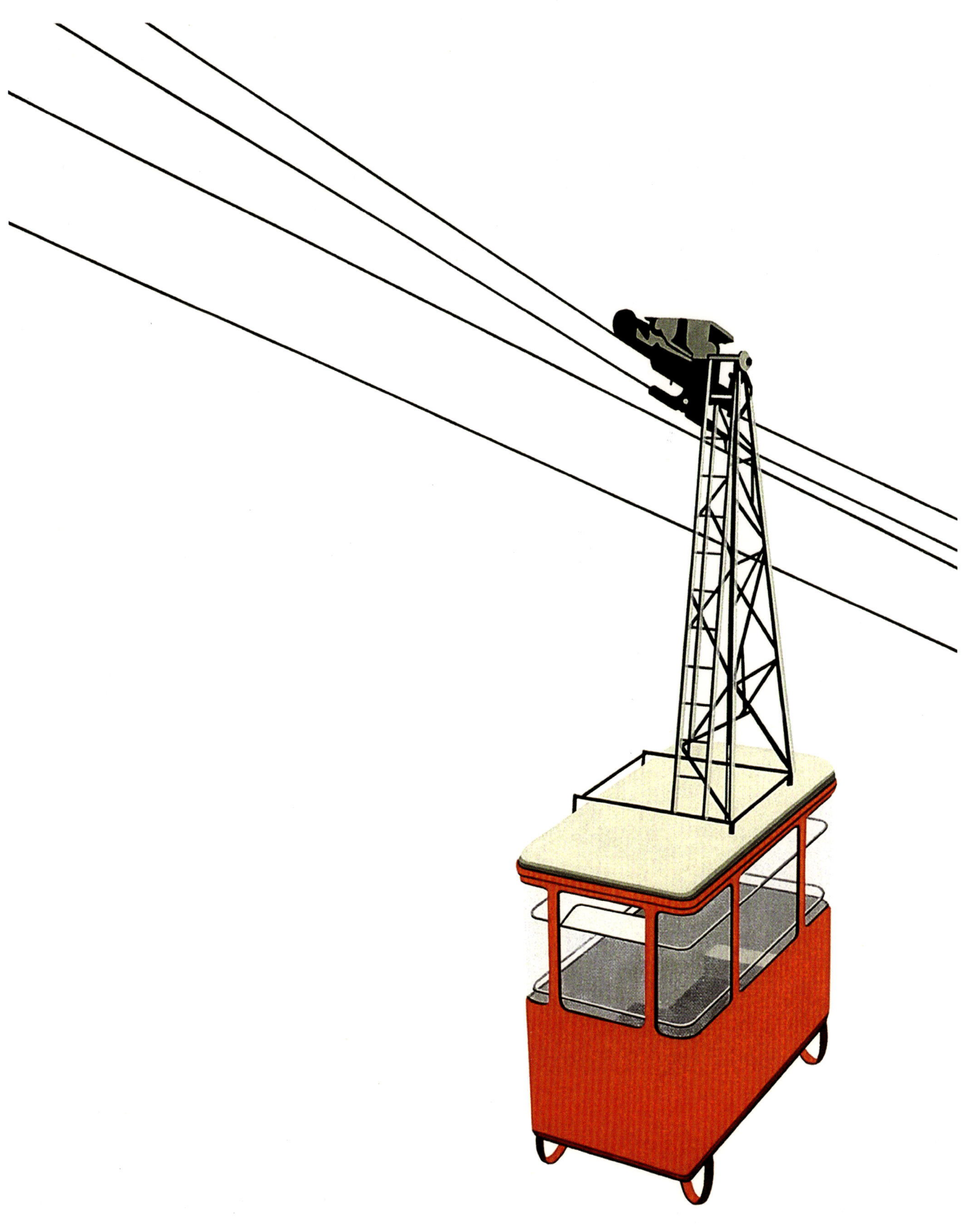

Plate 126. **Aerial Tramway II**, 2005, oil on linen, 30 x 24 inches. Collection of Barbara Hewson.

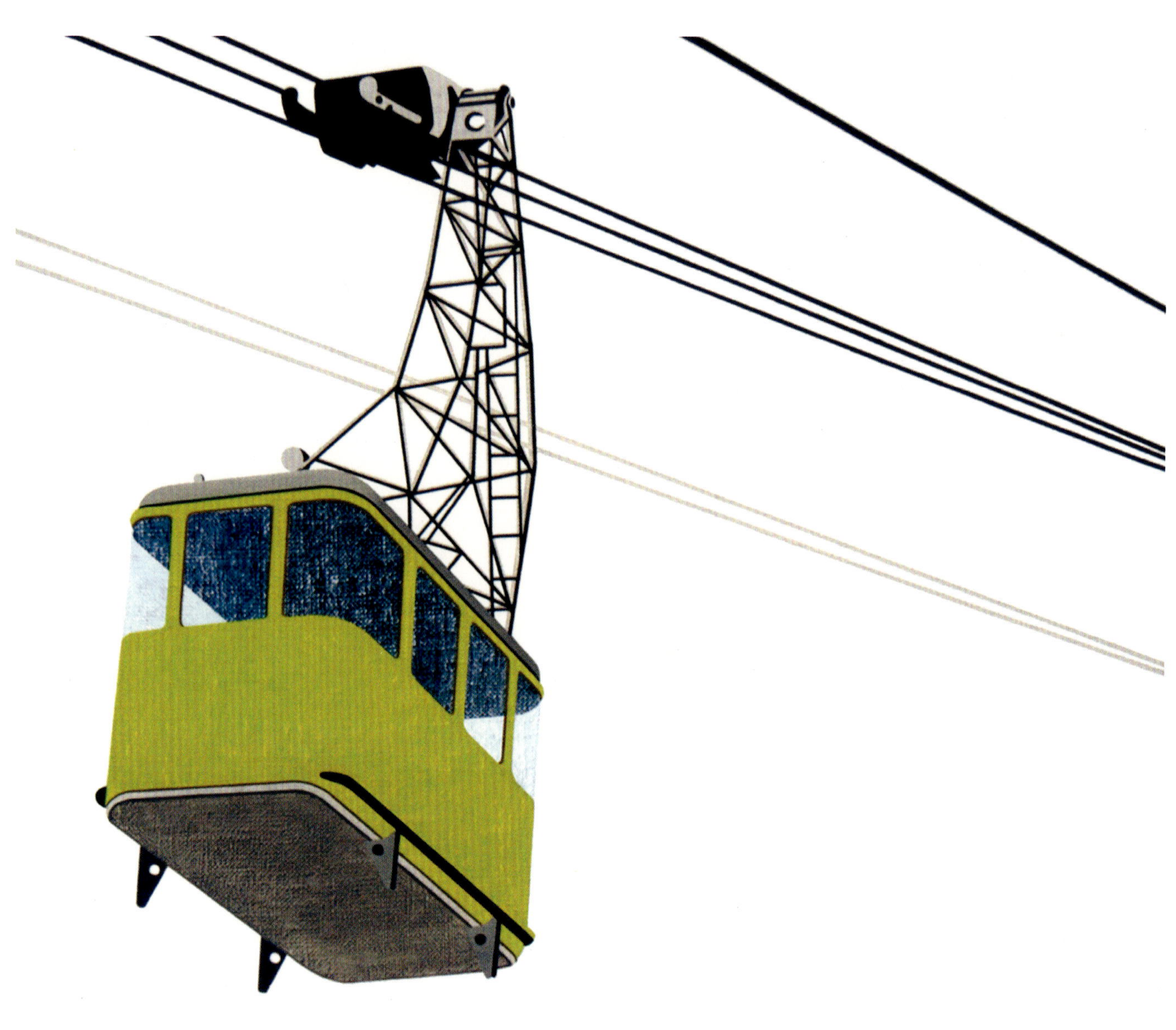

Plate 127. **Green Cable Car**, 2005, oil on canvas, 25 x 20 inches. Private collection.

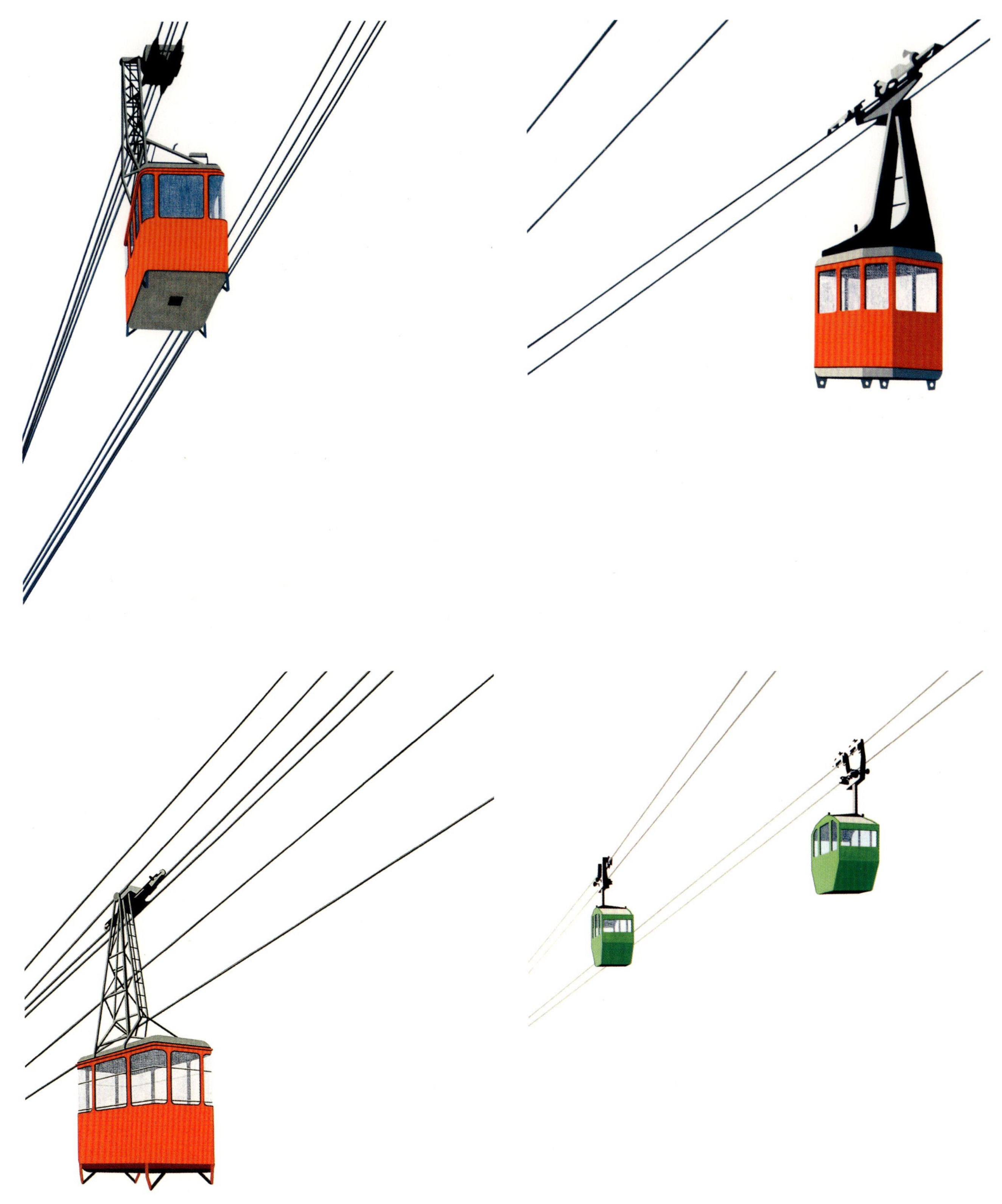

Plate 128. **Aerial Tramway #1**, 2005, oil on linen, 30 x 24 inches. Collection of Steven Nothern.

Plate 129. **Tramway**, 2006, oil on linen, 20 x 16 inches. Collection of John Robertshaw.

Plate 130. **Aerial Tramway III**, 2005, oil on linen, 30 x 24 inches. Collection of artist.

Plate 131. **Green Cable Cars**, 2007, oil on canvas, 60 x 48 inches. Courtesy Roy Boyd Gallery.

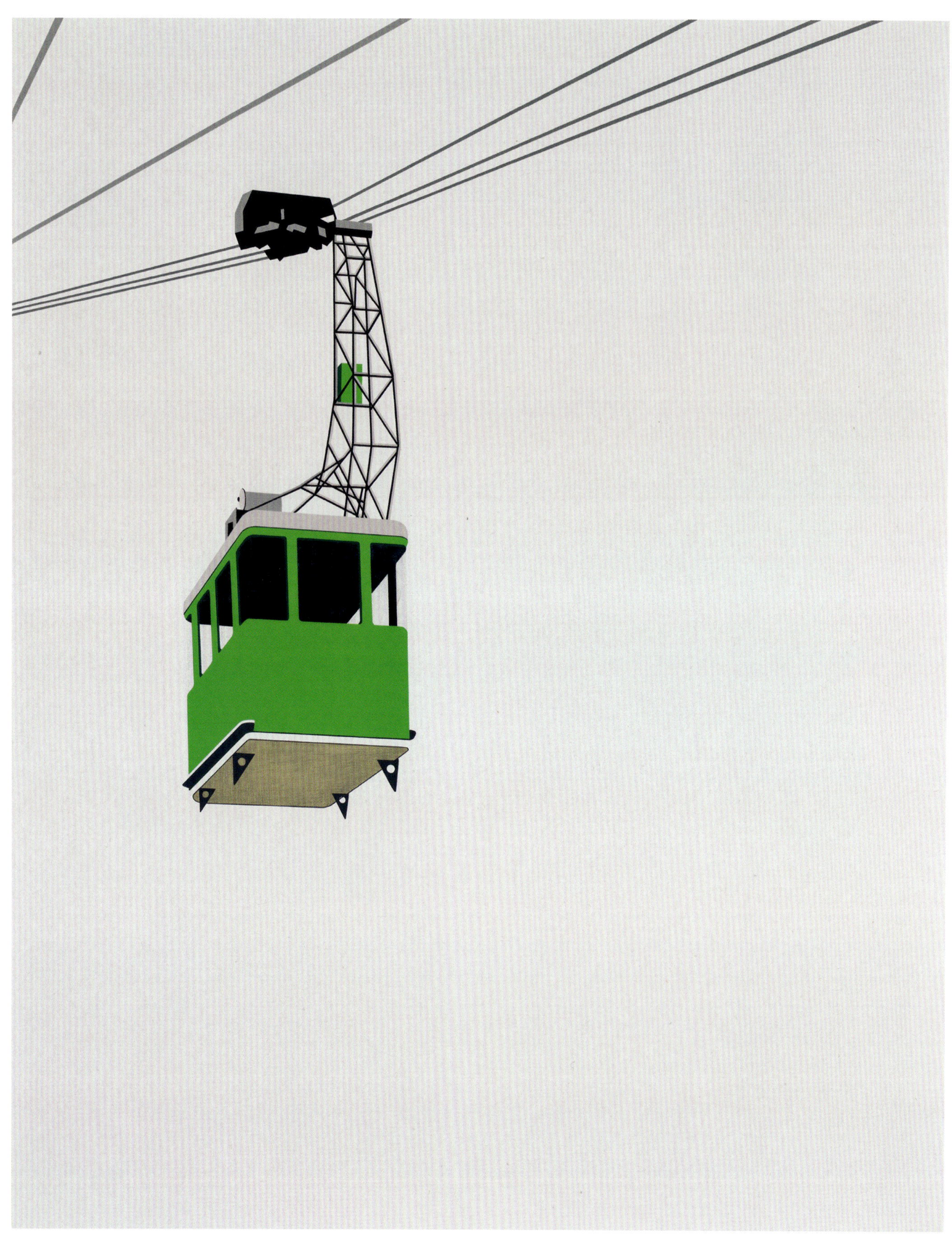

Plate 132. **Aerial Tramway Green I**, 2008, oil on linen, 60 x 48 inches. Courtesy Margaret Thatcher Projects.

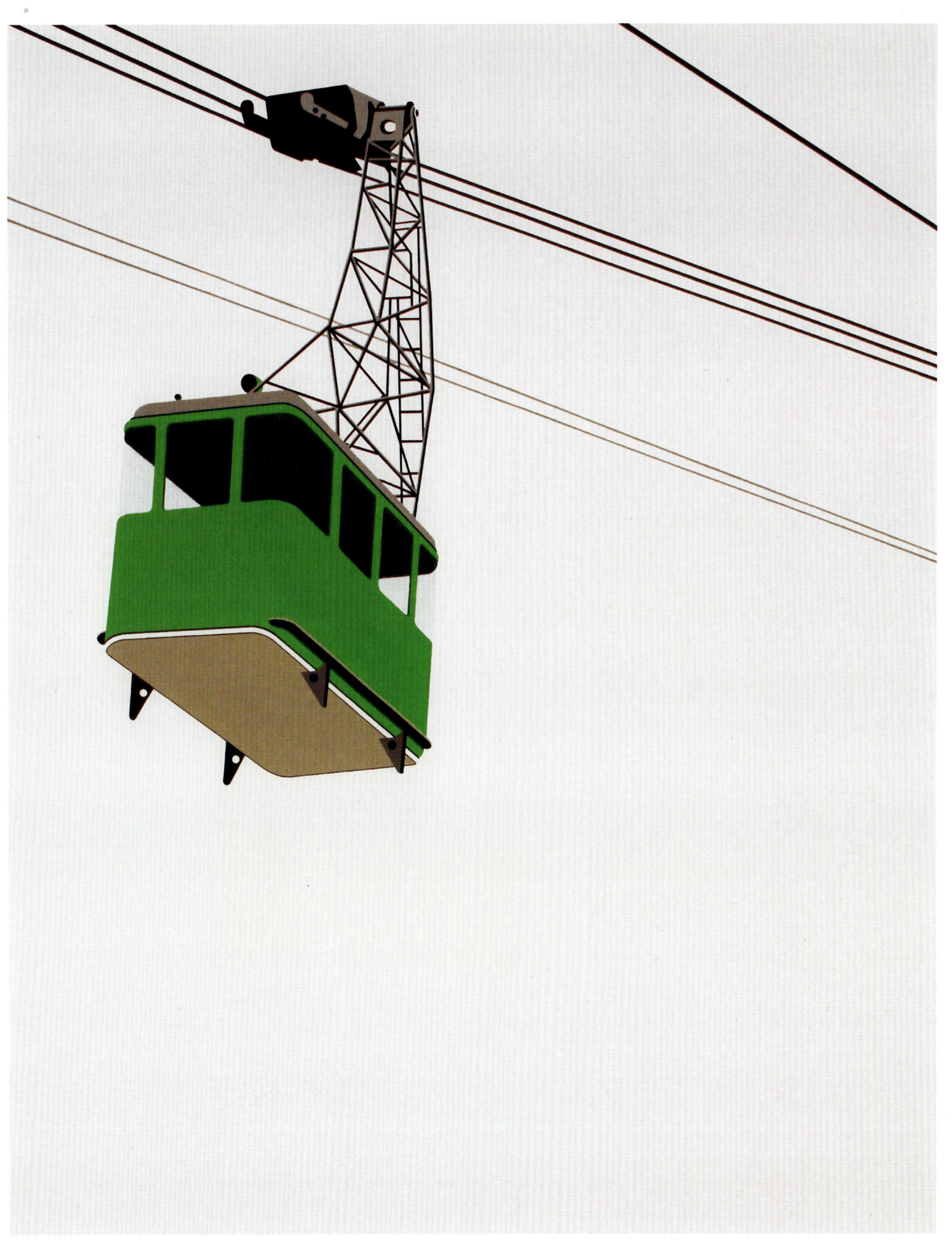

Plate 133. **Aerial Tramway Green II**, 2008, oil on linen, 60 x 48 inches. Courtesy Holly Johnson Gallery.

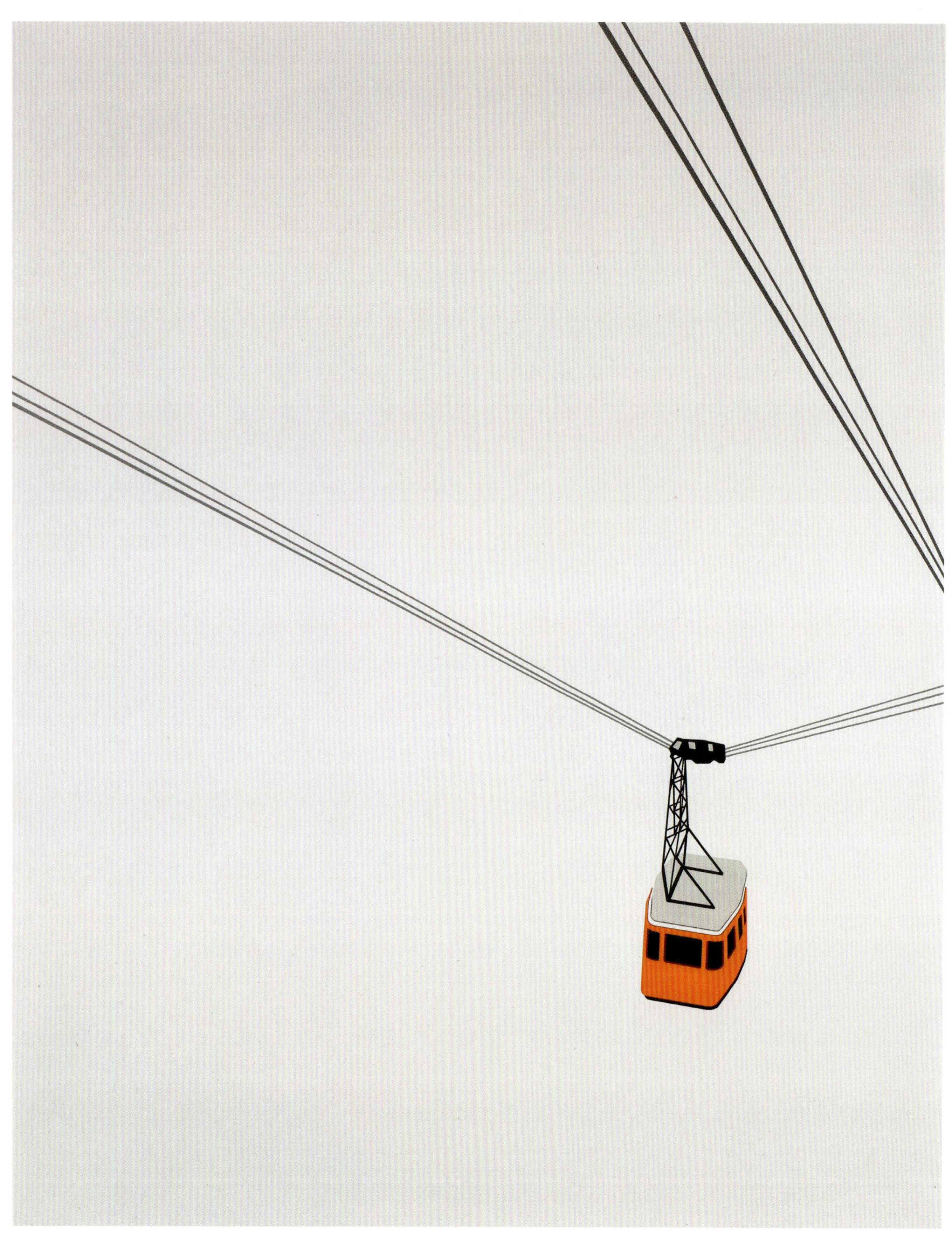

Plate 134. **Aerial Tramway Red**, 2008, oil on linen, 60 x 48 inches. Courtesy Holly Johnson Gallery.

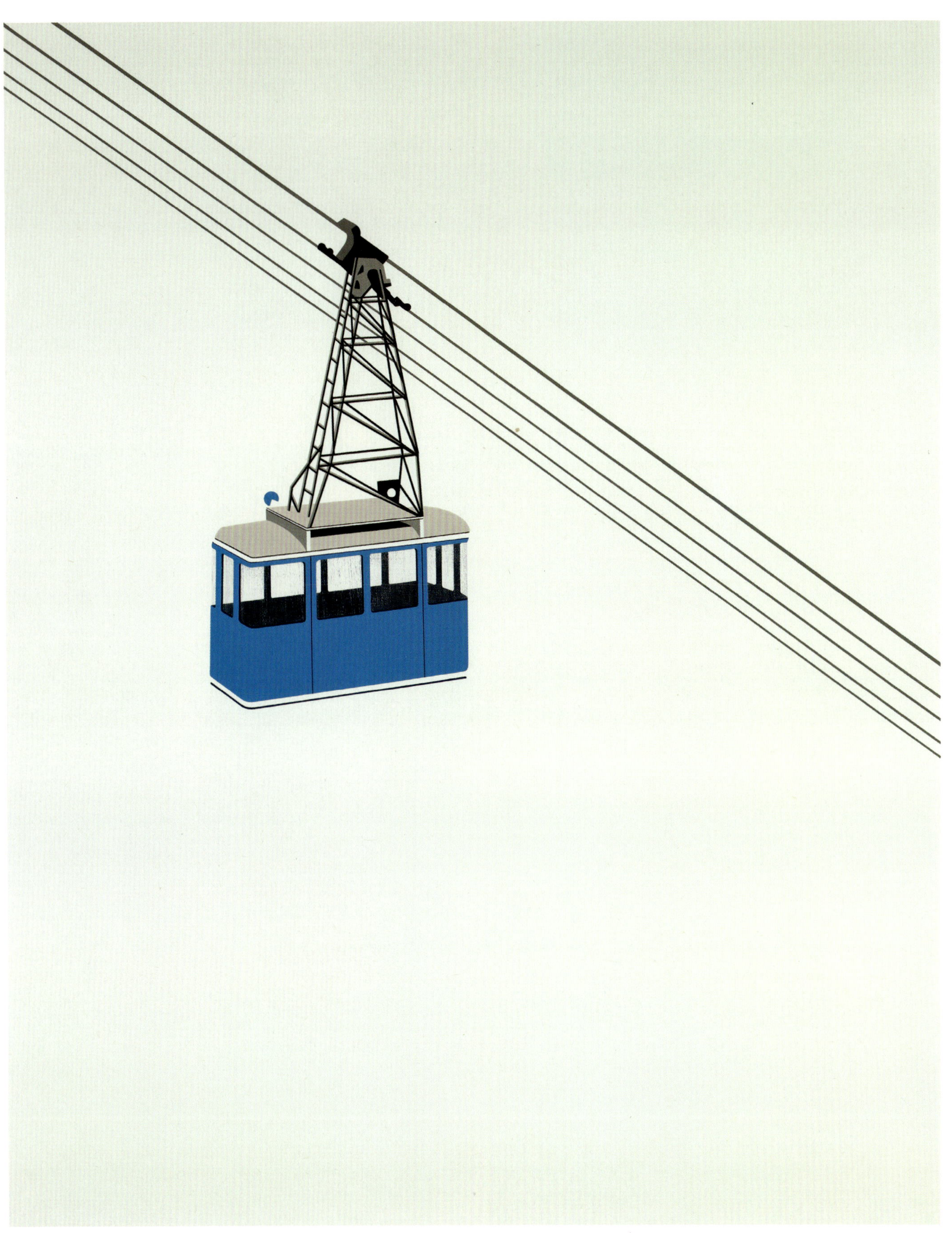

Plate 135. **Aerial Tramway Blue**, 2008, oil on linen, 60 x 48 inches. Courtesy Margaret Thatcher Projects.

WILLIAM STEIGER HAS MANAGED TO DISTILL the vision of the architect to its most essential
forms. In his amusement park paintings, the architecture is sometimes the subject and often,
perhaps always, it seems to be guiding the hand of the artist. I most enjoy his work when I
don't know immediately what the subject matter is; there is great power in that abstraction.
Only slowly can I decipher the original form and motivation. It is a revelation that teaches me
much about the nature of the object presented. Steiger has managed to join and transform
architecture and art—not an easy task. (C.P.)

MOVEMENT IS A CENTRAL OBSESSION of contemporary life. As depicted in William Steiger's
paintings of thrill rides and gravity machines, movement becomes stillness and risk galva-
nized into the intensity of poetry. The tenuous protection offered by their delicate webbed
networks of steel lines and wooden frames, and the precariousness of tiny passenger con-
tainers hung in empty space, portrays a world that is simultaneously beautiful and terrifying.
Seen against horizonless skies, the embodied energy implied in the frozen torques, twists, and
stark silhouettes of Steiger's weightless monuments is serene, yet profound. (F.C.)

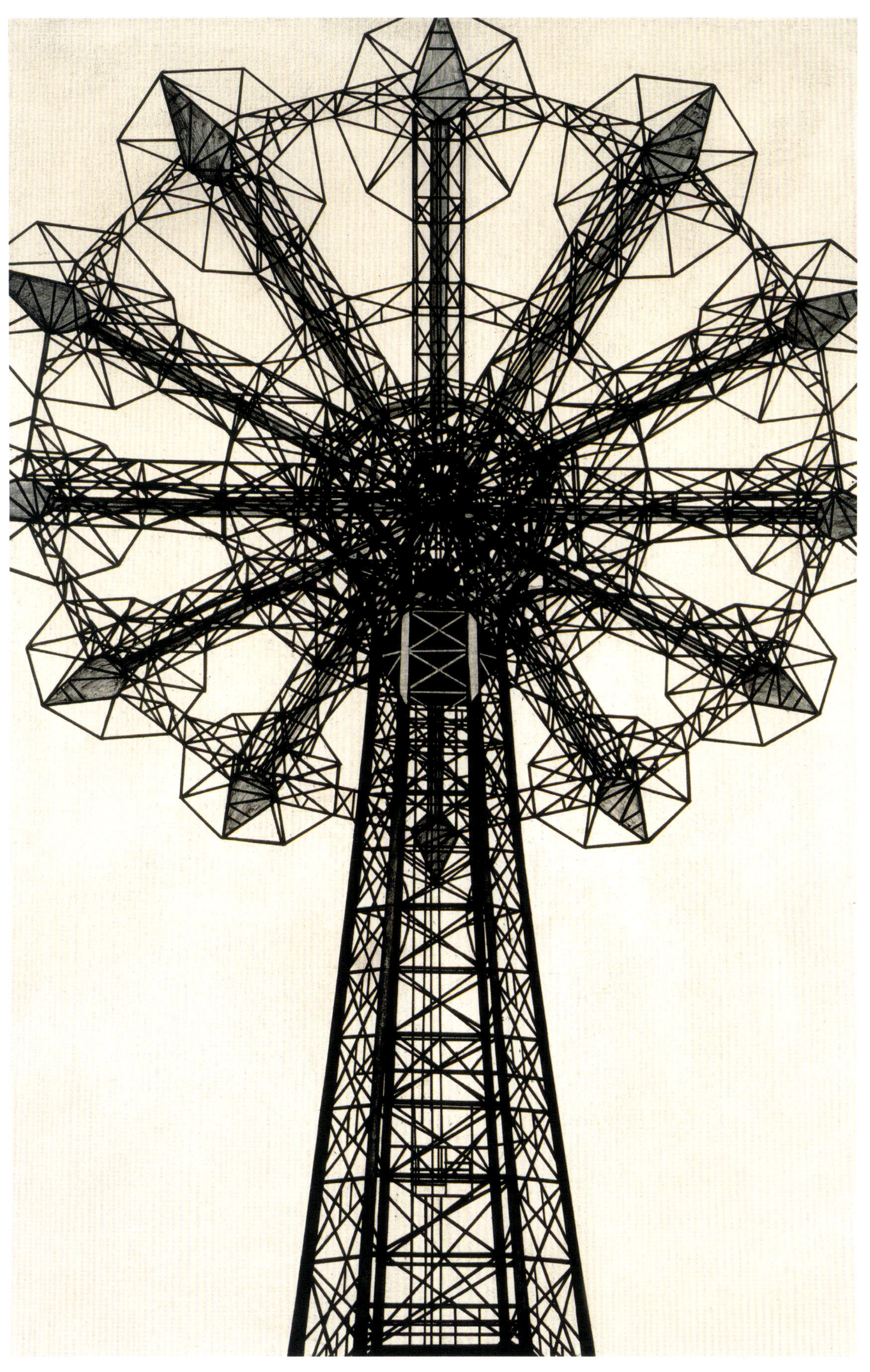

Plate 136. **Parachute Drop**, 1998, oil on canvas, 45 x 30 inches. Collection of artist.

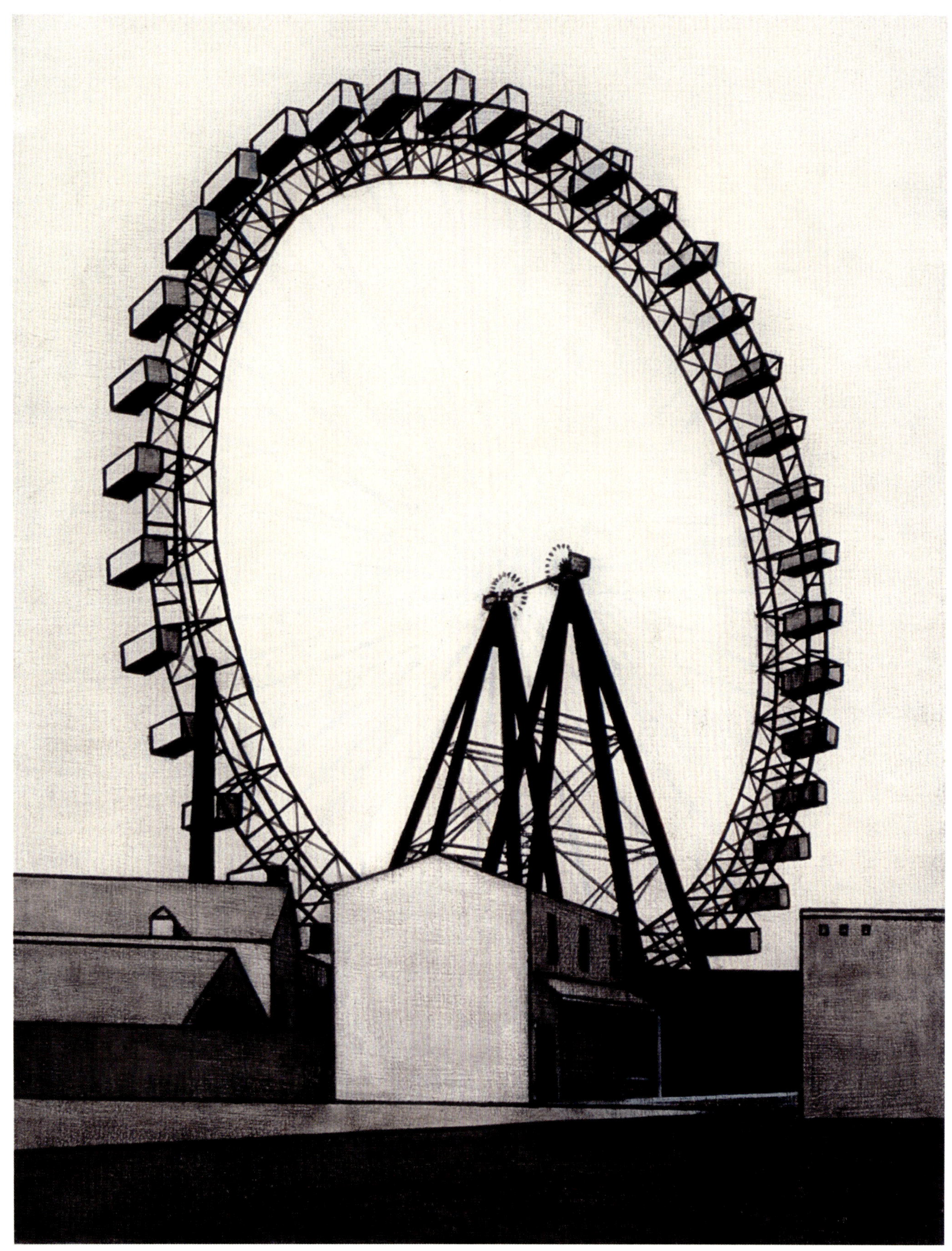

Plate 137. **Vue sur la Grand Roue**, 1994, oil on canvas, 20 x 16 inches. Private collection.

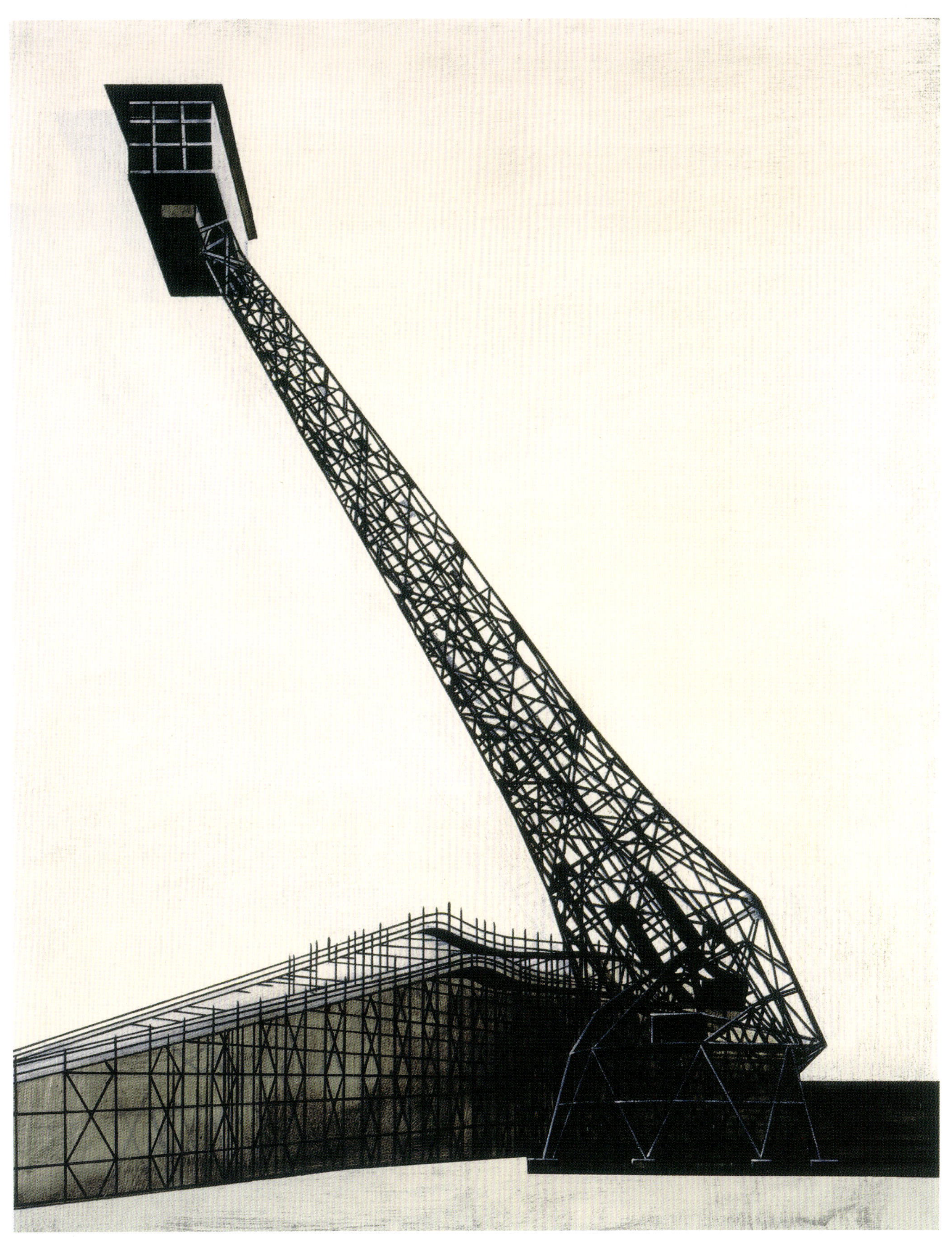

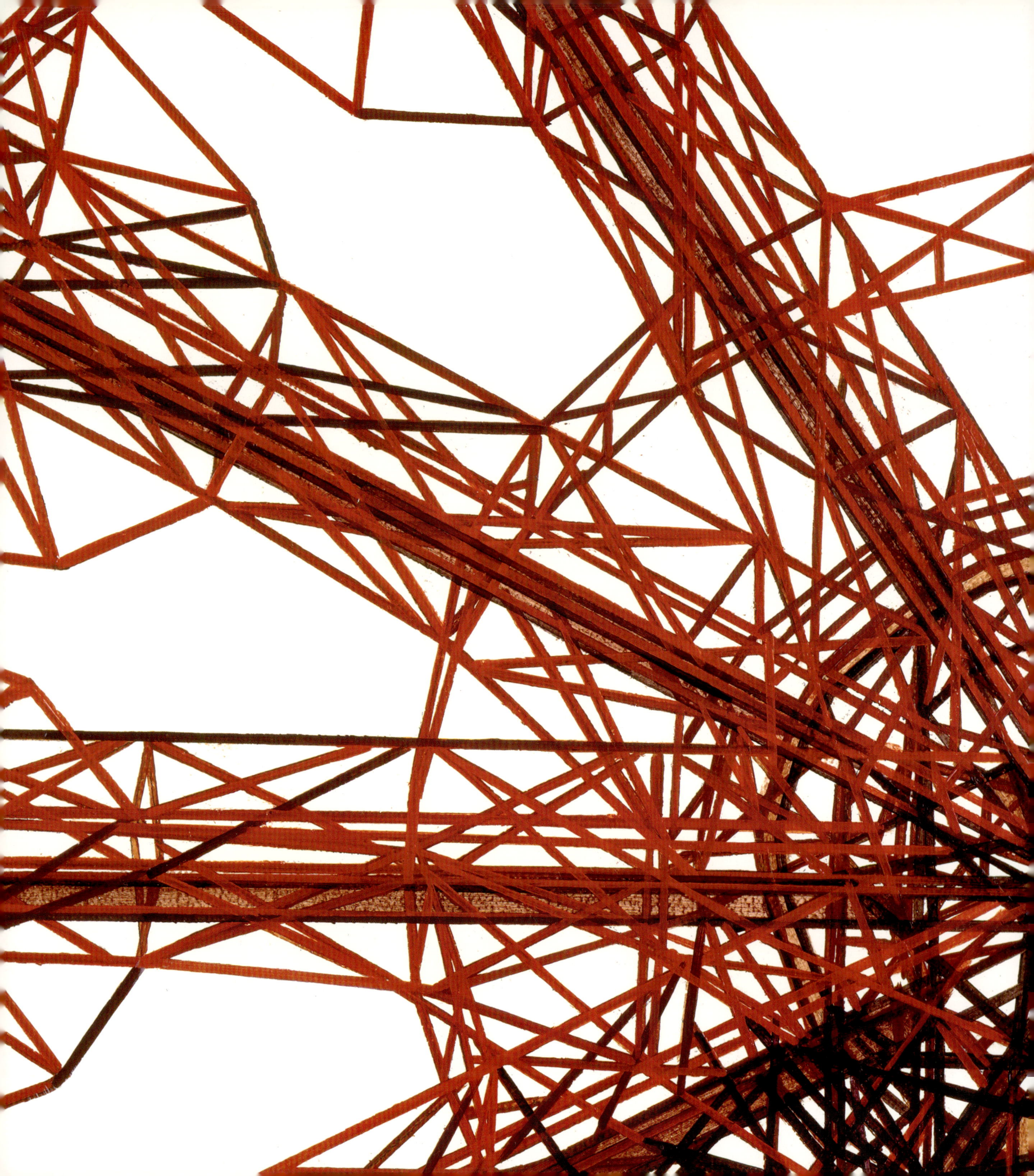

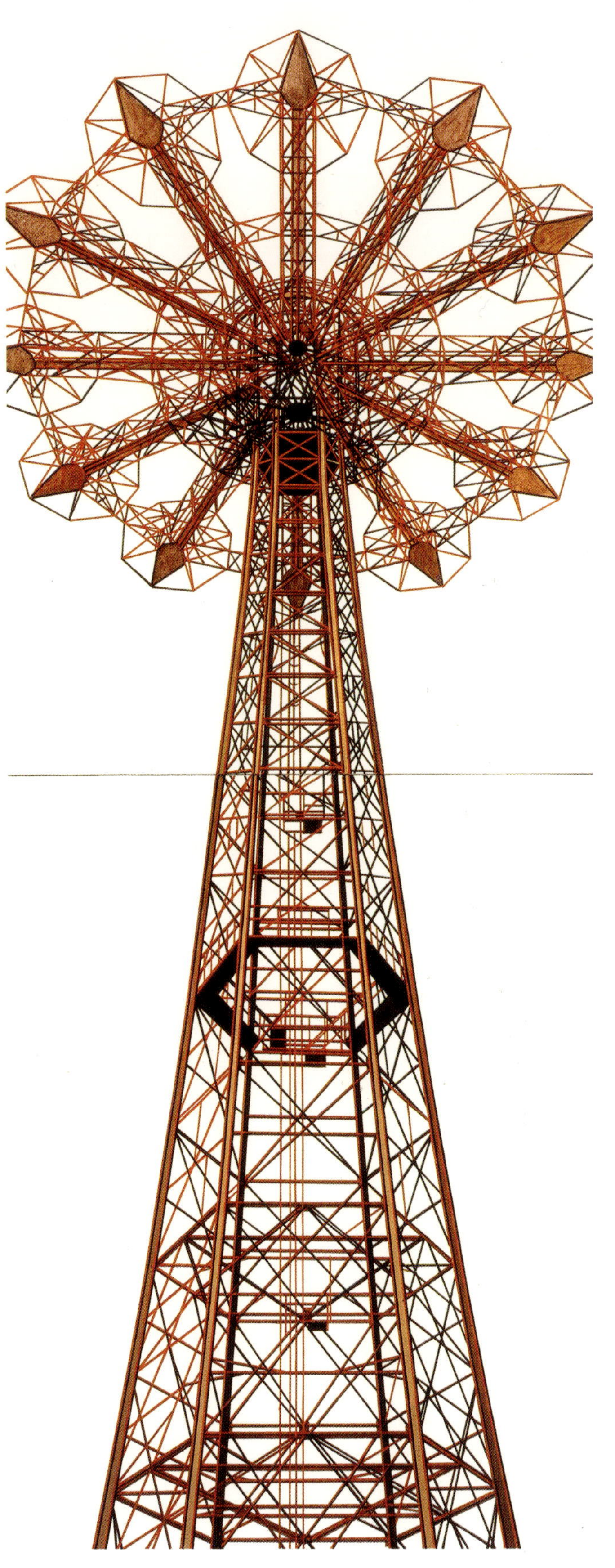

Plate 139. **Parachute Drop**, 2000, oil on canvas, 60 x 24 inches (in two panels). Collection of Adam Singer.

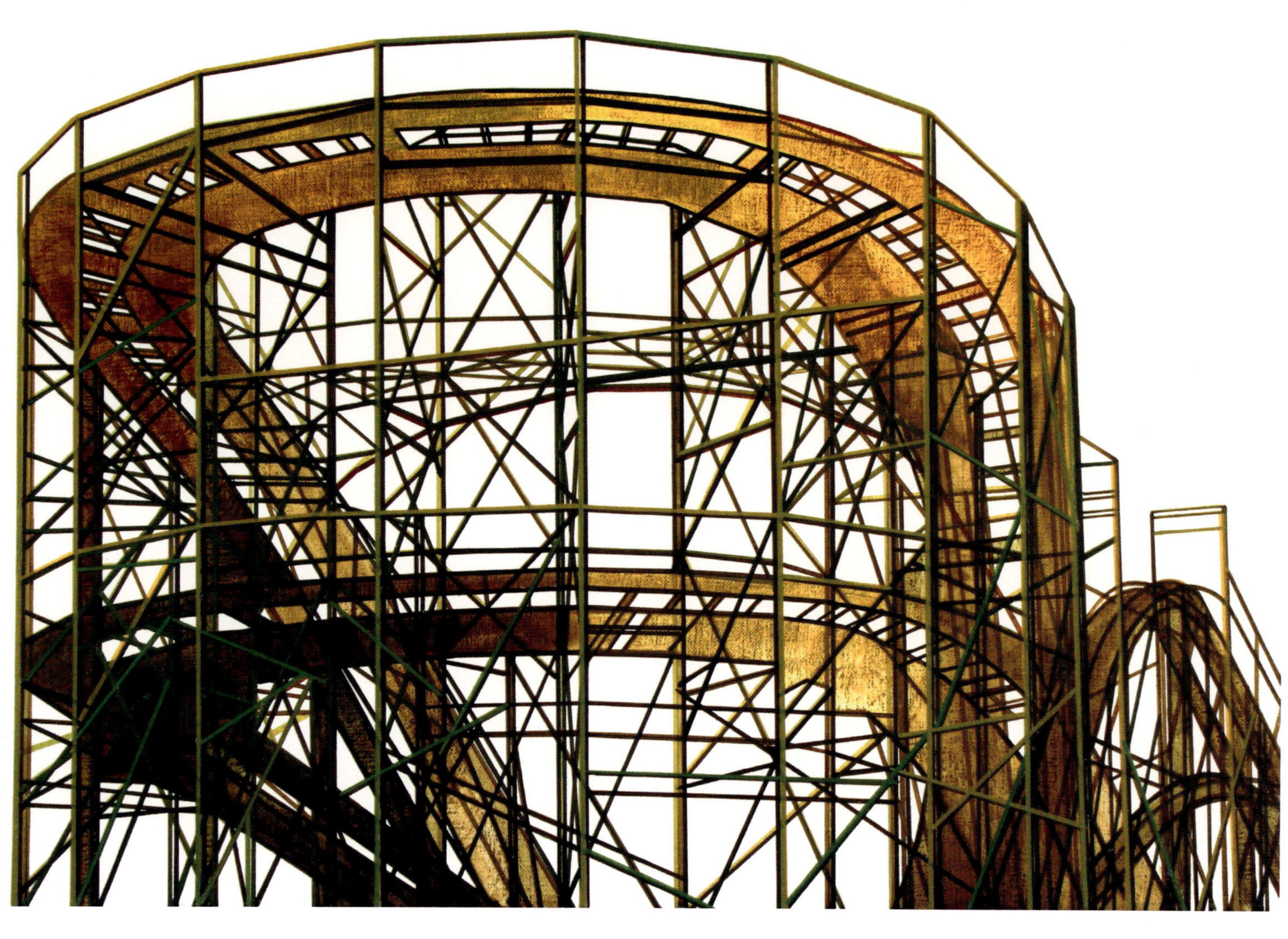

164   Plate 140. **Thunderbolt**, 2007, oil on linen, 20 x 30 inches. Collection of Chad A. Rice.

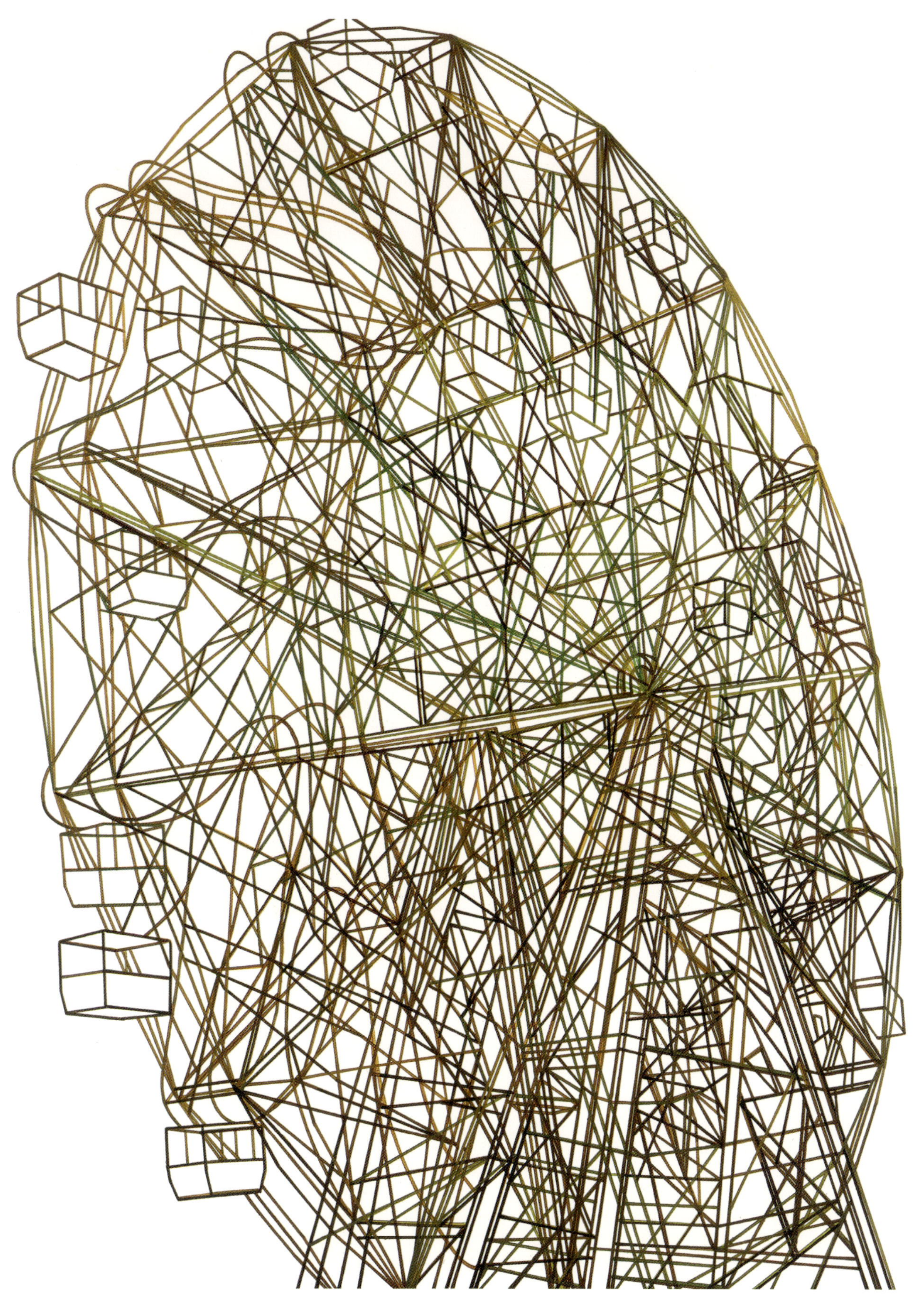

Plate 141. **Wonderwheel**, 2002, oil on canvas, 60 x 48 inches. Collection of Richard Lorenti and Andrew Flatt.

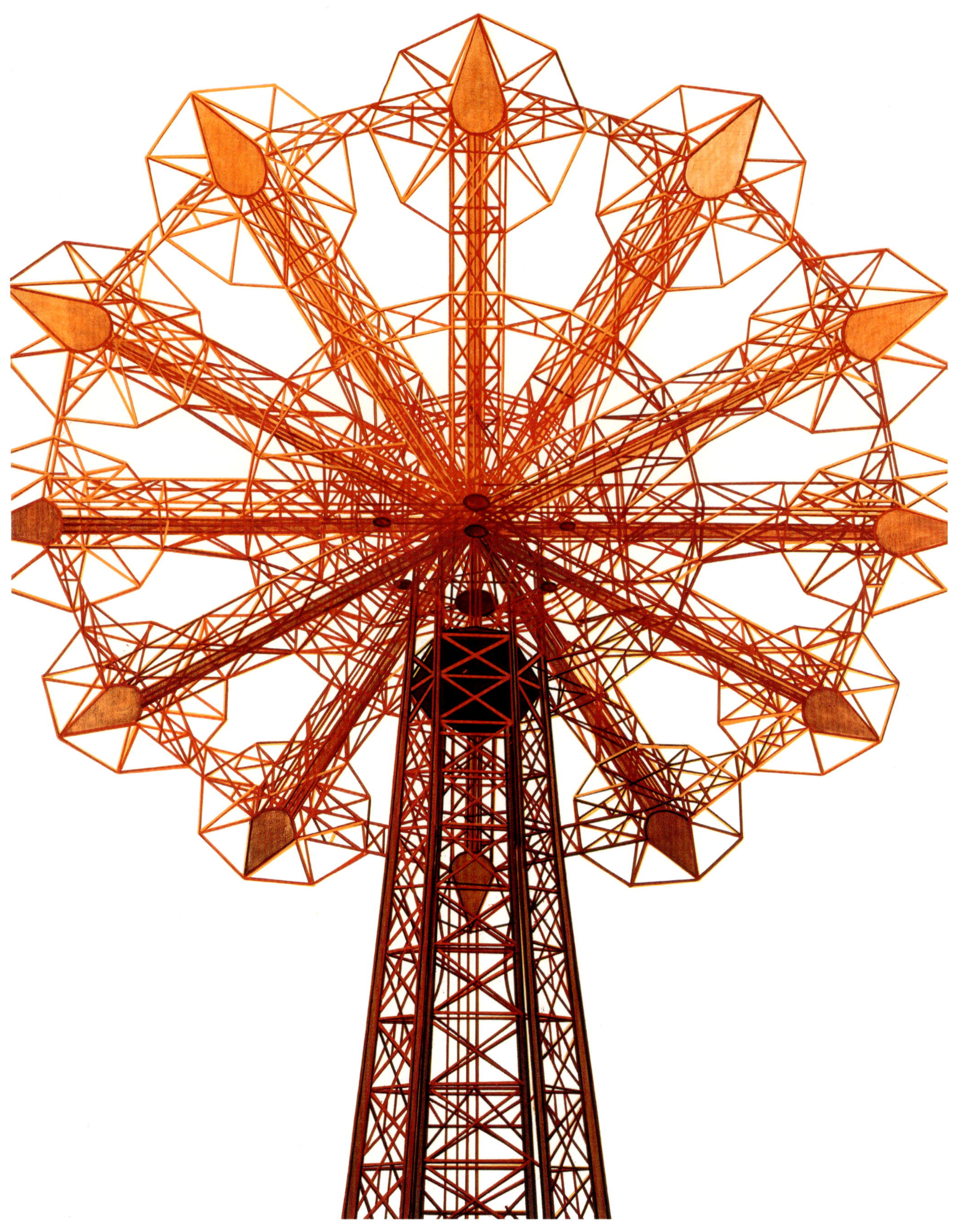

166 Plate 142. **Parachute Jump**, 2003, oil on canvas, 60 x 48 inches. Collection of Bank of America.

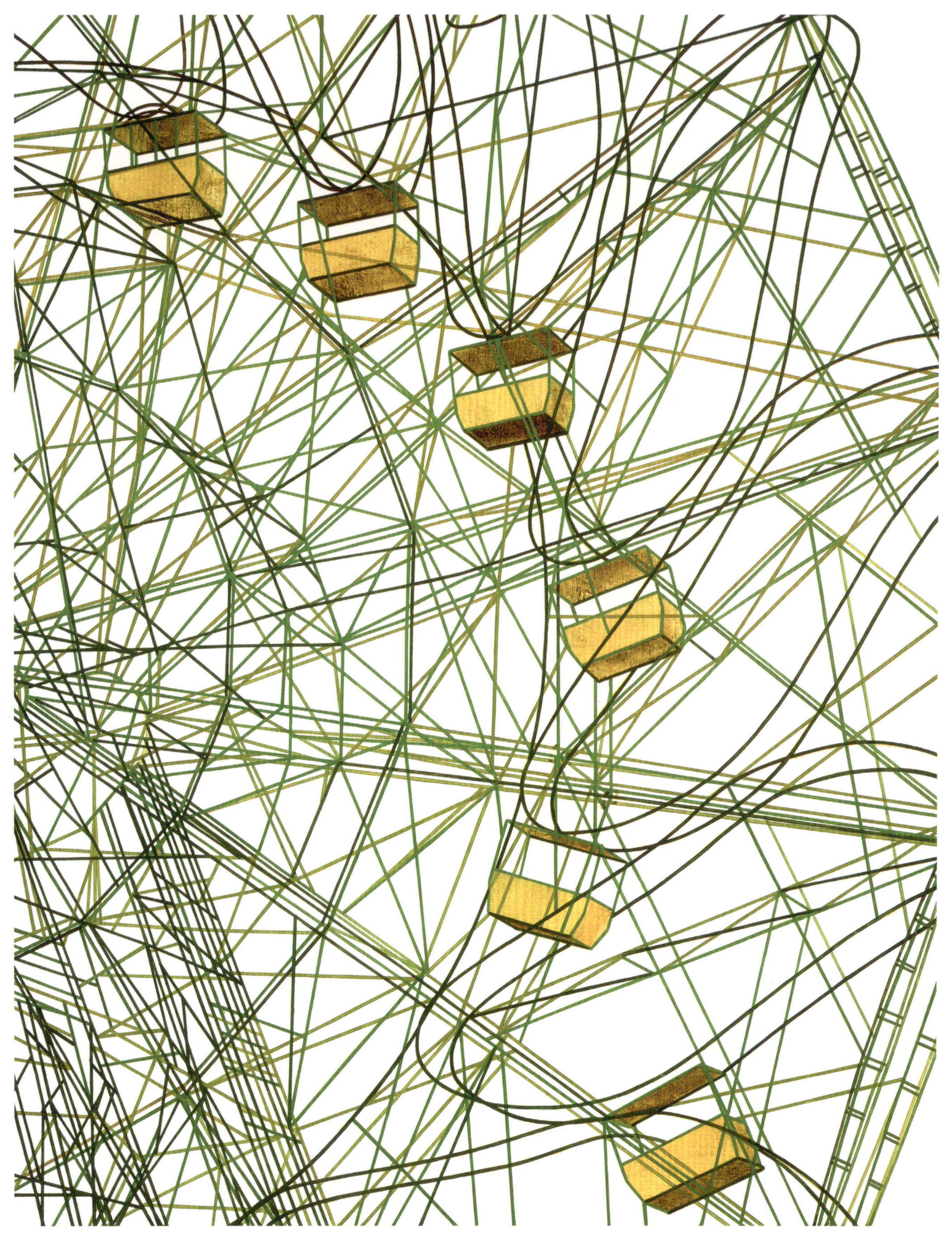

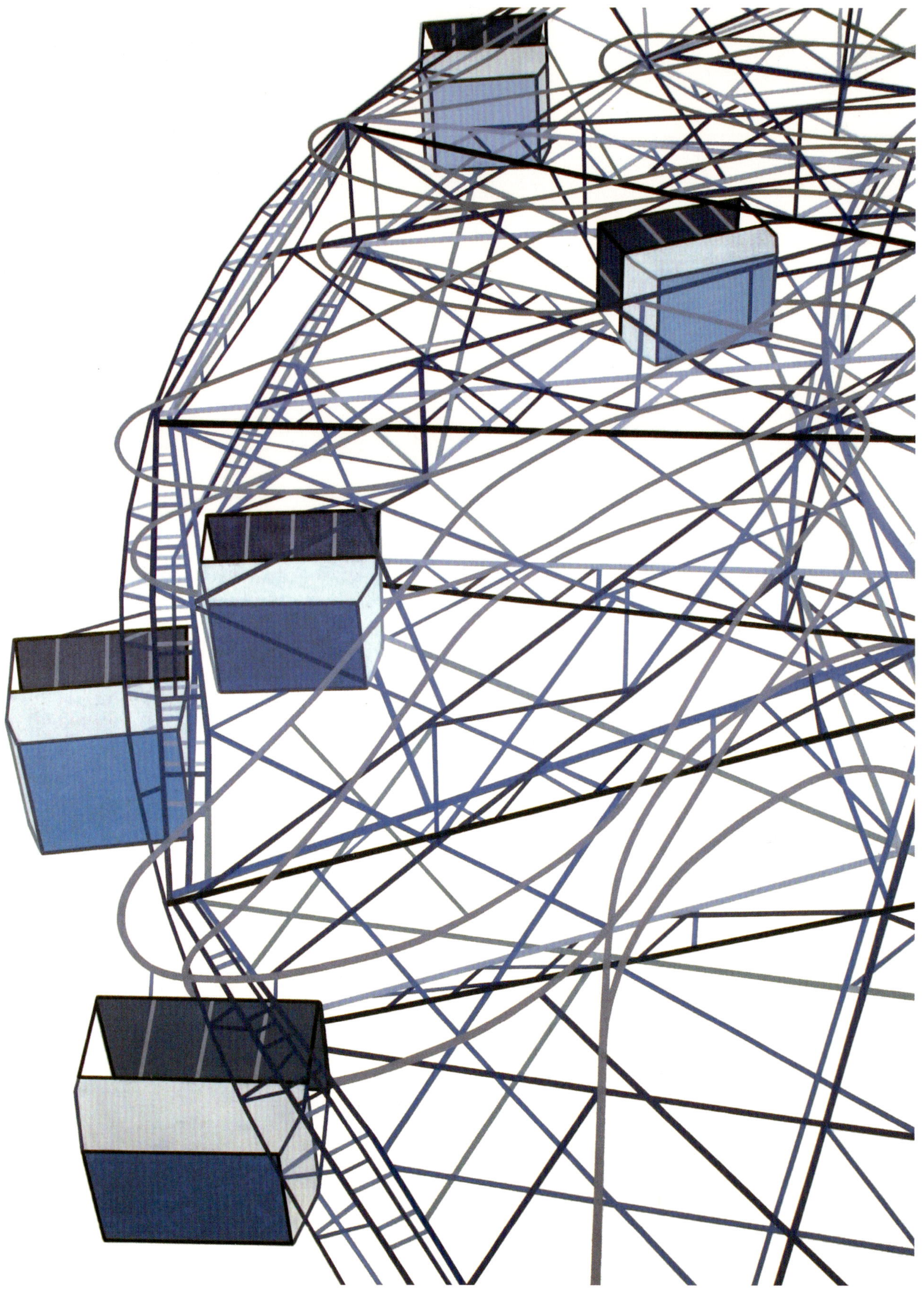

Plate 144. **Blue Wonderwheel #2**, 2007–2009, oil on canvas, 60 x 48 inches. Courtesy Marcia Wood Gallery.

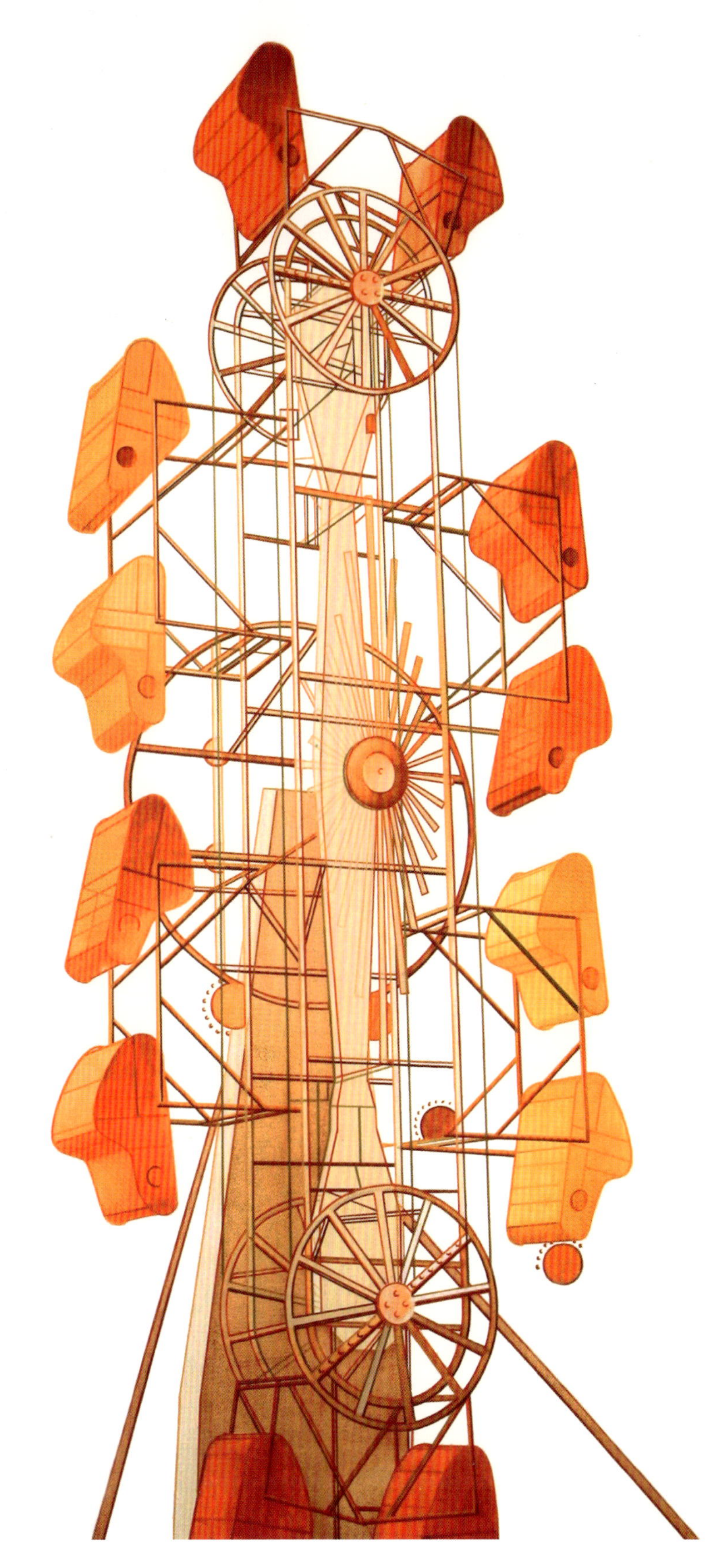

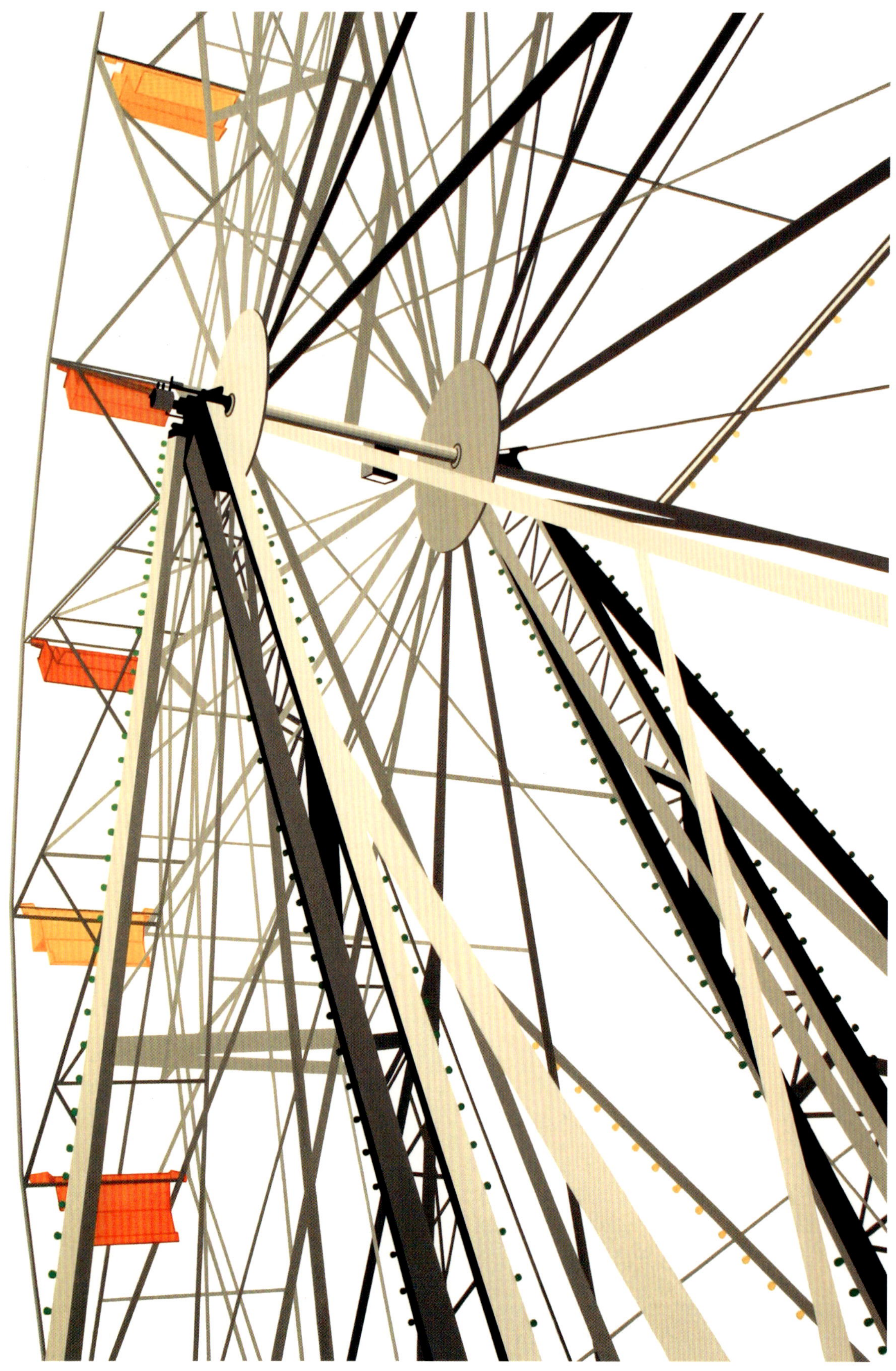

Plate 146. **State Fair,** 2007, oil on linen, 60 x 48 inches. Collection of Bradley and Jeanne Stevens.

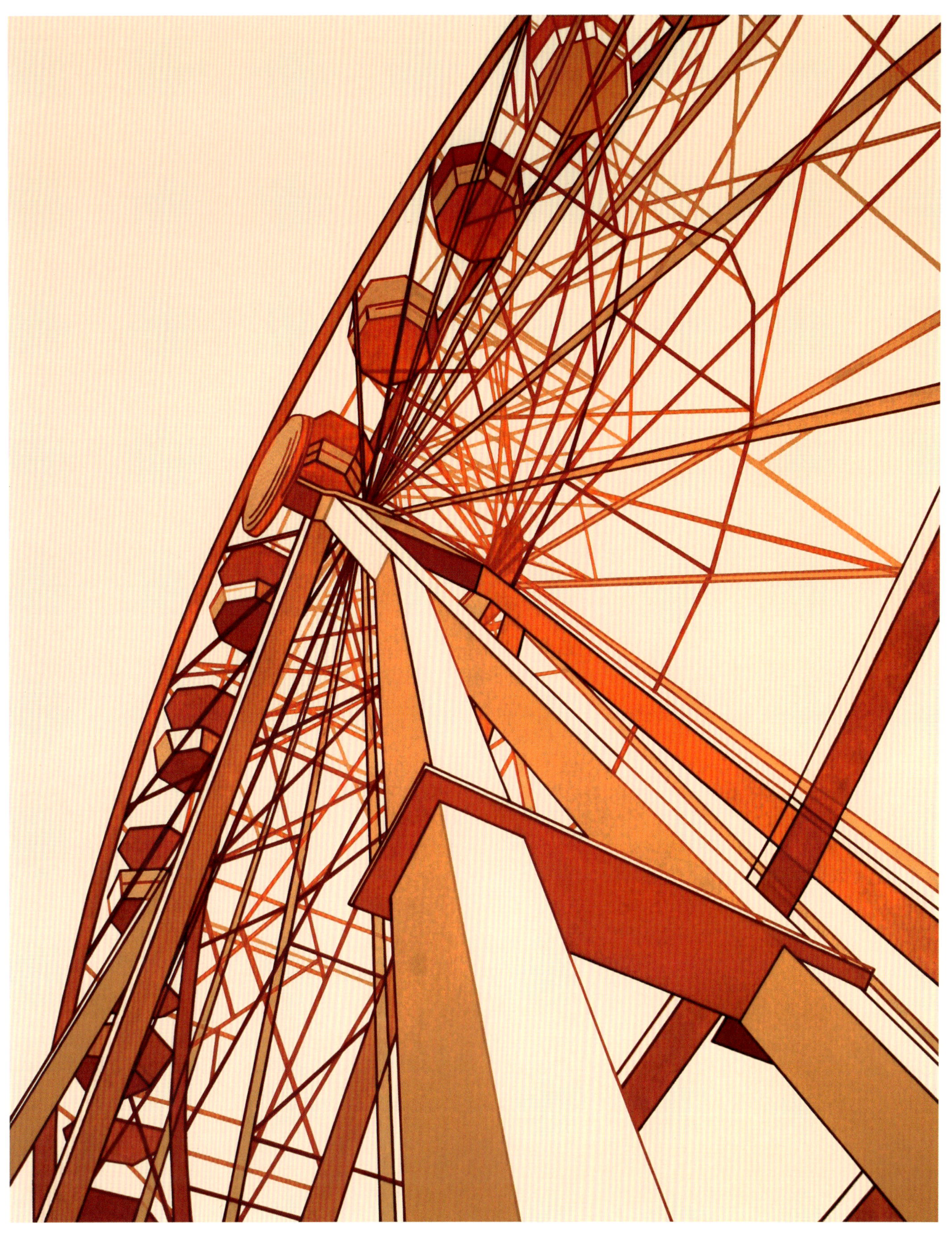

Plate 147. **Red Gondola Ride**, 2009–2010, oil on linen, 60 x 48 inches. Courtesy Marcia Wood Gallery.

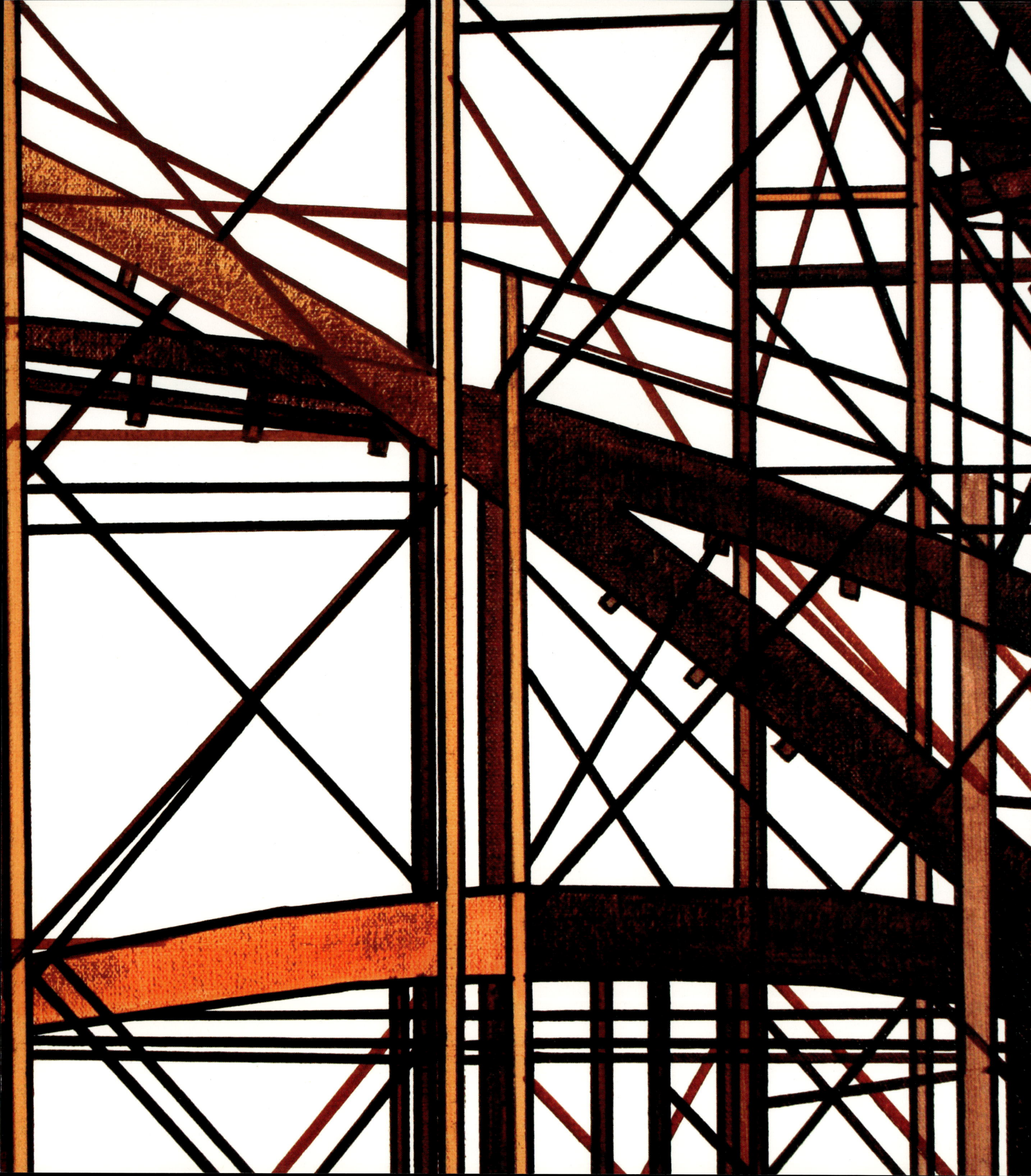

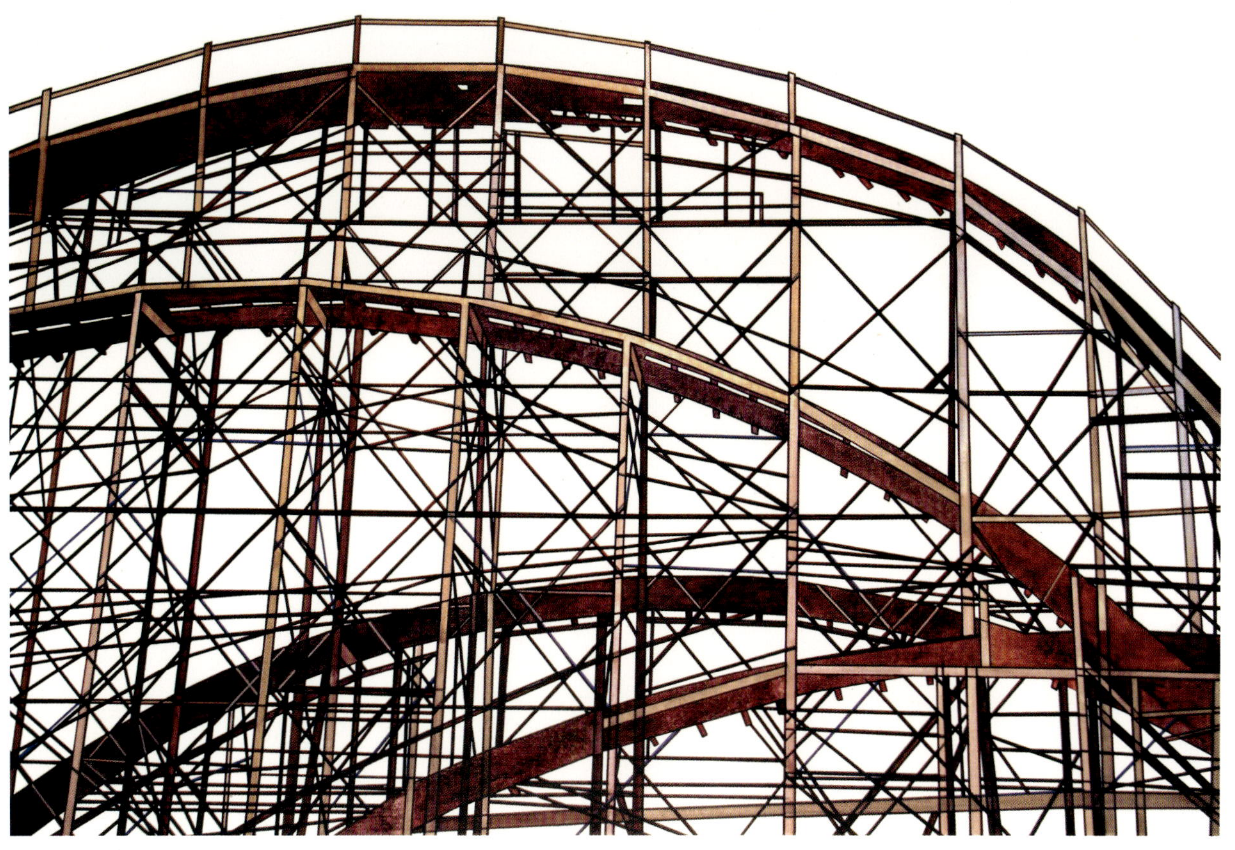

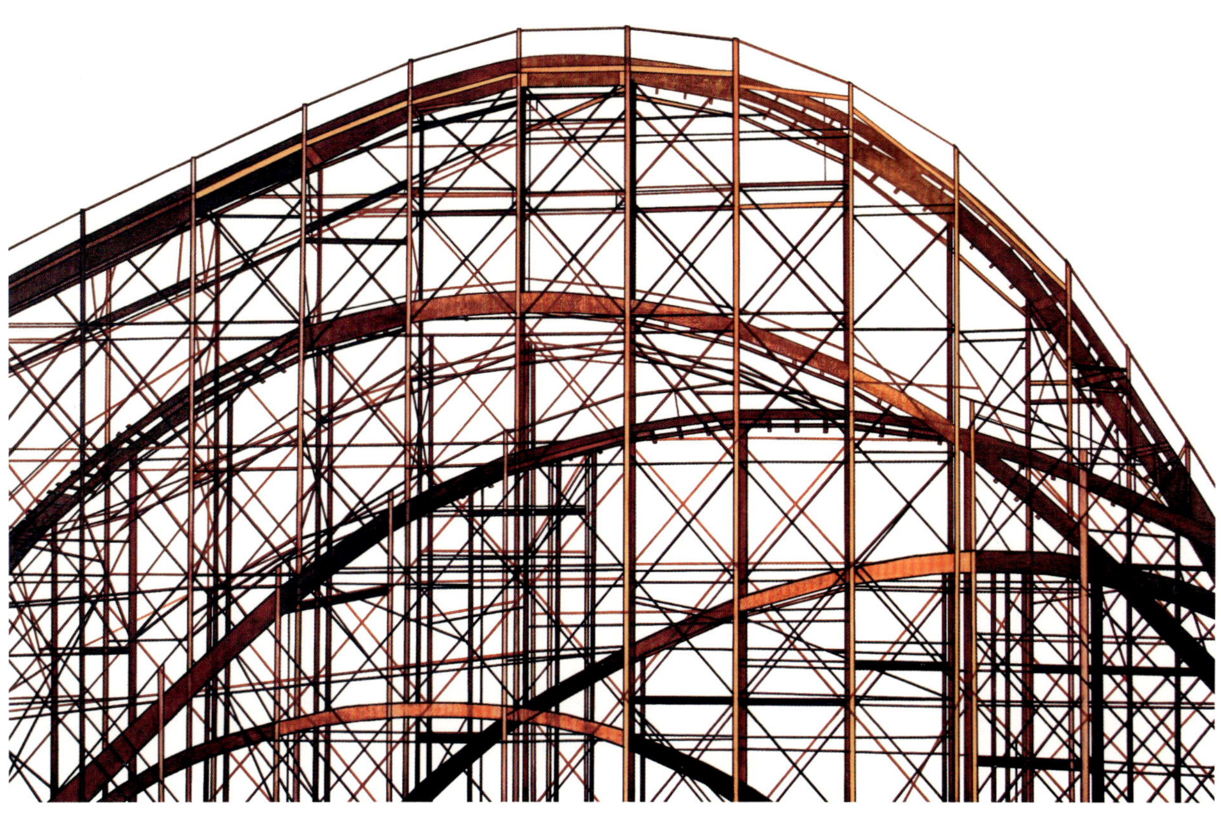

Plate 148. **Cyclone**, 2006, oil on linen, 40 x 60 inches. Collection of Mr. and Mrs. Jeremy Schwalbe.

opposite: **Cyclone II** (detail).

Plate 149. **Cyclone II**, 2007, oil on canvas, 40 x 60 inches. Collection of Martine Beamon.

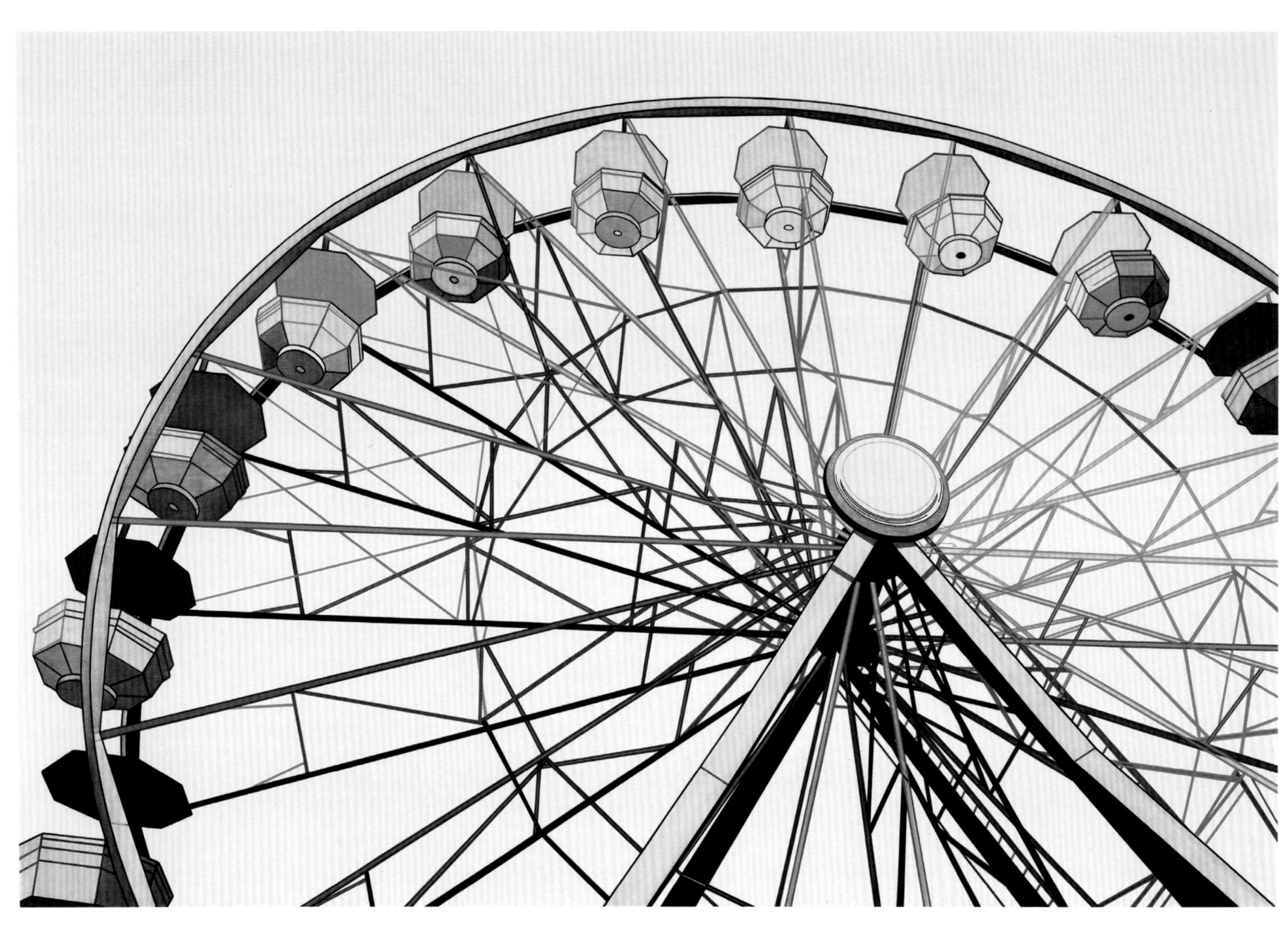

Plate 150. **Gondola Wheel**, 2008, oil on canvas, 40 x 60 inches. Courtesy Holly Johnson Gallery.

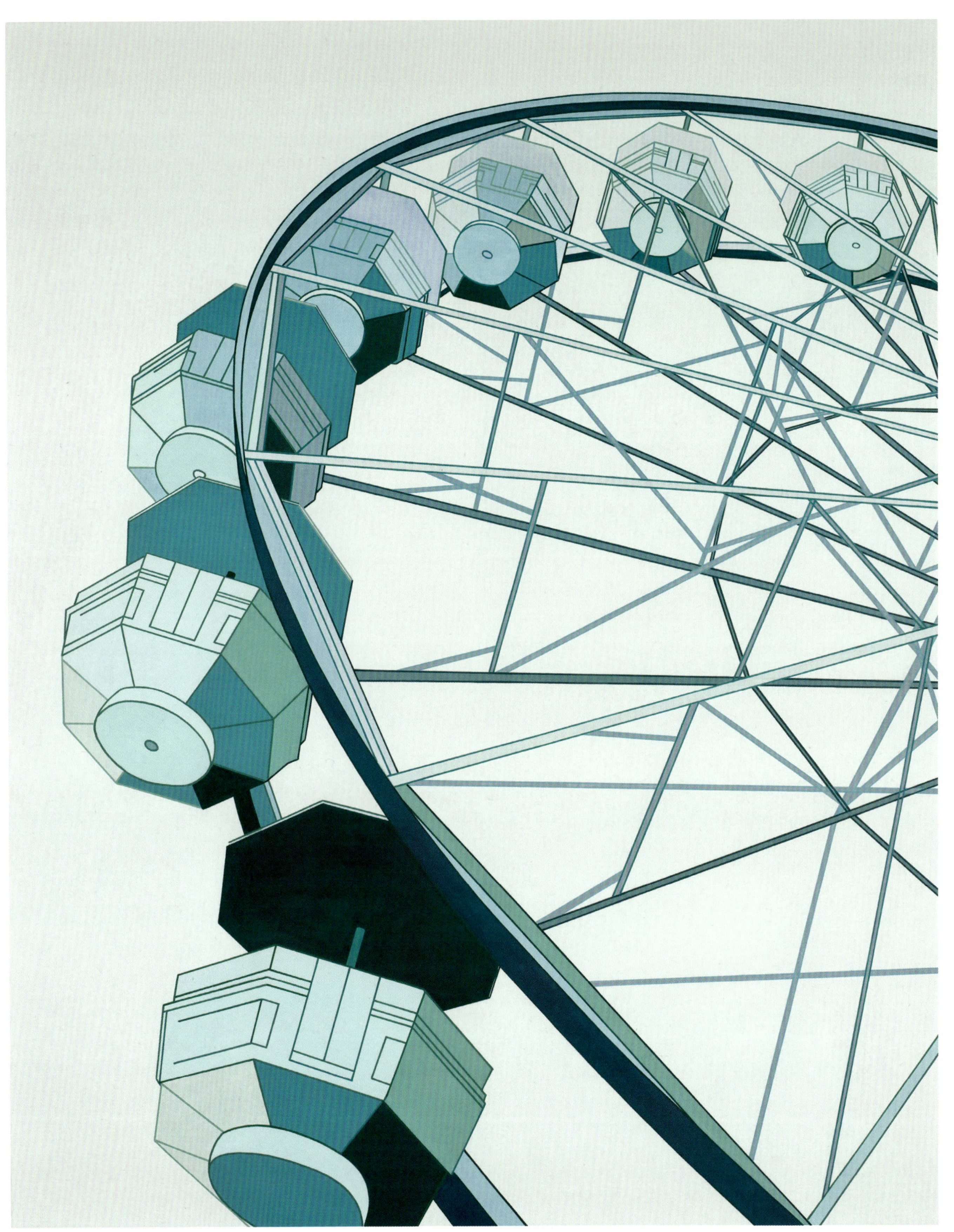

Plate 151. **Gondola Wheel II**, 2008, oil on linen, 60 x 48 inches. Courtesy Margaret Thatcher Projects.

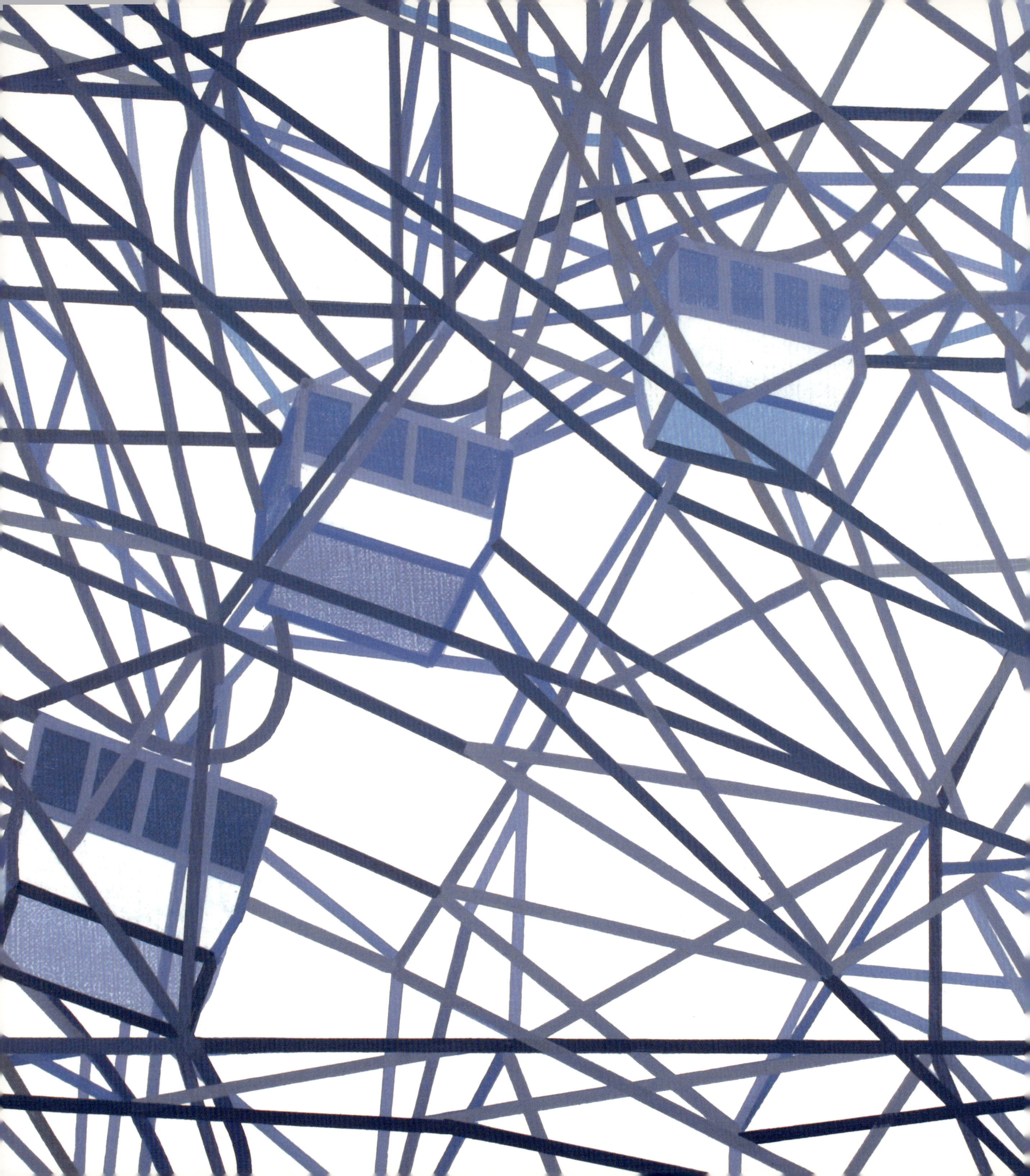

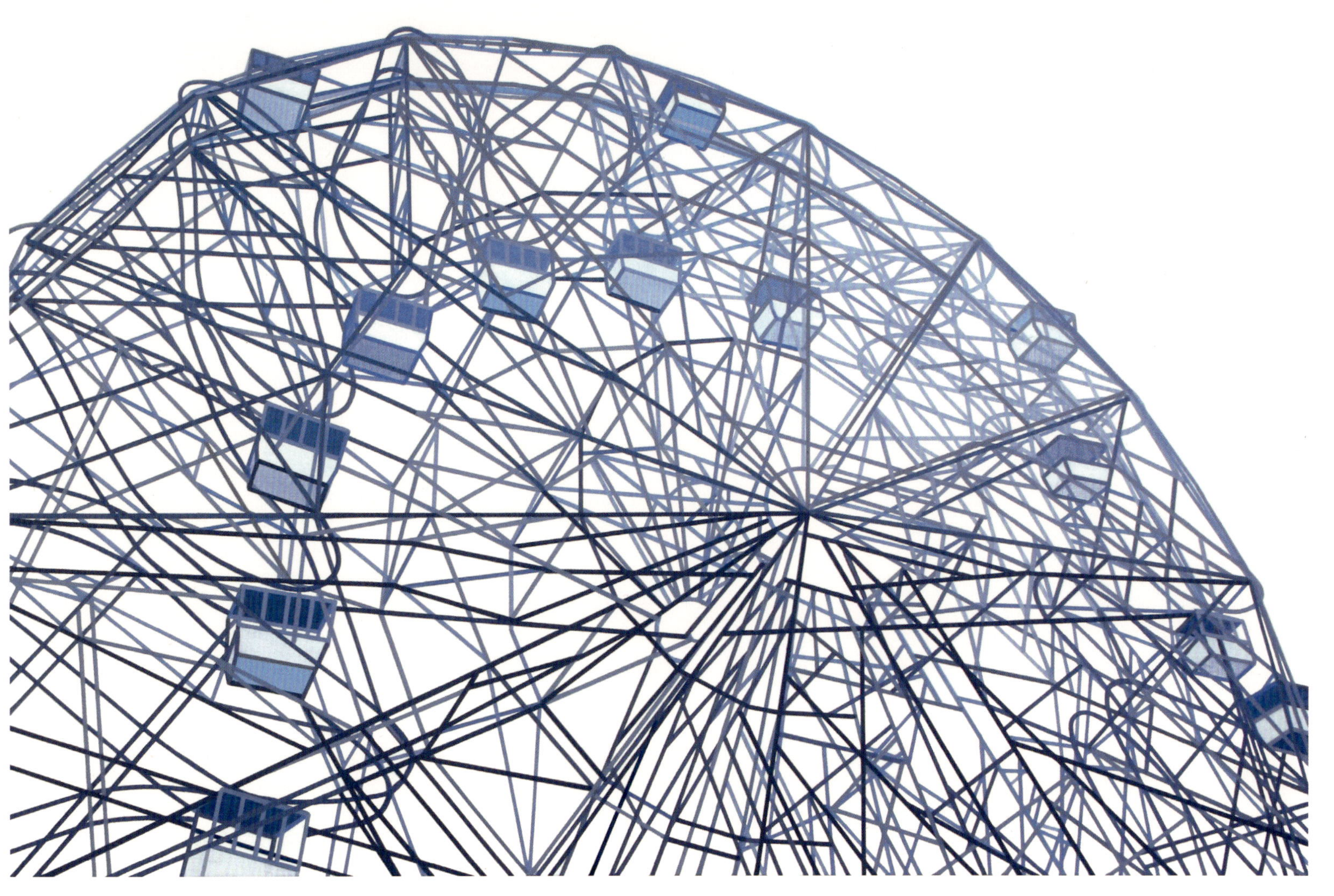

Plate 152. **The Wonderwheel Blue**, 2009, oil on linen, 30 x 45 inches. Collection of Phillip G. Bernstein and Nancy Alexander.

EVER SINCE MY FIRST ENCOUNTER with a William Steiger building, I have been fascinated by the artist's ability to give traditional realism a refreshing new look. Be it a farmhouse, a railroad signal, a roller coaster, the bend of a river running through a field, or any static or moving image on which he focuses his eye, Steiger introduces a spatial abstraction that tantalizes the viewer's perception. He defines his shapes very clearly with a cool sense of color harmony and a surreal starkness, enhancing the feeling of three-dimensional objects defying the force of gravity. There is no hint in his works as to the source of illumination and this emphasizes the purposeful absence of sentimentality. Technical skill and an obsessive precision is evident throughout Steiger's body of work, so it is not surprising that he has successfully adapted his imagery to printmaking, a medium which, to be effective, relies on these faculties.

PRINTMAKING
RICHARD SOLOMON

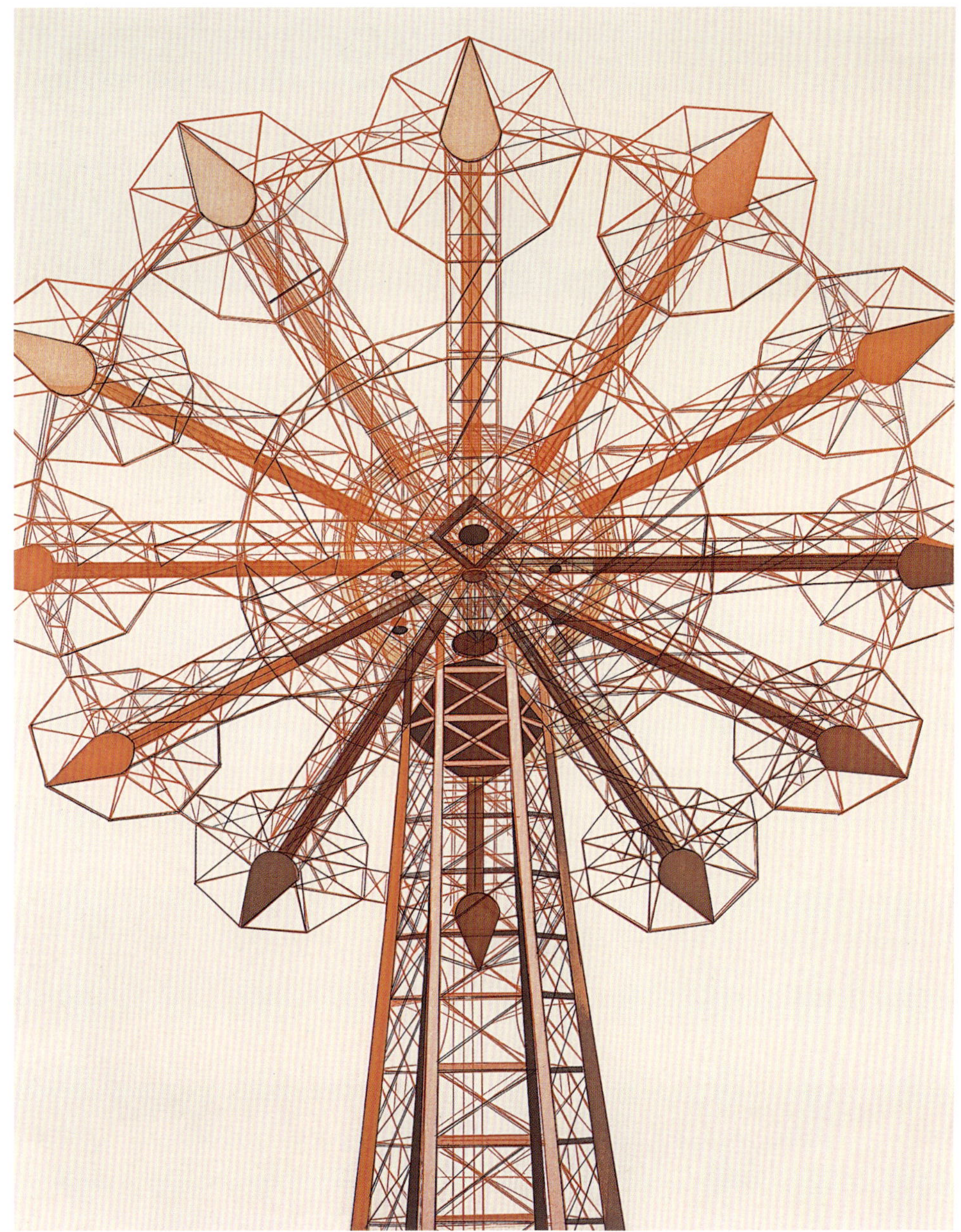

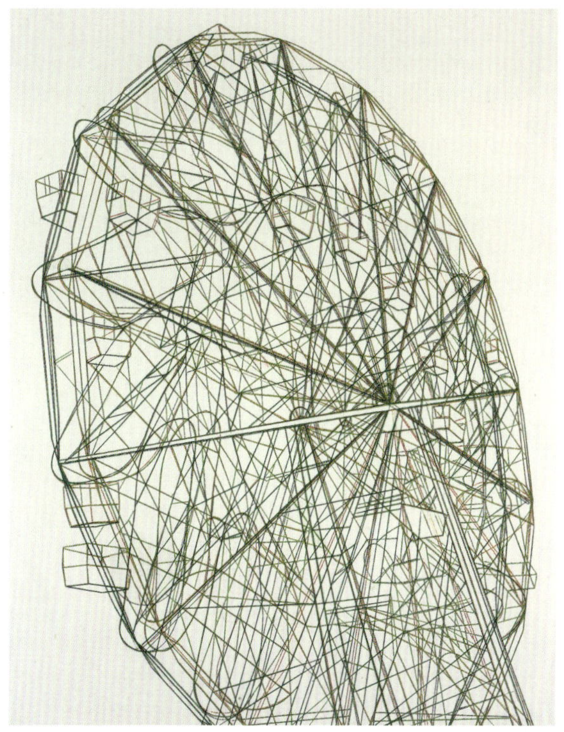

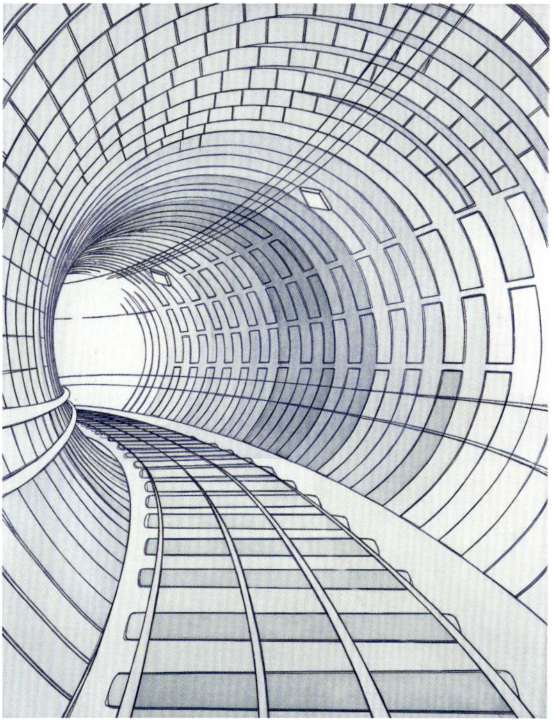

Plate 153a. **Parachute Drop**, 3-color hardground and aquatint etching, paper size: 26 ½ x 22 ½ inches. Printed 2002, Spring Press, New York City. Edition 25.

Plate 153b. **Wonderwheel** (as above).

Plate 153c. **Tunnel** (as above).

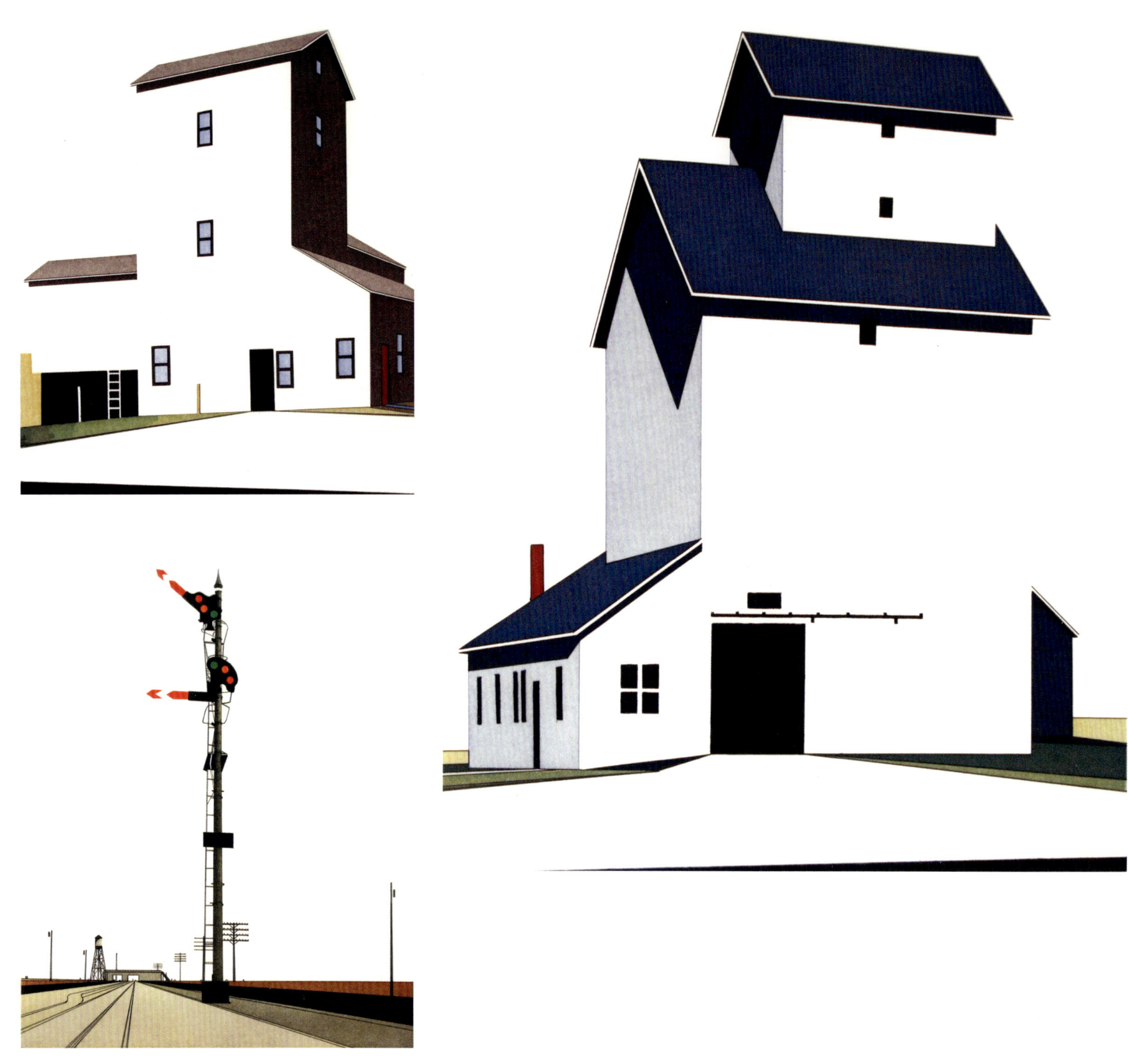

Plate 154a. **Elevator I**, 7-color hardground and aquatint etching, paper size: 21 ½ x 18 ½ inches.
Printed 2003, Spring Press, New York City. Edition 30.

Plate 154b. **Elevator II** (as above).

Plate 154c. **Semaphore** (as above).

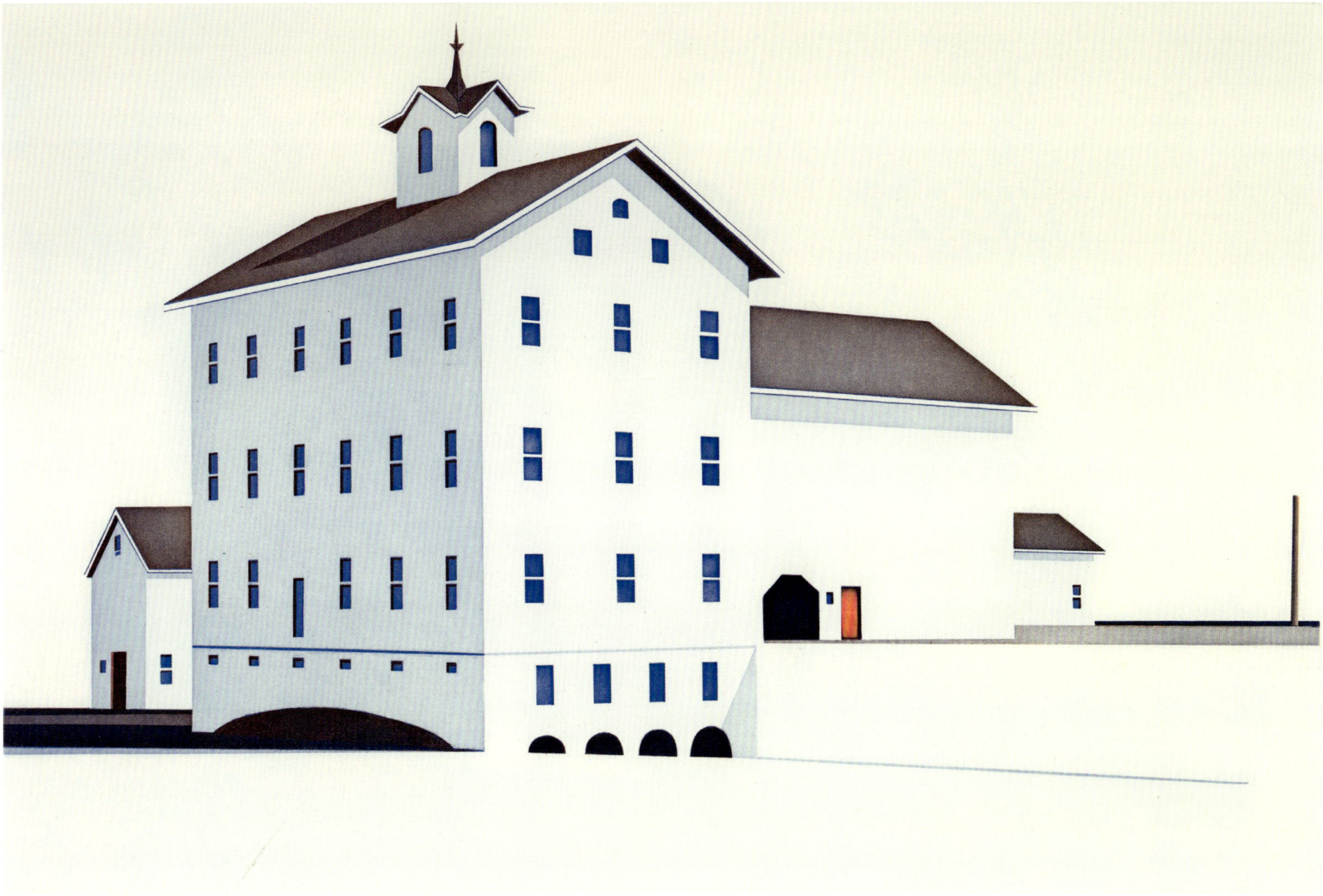

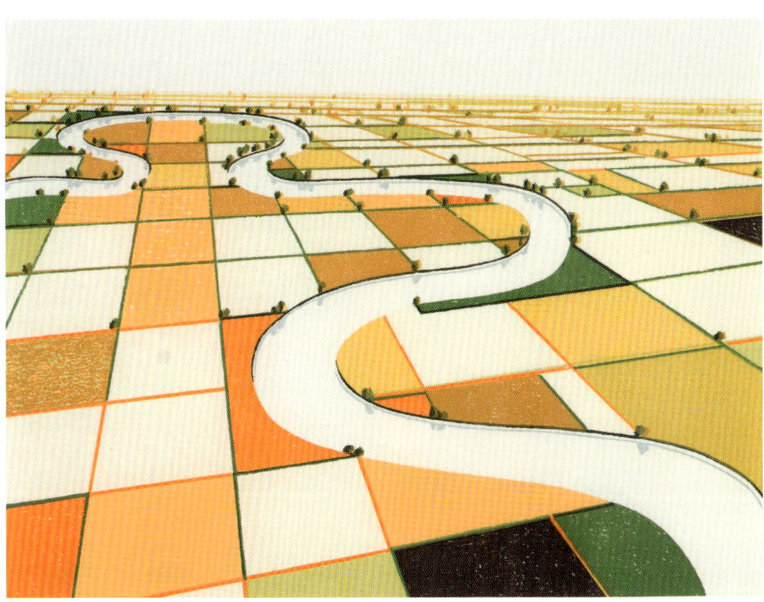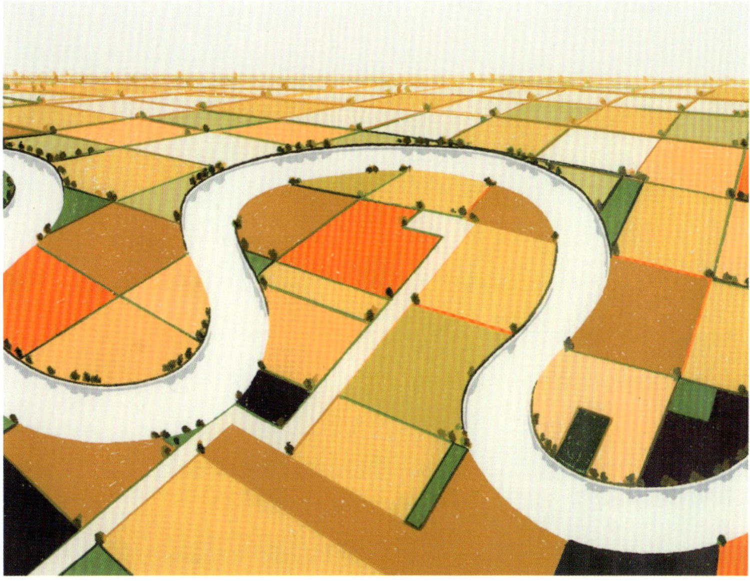

Plate 155. **The Mill**, 2-color softground and aquatint etching, paper size: 20 x 27 inches. Printed 2004, Pace Editions, New York City. Edition 30.

Plate 156a. **Curves**, 9-color relief print, paper size: 18 x 24 inches. Printed 2006, Pace Editions, New York City. Edition 35.

Plate 156b. **Winding River** (as above).

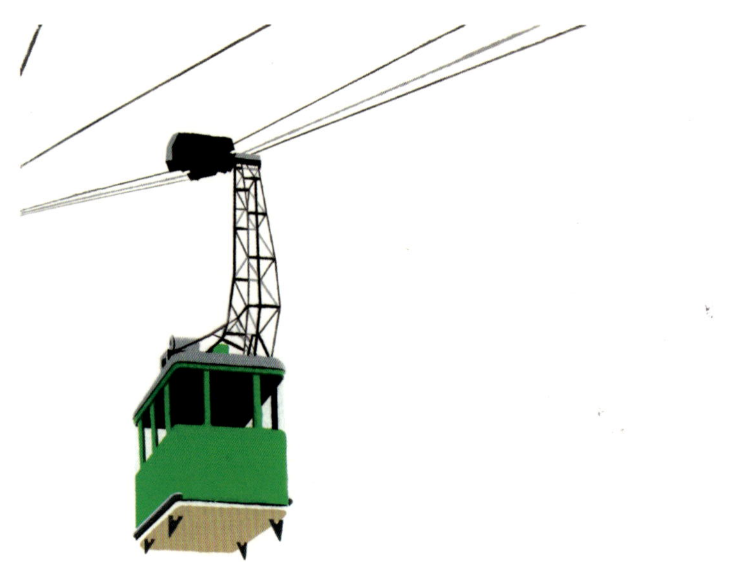

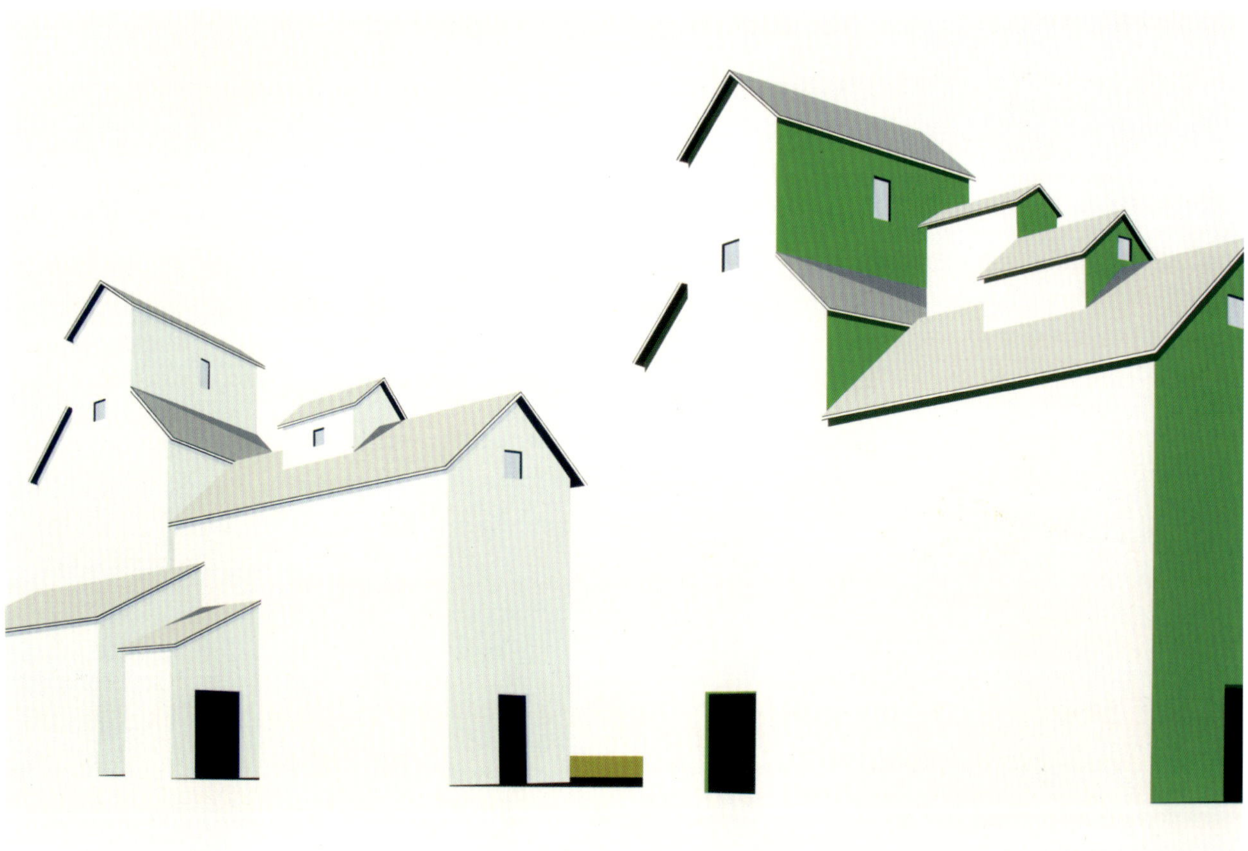

Plate 157. **Aerial Tramway-Green**, 7-color stenciled linen pulp paint on cotton base sheet, paper size: 20 x 16 inches. Printed 2008, Dieu Donné, New York City. Edition 20.

Plate 158. **Wheat Pool**, 14-color screen print, paper size: 28 x 40 inches. Printed 2008, Pace Editions, New York City. Edition 50.

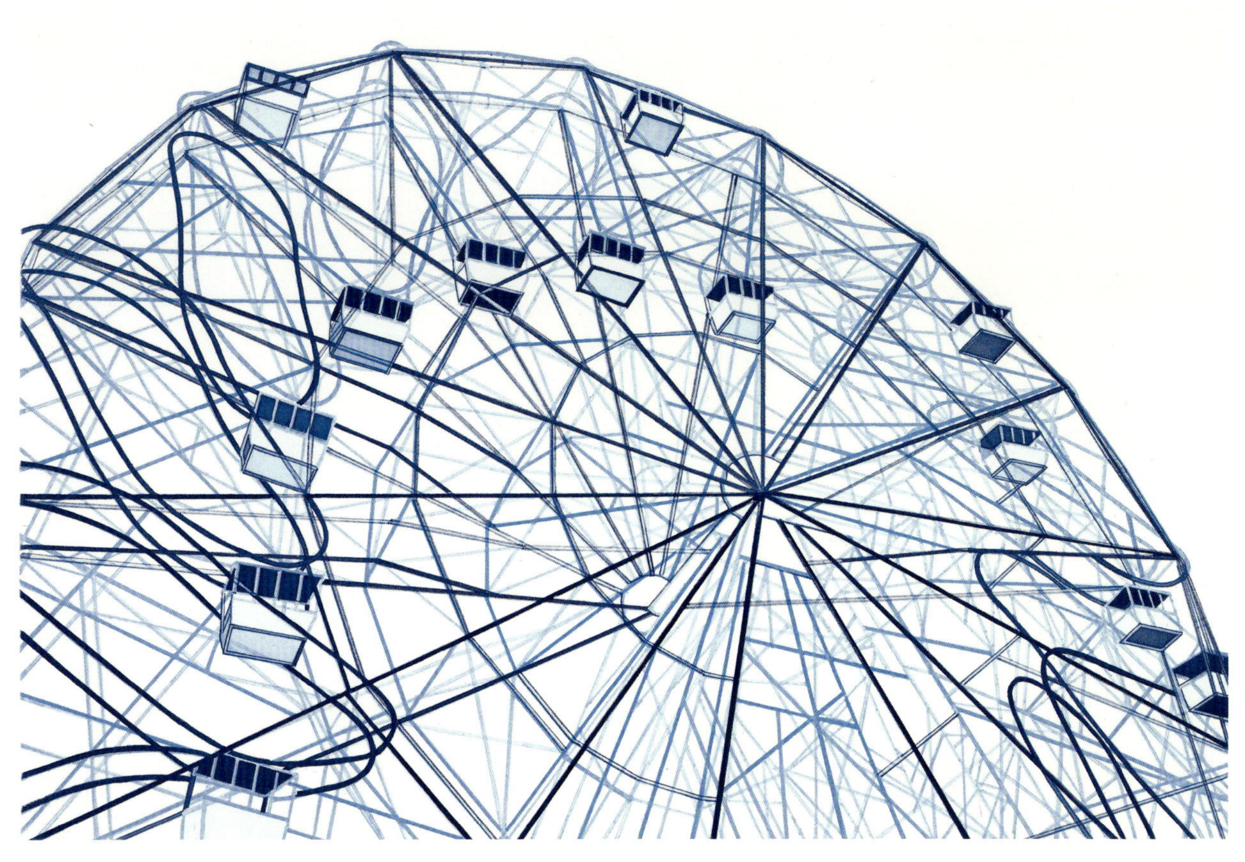

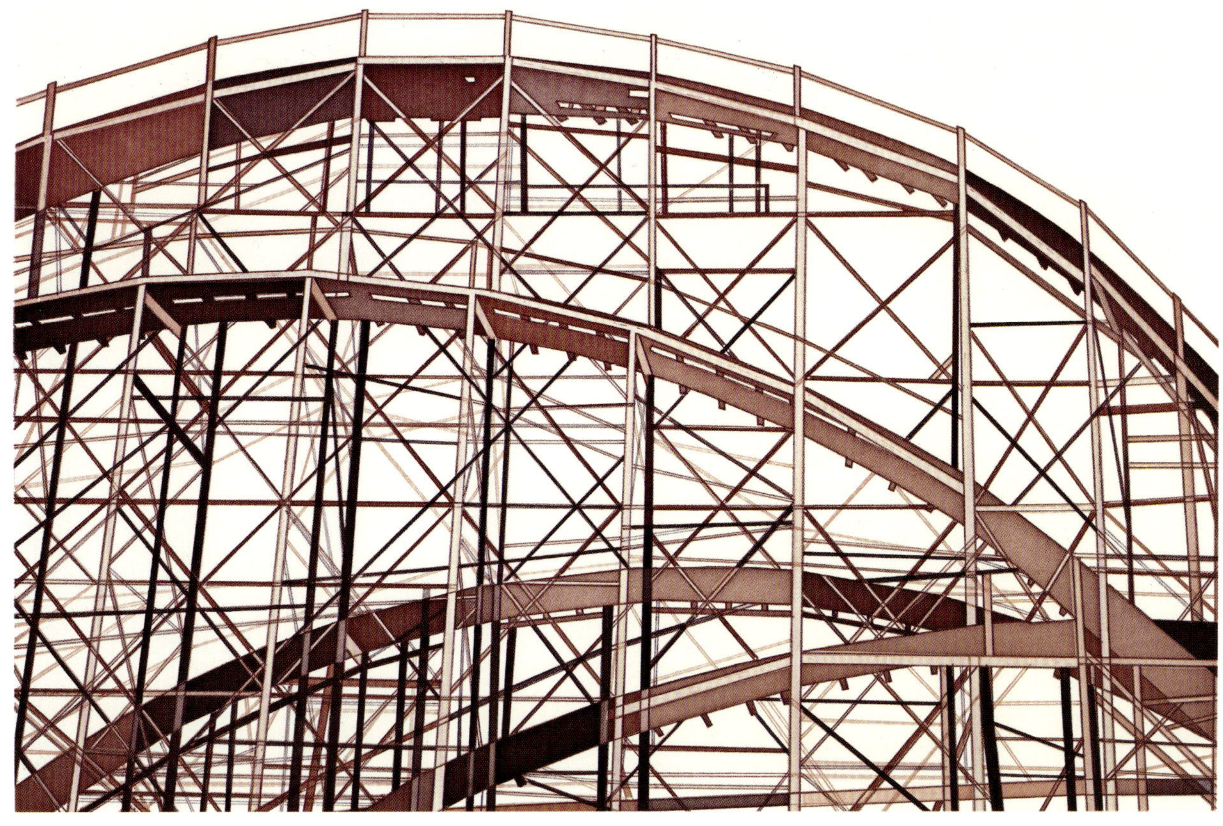

Plate 159a. **Blue Wonderwheel**, 2-color softground and aquatint etching, paper size: 21 ½ x 29 inches. Printed 2009, Pace Editions, New York City. Edition 30.

Plate 159b. **Cyclone** (as above).

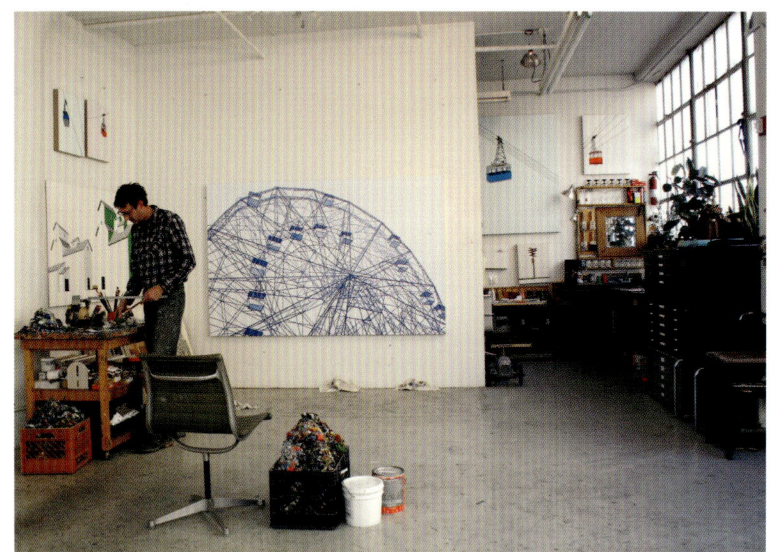 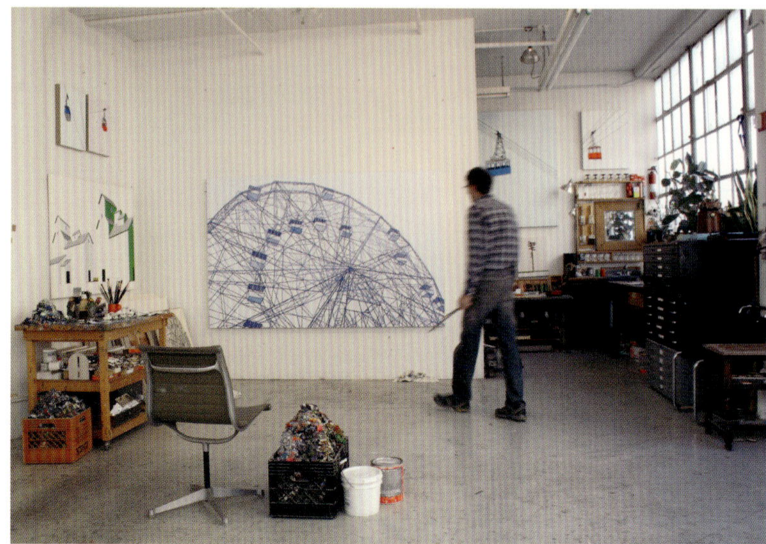

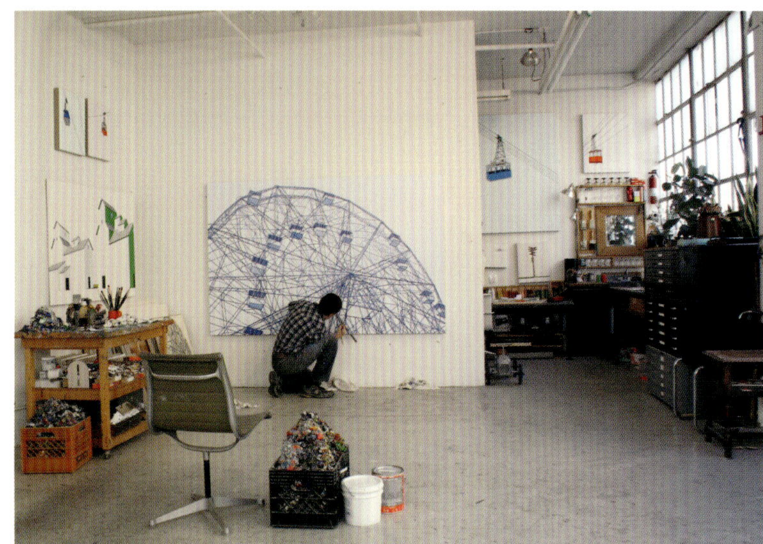 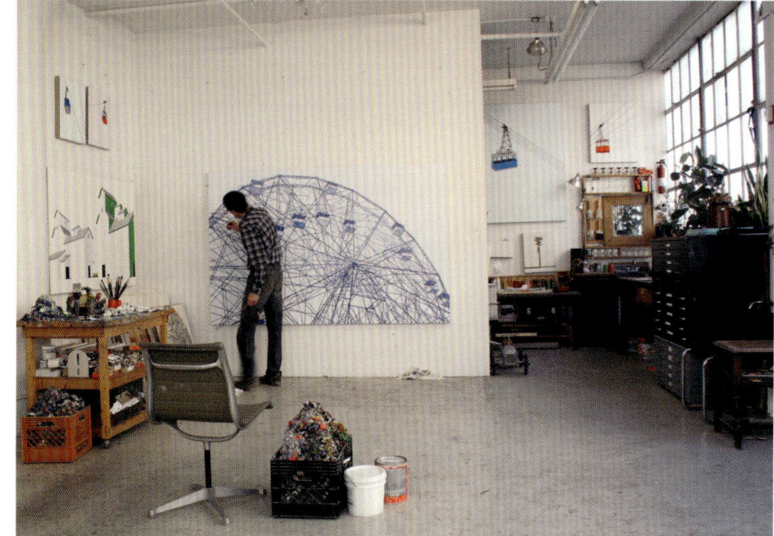

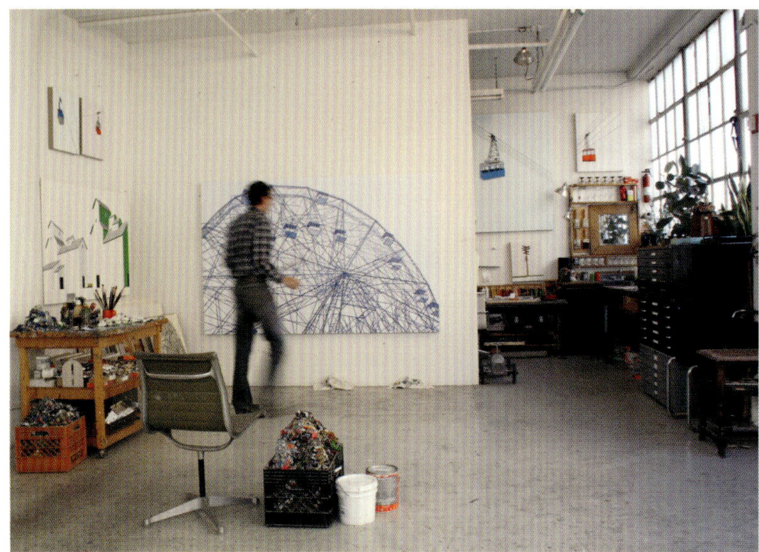 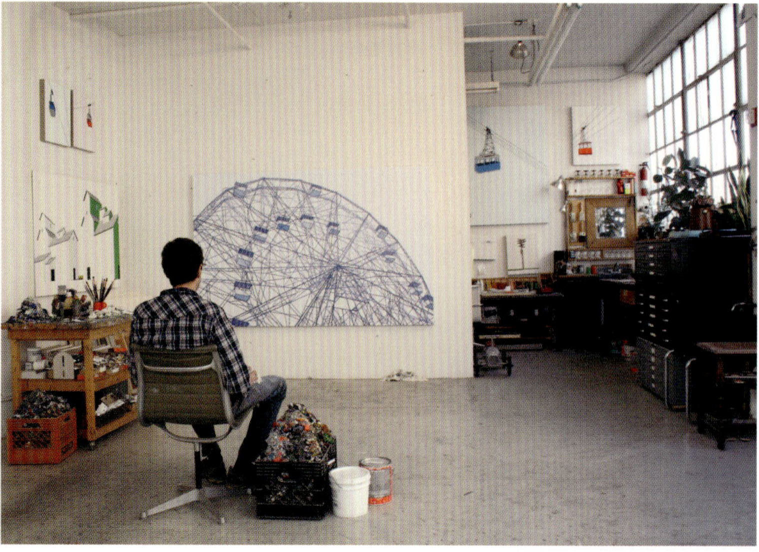

Figure 26. **Studio**, 508 West 26th Street, New York City, 2010. Photography: Foster Witt.

ACKNOWLEDGMENTS

THIS BOOK WOULD NOT HAVE BEEN POSSIBLE without the time and talent devoted by a diverse group of writers, particularly the insightful essays of Richard Vine (*Art in America*) and Christopher Gaillard (Gurr-Johns International). The chapters were thoughtfully introduced by the following people, listed chronologically: Turan Duda (Duda/Paine Architects), Bettina Prentice (Bettina Prentice Communications), Allison Peters Quinn (Hyde Park Art Center), Melissa Milgrom (journalist, author), Lisa Hatchadoorian (Nicolaysen Art Museum), Lowell Pettit (Pettit Art Partners), Maura Robinson (artist), Bruce W. Ferguson (independent curator and critic), Cesar Pelli and Fred Clarke (Pelli Clarke Pelli Architects), and Richard Solomon (Pace Prints). These individuals contributed unique perspectives on the work and their thoughts lent eloquent context to each theme.

The following people provided valuable assistance along the way: Kenise Barnes, Roy Boyd, Bill Butler, Craig Copeland, Eric Janssen, Holly Johnson, Natalie Tackett, Margaret Thatcher, Foster Witt, Carolyn Wood, Marcia Wood, and Ihn Yang. The team at Pace Prints is exceptional and they deserve many thanks for their excellent collaborative work. Molly Steiger's encouragement has been essential to this project from the beginning. Special thanks for the guidance of Leslie Pell van Breen at Hudson Hills Press and to designer David Skolkin.

This book is dedicated to Eleanor G. Steiger.

WILLIAM STEIGER
DECEMBER 2010

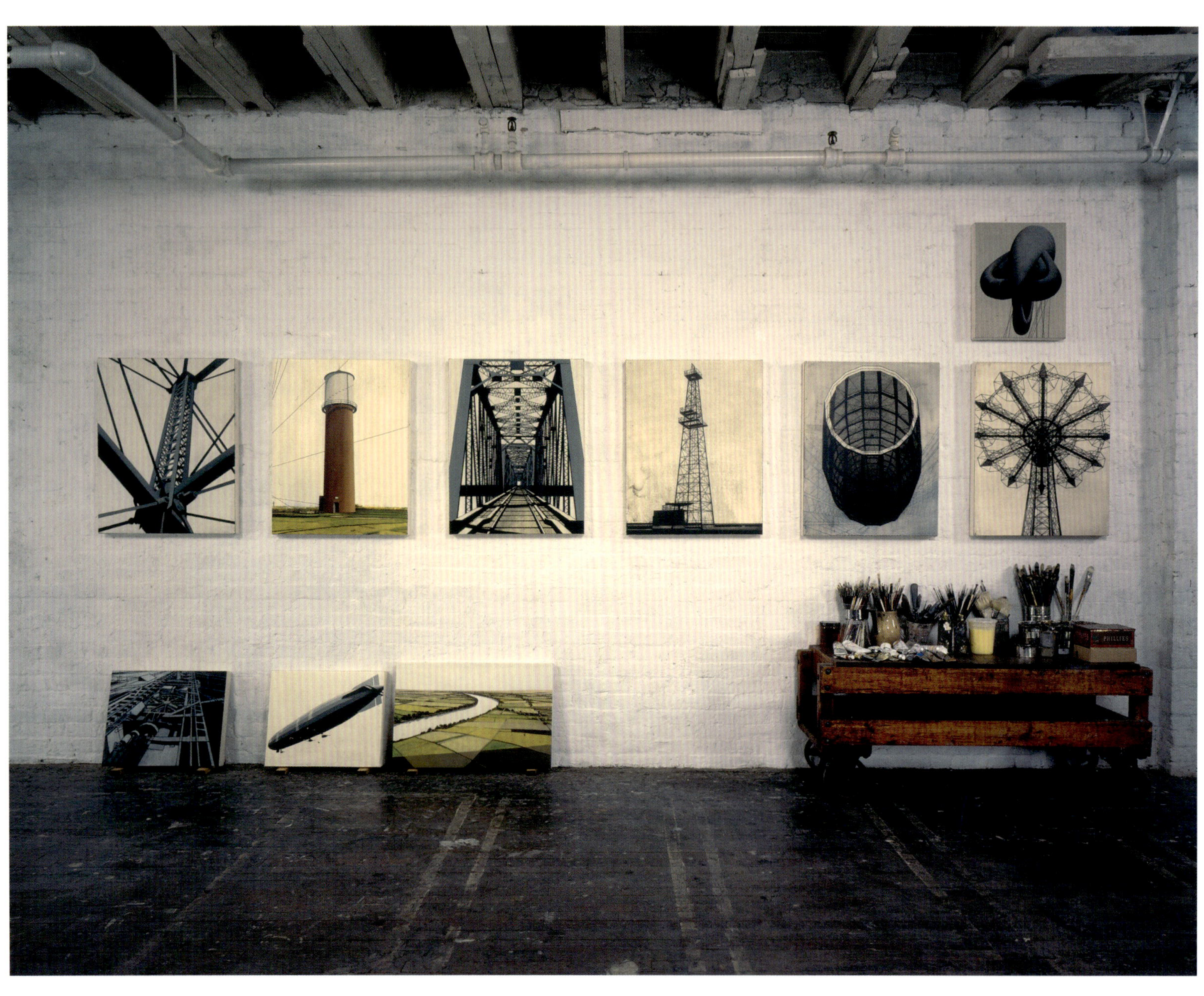

  Figure 27. **Studio**, 57 Front Street, Brooklyn, New York, 1996.

CHRONOLOGY

1962   Born August 26 in Summit, NJ. Fourth child of Leonard and Eleanor Steiger.

1968   Steiger family moves to Chicago, IL, area

1978   Steiger family moves to San Francisco Bay Area

1986   BA in Art and Fifth-Year Certificate in Art, University of California at Santa Cruz, Santa Cruz, CA. Studies with Patrick Aherne, Hardy Hanson, Robert Poplack, Terry St. John, and Don Weygandt

1989   MFA in Art, Yale University, New Haven, CT. Studies with artists William Bailey, Frances Barth, Jake Berthot, and Mel Bochner, architect Frank Gehry, and filmmaker Michael Roemer

1990   Moves to New York, NY. Locates studio space in Dumbo area of Brooklyn, NY

1990   Begins exhibiting with Condeso Lawler Gallery, New York, NY

1991   Begins exhibiting with Hackett Freedman Gallery, San Francisco, CA

1996   Relocates studio to Chelsea area of New York, NY

1998   Begins exhibiting with Marcia Wood Gallery, Atlanta, GA

1999   Begins exhibiting with Margaret Thatcher Projects, New York, NY

2004   Begins working with Pace Editions

2006   Marries Molly Longnecker in New York City, November 18

2008   Birth of son, August William, May 19

2011   Major monograph *William Steiger: Transport* published by Hudson Hills Press

SOLO EXHIBITIONS

2011   Roy Boyd Gallery, *Rolling Stock*, Chicago, IL

2011   Margaret Thatcher Projects, *Manufactory*, New York, NY

2010   Marcia Wood Gallery, *Whirl*, Atlanta, GA

2010   Margaret Thatcher Projects, *New Collages,* New York, NY

2008   Margaret Thatcher Projects, *Transport*, New York, NY

2008   Holly Johnson Gallery, *Destination*, Dallas, TX

2008   Richard Levy Gallery, *Sugarloaves*, Albuquerque, NM

2007   Roy Boyd Gallery, *Junction—paintings 1997–2007*, Chicago, IL

2006   Margaret Thatcher Projects, *Under a Telephone Pole*, New York, NY

2005   Marcia Wood Gallery, *dreamland*, Atlanta, GA

2005   Kenise Barnes Fine Art, *Draw>Paint<Draw*, Larchmont, NY

2004   Pentimenti Gallery, *Indication*, Philadelphia, PA

2004   Margaret Thatcher Projects, *Land : Mark*, New York, NY

2003   Pentimenti Gallery, *New Paintings*, Philadelphia, PA

2002   Margaret Thatcher Projects, *Signal*, New York, NY

2002   Queens Museum of Art, *130 ft high, 65 thou gal, 1/2 mile deep…*, Queens, NY

2002   Rudolph Projects, *Paintings*, Houston, TX

2002   Marcia Wood Gallery, *New Work*, Atlanta, GA

2000   Margaret Thatcher Projects, *New Paintings*, New York, NY

2000   Marcia Wood Gallery, *New Work*, Atlanta, GA

1999   Hackett-Freedman Gallery, *Landscapes and Mechanical Interventions*,
        San Francisco, CA

1999   Margaret Thatcher Projects, *New Paintings*, New York, NY

1997   Marcia Wood Gallery, *American Landscapes*, Atlanta, GA

1996   Condeso/Lawler Gallery, *Paintings*, New York, NY

1996   Hackett-Freedman Gallery, *Recent Paintings*, San Francisco, CA

1994   Condeso/Lawler Gallery, *Paintings*, New York, NY

1994   Hackett-Freedman Gallery, *Recent Paintings*, San Francisco, CA

1992   Condeso/Lawler Gallery, *Paintings*, New York, NY

1991   Hackett-Freedman Gallery, *Paintings From New York & California*,
        San Francisco, CA

1990   Condeso/Lawler Gallery, *Paintings*, New York, NY

1990   John Slade Ely House, *New Work*, New Haven, CT

SELECTED GROUP EXHIBITIONS

2010   Richard Levy Gallery, *The Painting Show*, Albuquerque, NM

2009   Pace Prints, *40th Anniversary*, New York, NY

2007   Silas Marder Gallery, *Country Side*, Bridgehampton, NY

2007   Holly Johnson Gallery, *Drawing Conclusions*, Dallas, TX

2007   Kenise Barnes Fine Art, *Surf & Turf*, Larchmont, NY

2007   Royal Academy of Art, *Summer Exhibition 2007*, London, UK

2007   Pace Prints, *New Editions*, New York, NY

2006   Gallery Ihn, *Beyond the Sensibility*, Seoul, South Korea

2005   Margaret Thatcher Projects, *Summer Sensation*, New York, NY

2005   Hunter College, *HEAVENLY, or A Slice of White*, New York, NY

2004   Galerie S65, *Landscapes*, Cologne, Germany

2004   Evo Gallery, *ART...CHITECTURE*, Santa Fe, NM

2003   Marcia Wood Gallery, *Tickled*, Atlanta, GA

2003   Pentimenti Gallery, *At Present*, Philadelphia, PA

2002   Apex Art Curatorial Program, *Sans-Absent Presence*, New York, NY

2002   Margaret Thatcher Projects, *Breathing Room*, New York, NY

2002   Marcia Wood Gallery, *Works on Paper*, Atlanta, GA

2002   George Billis Gallery, *LandEscape*, curated by Lisa Hatchadoorian, New York, NY

2002   Percy Miller Gallery, *In Your Time*, London, UK

2002   Dumbo Arts Center, *Theme, Source, Resource*, curated by Robert Poplack, Brooklyn, NY

2000   Gallery Korea, *Stark Narratives*, New York, NY

2000   Kenise Barnes Fine Art, *Great Escapes*, Larchmont, NY

1998   Margaret Thatcher Projects, *What's on the Wall*, New York, NY

1998   Rudolph Poissant Gallery, *New Work*, Houston, TX

1997   Caldwell College, *Relocating Landscape: East and West*, Caldwell, NJ

1995   Albright-Knox Museum, *New York Selections*, Buffalo, NY

1993   Condeso/Lawler Gallery, *Landscapes*, New York, NY

1990   Munson Gallery, *Landscapes*, New Haven, CT

1985   Eloise Smith Gallery, *Landscapes*, curated by Terry St. John, Santa Cruz, CA

1985   Glastonbury Gallery, *Done in the Open*, San Francisco, CA

SELECTED COLLECTIONS

Altria Group, Inc. (formerly Philip Morris)

Amy Lau Design

AXA (formerly Equitable)

Bank of America

Crocker Art Museum, Sacramento, CA

Dufner Heighes Design

Exxon Corporation

Geoffrey Beene

Gibbons P.C.

Hana Bank

Microsoft Corporation

Pfizer Corporation

Savannah College of Art and Design Galleries

Silicon Valley Bank

Swiss Re

The Progressive Corporation

Wellington Management

SELECTED BIBLIOGRAPHY

Alan Artner. "William Steiger," *Chicago Tribune*, July 6, 2007.

Jenifer Borum. "William Steiger at Condeso Lawler Gallery," *Artforum International*, October 1992.

Cathy Byrd. "Point of View," *Atlanta Creative Loafing*, March 2002.

Kriston Capps. "William Steiger at Holly Johnson," *Dallas Morning News*, November 2, 2008.

Samuel T. Clover. "Art to Start With," *New York Post*, October 30, 2004.

David Cohen. "William Steiger, Land : Mark," *New York Sun*, November 11, 2004.

Jerry Cullum. "American Landscape," *Art Papers*, May/June 1998.

———. "Paintings Capture a Nation Waiting for a Jump Start," *Atlanta Journal-Constitution*, November 1997.

Jennifer Elaine Davis. "William Steiger: Destination," *Dallas Observer*, October 14, 2008.

Felicia Feaster. "Ghosts in the Machine," *Atlanta Creative Loafing*, March 2000.

———. "William Steiger: Ghosts in the Machine," in *New Paintings*. New York: Margaret Thatcher Projects, 2000.

Bruce W. Ferguson. "William Steiger: Blind White," in *Under a Telephone Pole*. New York: Margaret Thatcher Projects, 2006.

John Forrest. "American Landscape," *New Art Examiner*, April 1998.

Micaela Giovannotti. "William Steiger," *Tema Celeste*, January/February 2001.

Margaret Hawkins. "Steiger Gets Maximum Impact from Minimalist Landscape," *Chicago Sun-Times*, June 29, 2007.

Hitomi Iwasaki. *William Steiger: 130 ft high, 65 thou gal, mile deep....* New York: Queens Museum of Art, 2002.

Julia Jacquette and Joie Rosen. *HEAVENLY, or, A Slice of White*. New York: Hunter College, College Art Gallery, 2005.

Ken Johnson. "William Steiger: Signal," *The New York Times*, November 1, 2002.

Melissa Kuntz. "William Steiger at Margaret Thatcher," *Art in America*, May 2005.

Hans Michaud. "William Steiger's Transport," *Whitehot Magazine*, December 2008.

Robert C. Morgan. "Immanence and Containment: Paintings by William Steiger," in *Paintings*. New York: Condeso/Lawler Gallery; San Francisco: Hackett-Freedman Gallery, 1994.

———. "William Steiger," *Review Art*, December 1996.

Peter Nesbett. "The Two-Color Miracle," *Art on Paper*, September/October 2004.

Bettina Prentice. "Transport at Margaret Thatcher Projects," *KiptonART*, December 2, 2008.

Daniel Rothbart. "William Steiger," *NY Arts*, January 1999.

Hilarie M. Sheets. "Paradise Lost? Artists Reinvent the Landscape," *ARTnews*, March 2001.

Edward J. Sozanski. "Painted Precisely," *The Philadelphia Inquirer*, March 21, 2003.

R. B. Strauss. "Steiger Creates the Ideal Idyll," *The Kennett Paper*, March 27, 2003.

"William Steiger's Destination," *Pegasus News*, October 13, 2008.

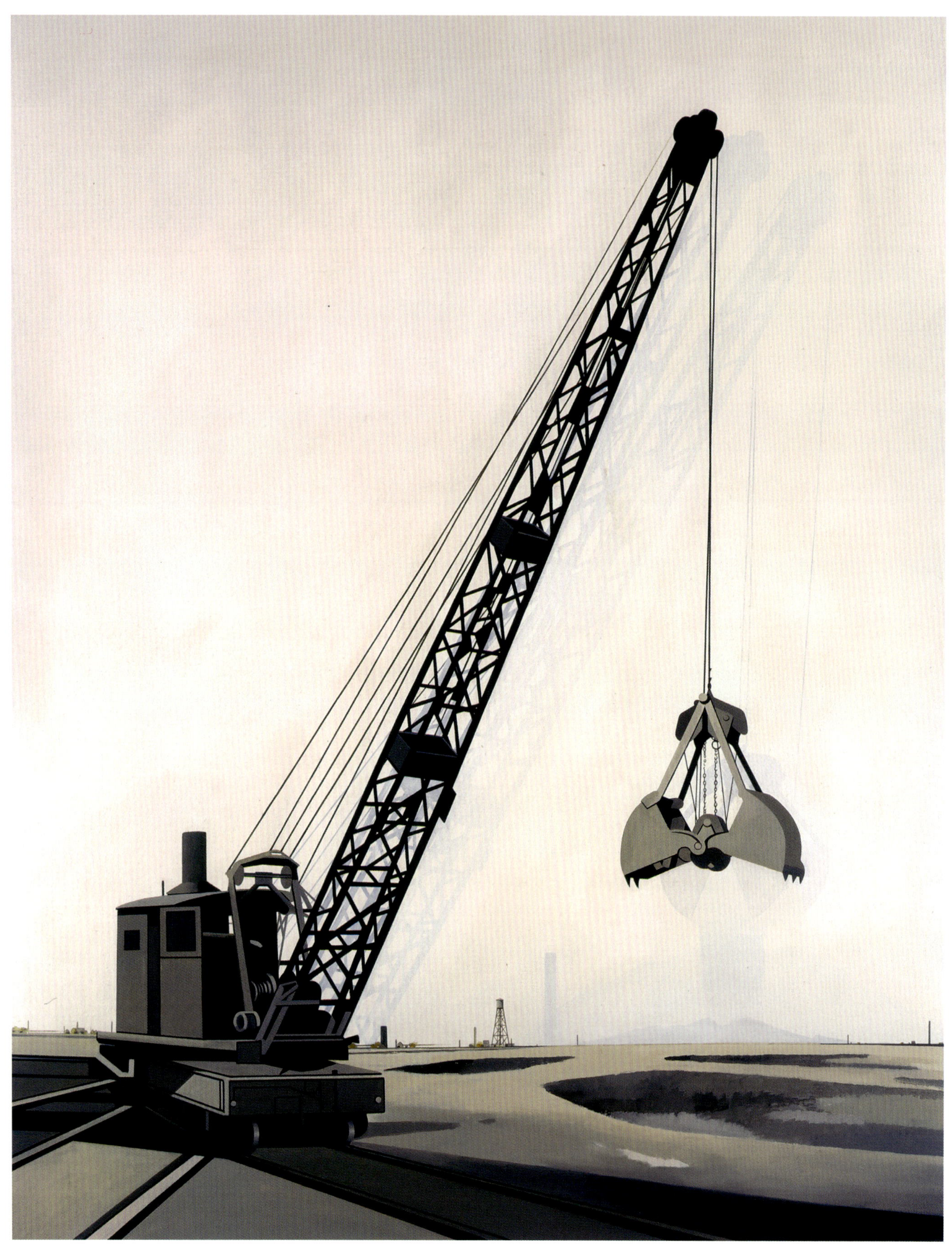

192 Figure 28. William Steiger, *Crane*, 2001–2002, oil on canvas, 60 x 48 inches. Collection of artist.

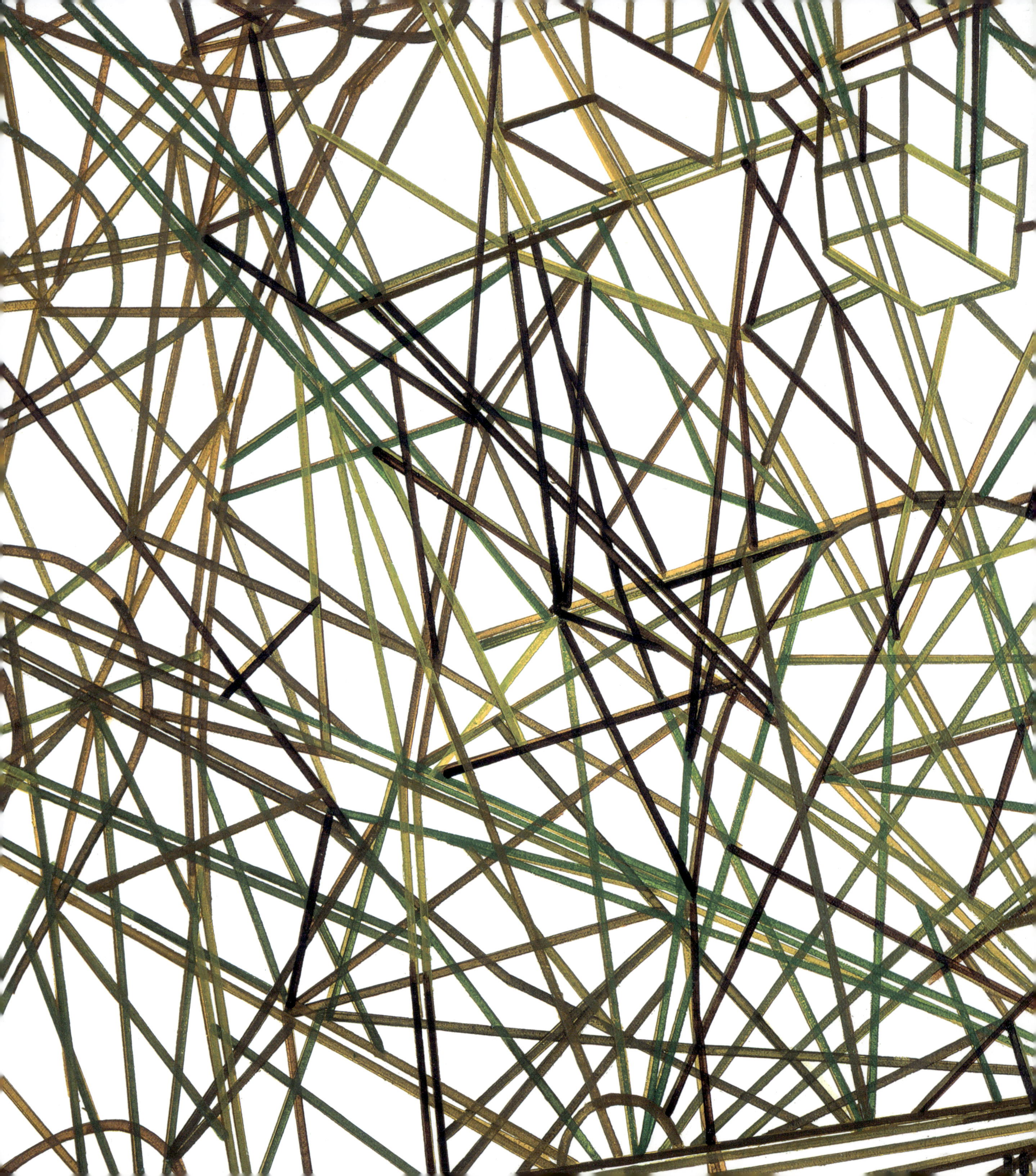